THE CRITIQUE OF
THEOLOGICAL REASON

Far from merely reinvigorating relativism, postmodernism has detected and expressed in our time a powerful nihilating process of which truth and reality itself are the final casualties; and with these morality and religion. Beginning, then, from the theological reaches of philosophy, this book argues that gods played a crucial part in modern philosophy, even when it was most critical of them; that the dominant nihilism of Derrida is really an excessive and misleading outcome of a contemporary philosophy which could otherwise resonate with all that is best in our evolutionary image of the universe; that moralists who turn to art in order to overcome the fact–value version of a concomitant and deadly dualism do not thereby rule out religion; and that a Christian theology which recognises the evolutionary/historical conditions of faith and revelation is once again producing a theology that builds upon the best of contemporary philosophy and science.

JAMES P. MACKEY is Emeritus Professor of Theology at the University of Edinburgh. A prolific author and broadcaster, he has taught extensively in the USA. His books include *The Problems of Religious Faith* (1972), *Jesus the Man and the Myth* (1979) and *Power and Christian Ethics* (Cambridge, 1994).

THE CRITIQUE OF
THEOLOGICAL REASON

JAMES P. MACKEY

University of Edinburgh

CAMBRIDGE
UNIVERSITY PRESS

PUBLISHED BY THE PRESS SYNDICATE OF THE UNIVERSITY OF CAMBRIDGE
The Pitt Building, Trumpington Street, Cambridge, United Kingdom

CAMBRIDGE UNIVERSITY PRESS
The Edinburgh Building, Cambridge CB2 2RU, UK   www.cup.cam.ac.uk
40 West 20th Street, New York, NY 10011–4211, USA   www.cup.org
10 Stamford Road, Oakleigh, Melbourne 3166, Australia
Ruiz de Alarcón 13, 28014 Madrid, Spain

© James P. Mackey 2000

First published 2000

Printed in the United Kingdom at the University Press, Cambridge

Typeset in Baskerville 11/12.5pt [VN]

A catalogue record for this book is available from the British Library

Library of Congress Cataloguing in Publication data
Mackey, James Patrick.
p.   cm.
Includes bibliographical references.
ISBN 0 521 77293 1
1. Philosophical theology. 2. Postmodernism – Religious aspects – Christianity. 1. Title.
BT40.M25 2000
230 – dc21   99–057403

ISBN 0 521 77293 1 hardback

Contents

PART ONE: HISTORICAL—CRITICAL

Prologue   *page* 3

1   The status quo: genesis   8

2   The status quo: current affairs   52

3   Beginnings: old and new   120

PART TWO: CRITICAL—CONSTRUCTIVE

Prologue   177

4   Morality and metaphysics   182

5   Art and the role of revelation   221

6   Revelation, religion and theology   265

Epilogue   323

Index   331

PART ONE

Historical–critical

Prologue

This essay on the nature, function and truth value of theology, and on the very prospects for theology in this very self-confidently proclaimed postmodernist era, is based upon two assumptions, and it makes use of a particular investigative hypothesis; and each of these had better be declared openly at the outset.

The first assumption concerns an intrinsic and essential link that binds theology to philosophy. This link can be explained and expressed from a variety of perspectives. From the perspective of the genesis of Western philosophy, explained as a move from *mythos* to *logos*, where *logos* named the rational investigation of the *physis ton onton* (the nature or dynamic centre of the things that are), theology was simply the name for that same rational investigation of all reality, at the point where it managed to meet the deepest entity that seemed to be the central source of all the moving universe. At that point, whenever and however it was thought to be reached, philosophy, without break in its nature or process, became the *logos* of *theos*; and by Plato's time had actually been named theology. From the perspective of those Fathers of Western Christian theology who borrowed not merely the method but so much of the content of this earlier Greek theology and put it at the service of the teaching of their own faith, we have this remark of Augustine about the Platonists: 'change a few words and propositions and they might be Christians'.

Even from the perspective of those Reformed Christians who are most hostile to any connection with philosophical or 'natural' theology, we expect, and normally find, not just a critique of this rival – even if the critique at times amounts to little more than an attempt to sustain a charge of idolatry, or to reveal the corruption of 'unaided' human reason – but also an intelligible, rational account of the truth which Reformed theologians proclaim. Indeed in that last exercise deeper links with prevailing philosophies can often be detected. For example, Barth's

3

central concept of God is that of a Supreme Divine Subject subsisting in three modes of being, rather than the older concept of a Supreme Divine Substance subsisting in three persons; and the contrast between a post-Hegelian and a Neoplatonic philosophical climate can scarcely be thought irrelevant to this exposition of a central doctrine of Barth's Christian faith.

Finally, from the perspective of philosophy itself: in any age philosophy invokes reason in its most expansive mode; searching as wide and as deep and as high in reality as possible, and looking beyond present fact to both remote origin and furthest prospect. Further, there is no set border between science and philosophy, any more than there is between philosophy and theology, so that philosophical development from the beginning has felt the spur of the most impressive scientific development. Except in the case of the most self-imposed reductivist views of science (or, of course, the most anti-metaphysical views of some philosophers), physics will always invite metaphysics as a natural extension of deeper and broader inquiry; and metaphysics always reveals, if not a theological dimension, then at least some important implications for any theology. From any and all perspectives, then, the intrinsic link that binds theology to philosophy seems obvious and inevitable; and that holds as well for the postmodernist era as for any other. One cannot ignore postmodernism as some Christian theologians would wish to do, not even on the basis of the hearty hope they express that it will deconstruct itself and disappear.

The second assumption is well caught in Heidegger's phrase 'the genesis of meaning' (*Sinngenesis*), particularly as that phrase is applied to a formed philosophy, a philosophical (or theological) system, a 'teaching' (or a doctrine), an 'ism'. The full and precise meaning-content of any such distinctive and named philosophical system, the phrase suggests, in addition to the most balanced assessment of its strengths and weaknesses, is available only through a study of its origins in its own time and place. It must be a matter of prudence to decide how far back one must try to trace the progenitors of any relatively well-formed or finalised and named philosophy; but in all cases it is as important to investigate how the earliest chosen progenitor's seed was modified by successive transmitters as it is to study that originary genetic formula in the progenitor's own *corpus*. In the case of prevailing postmodernism – and it has now prevailed to the point of supplying the chattering classes with their most common cliché – it would not be prudent to go back beyond Descartes; but it would be foolish to fail to pay the closest attention to the fate of Cartesian philosophy, as of any other contributory philosophy, in the time that intervened between the progenitors and the present. If one wishes, that is, to come to a competent understanding of the inherited strengths and weaknesses of postmodernism at this time.

The investigative hypothesis is also made up of two parts. In its first part, the hypothesis entertained after much thought on the subject is this: that the most significant feature of postmodernism is not the apparently rampant relativism it is thought to entail, but the loss of the subject (to which some would add, the loss to view also of the rest of reality). To those worried about relativism, one can respond in words similar to those of Jesus about the poor: relativism you have always had and always will have with you. For every age has been threatened by relativists, and has felt the cold consolation of the logical incoherence of absolute relativism. Each age has found its own answers, with varying degrees of satisfaction; and if relativism is decreed to be that which is most seriously significant about postmodernism, then there is ample precedent for adopting past answers and adding new ones. But the hypothesis here is that it is the loss of the subject that is most seriously significant about postmodernism, together with the much more radical consequences for concepts of truth and the nature and knowledge of reality which are then entailed. And if the unworthy suspicion should arise that this choice of the most seriously significant feature of postmodernism is made because of its obvious relevance to prospects for theology, then a brief perusal of books on the death of the author by scholars of literature should help to allay any such suspicion.

The second part of the investigative hypothesis, formed once more after much thought about modern philosophy, is more elaborate, and forms the investigative analysis of the first two chapters. Briefly, it is to the effect that the loss of the subject (and of reality) resulted from an insidious and rapidly developing mind–body dualism; a very strong form of mind–body dualism which can be called Cartesian, not because it is found as such in Descartes's own *corpus*, but because its long genesis goes back to him through influential transmitters who followed him. This genesis through the intervening centuries can be traced through two separate streams – though they do at times intertwine: the predominantly phenomenological stream which found increasing difficulty in relating to any realities beyond them the mental entities with which it seems initially to be exclusively concerned. And the more materialist stream, which was soon thought by its most radical admirers to be singing on its merry way, a song of reality as a historical process without a subject. When these streams did coalesce, and were swollen by certain other 'scientific' methods of studying signs, both subject and reality tended to disappear from view, and language seemed all that was left, as Beckett's *Unnameable* put it: 'I'm in words, made of words, others words, what others, the place too, the air, the walls, the floor, the ceilings, all words'; language playing with itself, precariously, infinitely precariously, in the intrusive and voracious void.

If this is the most significant feature of postmodernism, it is also its most extreme implication, and the question inevitably arises as to what to do about it – a question, surely, that is not just for theologians. Two things can be done. One is to observe that the subject never wholly disappeared from the dominant postmodernist texts, even in the texts that most stridently announced its death. What disappeared was a subject in the form of a divine *Logos*, a subject 'sitting above the ever-changing world', always already replete with all the intelligible content which ever was, is or will be. And what might be seen to emerge from the grave of that one is a subject that always creatively transcends all current content; and as a consequence a reality in unceasing evolution and, yes, a language that is correspondingly and literally marginless. For postmodernism has retained the best of its philosophical inheritance also, no matter how much it might seem to have betrayed it in some of its more excessive posturing.

The second thing that can be done is this: to realise that one does not have to single-handedly remodel postmodernism so as to relieve it of its excesses and restore to it the best of its own inheritance, even if one had the philosophical ability to do this. The coffers of philosophy have been replenished not only by the gathering and mutating inheritances of the past, but by new gold of knowledge mined in each and every age by the intense investigators of *ta onta*, the things that are. The continuity between science and (the love of) wisdom, between physics and metaphysics, does still obtain, even if the modern era has seen more denials of it than the past ever saw. And so the third chapter of this part considers two scientific movements, both with quite self-conscious philosophical interests, one more focussed on the psychological and the other more on the physical side of reality – just to keep the symmetry going – and these singly and together reveal a picture of ever evolving reality at the heart of which is indeed a very knowledgeable and, yes, even a moral kind of subjectivity. Postmodernism too, if it itself is to have much of a future, must keep in contact with such elemental growing points of humanity's knowledge of itself and its world. But, whether it does or not, the question of the nature, function and truth value of theology, and of its prospects in a postmodernist era, is best answered by wedding the best of what postmodernism has inherited to the best that the current questers after knowledge of our multivarious universe have to offer us. The prenuptial interrogation both of the philosophical genetic pool from which postmodernism developed, and of the most ambitious advances of contemporary science, will be regularly focussed on implications for theology. And any more detailed and constructive proposals for a future for theology that may come as the fruit of that wedding are the business of Part Two.

CHAPTER I

The status quo: genesis

CARTESIAN PHILOSOPHY TODAY

The most common assessment of the legacy of Descartes is that he left us with a picture of mind–body dualism more clearly drawn and more deeply and widely influential than Plato had produced, or Plato's less sophisticated followers had managed in the centuries between. Two examples of such an assessment must suffice. The first is from a piece on neurophysiology by Peter Fenwick. 'Descartes, in the seventeenth century, maintained that there are two radically different kinds of substance, the *res extensa* – the extended substance, that which has length, breadth and depth, and can therefore be measured and divided; and a thinking substance, the *res cogitans*, which is unextended and indivisible. The external world of which the human body is part belongs to the first category, while the internal world of the mind belongs to the second.'

Fenwick goes on from this general account of Descartes's legacy to a brief survey of the philosophies of mind that dominate the current scene. At one extreme he places Dennett's neurophilosophy: consciousness and subjective experience are just the functions of neural nets, and nothing is required to explain these except a detailed knowledge of neural nets. At the other extreme stands Nagel: subjective experience is not available to scientific method, as it is not in the third person and cannot be validated in the public domain. Searle, he argues, occupies an intermediate position: for Searle regards subjective experience as being a property of neural nets, but he does not think that a full understanding of neural nets is sufficient to explain subjective experience; indeed Searle awaits another Newton to provide a means of understanding, in some verifiable manner, the subjective substance. Subjective experiences, then, in the dual connotation of the experiences of being a subject and the experiences distinctive of subjects, are private, inner entities

8

which cannot (as yet) be understood or explained in any publicly verifiable manner. In this they differ radically, as a different kind of substance, from external entities available to public investigation, explanation and verification – such as neural nets. Hence the point of the reductionist approach, which maintains that subjective experiences are nothing other than neural nets, their properties and behaviour.

Of course, the dualism does not often appear to be quite as dichotomous as Fenwick's and other such brief accounts of it as that adopted here might suggest. On the Dennett side of the argument there is commonly said to be more than merely neural processes. There are said to be rule-governed systems of symbols, like computer programs, or some such systems composed also of causal connections; and these are described as epiphenomena with respect to neural states and processes. However, since these bear little resemblance to our actual experience of on-going consciousness and its procedures, and since they are in any case as difficult to establish in reality as anything other than the ever developing results of the latter's continuous investigative creativity, they can scarcely function to relieve us of the dichotomously dualist choice between merely physicochemical processes and something called mind or consciousness, particularly when we try to choose between the Dennett and the Nagel side of the current argument. In a phrase of Ted Honderich's, from his review of Searle's latest book, proponents of these rule-governed systems 'aimed at rescuing consciousness from being ghostly stuff, and turned it into yet less'.[1]

Just such a simple mind–body dualism of dichotomously distinct kinds of substance is assumed, in fact, by many of those engaged in cognitive science today, and not only by those who specifically study the brain and nervous system. The common linguistic currency of this dualism is that of internal or inner, private, subjective, for the substance variously named mind, soul or spirit; and external or outer, public (as in publicly verifiable) and hence objective, for bodily or physical substance. And much the same linguistic currency is used by philosophers; indeed it is most likely philosophers who put it into circulation, as it was philosophers rather than scientists who in the modern era attributed it to Descartes. D. Z. Phillips, to take but one example from contemporary philosophy, in his challenge to the very existence of such an entity,

[1] Peter Fenwick, 'The Neurophysiology of Religious Experience', in Dinesh Bugra (ed.), *Psychiatry and Religion* (London: Routledge, 1995), p. 168. John Searle, *Mind, Language and Society* (London: Weidenfeld and Nicolson, 1999); and Honderich's review in *Times Literary Supplement*, 25 June 1999, pp. 1–2.

describes a Cartesian self as an inner and necessarily private subject, whose very existence, not to say its nature, we must infer from publicly observable bodily behaviour.[2] Hence we have in contemporary discourse the widespread assumption of a simple dichotomous dualism of inner, private, subjective mind-self and outer, extended, public, objective body. This assumption governs a very great deal of the contemporary discussion of selfhood and personhood and of its place and prospects in the whole range of reality. In fact, until Searle's Newton of neurophysiology comes along, it rather favours those who either deny the existence of mind-self in any sense exceeding that which the most physical of sciences study as the extended substance of body. Or, at the very least, it restricts views about mind-selves to the realm of private, subjective opinion – a realm to which religion (and morality?) may then also be restricted – and debars these in any case from expression in verifiable or falsifiable propositions.

This state of affairs is commonly fathered upon Descartes. Now, it undoubtedly represents a most common caricature of Descartes, even if there are features of Descartes's philosophy which still invite the caricature. But does that matter any longer? Is it worth even a small expense of time attempting to rehabilitate Descartes? Would it not be better to criticise the status quo as we find it? Descartes is long dead.

Well, there is a case for a brief revisit of Descartes. On such a visit it is possible to discover larger perspectives and more promising developments in Descartes's own philosophical investigations of human nature, perspectives and developments which dominant impressions of too dichotomous a dualism serve to hide from view. It is also possible that, had these larger perspectives been followed further by himself or his successors, Descartes and his followers might well have left us today with more adequate philosophical views, and with more adequate philosophical underpinnings for the progress of science. A revisit of Descartes, then, can throw some light upon the critical role of those who followed him in the company of Western philosophers: including those who resisted his influence, those who shaped it more crudely and those who, in response perhaps, then tried for a greatly improved version. For then one can review the present state of the Cartesian inheritance with some real prospect of recovering some lost and better parts of it, and of deciding to move forward with it or from it.

[2] D. Z. Phillips, *Death and Immortality* (London: Macmillan, 1970), p. 5. See also Ilham Dilman, *Philosophy and the Philosophic Mind* (Basingstoke: Macmillan, 1992).

Descartes made much reference to 'primitive notions'. These are foundational ideas in our knowledge of reality, which could be critically analysed and deployed, certainly, but could neither be substituted for nor produced by any prior process of reasoning. In this matter of current concern, these contemporary references to Descartes which we have just seen seem to assume that he operated with but two primitive notions, namely, that of inner mind and that of extended matter. But this is not so. Descartes's investigation into human nature begins in fact from three primitive notions: the two just named are followed or, perhaps better, preceded by a third, the notion of the one united human being, 'une seule personne, qui a ensemble un corps et une pensée'. This is quite clear from the *Meditations* of 1641. It is also quite clear to the attentive reader of Descartes that from 1641 to the publication of the *Traité des passions* in 1649, later to be called *Les Passions de l'âme*,[3] he became increasingly preoccupied with the issue of the one united person, viz., the union of body and soul, and with the best means of investigating and describing this. His correspondence, and particularly his correspondence with Elizabeth, shows this preoccupation.

In the sixth of his *Meditations* Descartes makes it clear that he did not accept the 'pilot in the ship' analogy, or any similar analogy which would suggest the 'ghost in the machine' idea so often employed in his name. The kind of analogy he does use is that of weight which is distributed throughout the whole body, while not itself being an extended entity, though it can be brought to bear through any particular point of a body.[4] And as far as the implications of talk of two substances are concerned, he does say that spirit and body are incomplete substances with respect to the human being they compose; but when they are taken separately they are considered complete substances.[5] As if the three primitive notions were interlocked in ways which analysis would at first threaten, and only further analysis would restore.

He came to believe that it is in the investigation of the emotions, *passions*, that the unity of the person, the union of soul (or spirit, or mind) and body, could best of all be seen and described. In his *Principia Philosophiae* (pt 1, paras. 66, 75) of 1644, when he is occupied with the nature and enumeration of clear and distinct ideas, he names three

[3] R. Descartes, *Les Passions de l'âme* , ed. G. Rodis-Lewis, (Paris: J. Vrin, 1955).
[4] R. Descartes, *Oeuvres*, ed. Charles Adam and Paul Tannery (Paris: L. Cerf, 1897–1913), vol. 9a, p. 240.   [5] Ibid. p. 173.

(again, not just two) in the matter which presently concerns us: the idea of body, the idea of soul; but now, as a third, he names the idea of those sentiments, affections and appetites which belong to the union of body and soul. Indeed, in one of his letters, to Morus, he claims that the *Traité des passions* contains his final thoughts on the union of soul and body.[6] It is worth rehearsing very briefly, then, Descartes's treatment of the emotions; not merely in order to come to grips with the kinds of dualism which have so much affected modern philosophy, but to anticipate already the role of emotion in coming to an adequate philosophy of moral behaviour and moral value, a matter that is of central concern to the second part of this investigation.

The emotions or passions are to be distinguished, according to Descartes, both from those perceptions which arise in the soul as a result of stimuli from external objects, carried through the nervous system, and from those appetites or affections which derive from motions or states peculiar to the body and are consequently felt in the soul; such as hunger, thirst, pain. Emotions or passions strictly speaking consist of sentiments which belong to the soul, but are aroused or sustained with the help of those 'animal spirits' for a further description of which one must have recourse to Descartes's detailed physiology. Suffice it to say here that the emotions truly belong to the united person, to the union of soul and body in the whole human being. They cannot be accounted for as activities or passivities of either the soul or the body as if these were separate entities accidentally conjoined at, say, the pineal gland.

There are two further features of Descartes's treatment of the emotions which are worth noting here. The first is this: that they are described as perceptions or 'knowings', *perceptions ou connoissances*, albeit confused and obscure. The appetites and affections, such as hunger and so on, which belong to the body and are felt in the soul, are also described by Descartes as certain confused ways of thinking; and of course stimuli from external objects also give rise to perceptions. The emotions, then, in combination with the affections of the body and the stimuli from external objects, all form part of the process by which human beings know reality; and the pivotal place of the emotions, belonging as they do to the *one person* ('une seule personne'), suggests an epistemology in which the emotions are as integrated as they possibly have not been since the early Stoics rejected the soul–body dualism altogether and made the emotions an integral part of that process of

----

[6] Ibid. p. 347.

judgement by which we establish as much of the truth about reality as is available to us.

Second, and as a consequence of realising their role in our thinking or knowing, attention to the nature and number of these emotions can actually cast some light on the nature of knowing, and in particular on the nature of the knowing process that is characteristic of human beings. There are, according to Descartes, six simple or primitive emotions: admiration, desire, love and hate, joy and sadness. All the other named emotions are either derivatives from, or mixtures of, these. Admiration, which some might be surprised to find named amongst the emotions, and even more surprised to see named first, enables us to detect that which may be important for us. Desire drives us to engage with it. Love and hate are engaged respectively with what is good or bad for us in it; and so on.

Now, these are brutally brief depictions, and they do not even begin to adumbrate the expansions and nuances which follow in the writings of Descartes, especially as the derivatives and mixtures of the simple emotions are investigated and described. But they suffice to make the point that is presently relevant, namely, that the process by which we know the world of which we are so integral a part, is a process in which our embodied spiritual presence is active in engagement with it and passive with respect to its active engagement with us. Further, the process of knowing is, in a central and pivotal part of itself, a process of evaluating. It would then follow that value judgements and judgements of truth and falsehood may not be separable in the manner in which some contemporary epistemologies and theories of morality suggest they are. And these important epistemological insights both the nature and the pivotal role of the emotions do a very great deal to secure, as described by Descartes.

It would be idle at this point to speculate how these very real developments in Descartes's own thought, had they been continued by his successors, might have yielded something other than a dichotomously dualistic notion of human being – a notion to which, as we may later note, some modern denials of the very existence of mind, soul or spirit are as much indebted as are most affirmations of the existence of these. It would be idle to speculate at this point how much sooner a more unified view of human being might have yielded some of the more promising philosophical insights that are just beginning to emerge today. These are, in particular, views of the absolute integrality of emotion and praxis in the very genesis and in the whole development of human cognitive endeavour, which the most advanced developmental psychology now proposes. And indeed, as some developmental psychologists now argue, views of an original and persistent intersubjective nature of that knowing process. For Descartes envisaged a prenatal stage in which four passions or emotions have already arisen, with the 'newly united' soul–body: joy, love, hate and sadness. These emotions already enable the foetus to react emotionally to what may affect the mother. Further, the first coincidence of an object or event with a particular emotion predisposes the brain to an association of such object with such emotion. However, and finally, since emotions consist in 'confused and obscure' perceptions or knowledge, experience and reason have a role in forming the emotions so that they become an ever more reliable adjutant and access to the good life; in short, the emotions are patient to a process of education and learning.

These elements in Descartes's treatise on the emotions certainly hold out the promise that, on a less dichotomously dualistic view of the matter, even if the self is identified with the mind, soul or spirit, yet, provided only that its real unity with the body is sufficiently established, it can be known directly through its emotional and embodied activity just as substantially as it itself knows all that it knows, including other selves, through these. In short, the knower is known, and just as directly known, by the same means by which it knows. It does not need to be inferred, as something 'inner', by arguing from 'outward' phenomena which, since they belong to an altogether different substance, serve mainly to conceal it. However, it would indeed be idle to speculate on how much sooner such developments of the fuller reaches of Descartes's philosophical investigations of human reality might have come about, on what form they might have then taken, and on how successfully they might have been established. In actual fact, it was the dominant dualist impressions of Descartes's philosophy, of the kind so confidently represented by Fenwick and Phillips and by so many others, that came to prominence in succeeding centuries; amply aided as they were by other philosophical movements to which our attention must shortly turn. And there is little doubt that much in Descartes himself rendered considerable assistance to this otherwise unfortunate turn of philosophical events. This is not altogether because Descartes failed to bring his whole planned philosophical system to published completion during his own lifetime.[7] For even in that part of his system in which impressions of too

---

[7] A convincing argument could be made that with the *Traité des passions* in particular, Descartes came closer to this completion than he is normally credited with doing.

dichotomous a dualism seem to be most impressively overcome, that is, in his treatment of the emotions, Des-cartes introduces in the end a dual system of emotions.

The soul, remember, is characterised by *pensées*, that is, the 'perceptions' of the understanding and the inclinations of the will. The body is characterised by its own actions, passivities and affections; the soul–body unity, by the emotions as already described. But then Descartes does introduce a parallel set of 'interior emotions'. These have the same names as the previous set: love and so on. However, they are based on judgements of the mind; they can in fact be called *pensées raisonables, plus claires*, when the corresponding emotions are *pensées confusés*.[8] They are not subject to the perturbations of the previous set; and on them the identification and advance to the *summum bonum*, our ultimate good, depends. In contexts such as these Descartes is describing a certain aloofness of the rational will with respect to the ordinary or 'exterior' passions which he had considered all along. For with respect to the latter the rational will, since it could not directly arouse or allay them, had to work with them – by directing attention to objects that aroused more acceptable emotions or, as a last resort, simply preventing the action to which an unwanted emotion would otherwise naturally lead. Here, then, with the introduction of these 'interior emotions' the reader can reasonably suspect the influence of a popular Platonism which envisages a separable mind or rational soul, and a level of dualism which tends at least to run contrary once more to the impressions of unity so carefully cultivated in the basic analysis of the emotions. Of course, in Descartes's assent to the traditional doctrine of the immortality of the soul, the separability of the soul is given in any case. In fact, unless that particular doctrine were to be subjected to a more constructive critique than Descartes apparently felt like devoting to his inherited Christian faith in general, the further development of the investigation of the unity of the *one person* ('une seule personne') was never likely to come to fuller fruition in his own writings.

THE SUBSEQUENT RECRUDESCENCE OF DUALISM

It is time, then, in pursuit of the fate of the subject in modern philosophy, to leave these thoughts of what might have been, and to turn to

---

[8] Descartes, *Oeuvres*, vol. 4, pp. 601ff.

those subsequent movements in modern philosophy which can be reasonably read as contributing to the eventual loss of the subject, whether by assuming or establishing too great a separation between mind and body, or in some other way. Immanuel Kant is the next philosopher whom even the briefest of investigations along the present lines must visit. But a slight diversion to take in the philosophy of Hume would seem to be indicated. This is not simply because Kant attributed to Hume the credit for awakening him from his dogmatic slumbers. Rather, the tradition of philosophy represented in Britain, the currently named Analytic tradition which is so influential in the Anglophone areas, has been much indebted to the philosophy of Hume, and Anglophone philosophy will loom larger in later reaches of the present investigation. There is a combination of effect and influence, therefore, which is apparent on the contemporary scene, and which requires a look to its origins, and a brief visit to Hume.

Hume's scepticism concerning the self

When Hume in *A Treatise of Human Nature* (bk 1, sec. 6) comes to consider what he calls personal identity, his first page could be construed as a direct attack upon Descartes. This is especially so if we consider that the *Cogito*, the thinking thing, the content of the foundational certainty of the Cartesian system, constitutes the real self for Descartes; and that the self is not constituted, rather, as further actual and potential developments of Descartes's thought might suggest, by the *one person* ('une seule personne').

Hume rejects at the outset the assertion by 'some philosophers' that we enjoy a direct and intimate consciousness of a self, that is, of something in us which maintains its identity and 'simplicity' over a continuous span of existence. For all our knowledge is based upon impressions made upon us, according to Hume the would-be empiricist, and there simply is no impression from which such an idea of a self could be derived. What we actually experience is a whole collection or succession of impressions in the forms of sensations, passions, perceptions. Each and every one of these is different, distinct or at least separable from the others. There is not amongst them any impression of an entity which maintains its own simple and undifferentiated identity through the flow or succession of the others; much less an impression of such an entity to which all the other impressions could then be seen to refer, as to their source or sustainer. Or, to put the matter slightly differently, one can never catch a glimpse of one's self in a pure and simple state; innocent, that is to say, of any (other) attendant impression, any particular and passing sensation, passion or perception. The self, then, which Hume does indeed equate with the mind or thinking principle, is likened by him to a kind of theatre in which a plethora of perceptions make their appearance, come into being and pass away, and combine together in an apparently infinite variety show. Except that we must not take the metaphor of the theatre literally; for there is no 'theatre', and only the successive and varied perceptions exist, and it is to that 'bundle or collection' that we must apply words such as mind, thinking principle; for 'self' suggests a mind or thinking person, something over and above, or beneath this bundle.

How, then, do I come to talk of my self, as of an entity that persists with its identity intact through the whole course of my life? According to Hume this fiction, for that is what it is, is created by the combined contributions of the memory, the imagination and what he calls the three uniting principles of the ideal world. Well, in actual fact, just two of these uniting principles are operative in this case, namely, the uniting principles of resemblance and causation. The third uniting principle, contiguity, is not applicable here, presumably because it can apply only when we are explaining similar fictions of unity and identity in the case of physical things such as plants or animals. The memory, then, is a faculty by which we are made aware of the continuity and succession of perceptions; but it is not on that account and of itself that which produces the fiction of personal identity. There is a role for imagination.

In short, the memory brings together in a kind of chain the images of successive and simultaneous perceptions, and as it does so by retaining and linking images of past perceptions, and images resemble their objects, the uniting principle of resemblance begins to operate by courtesy of the imagination, which can move smoothly then from one link to another of the chain of images which memory creates. Much the same may be said for the uniting principle of causation which the work of memory also enables to operate, as impressions are imagined to be linked causally with ideas which habitually succeed them, and vice versa. And so the work of memory enables the imagination, through the operation of the uniting principles of the ideal world, resemblance and causation, to move so smoothly from one link in memory's chain to another, that the whole bundle or collection is made to seem like the continuance of one and the same object, or in this case of one identical self or subject.

In Hume's own words, then:

The whole of this doctrine leads us to the conclusion, which is of great importance in the present affair, viz. that all the nice and subtle questions concerning personal identity can never possibly be decided, and are to be regarded rather as grammatical than as philosophical difficulties. Identity depends upon relations of ideas; and these relations produce identity, by means of the easy transition they occasion. But as the relations, and the easiness of transition may be diminished by insensible degrees, we have no just standard, by which we can decide any dispute concerning the time, when they acquire or lose a title to the name of identity. All disputes concerning the identity of connected objects are merely verbal, except so far as the relation of parts gives rise to some fiction or imaginary principle of union, as we have already observed.

It is difficult to respond critically to any element in Hume's work without taking a general view of his philosophy as a whole, and then arguing in some detail for that view. That cannot be done at this point. In the meantime, may it not be permissible to see the strength of Hume in his relentless scepticism – in 'setting aside some metaphysicians', for example, as he puts it – rather than in any constructive positions we might be able to attribute to him? For we might be tempted to attribute to him the following construction of reality; even if, in deference to himself and his followers, we were to refrain from calling it a metaphysic:

There is a physical world and an ideal world. That latter phrase is his, but it simply means a 'world' of sensations and emotions, in short, impressions or perceptions, ideas and relations of ideas, and so on. We can only know with any certainty (probability?) that discrete objects in the former world make impressions in the latter world and give rise there to perceptions. Our beliefs that there are souls, selves and substances, forging continuous identities where there is only the flux of discrete objects and perceptions, are fictions based on relations of ideas rather than on received matters of fact. One is reminded of Bertrand Russell's translation into the categories of this Humean tradition of Descartes's *Cogito* as 'there is a thought now'.

But if we were to foist this construction of reality on Hume, on the merest pretence that this is what his talk of objects and perceptions on the whole suggests, we should immediately have to ask some awkward questions of him. To take but one example from the small but central section of his philosophy just now analysed: if he were to apply to his notion of memory, say, the very same technique of critical questioning which he applied to the notion of mind, how would it fare? He calls it a faculty. Never mind the question, a faculty of what or of whom? Ask merely, do we have an impression of some stable identity which retains the images of a great variety of distinct and different perceptions, affections and so on, and in particular of those that succeeded each other over a period of time? And if we have not, then how on his own philosophical methodology can we know that there is such a thing? And if we cannot know that there be such a thing, then how can he say that it plays such a pivotal role in the creation of the fiction of a mind or self? Much the same point could be made concerning the imagination and the very substantial role it is called upon to play in Hume's philosophy. In the end, indeed, would it not be just as simple to say that mind exists, and we know it, as it is to talk as if memory existed, and as if we knew that?

It is possibly best, then, to see Hume simply and solely as a sceptic. A man, perhaps, in a small way – a very small way – like Socrates; convinced only of his ignorance, intensely aware of what he realised he did not know, and wielding his *elenchos* (probing interrogation), and urging all of his followers to wield it, so that what is received as truth should never escape the closest critical appraisal, and so also that some advance might thus be made, if only through the long conversation of the company of questers after wisdom down the centuries. Indeed from the moment when A. J. Ayer said that, like Hume, he divided all genuine propositions into two classes, those which concerned relations of ideas and those which concerned matters of fact, that the former make no assertions about the empirical world, and the latter, in respect of which the matter of truth arises, can be probable but never certain,[9] the philosophical movement then known as Linguistic Analysis was often presented and received as a technique for separating sense from nonsense, rather than one which wished to propose its own construction of reality, a task it seemed to want to leave to the empirical sciences. Seen in such a role, then, Hume can certainly take his place in the story of the loss of the subject in the course of the modern era of philosophy. But then that achievement of his, in this matter which presently concerns us, must be suitably qualified. Hume did not bring about the loss of the subject in the sense that he achieved a critical and valid construction of reality from which anything which we could rightly call a self or subject was demonstrably absent. Instead, he mounted a devastating critique of the notion of a mind-self which was the received notion of his time and place, and the only one which he, as a practising sceptic, was

---

[9] A. J. Ayer, *Language, Truth and Logic* (London: Gollancz, 1954), p. 31.

obliged or perhaps enabled to consider. This was in fact the notion of self of a kind which was thought to derive from Descartes, particularly by those who keep the focus upon Descartes's distinction between mind and body, and provided that these also ignore the material in Descartes's works concerning the mind–body union, and the actual and possible development of that material towards a possibly more advanced notion of self or subject.

To be more precise, the proposal is, first, that Hume's philosophy should not be treated as an attempt to construe reality in the broadest available sense of that word; treated, that is, as metaphysics, in traditional terminology. The reason for this suggestion is not that Hume's philosophy, after a fashion established by Descartes for virtually all of modern philosophy, is initially and predominantly epistemology. In most, if not all, modern philosophy the issue of what is or can be known is inextricably bound up with the issue of the nature and prospects of the knowing process itself; and this bond differs considerably in degree from any previous era in the history of Western philosophy. For, as Sartre quite rightly observed, 'If every metaphysics in fact presupposes a theory of knowledge, every theory of knowledge in turn presupposes a metaphysics.'[10] And it would take no great ingenuity to detect the construction of reality entailed in Hume's philosophy. Reality would consist of a multitude of discrete objects in the physical world – although 'world' would need to be queried as a metaphysical term, since it suggests a unity that is apparently not given. In addition, there would exist the impressions and affections of which these objects are somehow the source, together with perceptions and ideas (there is a thought now, there are thoughts now and then . . .), and some very odd entities such as memories and imaginations; but no minds, souls, selves – definitely none of these.

The proposal, then, that Hume's philosophy should not be treated as an attempt to construe reality in the broadest sense traditionally known as metaphysics, is to save Hume, and his followers, the embarrassment of seeming to subscribe to such a truly unintelligible metaphysics as that just described. The proposal is certainly not meant to give any credence to the followers of Hume in their assertion that he or they have rid philosophy of metaphysics; it is too blatantly obvious, even if Sartre had never said so, that every theory of truth and logic entails a metaphysics. Nevertheless, it is surely permissible to take the philosophy of Hume and

---

[10] J.-P. Sartre, *Being and Nothingness* (New York: Washington Square Press, 1966), p. 10.

his successors as a thorough questioning of received certainties concerning the make-up of reality. And to deal with the very scepticism that ensues, not by an all too easy pillory of the alleged attendant metaphysics, but by critically revisiting the received certainties that are most clearly challenged.

To continue to be more precise, the proposal is, second, that the focus should be on Hume's argued scepticism concerning the single, not to say solipsistical, mind-self of the *received*, 'Cartesian', dichotomously dualistic notions of mind-self and body. For it is on such strictly dualistic notions of mind and body, in which mind in and of itself partakes of nothing of the body (and initially at least partakes of nothing of another mind), and body in and of itself partakes of nothing of the mind, that Hume's arguments against the real existence of mind can be deemed successful. On such a strictly dualistic account of the matter, bodies are the source of impressions which the single and initially solipsistic mind receives, thereafter to become the locus of those ideas of perceptions, affections and so on which follow on from the impressions. Hence the force of Hume's question: What impression of mind itself is there, lying behind or beyond the impressions that have their source in bodies? Hence his confident assertion that he comes upon no such purely mind-originated impression of something that could be thought of as mind, as an entity that continues its existence and identity through the passing parade of the impressions collected in memory. Hence, the loss of the subject which Hume secures – as a piece of negative metaphysics? – is the loss of a subject conceived according to the kind of received dualism that still to this day claims Descartes as its father.

If this view of Hume is at all acceptable, even as a practical manoeuvre, then it is time to turn to Kant, in order to see how Kant in his critical stage managed to set philosophy on a course which might carry it safe from the scepticism of Hume. Needless to say, the nature and position of the subject in the ensuing construction of reality – for Kant does certainly include as an essential part of his philosophy an attempt to construe reality – must continue to provide the focus on this wider question.

Kant's countermove, and the phenomenon–noumenon divide

The broad outlines of Kant's attempt to secure the future of knowledge, whether philosophical or scientific, from the scepticism of Hume, are well known and need only the briefest of rehearsals here.

In the transcendental aesthetic of *The Critique of Pure Reason* Kant
establishes to his own manifest satisfaction that since all sense perceptions (or intuitions, as he calls them) are always characterised by being in
time, and perhaps also in place, then time and space themselves cannot
be counted as things that exist in their own right (things in themselves)
and independently of the perceiving subject; for then time and space
would themselves have to be perceived in a time and a space, and an
infinite regress would ensue. We are left with no option, then, in Kant's
view, but to regard time and space as *a priori* mental forms of sense
intuition. Whether time and space are also characteristics of things in
themselves, independently of the process of our perceiving them, we can
by the very nature of sense perception never know.

Having established these *a priori* forms of intuition, Kant then proceeds to investigate the next level of knowing, the level at which we think
things through or understand things. At this level also he establishes the
existence of forms of understanding which serve to synthesise what
would otherwise be the discrete manifold of impressions made, as Hume
saw the matter, by a discrete manifold of objects in the outside world.
And once again at his level, it is the synthesising processes of these forms,
now referred to as the categories of the understanding, that enable
knowledge to take place, rather than an incoherent sequence of impressions. Thus, the synthesis of the manifold takes place at the level of
intuition through the *a priori* forms of space and time; and it takes place
at the level of thought through the *a priori* categories of the understanding, namely, the categories of quantity, the categories of quality, the
categories of relation and the categories of modality. But thought
according to the categories allows us to make no more claims to the way
it is with things in themselves, before or beyond our understanding
them, than happened in the case of the intuitions. The understanding
cannot bypass the intuition in such a way as to find a more direct route
to things as they exist in themselves. It operates, rather, by adding a
further level of formal, *a priori* structures to the process by which we
receive impressions from the world without.

Finally, Kant considers the process by which we apply these categories of the understanding to the objects that one intuits according to the
forms of sense perception. We do this, he argues, by means of the
schemata. Now, a schema is itself a mental construct, a product he says
of the imagination, which enables us to apply an idea to its object. And
the schemata are, as Kant put it, determinations of time. The schema of
cause and causality consists in the succession of the manifold, in so far as

that is subject to rule. The schema of substance consists in permanence in time. The schema of reality consists in existence at a given time. The schema of necessity consists in the existence of an object at all times. And so on.

So, from the first (level of) intuition, through the thinking or understanding, to the final issuing of a judgement, or the application of ideas to objects, the whole process of knowing is characterised and controlled as much by already existing (*a priori*) structures of the mind itself – forms of intuition, categories of the understanding, schemata of the imagination – as it is by the input of the objects in the world which one claims to know. One obvious result of this theory of knowledge, designed to save knowledge itself from the effects of Humean scepticism, was a new and more extensive kind of dualism than Descartes or his followers had contemplated. And it was a result which Kant himself was quite happy to acknowledge and indeed to assert. The dualism in question is that between the 'thing as it appears (to us)', or the phenomenon, and the 'thing (as it exists) in itself' independently of our knowing anything about it, or, in Kant's terminology, the noumenon.

Furthermore, a kind of quite radical agnosticism followed upon this dualism, and once again it was something which Kant was quite happy to acknowledge and indeed assert. We could never know the 'thing in itself'. Could we even know that such a thing or things existed at all? Kant argued that we could, and he argued in a manner that has been repeated by later philosophers of like-minded phenomenological persuasion. He argued, for example, that some permanent reality must exist beyond the flow of consciousness, since we experience this as a flow rather than as a number of discrete and unrelated impressions.[11] But it is not the success of such arguments for the existence of a world beyond our knowledge of it that needs concern us here. Such arguments are needed, and are forthcoming, from most if not all theories of knowledge. What must concern us here are two related questions, namely, does Kant's knowledge of the thing-as-it-appears, the knowledge of the phenomenon only, leave the prospects of knowing any better off than Hume left them; and more particularly, does it leave us with any more secure knowledge of self?

In order to answer these questions, it may be useful to remark that just as modern philosophy may be characterised in general by the fatherhood

---

[11] I. Kant, *The Critique of Pure Reason* (New York: Doubleday, 1966), p. 175.

of Descartes, so it may be characterised somewhat more specifically by the early and progressive influence upon it of a newly born and precociously successful science. One thinks of Roger Bacon's manifesto for philosophy, of Descartes's initial exemplary references to analytic geometry, or of Kant's to mathematics and physics. Paul Hazard, in his lucid survey of the end of the seventeenth and the beginning of the eighteenth century, wrote: 'A political system without divine sanction, a religion without mystery, a morality without dogma, such was the edifice man had now to erect', and his very next sentence acknowledged something of the extent of the contribution which the new architects expected of the newly burgeoning science: 'Science would have to become something more than an intellectual pastime; it would have to develop into a power capable of harnessing the forces of nature to the service of mankind. Science – who could doubt it? – was the key to happiness.'[12]

But if it is useful to notice the influence of the new science in these formative centuries of the modern era in philosophy, it is necessary to avoid a certain anachronism in so doing. (Indeed there may be a hint of such anachronism in the words of Hazard's second sentence above.) In much more recent times science and philosophy have tended to move apart. In the earlier Analytic philosophy, philosophy is generally regarded as a second-order study; in Continental philosophical movements, it is thought in general to deal with human concerns or human features such as language, or symbolism in general, when the different sciences deal largely with the physical features of the world. As a result of this more recent falling apart, philosophers are inclined to think of scientists in a number of ways. For some scientists provide the accounts of what can be known, and philosophers provide a logical service, mainly sifting sense from nonsense in popular accounts of reality; occasionally, as with Quine, preparing the analytic ground from which perhaps new hypotheses can arise. These philosophers tend in the main to be reductionists: just as science is dominated by the more physical sciences, so these feel that everything that needs to be explained or can be known is to be reduced to empirical, predominantly physical components and processes. Other philosophers do not welcome such reductionism. Those who do, take the second-order-study approach; those who do not, attempt to secure for philosophy the treatment of such human features as morality and, perhaps, religion; but because of the

---

[12] Paul Hazard, *The European Mind* (New Haven: Yale University Press, 1953), p. xvii.

dominant influence of the more reductionist tendencies, the latter feel constantly under siege concerning the objectivity, the verifiable truth, of what they assert about the human features taken to be the subject matter of philosophy.

Now, it is obvious, even from the words of Hazard just quoted, that it would be quite anachronistic to attribute this kind of relationship of philosophy and science to the philosophers and the centuries presently under investigation. The current separation between philosophy and the empirical sciences, a separation which can facilitate mutual estrangement to the point of depriving the scientific quest for truth of its inherently moral and human dimension, and the wider philosophical and theological quests of their very claim to verifiability, simply cannot be thought to characterise an age in which, for example, Newton's masterpiece could be entitled *The Mathematical Principles of Natural Philosophy*. In this early-modern period, on the contrary, the new science and the new philosophy were thought to form a kind of seamless robe, much as they formed in fact at the very dawn of Western philosophy, when the first philosophers set about a critical rational investigation of all the things that are, *ta onta*; wishing to rule nothing out in advance, least of all on some dualist conceit concerning mind and matter, with the exception of those imaginary entities of doubtful moral influence which had survived from a corrupt mythic past.

The more recent separation of science from philosophy results, no doubt, from a number of factors. Amongst them the increasing specialisation in academia. Amongst them also the myth created largely by Thomas Huxley on the back of his defence and popularisation of Darwin's theories that science and religion, and hence also science and theology, were intrinsically inimical to each other and inevitably, therefore, at war. When in actual fact, even at that time, theologies in their inherently critical-analytic mode were adjusting, as they had done from their beginnings as part of the seamless robe of pre-Socratic thought, to the advances in scientific investigation of the world.

But the main factor in bringing about the current mutually compromising separation between philosophy and science may well consist in some failure in the successive philosophies now under investigation to establish critically the prospects of verifiable claims to know the things that are, both knowers and known. For if such a failure were to occur and were not to be subsequently corrected, then it would be small wonder if the sciences were tempted to get on with the investigation of the restricted areas or aspects of reality to which they devoted their ever

more specialised attention; to renegue on the wider ambitions to speculate on the influence of their findings on the understanding of reality as a
whole (except, of course, in the form of reductionist claims they might be
tempted to make); and to ignore as largely, if not entirely, irrelevant the
products of philosophy which itself in any case no longer included any
comprehensive ambitions.

Hence the importance of the question to Kant: does his knowledge of
phenomena leave the prospects of knowing any better off than Hume
left them? And hence also, in view of the large and increasing influence
which the success and prestige of the new science exercised on these
philosophers, the need to ensure that this question is not asked anach-
ronistically from the perspective of a more recent and largely unhelpful
relationship between science and philosophy; and particularly between
science and that part of philosophy which remained theological or,
rather, that kind of theology which in this early-modern period was so
resolutely philosophical.[13] In their efforts to save the prospects of true
knowledge of real things and real processes, none of these early-modern
philosophers were even tempted to save knowledge of some compartments or aspects of reality, at the possible expense of knowledge of
others. So then what is to be said of Kant?

The understanding, Hume had declared, never observes any real
connection amongst the objects of which perceptions are available to it.
There exist a plethora of affections and sensations, impressions or
perceptions, and the ideas to which these in turn give rise. But the
understanding never observes behind this variegated pluriformity any
subsisting entity, any substance retaining its identity through any number or succession of such sensations and affections, or their related ideas;
it never observes any identical entity to which this variety may be
referred. The feeling we may have of some subsisting identity that unites
these varied and manifold perceptions in the case of the human mind, as
indeed in the analogous cases of plants or animals, houses or ships, the
ever changing parts of which we also observe, is a fiction produced by
memory and imagination. That latter in particular is enabled to pass
smoothly and effortlessly from one idea of a perception to another,
taken either as a perception simply or as a perception of a part or aspect

[13] In the history of Western philosophy there is no atheistic philosophy, no philosophy that does not
    contain a formal and explicit theological dimension integral to it, until some left-wing Hegelians
    arrive on the scene, and particularly Karl Marx. Modern historians of philosophy and classical
    scholars who describe early philosophers, such as Socrates for instance, as atheistic, or in such
    equivalent terms as secularist, engage therefore in a most unscholarly anachronism. See Mark L.
    McPherran, *The Religion of Socrates* (University Park: Pennsylvania State University Press, 1996).

of a plant, animal, house. This smooth and effortless passage is facili-
tated by such relations between ideas as resemblance, contiguity, causality; and that last at least is already itself no more than the result of a
habitual association of ideas of impressions of things that follow regularly one on the other. And it is this smooth and effortless transition that
creates the fiction of subsistent entities such as selves, souls or substances. But it is, of course, a fiction.

Now, science, or natural philosophy, proceeds by categorising the
entities we encounter in our empirical world according to their properties and behaviour, and by investigating the ways in which these entities,
particularly through their specific properties and behaviour, bear upon
other entities. In this way science, and any philosophy of which this
science is both model and content, leads to an understanding and
explanation of the very fabric of reality, and of all the entities that form
part of that fabric, at least in so far as such understanding and explanation is within our presumably limited human grasp. However, if the
categorising in which we engage, and the causal relationships which we
say we uncover, are to be attributed to an imagination which itself is
regarded as the source of nothing better than fictions, what can now be
said for science, irrespective of how comprehensively or narrowly
science is conceived? Little or nothing, is Kant's answer. But do Kant's
own life-saving efforts on behalf of *scientia*, knowledge, leave us any
better off?

The point of putting the question in this rather elaborate and slightly
repetitive form is to suggest a negative answer. It appears clear from this
way of asking the question that Kant simply takes these structures of the
knowing process which Hume had analysed, that he adds perhaps some
similar ones, and then, instead of treating them as processes predominantly of the imagination which therefore give rise to mere fictions,
Kant distributes them between the sensing faculty (as forms thereof), the
understanding (as categories thereof) and the imagination (as schemata
thereof), and declares that through them we know the entities we
encounter, because they represent the *a priori* structures of the mind
through which alone the entities we wish to know appear to us.

For example, according to Kant, I know of substances which are
related to each other causally, by the combined operation of schemata
of the imagination upon the intuitions I receive from entities in the real
world; in this case, the schema of permanence in time and the schema of
succession of the manifold, in so far as that succession is subject to a rule
(as a rule). This knowledge, therefore, is a fiction, at least in the literal

sense of a fabrication by the forms, categories, schemata, acting upon the input of the thing-in-itself. And the difference between Hume and Kant would seem to consist only in this: that Hume considers the work of the imagination to result in a fiction that the understanding can unveil as such. Kant, on the other hand, allows the understanding no such disillusioning or deconstructive role. Instead, all the structures of our knowing, including the structures of our understanding, are reissued by Kant as the known *a priori* conditions of all our knowing; and the validity of knowledge is thus secured at the cost of the qualification that we only know things as they appear to us and we cannot know that we know them as they are in themselves.

Hume's position may result in scepticism, and nothing more than scepticism, that is to say, in a total failure to do anything himself to save knowledge. A haphazard plurality, even a sequence of different perceptions, does not constitute anything we could possibly call understanding or explanation, and certainly not anything we could call science. Even when Hume calls the mind nothing other than a bundle or collection of different perceptions, he exaggerates and hides the true disintegration of our idea of mind in which he is engaged. A bundle and a collection needs a binder and a collector; otherwise we are really talking about a mere plurality of potentially infinite number, all different and unrelated. And there is then as yet nothing that could even minimally be called mind; there is neither knower nor known. If the focus is now directed, finally, to Kant's account of the self, does the assessment of his advance on Hume improve?

Kant's understanding of the mind-self – for in this philosophical climate mind or soul still constitutes the real self – is best gleaned from that part of his philosophy in which he investigates the moral behaviour of the human being. Kant insisted that where the mind, its understanding and will, is driven by emotions such as desire for pleasure and repulsion from pain, the kind of categories available to Hume in the matter of morals, no genuinely moral behaviour takes place at all. Moral behaviour does indeed require the willing of good, but that good must be the *summum bonum*, the coincidence of total wellbeing with good moral behaviour; and as such it must be willed by each for all rational beings,[14] where the emotions envisage merely the satisfaction of individuals or, at best, close groups of fellows.

It follows for Kant that rational beings must act for this universal end

---

[14] I. Kant, *The Critique of Practical Reason* (New York: Liberal Arts Press, 1956), pp. 40ff. *Fundamental Principles of the Metaphysic of Ethics* (New York: Bobbs-Merrill, 1959), p. 40.

rather than act on individual or group emotions, even though they cannot individually guarantee such coincidence of happiness with virtue – it is the chief office of God to do that for them, in Kant's view. It follows also, then, that the main maxim by which rational beings must act, and the maxim which should form the one criterion of all more specific maxims of action, is this: act only on that maxim which you can at the same time will should be a maxim for all rational agents. The source of this maxim, and as a consequence the source of all behaviour which is truly moral, is the pure rational will. However – and here from the perspective of the present investigation is the rub – that pure rational will can be known to exist only indirectly, only as a postulate, as Kant would say, supported by such tainted experience of being moral as rational agents enjoy and by the ideal of the *summum bonum* which they inevitably entertain. The mind, reason and will, the rational will *as it appears*, the phenomenon, always appears enmeshed in the desires and aversions, the loves and hates and so on, of actual human individuals. Furthermore, all of the empirical behaviour of human agents appears to them to be under the same determination of the chain of causality which applies to all entities and activities in the world, as these appear to the human intuition, imagination and understanding. The pure rational will, therefore, the mind which is composed of uncompromised reason and free willing, is a noumenon, in Kant's terminology, not a phenomenon. As a thing-in-itself we do not know it as such; we only know it as it appears through the structures of intuition, imagination, understanding, like everything else that exists.

It was Beck, a pupil of Kant's who was also his chief disciple and the principal expositor of his system, who felt that the system would remain flawed unless some higher synthesising factor were identified, over and above the synthesising structures already in place. And he seems to have won some measure of agreement from Kant on this point, though Kant himself does not seem to have developed his system any further as a result.[15] For it only takes a moment's thought to realise that the *a priori* structures of intuition, of imagination and of understanding, are themselves a plurality which, unless they are functions of some more unified knower, leave us with a variegated plurality of intuitions, images and ideas; even though the variegated plurality may now be said to be reduced, in that some of these, the intuitions, are collected into groups by the (combined?) operation of others, the categories and schemata.

---

[15] I. Kant, *Philosophical Correspondence 1759–1799* (University of Chicago Press, 1967), esp. n. 500.

Furthermore, since we cannot know things as they are in themselves (even if we are satisfied with Kant's argument that things-in-themselves do exist), we cannot know if reality as it is in itself exhibits those features of permanence through change, and the further features of an interactivity that synthesises the entities-in-themselves of that real world. We cannot know if such features in the real world then correspond to the admittedly flawed synthesising features of the knowing process. We cannot know if we are not after all just recipients of a haphazard plethora of discrete impressions, or of some other type of input which the structures of our knowing processes radically distort. Beck, then, was suggesting a more basic synthesising agent or process which operated on knower and on reality, and even on their intrinsic interrelationship.

Whatever it is that could synthesise to the point of exhibiting the unity of the apperceptive ego, as Kantians would say, beyond its described structures; whatever it is that could synthesise the manifold of things-in-themselves to the point of exhibiting a formed and structured world, a *uni*verse, or at least a universe of interrelated universes; whatever it is that could then synthesise the former with the latter (for even Kant insisted we human knowers belong amongst things-in-themselves as an integral part of that unknown reality); whatever such an overarching, synthesising factor could be, of it the system developed by Kant himself remains innocent. As a result we are still left without an account, much less an explanation of how *we* actually *know* any *thing*. We cannot know, we can only postulate, the real knowing, thinking self which Hume was anxious to deconstruct; and the same has to be said of the real world as it exists, and of which we appear to be such an integral part.

The upshot of all of this busy philosophising, from the alleged mind–body dualism of Descartes, through the opposing commentaries of Hume and Kant, would appear to be this: that we have now lost sight of both ends of the equation, the thinking subject and the 'objective' entity. The attention has remained upon knowledge, as if epistemology is first philosophy. Yet knowledge, both the active process and its content, seems to have become somehow semidetached, from the knower on the one side, and from reality as it is actually fabricated on the other. An uncanny anticipation, some might say, of much more recent philosophies which present themselves as essentially semiology, and leave us with a play of signifiers amongst themselves. Indeed; and such causal connections as may exist must yet be investigated. But not before noticing what happened with Hegel, who saw clearly what had happened with Kant, and who tried manfully to reverse it.

HEGEL: DEVELOPING DUALISM REVERSED

Hegel was not very kind to Kant, and the older he grew the more unkind he was inclined to be. In the posthumously published *Lectures on the Philosophy of Religion* Hegel considers the position described above, the position, namely, in which knowledge seems to have become detached from both the knowing self and the entity to be known. He is immediately aware of the paradox that the very attempt to establish the validity of the knowing process as one which enables a real knowing subject to know a real object, has proved to be nothing more than a rational investigation of knowledge itself, an investigation which never actually catches sight of either the subject-in-itself or the object-in-itself. And he has this to say:

Criticism of the faculty of knowledge is a position of the Kantian philosophy, and one which is general in the present time, and in the theology of the day. It was believed to be a great discovery, but as so often happens in the world, this belief proved to be self-deception . . .

Reason is to be examined, but how? It is to be rationally examined, to be known; this is, however, only possible by means of rational thought; it is impossible in any other way, and consequently a demand is made which cancels itself. It we are not to begin philosophical speculation without having attained rationally to a knowledge of reason, no beginning can be made at all, for in getting to know anything in the philosophical sense, we comprehend it rationally; we are, it seems, to give up attempting this, since the very thing we have to do is first of all to know reason. This is just the demand which was made by that Gascon who would not go into the water until he could swim.[16]

But it is in Hegel's seminal work, *The Phenomenology of Spirit*, that this criticism of a prevailing philosophical mode occurs in its most constructive form; in a form and a context, that is to say, in which this Kantian theory of knowledge is made to reveal, quite positively, both what in process and content it actually presupposes, and what it in effect promises. There are three things to be said briefly about Hegel's *Phenomenology of Spirit* before attempting the briefest outline of the alternative construction of Science, as he called it, which Hegel himself attempted.

First, it is in the form of a *Bildungsroman*. Its place in the history of Western thought is beside the works of Augustine, in particular the *Confessions*, and the *Enneads* of Plotinus. It is a journey of discovery in which the reader is drawn to participate. It is not a journey across a landscape, if that suggests traversing a series of objective cantons and

[16] G. W. F. Hegel, *Lectures on the Philosophy of Religion* (London: Routledge and Kegan Paul, 1968), vol. I, pp. 52–3.

mountains previously uninhabited by mind; if such a contrast be allowed at all, it is rather a journey in the form of an inscape, such as
Augustine made, or Plotinus; an inscape of the mind towards the true
Reality. But the point will be, of course, that the contrast must not be
allowed to operate, and in this seminal work of Hegel's the first and
permanent discovery to be made is precisely that the contrast between
journeying inward through mind, and journeying outward through
objective reality, does not obtain. In this journey, then, consists the
education, the bringing up, the coming to its full adult self of the
questing human spirit. Thinking, no doubt, of the kind of structures of
mind and reality which in Kant had come loose from mind-reality,
Hegel envisages a journey through these which will bring us to the
fulness of mind-reality, which he calls the Absolute. 'The series of
configurations which consciousness goes through along this road is, in
reality, the detailed history of the *education* of consciousness to the
standpoint of Science.'[17]

Second, in offering even the briefest summaries of Hegel's philosophy, the relationship of the *Phenomenology* to his other works needs to
be decided and explained, and in particular the relationship of the
Phenomenology to the Encyclopedia of Philosophical Sciences, which
comprised Hegel's *Logic*, his *Philosophy of Nature* and his *Philosophy of
Mind*; since the Encyclopedia presents the reader with the System,
where the *Phenomenology* invites the reader on the journey. This relationship between the *Phenomenology* and the System, it may be suggested, is
the relationship between a travelogue which one uses as a guide in
making an actual journey, and those holiday brochures which depict
all the places people have occupied. The former constitutes a dynamic
process which can be improved, or disimproved, by each successive
user. The latter represents a more static achievement in which the ones
who have arrived abstract from the process of arriving a systematic
account of themselves and others in place. It too can be changed by
new arrivals, for they are new ones who have each made the journey to
the place, and they will not leave the place the same as if they had not
arrived. Now, if this metaphor is at all useful, it will yield the insight
that the primacy in Hegel's philosophy always belongs to the *Phenomenology*. The System is an abstract, conceptual out-take from a dynamic
process which consists in being acted upon and acting, the process in
which education, becoming, actually and permanently consists. As an

[17] G. W. F. Hegel, *The Phenomenology of Spirit* (Oxford: Clarendon Press, 1977), p. 50.

out-take it is useful for orienting oneself at any and all points of the journey; but it remains nevertheless under the continuous creative influence of the pilgrims and of their tales; at least until all journeys end, if they ever do end.

Third, Hegel's philosophy is theology from beginning to end. More is intended in that remark than reference to the fact that his earliest vocation was to religion and theology; and his early, probing works before he launches out on the great journey-to-the-end of the *Phenomenology* are largely theological in theme and content. What is intended, rather, is that in Hegel's view of the matter, the Absolute is present to and through the process of knowledge from the beginning. Now, this does not mean that we do, or should attempt to, prove the existence of God at the start of the quest for wisdom, much less that we should think that we know from the beginning the meaning of the word 'God' or, for that matter, the meaning of 'the Absolute'; as indeed all proofs of God's existence must presume that we do. Hegel was particularly dismissive of the rationalist philosophy and theology of his time. He had in mind those who first define God in terms of certain attributes, for example, attributes of power and knowledge, but then attempt to do justice to the transcendence of God over creatures by qualifying each of these attributes in turn with an 'omni', as in 'omnipotent', in order to denote the infinity of the attributes and of the Being. All that is achieved by such manoeuvres is a concept of God which is hollow, empty and poor; one from which all accessible content of meaning has been removed in advance. In reality, we discover, or uncover God or the Absolute in a very different way.[18] Therefore, Hegel's philosophy is theological from beginning to end, in the sense that the Absolute appears to and in our knowing at the beginning of our formational journey in a manner that, if we respond with full analytic attention, will lead us in the end to the fullest knowledge of, and participation in, the Absolute of which we are capable.

So, then, in the introduction to the *Phenomenology* Hegel already considered the position of those who first rationally investigate knowledge itself, under the illusion, or on the pretext, that knowledge is either an instrument for bringing near or making present the Absolute, or a

---

[18] Hegel, *Lectures*, vol. i, p. 30. It is a great pity that contemporary philosophers who treat philosophy of religion as if it somehow centred upon such proofs of God's existence do not pay more attention to Hegel. See for example Anthony Kenny, *The God of the Philosophers* (Oxford: Clarendon Press, 1979): Hegel could have saved him the trouble of such laborious analysis and critique of a God already defined in the questionable categories of omniscience and omnipotence.

medium through which the Absolute might be known. The Absolute at this point simply denotes that final (form of) reality which comprehends (because it is source of?) all that exists, has existed or will exist; and we do not know at the beginning much if anything of what the term connotes. Yet the Absolute is already present to us in and indeed also as knowledge, for knowledge is a part of reality, and a very creative one at that. For if knowledge, as both process and content, initially separated us entirely from the most comprehensive knower or knowledge-bearer and all that it comprehends or originates, all that participates in it – as the model of knowledge at first detached from both subjects and objects suggests, and as the images of instrument and medium merely illustrate – then we could never even begin to come to a true and full, that is to say, to as comprehensive a knowledge as is possible for us of the reality, the whole reality and nothing but the reality, in which we participate as integral and active parts. And that would mean also that we could never *be* as fully as we could be, in that reality. If knowledge were an instrument between us and reality, its use upon reality would alter it, and we could never know the extent of the alteration, that is to say, we would never know we had used such an instrument unless reality was present to us all the time. And a similar point would prove true of knowledge imagined as a medium between us and reality. The medium would deflect the ray by which the light from the real reached us; but we could only know that if at all times we could also see even the merest glimmer of the undeflected ray.

Hegel, then, begins the journey with appearance; the book after all is called a *Phenomenology*. Yet not, and quite explicitly not, with any distinction between appearance and reality such as had become the fashion after Kant, and to which the noumenon–phenomenon in effect amounts. In fact, Hegel says, all knowledge initially is appearance; and in this there is no distinction between our initial knowledge of the Absolute, which he calls Science, and our knowledge of other entities and aspects of reality.

At this point he introduces the term 'consciousness'. Consciousness consists also of appearance. In fact it is appearence to and of itself. In all consciousness of an appearance of an object, consciousness simultaneously distinguishes itself from the something-that-appears and relates itself to that determinate appearance – this is called knowing. But there is entailed already here another dimension of consciousness. In being conscious of itself, in the course of being conscious of the appearance of something which it distinguishes from itself, it reveals itself to be something simultaneously limited and yet transcending, going beyond these limits in and of itself. That seems clear enough. Even if one thinks of this self-consciousness in the spatial imagery of something bent back over itself, something reflective, one can then envisage an overview perspective which belongs to the part of the thing bent back over itself. So, even if consciousness always has a determinate, limited content as consciousness of some thing, it is also conscious of being conscious of that, and so goes beyond that, transcends it, always. Consciousness therefore transcends itself.

Hegel introduces a further feature of this reflective dimension which consciousness possesses as self-consciousness. He describes a consequent and permanent openness of consciousness which troubles its repose whenever it tries to rest with its current content of knowledge. Further still, he writes of a violence that consciousness experiences in this respect; a drivenness in consciousness that can only be reminiscent of the role of Eros in Plato, of the inclinations of the will which Descartes numbered amongst the *pensées*, of the rational will in Kant's philosophy; the dimension of consciousness, in short, that appears to drive it onward to envisage, to comprehend, to master what is good for us, and what promises continuance in being, life and life more abundant. And then, not unexpectedly, the word 'soul' occurs in this context as a synonym for consciousness: 'the way of the soul which journeys through the series of its own configurations as though they were the stations appointed for it by its own nature, so that it may purify itself for the life of the Spirit'.[19]

Commentators have rightly interpreted these stations as a veiled reference to the Christian imagery of the stations of the Cross, the stages which led to the death of Jesus. Hegel does see the progress of the soul as a successive putting to death, a negating by a restless and driven consciousness of its own configurations. In other words, since these configurations of phenomenal knowledge themselves constitute consciousness, this is a process in which consciousness continually dies to itself so that it may continually rise in a higher form, to be resurrected into the absolute status of Spirit. The raising at each stage and overall is the Hegelian *Aufhebung* – a negation which preserves that which it negates in a higher form. Spirit is the absolute status of consciousness or soul; the state, it would seem, in which it now knows as appearances of or from it, what before were known as appearances to or in it. It is difficult to avoid the implication that this means soul knowing as its

[19] Hegel, *Phenomenology*, p. 49.

creation, and thereby uncovering itself in, all that before appeared as object to it. One thinks of Paul's promise in the New Testament: 'then I shall know even as I am known'. And if one combines this with Hegel's own insistence that the only true knowledge of God is knowledge of God as subject, one can only assume the following as Hegel's final scenario. God knows everything as its creator; as souls complete their journey and so come into union with God, they participate together in this ultimate knowing-being; and that is Spirit, now all-in-all, Absolute.

This is very traditional stuff indeed. Augustine's journey through the inscape of soul is described in terms of memory, will and understanding; where memory connotes the fund of knowledge one always already possesses, however obscure or inchoate the presence of the most profound of it may be; will is that erotic drive to attend to what is deeply but dimly known, the drive to apprehend, indeed to live it; and understanding names that final appropriation or union with all that is known. The journey to this final goal is in fact described by Augustine as a journey through science to wisdom – although Hegel would probably prefer to say through the sciences to Science. And finally, the reason why this structuring of the human soul as memory, will and understanding is the best 'trace' of the divine in the world, which we may follow to union with God, is because the God who continually creates the world is triune: Will (Spirit) dynamically secures the unification of the Knower (Father) with the Known (Son), and shines in our hearts and minds.[20]

But how, one may ask with some exasperation, can such massive deployment of metaphysical, indeed theological, terminology in the very introduction to the *Phenomenology* be cached in its staid language of appearance? The answer to that question begins with the realisation that the distinction between consciousness (of itself) and that something which appears to it in determinate appearances, is a distinction that falls within consciousness itself. Consciousness, as we saw, relates itself to that something which appears to or in it, which may be called the object or the thing-in-itself, and in that relationship knowing consists. But it is only when we realise that it is consciousness itself that distinguishes between itself and that which appears to or in it, that we also realise that the task of establishing the truth of our knowing cannot involve any stepping outside of consciousness in order to watch and measure the relationship between consciousness and object. On the contrary, when

---

[20] Augustine, *De Trinitate*, esp. bks x–xiv.

consciousness tries to establish the truth of its knowledge, it will always find itself confined, indeed driven, to attending critically at any of its phases or 'stations' to the relationship between itself and the object which appears in it and forms the determinate content of it. As the distinction between consciousness and its object falls within consciousness, so too does the critique and criterion of the relationship between these. Consciousness thus discovers the role it itself plays in the construal of reality. It discovers this gradually by attending critically to each form or phase of contentful or determinate consciousness, in a process that will cause the death or negation of each distinguishable phase. From this there results for consciousness its gradual and increasing realisation that the work of consciousness in the construction of reality at each level or phase will, indeed must, lead to a final realisation of the whole of reality as the creation of consciousness; in which it will then have both recognised and realised itself.

Before taking from Hegel's *Phenomenology* a few concrete examples of stages on this path to absolute truth, examples which certainly make concrete sense of these awesomely abstruse propositions, it might help to anticipate just one aspect of the matter that will come under consideration later in this essay. The notion of the role in the very construction of reality of something that is explicitly called knowledge; the notion of truth, as a consequence, consisting in part at least in correctly knowing that knowledge – that is not at all alien to some contemporary scientists. And if one remembers the close relationship between the notions of consciousness and knowledge in Hegel, that feature of modern scientific philosophy should help in the present context. For example, in the metaphysics of David Deutsch the 'theory of everything', the account of the whole fabric of reality, for which he argues, comprises four constituent theories.[21] Amongst these four he counts epistemology, or theory of knowledge; and this is precisely because of the role of knowledge in the very process of the construction of reality. To say that in Deutsch's eschatology the knowledge which constructs reality is that of our distant future successors would be to anticipate too much; but it would also give some preliminary hint of the fact that Hegel's ways of thought are neither idiosyncratic nor *passé*. So to some of Hegel's particular examples.

Hegel keeps faith with the philosophies he inherited, at least to the extent that he begins the description of the soul's journey to Absolute

---

[21] David Deutsch, *The Fabric of Reality* (London: Penguin, 1997).

Reality, which is also Absolute Truth, with the phase of consciousness characterised by sense-certainty; what Kant called the mind's most elementary intuitions. This sense-knowledge at first appears to be the richest and truest kind of knowledge; richest in that it promises an infinite wealth of object-contents; truest in that it seems to take its objects immediately into itself in their entirety, without altering anything in them. Yet as soon as consciousness distinguishes from itself this appearance to itself, as soon as it reflects in its transcendent openness on this determinate form of itself, just as soon does transcending consciousness negate this level of knowledge, this determinate consciousness, as the poorest in offering and promise, and the most abstract form of truth. And consciousness as a result dies to that form of itself in order to rise to a truer self.

For at that most elementary level of consciousness of things I can only point, or say 'this', 'here', 'now'; and the 'I' involved is no more than a this, here, now. Then on reflection the now quickly becomes a then, or not-now; the here, a there or not-here; and the this then asserts the merest existence of the thing as it appears and the merest existence of the I at this level of consciousness. I know nothing more about it than that it is an instance of reality; and that is the most abstract, the poorest kind of knowledge, the knowledge that things are, that being is. Yet in the course of reflection which negates this consciousness, consciousness raises all of that content, and itself, to a higher level. Simultaneously it alters both itself and its object. For it now sees a here as one amongst many heres, a this as one amongst many thises; so that where immediate intuition was merely a source of instances of being, perception now witnesses the appearance of something composed of many; a thing with many properties, for example. To this new level of consciousness called perception, then, the wealth of sense-knowledge, and a fuller truth about it, really belongs. But this determinate consciousness too dies at the reflective realisation of the negative effects of difference in the manifold. Until consciousness construes the reality which appears to it as the result of patterns of deployment of properties across different things, and the causal or dispositional interactions that mutually involve these things through these properties. This new stage of consciousness which rises from the grave of the former stages, and which construes in this manner the reality which appears, is called understanding. It understands reality through notions of natures, forces, laws. The differentiated manifold of perception now rises up as a universe at this level of its construal by consciousness.

All the time, through all these stages of death and resurrection, the soul or self is learning of its role in the construal of reality; and since, throughout the series consciousness changes *pari passu* with the objects that appear, it learns something about the dynamics of the self itself. The provisional result of this lesson Hegel outlines in the section of the *Phenomenology* entitled 'Self-Consciousness', where he uses the famous master–slave analogy. Considered as self, consciousness seems to be inherently intersubjective: it is named self-consciousness in that in all the processes already described, as indeed in all others that might be added, it appears as if a (conscious) self is conscious of a (its) self. That could be made a little more concrete if each process – for they are all of one kind in a sense – is represented as a transcendent self attending to a determinate self, where the latter continually construes the world, or indeed constructs it if the subject moulds things in the course of labour, according to the present configurations of the subject's determinate consciousness or determinate self. The transcendent consciousness-self is then constantly killing, negating, the determinate self, or seems to be trying to do just this. But it is really driving the determinate self, or the empirical self as one might say, to rise up to transcend itself, since it, after all, is doing all the work of construal or construction, and the transcendent self, in so far as that can be distinguished from the other, is in a sense doing nothing, merely negating. The master kills the self of the slave, but the slave is the creator nonetheless, and more essential to the master than the master is to the slave. Yet without the transcendent self, creation would not take place.

In this complex manner Hegel essays the dynamics, the metaphysics, of self. It is essentially intersubjective; that at least is a simple outcome of the analysis. But it is quite intriguing to note that in all of the section on self-consciousness where Hegel is writing about the self and its other, it is impossible to decide whether he is thinking simply of the intersubjectivity of consciousness *simpliciter*, or of the intersubjectivity of numerically distinct human selves, or of the intersubjectivity of God as supreme transcendent self with a race of individual empirical selves. And if he is thinking at different times of all three forms of intersubjectivity, what is the relationship between them? Is it that that question should not be put in that form to his text at all? Is it that the relationship between these selves, all intrinsically involved in inevitable intersubjectivity, is a much more subtle and profound one than a question phrased from such impressions of numerical distinctions could ever elicit? Perhaps the transcendental self is God working in all empirical selves, and working through them in co-construing and co-constructing the world?[22] God is in us in the world, and we in the world in God, and the eschaton, the end of the journey, involves the fullest conscious realisation of that state? There is much in Christian theology and scriptures that paints such a picture: the Spirit that is the risen Lord making us all one body in the world, by being the transcendent spirit of that body, in a way analogous to that in which my soul or spirit makes of its members one body of mine.[23] But, however we answer these questions, the ultimate nature of reality and truth for Hegel, in any case, remains clear: self, which construes and constructs reality, reconciling to itself, realising itself in all that is. For us this realising is pictured as a journey of the soul through the configurations of itself by which it construes and constructs reality. For the Absolute itself it is always already realised.

It is not the business of this essay, and certainly not of this part of it, to make any final suggestions in Hegelian exegesis. It is sufficient for present purposes to see in outline a philosophy that avoided dominant dualism and not only recovered the subject, but set the subject quite resolutely at the creative centre of reality.[24] Since even Hegel himself, in his more modest moments, realised that successive ages cannot reproduce the same philosophical moves in the same terms, he would presumably wish us to search our modern minds for a philosophy which would succeed in the same way as his did for his time, rather than reissue his. And the reference to Deutsch above gives a slight hint of the possibility of doing this. However, dualism did re-emerge – and such a dualism as involved the loss of the subject – and we must describe how that happened before ending this chapter, for that will have its own negative bearing on prospects of achieving something similar to what Hegel achieved.

---

[22] In the considered opinion of one of the finest of Hegelian scholars, Franz Gregoire, 'Dieu est . . . l'ensemble des esprits finis, ou mieux leur système, c'est-à-dire les esprits finis groupés en différentes religions et différentes philosophies enchaînées entre elles dialectiquement.' See his *Aux sources de la pensée de Marx, Hegel, Feuerbach* (Publications Universitaires, Louvain–Paris, 1947), p. III; also his *Études hegeliennes: les points capitaux du système* (Publications Universitaires de Louvain, 1958). But this rather begs the question of the source or outcome of their 'enchainment'.

[23] Saint Paul in I Corinthians chs. 12–15.

[24] There is a comment by Richard Kroner in his introduction to G. W. F. Hegel, *Early Theological Writings* (Chicago University Press, 1948), p. 37, which is interesting from the point of view of the interrelationship of theology and philosophy, and for the corresponding links in modern philosophy between the fates of divine and human subjects: 'Because Kant saw the connection between the theory of knowledge and the knowledge of God, he denied all knowledge of things as they are in themselves. This philosophic decision, Hegel says, and the method of reflective subjectivity which it entailed, are fruits of the tree of Protestantism.'

AFTER HEGEL
THE SPECTRE OF STRONG DUALISM BEGINS TO APPEAR AGAIN BUT NOT WITH MARX HIMSELF

'Philosophy since Kant has never achieved a freely mobile and genuinely critical relationship to Hegel's thinking, nor, *a fortiori*, to the inversions structuring modern subjectivity and ethical substance in which it embroils itself more blindly and deeply with the totalising invocation of metaphysics overcome.' So wrote Gillian Rose.[25] Yet these inversions structuring modern subjectivity did not immediately after Hegel amount to the total loss of the subject which has recently characterised postmodernism, at least in the express view of some of the leaders of the postmodernist movement. The steps by which the larger loss came about must be rehearsed here, then, as briefly as possible.

It was the so-called left-wing Hegelians – Strauss, Bauer and most notoriously Feuerbach – who first sharpened critical pens against the subject in Hegel's philosophy; but it was to the divine subject that their objections were directed. Apparently unaware of the fact that, in Gillian Rose's words again, the Hegelian Spirit never leaves its body in the world; inattentive at best, that is to say, to the permanent immanence of Spirit in the world; oblivious to the hints of such mutual immanence of divine and human consciousness in Hegel as we have seen so fleetingly above, both in the general account of the journey of spirit to the Absolute through its own configurations and, more specifically, in a passing question concerning the forms of intersubjectivity and the relationships between these in Hegel's text, Feuerbach convinces himself that the divine subject in Hegel's philosophy is an additional other individual person which, as the supreme subject of all that happens in creation and history, simply sets the human subject at nought. Unlike Strauss, though, Feuerbach considers this divine subject, which he thinks is Hegel's Spirit, to be a projection onto an empty heaven of the human subject by the human subject. For this reason Feuerbach himself characterised the central achievement of his own philosophy as the discovery that the secret of theology was anthropology, whereas the secret of the speculative philosophy of Hegel remained theology. He secured Marx's endorsement for this self-assessment, albeit rather grudgingly, as the one important idea that the whole of his published work had managed to produce.

---

[25] Gillian Rose, *Mourning Becomes the Law* (Cambridge University Press, 1966), p. 65.

It is probably worth pausing briefly here in order to point out that Feuerbach's dismissal of the kind of divine subject he thought he saw in Hegel's philosophy may not in fact be amenable to those projectionist-reductionist-type philosophies of religion with which more recent writers like Freud have made us familiar. There is a reading of Feuerbach which makes him say not that any subject that might reasonably be called divine is now critically dismissed, but rather that any divine subject other than that which coincides with human subject is to be critically dismissed. In short, Feuerbach is critical of the move by which humans have projected as an Other, additional and external to humanity in this world, what is in effect humanity's own infinite, that is, divine nature. On this reading, the phrase 'the secret of theology is anthropology' can be interpreted in a non-reductionist sense: Feuerbach's anthropology, his analysis of human nature, yields the true theology. In other words, the reversal of the projection is not a reduction of the divinity to the non-divine, but rather a discovery of the truly divine.

The clues which recommend this reading are everywhere in Feuerbach's most popular and influential work, *The Essence of Christianity*. They are found already in the very title of that work, especially when that is taken in conjunction with a key argument of Feuerbach's in the course of the book, to the effect that the central doctrine of Christianity, the doctrine, that is to say, of the incarnation, has God take human form, and that not as a temporary expedient for the purpose of delivering some revelation, for example, or of performing some essential salvific act, but as a permanent feature of the divine being.[26] Clues to this reading of Feuerbach are also found when the careful comparative reader notices how many key moves in Feuerbach are lifted straight out of Hegel's text. For example, when Feuerbach says that the usual content of the meaning of the word God is found in fact in the attributes – God is love, truth, goodness, creator and so on – so that the subject of these sentences, God, is left empty of content; and when he later makes the point that the only true knowledge of God is knowledge of God as

---

[26] Christians who read Feuerbach in this way gain an insuperable impression of the awesome immanence of God recorded in their scriptures. At the same time they gain an insight into the fact that transcendence and immanence are correlates, not contraries. And all of this as a result of the fact that Feuerbach does not merely state his thesis concerning religion in the abstract and then select Christian texts in support. On the contrary, he undertakes a critical analysis of all major Christian doctrines, rituals and practices, in order to show from them both how God can be seen to coincide with humanity, and how even Christians have projected a Wholly Other God to the diminishment of humanity.

subject, he is pretty well paraphrasing Hegel.[27] And all of this before one concentrates on explicit statements of Feuerbach's to the effect that religion is identical with the consciousness which humanity has of its own not finite but infinite nature – a statement supported by his analysis of the limitlessly self-transcending dimension of human consciousness, and protected by his warning that we are not to confuse the very real limitations which we as individuals or groups experience at any particular time with limitations of humanity, of the species-being as such – or the even more explicit statement to the effect that 'what today is atheism, tomorrow will be called religion'.[28]

Finally, and more generally, and this is a point that applies equally to Marx: when one notices how humanity, not as a collection of individuals but as a species-being, now enjoys the role of inner-worldly creator of what appears to the unlimited nature, surely, as limitless possibilities, one is bound to wonder at the very least if this subject of the continuously created world and of its history, which has so allocated to itself the traditional attributes of divinity, is not itself then of the status of a divine species-being in which all we limited individuals participate? It would then represent the transcendent embodied spirit, immanent in each of us in the world. In sum, Feuerbach does everything necessary to allow himself to be read not as someone who dismissed divine subject *simpliciter*, but rather as someone who dismissed a type of divine subject which would comprise an individual, discrete divine being, additional to all that we experience in ourselves and in the world of which we are so integral a part. Much congratulatory noise is heard about people, and in particular Marx, who stood Hegel on his head; and perhaps here in Feuerbach what we are really seeing is an admittedly lesser philosopher who situates the pivotal creative role of empirical human subjects more prominently than the role of the more elusive transcendental subjectivity operative in and through the species-being. Even so, it would be well to try to listen, beneath the prevailing noise, to a more restrained voice of critical reason whispering: ah yes, but Hegel upside-down is still Hegel. Even in the case of Marx.

Marx did believe that Feuerbach's pivotal philosophical move had rid us of the divine subject and left us with the human. Yet in his *Theses on Feuerbach* he criticises Feuerbach for his conception of human nature as something abstract – an abstract being squatting outside the world, as

---

[27] Compare L. Feuerbach, *The Essence of Christianity* (New York: Prometheus Books, 1957), chs. 1 and 23, with Hegel's *Phenomenology*, the Preface and particularly p. 12.
[28] Feuerbach, *The Essence of Christianity*, pp. 2, 7, 32.

he puts it elsewhere – which then comes to inhere in each single individual; and he correspondingly criticises Feuerbach's work of reinstating the human subject in place of the divine as something which is achieved in theory and not in praxis.[29] It is significant that the terms in which Marx criticised Hegel are quite similar. In Marx's 'Critique of Hegel's Dialectic', in which he begins with Hegel's *Phenomenology*, 'the true birthplace and secret of Hegel's philosophy',[30] he decides that Hegel defined the human essence in terms of consciousness, and especially self-consciousness, and further, that in doing so Hegel permanently privileged the conscious or thinking element over the real entity that is conscious or thinks.[31] Hence, Marx has convinced himself, Hegel's whole account of the journey of the soul through its own configurations to the Absolute is an account of a thoroughly theoretical procedure, a consciously conceptual procedure through-and-through. And it ends in a mind, now in Hegelian terms fully spirit, self-consciously thinking its own thoughts, replete in its own knowledge. Admittedly there are steps on the way which consist in some form of 'objectification' in which consciousness is seen to wrestle with what appear to be real objects alien and independent. But in the end the objective status of reality is overcome, and mind and all else return to the pure status of mind itself. A purely theoretical victory, Marx concludes, over real human suffering and alienation; and yet, Marx concedes, a mystifying account of the real dynamics of alienation and its eventual overcoming in atonement (at-one-ment).

Marx, on the contrary (and here is Hegel on his head again), and in an advance also on Feuerbach, defines the human essence in no abstract manner; for an abstract being squatting outside the world is in some ways hardly distinguishable from a god. For Marx, as the Sixth Thesis on Feuerbach has it, the human essence is defined as 'the ensemble of the social relations', or, as he put it in the introduction to the *Critique of Hegel's Philosophy of Right*, 'man is the world of man, the state, society'. These social relations which define humanity as a concrete entity in the real world are in turn constructed, first, according to the nature of the means of subsistence, and then according to the ways in which human

---

[29] See Marx's *Theses on Feuerbach* and his introduction to the *Critique of Hegel's Philosophy of Right* in D. McLellan, *Karl Marx: Selected Writings* (Oxford University Press, 1977), pp. 63, 156ff.

[30] See McLellan, *Karl Marx*, pp. 96ff.

[31] See K. Marx and F. Engels, *On Religion* (Moscow: Foreign Languages Publishing House, 1955), p. 74, where Marx makes the point by comment on the German word *Bewusstsein* and the possible ambiguity of the word, literally translated 'conscious-being' – consciousness of (some concrete) being, or (some concrete) being that is conscious.

beings successively reproduce these for themselves. Thus human nature constantly and actively creates itself as it acts creatively in the world. The single most succinct and genetic account of Marx's concept of human nature is found in *The German Ideology*, which Marx composed, with Engels, as a final riposte to the young Hegelians, particularly Feuerbach, and as a definitive explanation of the materialist conception of history. To quote one brief summary introductory passage:

The way in which men produce their means of subsistence depends first of all on the nature of the actual means of subsistence they find in existence and have to reproduce. This mode of production must not be considered simply as being the production of the physical existence of the individuals. Rather it is a definitive form of activity of these individuals, a definite form of expressing their life, a definite mode of life on their part. As individuals express their lives, so they are . . . This production only makes its appearance with the increase in population. In its turn this presupposes the intercourse of individuals with one another. The form of this intercourse is again determined by production.[32]

Now, and in consequence of such definition, the concept of humanity by which Marx wishes to set Hegel on his head is this: it is an inherently relational, intersubjective or social species (as Hegel indeed explained, albeit in his own peculiarly mystifying manner); but it is a community permanently, progressively and consciously active in reproducing simultaneously its own concrete reality and that of the physical world which is, in Marx's own language, its own sustaining inorganic body. Truth correspondingly consists in the success of praxis rather than the adequacy and accuracy of theory, as the human species-being reaches its specific fulfilment in a world simultaneously and adequately humanised; 'for [man] duplicates himself not only intellectually, in his mind, but also actively in reality and thus can look at his image in a world he has created'. Nor does this mean that humanity can use the natural universe in an arbitrary and entirely chauvinist manner: it would be as counterproductive for humanity to use arbitrarily its 'inorganic body', which after all provides the original means of sustenance designed for itself, as it would be for me to use arbitrarily my own organic body. Hence, 'man knows how to produce according to the measure of every species and knows everywhere how to apply its inherent standard to the object; thus man also fashions things according to the laws of beauty'.[33] Here are fleeting, intriguing intimations, surely, of the coincidence of truth with goodness and beauty, accompanying the coincidence of truth and praxis.

[32] See McLellan, *Karl Marx*, p. 161.
[33] From 'Alienated Labour' in *Economic and Philosophical Manuscripts*, as in McLellan, *Karl Marx*, p. 82.

But for the moment it is the alleged contrast of Marx's philosophy with Hegel's that is of concern, and there are just two things to be said about this before putting in place the final episode in the history of the origins of the contemporary status quo. First, as to the complaint that Hegel overcomes the evil and reaches the good, the (Absolute) good of existence, only in theory: it has to be said that Marx produces a possible, but equally a highly controvertible, reading of Hegel, and in doing so indulges in a form of criticism that could in part be turned against himself. For Hegel in his famous *Bildungsroman* pays at least as much attention to the construction of reality (praxis) as he does to the construal of reality (theory), as his substantial sections on labour, on politics and on morality show. Indeed these twin features of human creativity, construal/construction or theory/praxis, seem to be not only equally necessary, but so inextricably intertwined that questions of relative priority may be impossible to answer. In a later chapter of this essay the issue will recur in the form of the question as to how the creation of virtual reality can be incorporated into prospects for the future of a rapidly evolving scientific and technologically adept humanity, in a physical universe over which it gains increasing control. For the moment, though, it is necessary only to make the *ad hominem* point against Marx that he himself spent his life theorising and teaching, envisioning, one might say, and preaching both the actual structures of reality and the praxis by which it would be changed for the best. And that activity, that mental, literary and rhetorical production, had its inevitable place in changing the world, rather than merely interpreting it.

Furthermore, the object of mind, the 'real' world in which it finally recognises and is reconciled to itself, at the stage and status known as spirit, is no more due for disappearance in Hegel than it is in Marx. But the issue of the relationship and priority between theory and praxis in a subject-based account of the universe, as indeed the issue of the relationship of both to (self-)consciousness, is deep and difficult and will arise again. Marx, it may be said in the meantime, may have issued a perspectival corrective to Hegel, rather exaggeratedly expressed in terms of standing the poor man on his head, and a necessary corrective perhaps in an age biased towards idealism; but this, if anything, serves to enhance the achievement of Hegel in overcoming the kind of dualism that Kant bequeathed, a dualism in which the subject, both divine and human, disappeared from the world of experience, and could only in the end get lost from view.

Secondly, Marx certainly assumed that he had rid us of a divine subject, in that double move by which he endorsed Feuerbach and at the same time put an end to lingering impressions of an abstract being squatting outside the world; and left us with the human subject in its communal form instead. But has he really? There is always the danger, already obvious from Feuerbach, that in replacing divine with (merely) human subject one may fit the latter out with functions and attributes that still suggest divine status. For gods, after all, are not first defined as a distinct species (often with only one member), and then proved to exist – despite the manner in which much that passes for philosophy of religion is conducted. They are discovered, rather, as the ultimate ontic and ontological/explanatory, that is, creative sources of our universe in its past and present states and future prospects; discovered as the ultimate creative sources which we have encountered, or which we sense, however obscurely and tentatively. And Marx does write of 'man' creating a world in 'his' image.

Furthermore, there is for Marx, as there is for others who hold views similar to Deutsch in *The Fabric of Reality*, a kind of question concerning the creative agency that operated to make this a human-friendly world before *Homo sapiens sapiens* arrived at reasonably adequate creative status. In Marx's case the 'means of subsistence' which 'man' progressively reproduces, originally made 'man' what he then was, that is, they structured the ensemble of social relationship which then defined the human essence. But who or what, then, made the world in the image of humanity? An obvious question, of course, but one which increases rather than decreases its inherent insistence when it occurs in much more sophisticated forms in more recent times, when the world is seen as a great computer of a kind which we humans are just beginning to reproduce in the new age of quantum physics and quantum computers.

It must be enough to say for the moment that, whether the subject in Marx is human or divine, or some combination of both, the subject is in any case as present and prominent in Marx as in Hegel. And that leaves only the minor task of ending this chapter with a very brief description of the disappearance, nevertheless, of the subject in subsequent Marxist theory; for the particular genre of Marxist theory in which the subject did eventually disappear undoubtedly ranks amongst the influences responsible for the loss of the subject in that far from coherent contemporary movement known as postmodernism.

The impression can sometimes be gleaned from some of those who talk about it that 'historical materialism' or 'the materialist conception of history' of itself involves the loss of the subject, in the sense in which this essay takes the term subject, the sense of a knowledgeable agent. But, as can easily be seen even from the little that has been said about Marx, this is not the case. There is very definitely a subject, a very human subject, as Marx would insist, that continuously creates the world and construes the course of history. The force of the word 'materialism' in the programmatic phrases in which it occurs, therefore, is to confirm that the creative agency involved here is no extra-mundane and entirely incorporeal spirit, but rather a quintessentially bodily species which progressively creates itself as it creates its world in its own image, and which does so by reproducing the very material means which originally enabled it to be and to live: the means of its subsistence. The force of the word materialism is also designed to include the conviction that such elements of this very human creativity as law and morality, art and literature, philosophy (theology) and religion, are predominantly derivatives in both structure and content from those processes in which the means of production of our bodily being, what-ever their nature at any particular time, are distributed and used so as to fashion the most vital relationships between person and person, the very ensemble of the social relations by which human nature is defined and progressively realised. That this derivation of the more 'spiritual' cre-ations from the more 'physical' does not amount to complete determin-ism of the former by the latter is clear from the little that has been said of Marx the philosopher who preached revolution. Indeed, it is also clear from the little that Marx himself said about the protest, albeit ineffective and inherently distorted, that religion as the cry of the oppressed makes on behalf of alienated humanity. Materialism must be understood in such highly nuanced fashion, then, if we are not to misconstrue Marx as a proponent of materialism in an altogether cruder sense.

THE EMERGENCE OF CRUDE 'MARXIST' MATERIALISM
AND THE SPECTRE OF STRONG DUALISM RETURNING

However, it must be said that materialism in much cruder form does make an appearance in the writings of Engels, Marx's most eager disciple and loyal supporter. In his introduction to the English edition of *Socialism, Utopian and Scientific*, Engels is acutely aware of the suspicion with which his English audience will greet the introduction of such programmatic phrases as 'historical materialism'. So he enlists the aid of the contemporary physical sciences in order to recommend the materi-alist conception of history. He paints a picture of the imminent success of modern science in explaining everything that has evolved, including life and the very highest forms of life in the universe, in terms of 'matter and motion, or as it is now called, energy'. 'Life', he declares in the jargon of the time, 'from its lowest to its highest forms, is but the normal mode of existence of albuminous bodies.' And his dismissal of spirit, as either of God or in humanity, is summary, almost impatient: 'as far as we are concerned, matter and energy can neither be created nor annihilated; for us, mind is a mode of energy, a function of the brain; all we know is that the world is governed by immutable laws, and so forth. Thus as far as he is a scientific man, as far as he *knows* anything, (man) is a materialist.'[34]

Marx himself was not a crude materialist of this kind. What he opposed to the purely and utterly disembodied spirit which he (wrongly) attributed in the end to Hegel, was conscious matter, thinking bodies. Consciousness, *Bewusstsein*, meant to him (a) being (*Sein*) (that is) conscious – *das bewusste Sein* – not a consciousness whose being was simply to be consciousness, a consciousness of consciousness, like Aristotle's God, the Thinking of the Thinking of the Thinking. (Descartes, too, both identified persons with minds or souls and believed that they encountered each other bodily in the street.)

Yet there did develop in Marxism after Marx a materialism which, though not quite as crude as that of Engels, was still cruder by far than the materialism which Marx himself espoused and explained; and a materialism, consequently, that resulted in the kind of loss of the subject that wielded its own specific influence on more recent thought. This kind of materialism, which was presented as true, mature Marxism, took a number of different forms. It emerged as the ideology of Soviet state Marxism, for instance, but also in the Neostructuralism of Louis Althusser. In essence the various proponents of this version of Marxism seized upon the definition of humanity as 'the ensemble of the social relations'; they saw these social relations to be not just the results of, but to be entirely determined by, the most material means and processes of the (re)production of human physical life; and the continuous development of such determinative means and processes of production they insisted were governed by an inherent, Hegelian-type dialectic operating as the kind of immutable natural law beloved of Engels. In this way they arrived at the programmatic phrase 'dialectical materialism' and, as an end result, at a view of history as a process without a subject, human or

[34] Marx and Engels, *On Religion*, pp. 297-8.

divine. The most recent emergence of poststructuralist and deconstructionist accounts of history as a sequence of periods without subjects, in
the form, for instance, of literary eras without authors, is enough to
suggest one important line of influence here. But that influence must be
traced in the next chapter, together with other lines of influence which
can also be seen to emerge from the account in this chapter of the
successive and varied philosophies which raised and resolved in their
various ways the issues that arise concerning the place of the subject in
the fabric of reality as we know it.

But what has any or all of this got to do with dualism, and more
particularly with the advertised and alleged re-emergence of strong
dualism? With a kind of dualism which, in deference to Descartes, on
the one hand, and to the thinkers who were called upon in the opening
pages to describe its current image, on the other, we shall have to refer
to from now on as 'Cartesian' dualism? With the alleged re-emergence
of a dualism which suggests a dichotomous distinction between mind (or
soul)-substance and body-substance? Two factors, perhaps, explain this
connection.

The first consists in an impression, or perhaps no more than a
suspicion, to the effect that many materialists must tacitly assume, and
hence conspire in the dissemination of, a dichotomous mind–body
dualism. This would appear to be the case where, as with Engels for
example, the securing of a materialist view seems to depend upon the
denial of the existence of mind or spirit. It would take a hard and
detailed argument to prove in any particular instance that such a dualist
world view is logically entailed in some professions of pure materialism.[35] But impressions are more easily ascertained; and there can be
little doubt that strong affirmations of materialism, such as those in
which Engels and many more recent exponents of materialism indulge,
do intimate a background scenario in which something which is utterly
other than matter is rejected in favour of something which is utterly
other than mind. This is the reason, or the excuse, for talking of strong, if
not crude, materialism, and of strong, if not crude, dualism.

The second factor is this: there now appears on the modern philosophical scene a kind of philosophising which resolutely begins with the
material realm; and in the main as resolutely attempts to remain there.
An alternative, a rival, thus appears; a rival to the kind of philosophising
which stems from Kant's (rather than Hegel's) view of the phenomenon;

[35] A fine example of such a kind of argument can be found in Deutsch's *The Fabric of Reality*, ch. 7,
where he shows how many critics of induction remain themselves crypto-inductionists.

a kind of philosophising which begins with the phenomenon (with knowledge itself, that is), and which will shortly be formally named phenomenology as we approach the contemporary scene. It is not the case that each philosophy encountered can be securely placed in one of these two categories: the story of their interaction and interactive influence must be told in the next chapter. But the very fact that philosophers can start from two such contrasting starting points reinforces impressions of a strong dualism as an insidious impression or underlying assumption of recent philosophy. This impression is occasionally strengthened by perceptions of the difficulty of those who start with the mind alone, or with the content of its empirical consciousness, to build a bridge that allows it to arrive at material reality; or the difficulty, or sheer unwillingness of those who begin with matter alone, to arrive at any apprehension and account of consciousness. And so all of this contributes to an understanding of the manner in which a strong dualism which derives more from the successors of Descartes than from Descartes himself, gradually returned after Hegel's mighty attempt at correction. Indeed, as the continuing story unfolds, it is seen to become the assumed basis on which people like Fenwick and Phillips set up their current philosophical problematics. And it is also the ground upon which, by a combination of influences and a kind of collusion of bridge-building failures from both sides, it is not only the subject that goes missing but also, eventually, reality itself.

CHAPTER 2

The status quo: current affairs

'"Mind" and "reality" have for too long been four-letter words in philosophy,' complained the colourful Umberto Eco in a newspaper interview.[1] 'Serious philosophers were thus forced to engage in self-contained, system-oriented approaches that had no need of these concepts. But', he immediately went on to assure us, 'a recent cognitive revolution is now changing things for the better.' It is of course that latter prospect that this essay hopes to investigate; perhaps even to contribute in some small way to it. But it is necessary, before it can be made good, to gain further insight into the nature and extent of that loss. Mind *and* reality gone missing from recent philosophy? One is tempted to paraphrase Oscar Wilde: to lose one of this primordial pair, to lose one's mind, might be passed off as a tragedy of sorts; to lose both, to lose reality as well, must surely raise the charge of carelessness.

From the brief preceding investigation of the modern origins of contemporary philosophy the surviving features which came to comprise the current mind-scape, or rather mindless-scape, can be clearly seen. The attack by Marx upon such priority of mind in the account of reality as would, in his view of Hegel, reduce non-mental reality to at best a transient phase in the history of being, gradually gave rise amongst his self-proclaimed successors to the view of reality as an evolutionary, indeed historical, process without a subject. In the course of that particular movement, mind, self, subject lost any effective presence in reality; and the course of that particular movement can be traced, as the reference to Althusser makes plain, still developing and wielding a broad influence well beyond professional philosophy, up to the boundaries of the contemporary scene. At the same time the study of the phenomenal world to which Kant had confined all prospects of actually knowing anything, continued into this century in the philo-

[1] *Guardian*, March 24 1998, p. v.

sophical movement known as phenomenology. Phenomenology characterised explicitly and by name the philosophy of Husserl; but it also
characterised in deep if differing degrees the philosophies of other major
influential figures in this century, such as Heidegger and Sartre. Now,
the phenomenology of this century, and in particular the phenomenology of Husserl, loosened its grip upon 'objective' reality from the very
outset. Consider the key example of Husserlian *epoche*; the bracketing-
out, in the course of the philosophical investigation of the appearances
(of objective reality) to the mind-self, of the question of the truth, of the
re*present*ational status of these appearances-phenomena vis-à-vis objective reality. This initial loosening of the grip of mind on objective reality,
however methodologically argued, posed the threat of losing that grip
altogether, and with it objective reality; in clear contrast with Hegel's
Phenomenology, which never loses, and indeed can never lose, sight of that
reality.

The historical causes of the coming about of such carelessness as may
be suspected in the very prospect of the loss of reality need not unduly
concern us. There appears to have been a regression to a pre-Hegelian
view of the mind-self and/or its characteristic forms of knowledge as
something that could be investigated by itself – in both senses of that
term: self-investigated and itself alone investigated – before objective
reality, or the objectivity of extra-mental reality comes into consideration. A regression, therefore, to the kind of dualism that had come to
be called 'Cartesian'. And Marx's critique of Hegel, together with that
of (other) Young Hegelians, contributed to the failure of Hegel's less
dualist philosophy of mind and reality to dominate the immediate
future of Western philosophy. This may have contributed, in other
words, to the return of a 'Cartesian'-like dualism such as one finds
methodologically invoked in Husserl's *Cartesian Meditations*, especially
for those who saw Althusser and his ilk as the true face of Marxism. But
it is the fact of the matter rather than the detailed tracing of causal
sequences that alone is of concern here. The fact of the matter being
that these two lines of influence – first, that represented by the materialist philosophy described above as a philosophy of history as a process
without a subject, and then that represented by the dominant phenomenological philosophies of this century – combined, as any history of the
origins of postmodernism can show,[2] to help bring about the kind of
philosophy that Umberto Eco excoriated for losing sight of both mind

---

[2] See for example one of the best critiques of postmodernism, Séan Burke's *The Death and Return of the Author* (Edinburgh University Press, 1992).

and reality, the currently dominant deconstructionist, postmodern philosophy presided over by the holy trinity of Barthes, Foucault and
Derrida.

Correspondingly, in this chapter of the essay it would seem to be
potentially more satisfying to treat more thematically the rise and rise of
postmodernism, rather than repeat the format of the origins chapter
and, by doing so, attempt to add unnecessarily to the many excellent
historical accounts of the related and successive philosophical, social-
scientific and literary-critical steps by which postmodernism came to be
and developed to its current status. All the more so since a thematic
account can encompass the occasional recall of some of the more
significant of these steps in any case. By a thematic account is meant one
which rehearses in general terms the problematic that we have seen
develop in the treatment of the self or subject, and the corresponding
treatment of reality, through the philosophical movements already
traced, and then offers a critical response to the manner in which the
prime ministers of the philosophy of postmodernism sought to resolve
the problematic. Of course, examples of such thematic acounts also
exist: Heidegger, for example, offers such an account, briefly, towards
the beginning of his seminal work *Being and Time*;[3] and it is an account of
the relevant problematic on which we might build at the beginning,
while leaving until later a critique of Heidegger's own attempt, amongst
those of other phenomenologists, to resolve it.

In Heidegger's view the subject is still dominant in the modern
philosophy which he himself encountered in his early years – and one
remembers that he succeeded Husserl at Freiburg. And that still dominant subject is purely of the nature of mind, consciousness or spirit
(*Geistding* is his word for it). In its own pure being or essence it is as yet
without any content from the material, empirical world. It is worldless,
or other (than) worldly. In other words – for this is how Heidegger
understands the term transcendental when used without his own qualifications – it is the transcendental subject that can only later, by some
process or other, come to be or to be seen to be related to this material
world of which even our bodies are part. It is in reality, he consistently
implies, God. That is to say, in this conception it is an entity truly
indistinguishable from the God of a traditional Western theology, a God
that first existed as pure spirit, conscious only of itself, and then came to
conceive of the things of this material world, as and when it wilfully

---

[3] Martin Heidegger, *Being and Time* (London: SCM Press, 1962), pp. 48ff.

construed and created them. Clearly Heidegger remained convinced that this transcendental ego that still dominated modern philosophy until he set about its removal is a carry-over from that dichotomous, dualist system of two entirely different substances which has long been attributed to Descartes. And the problem, the problematic? First, can such an utterly transcendental *Geistding* admit of real others? and if others like itself actually existed, how could it have any knowledge other than inferential knowledge of some kind about them? Indeed how could it have anything other than an always and easily defeasible inferential knowledge of anything other than itself? Would not solipsism be its natural state? But the problem, you may say, can be put in more concrete terms, in terms less theological than those Heidegger uses, and more accessible from our ordinary human experience. For our consciousness is always self-evidently replete with content that appears to be from the material world. Yet a problem would remain; for that empirical consciousness still appears to us to have a transcendental dimension, and so we should still have to account for that dimension in such a way as not to see the full reality of our consciousness still take on the features of a traditional divinity to whom the material world, including other subjects within that world, is purely adventitious, and is in addition in our case purely conjectural, since, unlike this traditional divinity, we do not appear to have created that world and the others who appear to inhabit it.

Now that is, in fact, an accurate statement of the problematic as it has developed in the modern era in the West. The theological terminology has not been added by a philosophical essayist who happens to have a predominantly theological interest. Indeed when the final act so far in this historical drama, when postmodernism and its critics come into view, the conflation of the idea of a transcendental subject or author with the idea of divinity will still prove to be a persistent feature of the philosophical manoeuvering. But the persistence of this theological terminology must await a later assessment. For the moment, it is necessary to engage in a critical thematic account of the genesis of postmodernism. It seems best to take separately the role of phenomenological philosophers in that genesis; then that of the materialist philosophers, and of the combination of the two. Begin then with a critical account of the phenomenological philosophers; and since Sartre has already provided just such a critique, begin by climbing on Sartre's shoulders.

THE RECENT GENESIS OF POSTMODERNISM:
THE PHENOMENOLOGICAL APPROACH

Sartre on his predecessors

In the course of Sartre's critique of the major figures in phenomenology
and particularly, for our purposes, of Husserl and Heidegger, he consistently queried their success in bringing about the resolution to the
problematic that Heidegger so well saw and described. He concentrated, very astutely as it turns out, on the security within their accounts
of these matters of our knowledge of other persons, using this as the acid
test of their accounts of reality. His critique, as it forms a major section
of his *Being and Nothingness*, is rigorous and fair, and so a brief résumé of it
will serve as a substantial part of the analysis we now need of the first of
the two major lines of influence, namely, the phenomenological tradition, that lead to the origin and development of postmodernism.[4]

Husserl, according to Sartre, in his two major works, *Cartesian Meditations* and *Formal and Transcendental Logic*, in his attempt to refute solipsism
makes the astute move of securing immediate certainty of other persons
as a central part of securing certainty of the world beyond the mind. He
does this by arguing that the existence and action of other persons is an
indispensable condition of the constitution of the world.

Whether I consider this table or this tree or this bare wall in solitude or with
companions, the Other is always there as a layer of constitutive meanings which
belong to the very object which I consider; in short, he is the veritable
guarantee of the object's objectivity. And since our psycho-physical self is
contemporary with the world, forms a part of the world, and falls with the
world under the impact of the phenomenological reduction, the Other appears
as necessary to the very constitution of this self. (P. 316)

In short, the world is constantly co-constituted by the other egos, of
indefinite number, and the world so co-constituted by them includes in
it my empirical existence as a professor of the University of Edinburgh,
writing a book called *The Critique of Theological Reason*. Indeed in this
perennial task of constituting the world, there is for Husserl, as Sartre
notes, no privileging of my own empirical ego over these others: 'it is *on*
the table, *on* the wall that the Other is revealed to me as that to which the
object under consideration is perpetually referred (as it is to me also) – as

---

[4] J.-P. Sartre, *Being and Nothingness* (New York: Washington Square Press, 1966), pp. 315ff. Page
   numbers in the text refer to this work.

well as on the occasion of the concrete appearances of Pierre or Paul (and of my concrete appearances to them)' – the additions in brackets are mine. The result of this account should be, then, a collusion, a congress of empirical consciousnesses together construing the world; where by empirical consciousnesses one means consciousnesses (in so far as they are) filled with content of representations of the world. And Husserl can then assure the solipsist that 'the Other's existence is as sure as that of the world' (and vice versa). (p. 318)

Indeed, but, as Sartre shrewdly points out, that retort of Husserl's really amounts to no more that this: the solipsist can be assured that the existence of the Other is as sure as the existence of the world is *to the solipsist*. Why? Well, Husserl did come upon an important truth when he said that the Other is a veritable guarantee of the object's objectivity, and this truth must figure somewhere in the more constructive chapters of this essay. But that truth could not be secured in Husserl's phenomenology. First, if the egos or consciousnesses involved are considered to be purely empirical egos, the Other which is reputed to co-constitute the world would be no more than a contingent and supplementary set of representations with respect to those that currently, at any point, constitute my own empirical ego, and such an entity, or congress of entities, could not achieve the unifying effect which the constitution of the world requires. A further transcendental dimension of consciousness, over and above its being a kind of container of representations 'beyond' the things in the world of which it is conscious, is in fact required for the constitution of these manifold phenomena/things as a world. Now, Husserl can supply this added dimension of transcendence, of course, by simply asserting that something like the unity of the apperceptive ego, in Kantian terminology, is intrinsic to my consciousness of my self in the course of being conscious of the world. But how can I arrive, other than by some inferred analogy, at *that* level of transcendence of consciousness in the case of alleged Others that he claims I encounter in all particular configurations of the world? These are no different from my perceptions of the empirical configurations of Pierre or Paul in their presence or in my concrete memories of them, and the unity of my own apperceptive ego is the only unifying, world-construing transcendence that I directly experience in either case. I do not, then, encounter in the case of other subjects that level of transcendence that makes them individual subjects co-perceiving, co-constituting a world with me; or at least there is nothing in Husserl's analysis of consciousness that makes me understand how I can encounter such subjects, other than his assertion that I do.

This coincides with a more general criticism of Husserl, to the effect that he really begins his philosophy with a mind and the mental contents it unifies within it, *as if* it were a separate entity or substance. The *epoche* is little more than a device for insisting that that is where one must begin. Or, as Sartre puts it, Husserl reduces being to a series of meanings, and being here includes the Other. But, having done this, he is faced forever after this move with the thankless task of making his way back to the world again and to an encounter with other persons that can replace some vulnerable inference. Notice, by contrast, that Hegel's *Phenomenology* describes the beginning of the journey of the soul through its own configurations by describing sense intuition, that is, that state in which the most physical world of sounds, smells, tastes, colours, shapes, softness and hardness immediately fills us with all its concrete variety and richness, and by tracing the transcending drivenness of consciousness in and through this fully present world, attired in all its most physical attributes, gradually discovers mind's own increasing role in construing and constructing this world; and how his model for explaining the encounter with other selves is that of the interchanging roles of master and slave in the construction of world. Phenomenology with Husserl has resiled considerably again from the overcoming of crude dualism which Hegel attempted and, *pace* Marx and Sartre, significantly achieved.

Does Heidegger fare any better, according to Sartre? One might expect that Heidegger should have fared better. If the simplest way into Heidegger's *Being and Time* 'is to read it as an attempt (historically the first of many) to free modern philosophy from its Cartesian inheritance', as Fergus Kerr says, and to do this by seeking 'to embed the subject properly in the world',[5] then one would certainly be led to expect that he would have succeeded in impressing, if not fully satisfying, Sartre. There are three significant facets to Heidegger's attempt to embed the subject in the world to the degree at which the 'Cartesian' cancer is killed. There is the role of *Angst* as it develops in the existentialist tradition after Kierkegaard. An emotion which, as such, plays its own part in explaining the unified soul–body nature of the human being. There is a corresponding mortality, the fact that human being is a being-unto-death, consciously sharing in the finitude that characterises every thing in this world. And, thirdly, there is the communal condition of *Dasein*, of concrete human being in the world; the 'crew' factor, as Sartre summarises it; the fact that I am always and inevitably with others in the

    5 F. Kerr, *Immortal Longings: Versions of Transcending Humanity* (London: SPCK, 1997), pp. 46–7.

world. And we are primarily at work there together; we are not there primarily in the role of detached observers, as too much traditional science and philosophy, still haunted by shades of the detached 'Cartesian' ego, might suggest. Heidegger has an interesting comment, in the course of outlining that latter facet of our being, on the Greek world *pragmata*. It is simply a word for 'things'; but it carries within its connotation the suggestion that the things that make up our world are not primarily objects of observation and contemplation; they are rather that which we do something with, pragmatic entities, for we are essentially a project in this world in(to) which we find ourselves always already thrown.

The picture Heidegger paints in *Being and Time*, then, is a portrait of very bodily human beings emotionally involved and working together in the only world there is, in which they must live and die. There is no longer even a hint of a mental or spiritual entity which could even potentially squat outside the world. World and human beings are inextricably bound together, their destinies intertwined, in fashioning what existentialists prefer to call the human condition rather than human nature. Yet Sartre is not satisfied. And his dissatisfaction is understandable. He has, as already remarked, and very shrewdly, chosen the encounter with others as the acid test of the philosophies under review. And he quite correctly requires an understanding of that encounter, an explanation of it, in which the being, the actuality of the encounter, yields the awareness, the consciousness of it; this, rather than an account of the encounter in which, because the other has first to be inferred, the encounter takes place really only in discursive thought or as inferential knowledge rather than in reality. This is part of a general proposition which Sartre also enunciates, to the effect that being, reality, must yield and therefore measure knowledge, rather than knowledge attempt to measure being. For philosophy really consists in an understanding of reality that at once derives from and is verified successively in the actuality of our faring in the world; and not an idea-system or logical system, at first in and of mind, by which we might first infer the world and afterwards encounter and manage it. Now, although Heidegger's philosophy of *Dasein* at first seems to be measured by being, rather than the reverse, in this crucial matter of the encounter with others it proves to be otherwise.

Sartre, then, to return to his assessment of phenomenological philosophers in *Being and Nothingness*, accurately summarises as follows Heidegger's account of 'being with' as the privileged mode of encounter with others: 'In so far as I make a world exist as a complex of instruments (*pragmata*) which I use for the ends of my human reality, I cause myself to be determined in my being by a being (i.e. another) who makes the world exist as a complex of instruments for the ends of his reality' (p. 331). But this account is no more than a general and hence abstract statement of something Heidegger appears to know about reality. What is missing from the account is precisely an explanation that will enable me to understand how I, one concrete self, make a bridge to and actually encounter another concrete self that is yet distinct from myself. As an agent who makes myself and my world by realising my own possibilities in the world, I relate to all entities in the world as instruments, which of course set up their own resistance to me as part of a world in itself in the making. Then how do I actually encounter another person rather than other things in the world? Is there a specific kind of reaction or of resistance, of 'opposition', to me from other selves (usually expressed in the language of 'for-itself/for others', and incapable, it would seem, of expression in the simple language of 'with' which is equally available for the 'in-itselves')? Is there something which will allow me to experience an encounter with another self as distinct from a thing? And which would then enable me to understand and describe that encounter with a real, concrete other; allow me to know another and to express that consciousness of another? Not in Heidegger's philosophy, at any rate. All there is in Heidegger's philosophy is an abstract statement to the effect that there are others with me, not just inhabiting the world but involved in the mutual making of the world. In other words, intersubjectivity appears in Heidegger's philosophy as an *a priori* structure of reality from which concrete encounter of real selves can neither be derived nor understood.

The matter becomes worse rather than better if we add to Sartre's account of Heidegger in this context the change in Heidegger's view of the world that characterises his later work. Briefly but not, one hopes, too crudely put: in Heidegger's later work the world takes more of the initiative, where in his earlier work the initiative was more with human beings working the world of things as *pragmata*. Now, in the later works, the world is a self-sustaining reality; an active process still, of course, rather than merely an object for science: the world 'worlds', as he puts it. And still as much as ever a human world, in that it is the world that constantly comes to be in and through its 'crew' of human beings. This world of which he still speaks in these ways can be analysed further as consisting of the four dimensions of earth, sky, mortality and divinity; its 'worlding' then consists in the play of these four. This is Fergus Kerr's paraphrase of the play of this quaternity by which the world 'worlds' through human beings:

Our life-world is established and sustained, establishes itself and sustains itself over and over again and all the time – by this quadrilateral structure of non-human non-subjective dimensions, these four 'quarters' of our world; the sky above, with all that the sky and heaven have meant and mean in the experience and imagination of the human race; the earth beneath our feet, mother earth, the soil, the land, bedrock, the dust from which we come and to which we return, and so on; death, the shadow under which we are born and always have to live, our transience, vulnerability, mortality; and fourthly and finally the sacred, the holy, intimations of something divine, something gracious.[6]

Divinity has appeared once more, one notices, even if the denotation of the term is uncertain; if only because its connotation remains, as Descartes would have said, obscure and confused. Divinities are messengers of the god, and the god refuses comparison with any of the things that are present, consisting instead of some element of reality that is undyingly determinative of the form of coming to be and passing away – invoked therefore in rites of passage. But however this theological dimension of Heidegger's philosophy may be analysed and explained, one thing at least is clear: the god is an inner-worldly reality. As with each other of the four in the play of the fourfold, the god is inconceivable outwith the *perichoresis*, as Greek theologians of old described the Trinity, the round-dance of the four. There is no extramundane divinity, no incorporeal mind or spirit that causes and explains our world. This world itself it is that 'worlds' in the course of the play of the fourfold, and as it does so it conditions our life without remainder. It is that last feature of Heidegger's later philosophy, rather than the persistence of theology as such, that is of primary interest here. For the more the initiative goes to the world as such in Heidegger's account of coming-to-be; the more the world is thought of as a 'quadrilateral structure of non-human non-subjective dimensions'; and the more it is thought to condition our human lives, all the more difficult will it be to explain and understand the existence of any self, or any other, either human or divine. First, what unifies the four, apart from Heidegger's assertion of their ontological inseparability in the dance? What makes them world, so that we can understand his talking in terms of a unified, continuously creative agency? And if even the god is a 'non-subjective' dimension by which

---

[6] Kerr, *Immortal Longings*, p. 61.

our life-world is totally conditioned, must we not conclude not only that we encounter no other self in the world, but that our own increasedly solipsistic impressions of the world, each one committed to reading its own possibilities in the world, are no more than an illusion? Quite similar in fact to the illusion of the God-self making a world, even from within it?

Sartre in any case was correct in his criticism of Heidegger. Heidegger's philosophy contains no explanation, no understanding, of an other self which could derive from and be verified in a real, existential encounter with an other self. His efforts to root out the entirely-different-substance-self of 'Cartesian' dualism carried him away, and he left us with a conviction of selfhood that is as solipsistic in the end as it is in Husserl's philosophical results. But, as has been pointed out before, a philosophy which ends in the denial of the self of 'Cartesian' dualism, if it fails to include, if only by default, any other form of self in its explanation of the world, actually falls back into a 'Cartesian' dualism once more. For the world in this philosophy must finally be defined, without remainder, by the denial of a 'Cartesian' self. That paradoxical state of affairs comes about more than once in the history of our subject in this century, as there may be other occasions to observe. In this case it results from the fact that Heidegger presents us with a world replete with a crew of selves, yet he is not capable of accounting for these selves positively; his only intelligible statement about them is that they are not 'Cartesian' selves. But then of course, one might well suspect, a 'Cartesian' worldview remains a necessary basis on which to structure his own alternative.

But before coming to the borders of postmodernism, with its final refusal of subjects or authors – and since Sartre has been used to show how poorly the major figures in the recent history of philosophy in the tradition of phenomenology had done – it would be well to ask the question: Did Sartre himself do any better? At least there is then the opportunity to discuss in more detail the finer points of the problems that phenomenological philosophers seem to meet in trying to get from mind to other minds to reality.

Sartre's own phenomenology

In the very opening pages of the introduction to Sartre's *Being and Nothingness* he sets about the dismissal of the crude dualism of appearance and reality, the kind of dualism epitomised in Kant, in which reality as it is in itself is forever hidden behind the phenomenon, the reality of the appearance; and with this he dismisses all derivative and attendant dualisms. The appearance, in the phenomenological meta-physics he is about to unfold, does not hide the essence or substance of a being; it reveals it. This is because the essence of a being is nothing other than the well-connected series of its manifestations. He does concede at this early point that a very different kind of dualism may already creep in here: the finite–infinite dualism, in the form of the infinite-in-the-finite. This is because the sole fact of there being subjects multiplies the points of view and, hence, the series of appearances prospectively to infinity. But although this fact may entail the admission that things can never be known in any total or totalising manner – and this is as much a welcome final conclusion to Sartre's philosophy as it is an initial obser-vation – neither does it weaken the dismissal of the self-defeating dualism, as he sees it, which characterised so much of philosophy after Kant.

The positive achievement of Sartre's opening aim begins with his distinctive analysis of the *Cogito*. Instead of defining the *Cogito* as a thinking substance, replete with ideas and *volontés*, and reflecting on these in a consequently self-conscious mode which yields its concomi-tantly transcendent and empirical self, Sartre seeks to define something altogether more fundamental and originary, which he calls the 'pre-reflective cogito.' This is a consciousness which is a being; and being a consciousness, it is conscious of being conscious. Yet we must not then describe it as being conscious of its self, for that would suggest that of its own nature and essence it has a kind of content to be conscious of, similar to the content of meaning of other things of which it may be conscious. For it would then no longer be consciousness *tout court*. Therefore we have to refer to its status as consciousness by writing 'consciousness (of its) self' if we are to bracket out at the beginning a creeping dualism of the Kantian kind. This prereflective cogito, then, is a being *sui generis*; Sartre names it the *pour-soi*, the For-itself. It is what we would generally call the subject; it is non-objectifiable. As Sartre puts the matter, once again in the sustained analysis in *Being and Nothingness*, it is of itself contentless, to the point where it can be described quite accu-rately as the 'absolute nothing which I am' (p. 349). It cannot, then, of itself and in his terms be *known*. Here is the context for Sartre's distinc-tion between being and being conscious (of) being, on the one hand, and knowing, in the sense of procuring contentful ideas of, or verifiable connotations of, a thing, on the other. This is the distinction he uses in order to show how Husserl fails to ovecome the solipsism attendant on 'Cartesian' dualism.

Yet this cogito is also conscious of things that are not, like it, nothing; it is itself 'no thing'; yet it is conscious of things other than itself that do have positive content and can be connoted as well as denoted. Indeed the 'also' in that sentence misrepresents a crucial feature of the role of such things vis-à-vis the prereflective cogito: the prereflective cogito, the *pour-soi*, can only be (self-)conscious, can only be self, can only be, precisely in so far as it is conscious of some thing, some contentful, connotable entity, other than itself. This entity that is other than the For-itself is called the *en-soi*, the In-itself. There is a terrible truth, therefore, in Descartes's 'I think, therefore I am.' But it is entirely missed by those who think that famous sentence can be paraphrased by 'I am a thinking thing' or, more pathetically still, 'there is a thought now'. I am a prereflective cogito, not a subject already made up of contentful thought, not a mind-substance replete with and identifiable by its conscious contents. As a consciousness of itself contentless, I am forever dependent in my innermost being and for my least existence on that which is always full of its own positive content of thingness, the In-itself. I *am* and can *be* (self-)consciousness only in the process of being conscious of something other than myself. The In-itself affords me the very possibility of being, in both the ontological and the ethical mode. That is to say, I both depend upon it and act to try to make myself into an In-itself, indeed at times trying, in bad faith, to pretend I have already succeeded in doing so: as on these occasions when I define myself as the past experiences and activities I select – professing at the university, writing a book, drinking coffee and so on – and use that definition to determine how I ought to act and be from now on; when I take myself to have a human nature, as other entities have fixed natures. But all of this is futile, and a refusal of moral responsibility. I must negate it all: it is not me and I can never be it. I am in constant flight from all of it, and from my constructed 'selves'. As For-itself I am negation: 'The For-itself, in fact, is nothing but the pure nihilation of the In-itself; it is like a hole in being at the heart of being' (p. 786). Being-consciousness, the prereflective cogito, depends for its being (consciousness) on the In-itself, through a process not of assimilation of the In-itself, but of perpetually denying that the In-itself is it(self) – a process of perpetually nihilating the In-itself.

There is no point in asking questions about the origin of either the For-itself or the In-itself; no point in trying to understand either in terms of ground, or cause, or reason for existence. In terms that sometimes rival the poetry of Parmenides, Sartre describes how the In-itself is always already there before its being can come into question, so it pre-empts all such questioning; and when it ceases to be, the question no longer applies. And the For-itself? It simply arises: 'it is precisely because consciouness is pure appearance, because it is total emptiness (since the entire world is outside of it), it is because of this identity of appearance and existence within it that it can be considered as the absolute' (p. 17). It is true that '*consciousness is a being such that in its being, its being is in question in so far as this being implies a being other than itself*' (the In-itself, on being conscious of which its being consciousness depends) (p. 24). So it might seem odd that a dependent being should be termed absolute? But it does not, indeed could not, derive its *ousia*, its being or substance, positively from the In-itself. It exists by nihilating the In-itself. It is in that sense equally original, equally without origin, without ground or reason for existence. It is a non-substantial absolute, a nothingness in being.

The upshot of all of this would at first blush seem to be a dualism, and a dualism withal that looks potentially more deadly than any which the so-called Cartesians, or better still Kant, had managed to design. Sartre does indeed describe For-itself and In-itself as 'these two radically separated regions of being'; and he asks himself the question: Since 'idealism and realism both fail to explain the relations which *in fact* unite these regions which *in theory* are without communication', how can he himself solve the problem of their separation? (p. 30). He cannot make the problem any easier for himself as a result of the number of times and manners in which he drives home to the reader the separateness of For-itself and In-itself; neither has any hand, act or part in the coming-to-be of the other. The For-itself, he has said already in his introduction, simply arises. It cannot create the In-itself: since it is pure subjectivity, consciousness (of) itself, (self-)consciousness, anything it might create out of nothing could never even have the appearance of emerging from the subjective state. In any case, the For-itself exists as negation. The In-itself, on the other hand, is simply a *plenum* of being, it simply exists, without origin, without reason for being there – it simply is. It cannot be said to act upon consciousness: 'transcendent being could not act on consciousness and consciousness could not "construct" the transcendent by objectivizing elements borrowed from its subjectivity' (p. 238). Indeed it cannot even be said to be present to consciousness, as some say who describe knowledge in terms of this presence of object to consciousness. The In-itself is so called – even though this involves a potential misreading of the term self – because it is entirely self-contained and bears within itself no relationship to anything else or other.

In Sartre's philosophy in fact this separation becomes most acute in the course of considering the very topic that can be more usually relied upon to narrow the gap, the topic, that is to say, of consciousness in its more empirical mode, or what we may call the empirical ego: that which is characterised by the sequence of perceptions, intentions, experiences that make up 'my' stream of consciousness, my life history. Sartre is adamant that this ego, this empirical entity of which I am of course conscious, is nevertheless *not of the nature* of consciousness as such: 'the Ego is in-itself, not for-itself . . . the Ego appears to consciousness as a transcendent in-itself, as an existence in the human world' (p. 156). It is the prereflective cogito, consciousness (of being) consciousness alone, then, that of its very nature constitutes this For-itself, the subject, subjectivity. Sartre drives this point further home in some comments on personhood. If we are inclined to confuse person with empirical ego, he tells us that, on the contrary, it is the nihilating presence to its own self that constitutes the personhood of For-itself in the prereflective cogito, and this then confers personhood on the (empirical) ego, and not vice versa as is at times suggested.

The dualism now seems as dichotomous, as crude as ever. On one side is a personal absolute, indistinguishable from a certain traditional divinity only by the Sartrian decree that it cannot create anything beyond itself. On the other side is a Parmenidean Being that neither comes to be nor passes away. Another impersonal absolute, then? How can the separation be bridged, even to the extent that one side could know (of) the other? Sartre's first answer is that the separation is bridged in that one side, the personal subject or For-itself, can know the other, the In-itself. But how; for to Sartre also knowledge is presence? Since it makes no sense to him to say that the In-itself is present to anything, knowledge consists in the particular type of presence of which For-itself is capable. This primordially is presence to itself; but its presence to itself as (self-)consciousness involves essentially the negation of every In-itself as being (any part of) itself. Hence it is present to the In-itself as negation of the In-itself, by which alone it is consciousness (of itself) as not being an In-itself. Which, Sartre thinks, allows him to conclude, negatively, that if the consciousness were not consciousness of something other than itself it would 'dissolve into nothing', and to conclude, more positively, 'that it is within and upon the being which it is not that the For-itself appears as not being what it is not'; and this is then described as the ecstatic condition in which the 'for-itself is outside itself in the in-itself' (p. 245). Sartre is not, then, he points out, trying to relate knower to known as substance to substance. That is a failed dualism of the kind he has determined to avoid from the outset. The In-itself is substance; the For-itself is not substance: 'There is nothing *there* but a pure nothingness encircling a certain objective ensemble and throwing it into relief outlined upon the world' (p. 349).

A complete and clear account of knowing? Perhaps not quite yet, because Sartre elsewhere describes 'world' as in a sense the creation of the For-itself. Now he is thinking of consciousness with respect to its *volontés*, of the sovereign freedom of the person as a free, undefined relation to itself, of its possibilities therefore. Of the possible he says: 'it has the being of a lack and as lack, it lacks being' (p. 155). It is thus not of the nature of the In-itself. The possibility of satisfying thirst, for example, is of the nature of For-itself; it is consciousness (of) thirst as a satisfied thirst which, like any (form of) consciousness, negates its concrete content – that is *not* what it is. Yet here again Sartre insists that consciousness must be present to something, some In-itself, which it 'encircles' in this negation. The consciousness (of) thirst is apprehended by means of a glass of water as desirable; so that in this particular possibility – of thirst assuaged – glass-to-be-drunk-from appears as a correlate of this possibility-consciousness. If one generalises from this instance, one arrives at this understanding of 'world': 'The world [is] mine because it is haunted by possibles, and the consciousness of these is a possible self-consciousness which *I am*; it is these possibles as such which give the world its unity and its meaning as the world' (p. 158). The In-itself, it would seem, has neither the unity nor the meaning which would allow us to call it world. World is constituted by the possibilities which consciousness is, in the form, as usual, of what it is not. Yet, as in the case of consciousness in its simpler mode as consciousness, consciousness in the mode of consciousness (of its) possibilities, Sartre again insists, must have something of an In-itself 'within and upon the being of which' it exercises its self-constituting negation. Otherwise, as with consciousness in its primary mode, its self-negation would entail its dissolution into absolute nothingness.

The whole enterprise of synthesising For-itself and In-itself, as of explaining how knowledge takes place within that duality – for these are two versions of one and the same enterprise – rests upon the assertion that (self-)consciousness of the For-itself could not be (self-)consciousness unless it were consciousness of something other than itself. For, so the point is developed, since consciousness establishes its being and nature by negating (by maintaining it is not that of which it is conscious), then, if there were no In-itself to negate, it would reflexively negate its own self and dissolve into absolute nothingness. Now, the problem with this complex assertion, upon which Sartre's whole enterprise rests, is this: its subject, in every sense of that word, is the prereflective cogito, the pure consciousness (of) consciousness, taken at first quite separately from everything else that is. And the problem with that, in turn, is that there seems to be no way in which he can or could encounter such a subject at the outset of our investigation, so as to then come to know how it relates to and how it knows things. There seems to be no way in which we could understand Sartre's explanation as to how this self, this pure conscious-ness, which of course he takes to be the human self strictly speaking, relates to other things and knows them; which is to say, there seems to be no way of knowing how Sartre knows what he so confidently explains to us in his complex assertions. These must remain mere assertions, neither verifiable nor, consequently, understandable.

There is another way of making that point, and it is a useful one for the further pursuit of the theme of this essay. There is one sense in which some of us have already encountered this pure (self-)consciousness, this primordial and absolute consciousness (of) self. We encountered it in A. N. Whitehead's reading of the works of Aristotle; in particular in his reading of Aristotle's investigations into the ultimate structures of real-ity, and of the kind of God that emerged at the end of that investigation. This is the God that Whitehead described as 'a divine aristocrat . . . serenely indifferent to the world's turmoil'.[7] By this Whitehead meant not merely that the God of Aristotle did not create the world *ex nihilo* as the Christian God, for instance, is reputed to have done, but that this God of its very nature is not even aware of the world. The fact that Aristotle's God does not create the world *ex nihilo* suggests a basic similarity with Sartre's For-itself, since the latter 'absolute' is also denied any creative role in the origin of the In-itself. And the fact that Aristotle's God according to Whitehead does not even know the world? There also is a basic similarity with Sartre's For-itself: for Aristotle's God is an eternally and essentially self-contemplating entity; conscious (of) self, thinking self; 'the thinking is the thinking of thinking', in Aristotle's own phrase. Now, at the very least this further, intriguing similarity should alert those who have encountered this God, if only in the history of

[7] Quoted by Gerard Watson, *Greek Philosophy and the Christian Notion of God* (Dublin: Columba, 1994), p. 30. Watson then proceeds to give a fuller and truer account of Aristotle's theology.

philosophy, to the problems ahead, when Sartre tries to explain how his very similar, very separate pure (self-)consciousness can come to any synthetic relationship with the other separate 'region' of being, the In-itself, precisely by a kind of presence to the latter that consists in knowing it. In his attempts to overcome these problems, Sartre relies heavily on his ideas of negating or nihilating.

Now, it is true that the concept of negation is necessary in order to account for any relationship, even the reflexive relationship of self to self that is constitutive of pure consciousness – it is necessary to say of each one in a relationship that that one is not the other. But that is not to say that relationship consists, or can consist, in negation pure and simple. Nothing, literally, consists of, or subsists in, negation alone. Negation rather has an essential part to play in the emergence and maintenance of that more complex entity which a relationship names, where otherwise the correlates which make this up would fall back into the more impoverished solitariness and limits of one or the other of them. At this point, however, Sartre unfortunately and in blatant disregard once again of Hegel's more sophisticated thought and concomitant warnings concerning indeterminate negation, invokes the idea of negation pure and simple. How else can we explain his assertion to the effect that For-itself, which, according to himself, exists as a separate region of being, which is absolute and underived, would yet dissolve into nothingness were the inevitable negating that takes place within it to be thought to operate only on the correlates of the pure consciousness (of) self in which it essentially consists?

In response to this position it can only be said, first, that we do not know how such pure, entirely self-sufficient consciousness could exist, at least until we encounter it directly, perhaps at the end of a journey of ours through the structures of reality, if even then; but neither are we in a position to say that it cannot exist. Those Christians who follow the traditional account of a Triune God in terms of subsistent relations believe that such an essentially self-sufficient consciousness does exist, and can someday be encountered.[8] But, second and much more seriously, Sartre seems to court self-contradiction. For that which he says would dissolve itself into nothingness if it tried to exist quite separately from In-itself, the pure For-itself, he also says does exist as a separate region of being. It exists, he insists, and not as a result of anything else either giving it origin or acting upon it so as to form or

[8] See my *The Christian Experience of God as Trinity* (London: SCM Press, 1983) for a full account of this Trinitarian theology.

fashion it in a manner that would enable it to exist as it is. To put the matter in a slightly different way: while maintaining quite explicitly of the For-itself that it must engage with some thing in the mode of negation, if it is not to dissolve into absolute nothingness, he really has in mind the more empirical consciousness, or what he calls the ego, which he nevertheless explicitly says is not of the nature of For-itself.

This simple, indeed crude, concept of negation, then, is more a part of his problem in relating his regions of being in the mode of the knowledge by one of them of the other, than it could ever be part of the solution. For even if we concede that the For-itself needs something other than itself on which to practise its necessary negation; and if in actual fact a thing, any thing which, though not brought into existence by the For-itself, just happens conveniently to be there, an act of pure nihilation of this thing would not constitute knowledge of it. In such pure and simple nihilating the For-itself is simply saying to itself: 'I am not a thing', where 'a thing' is equivalent to 'any thing'; or, better still perhaps, where 'a thing' is equivalent to 'an unconscious entity'. So that what the For-itself is really saying to itself is: 'I am not what I am not', for – and this is the point of all of this convoluted conceptualisa-tion – such pure and absolute nihilating could not of itself yield any actual knowledge of any actually existing thing; and Sartre has already made sure that no such knowledge could precede in any way the exercise of this nihilating activity of pure consciousness – when he said that there can be no presence of the In-itself to consciousness. In short, all the talk in the world about negating, if this is taken in this crude sense of simple nihilating, cannot explain the existence of a relationship of knowledge-presence between persons and things. So all Sartre's talk of his For-itself negating, as an ecstatic process by which the same For-itself appears outside itself, and thus appears within and upon the thing which it is not, is really a tissue of unsupported and unintelligible mystification.

That this is the case is made clear by quick consideration of the two related topics: first, Sartre's account, already summarised, of the (more empirical) ego and of the world; and, second, his account of the For-itself's knowledge of, or as he would prefer to say, conscious encounter with, other persons. The ego, it will be recalled, is not of the nature of the For-itself. It is rather an In-itself that is described as existing in the human world. Yet this world, as we have seen, is very much a product of the For-itself, as a universe of the possibles; the possibles being the possibles which the For-itself *is*. Now, this ambiguity appears to stem from, and corroborate, the deeper confusion in Sartre's account of the relationship between the two separate regions of being. For when he is insisting that the For-itself remains a person, and does not in the least come to share in the nature of the In-itself, he describes its relationship to the In-itself as that of a 'pure nothingness' which merely encircles a certain objective ensemble. Yet when describing the equally essentially ecstatic feature of the For-itself, he talks, as we have seen, of the For-itself appearing within and upon specified In-itself things, the 'thises' with all the characteristic features which make each a 'this' and thus make up a certain objective ensemble. How can anything be at one and the same time an encircling nothingness or emptiness, a hole, and yet appear in or on the concrete features that make this thing to be this thing?

The answer must, one supposes, be found on the analogy of students in an art class who are told not to draw the chair but rather to draw the empty spaces around the chair. The result will be, then, that it is the ecstatic procedure of the For-itself, rather than the activity of the In-itself, that yields the circling-appearances which result. And this may be what is meant by talking about a pure nothingness encircling a certain objective ensemble *and throwing it into relief upon the world*. The world will then remain as it has been described in terms of possibles, a projection of the For-itself; but the phrase about the (more empirical) ego being an existent in the human world will then correspondingly negate the force of calling the ego an In-itself. And the end result must then be that the ecstatic process, allegedly constitutive of the For-itself, cannot know the In-itself in itself, but can only know the figures it has itself drawn in the course of its nothingness-encircling. In a 'Key to Special Terminology' at the end of my copy of *Being and Nothingness*, in a comment on the term world as used by Sartre, I read: 'strictly speaking, without the For-itself, there would be not a world but only an undifferentiated plenitude of being'. Quite so; but this of course means that we have not had explained to us, and so we can neither verify nor understand, how or indeed if the For-itself knows the In-itself in itself. Indeed we do not know how the For-itself can even know if there be an In-itself beyond its own projections. The unknowing known would appear to have gone missing. But perhaps there still remains the possibility of understanding the For-itself as conscious encounter with an other For-itself; and since explanation of encounter with others was the acid test that Sartre applied to Husserl and Heidegger, it might be worth asking briefly if he himself can pass that crucial test.

In his chapter in *Being and Nothingness* 'The Existence of Others', Sartre actually begins with a point that seems to concede all that has just been said in criticism of his account of the knowledge relationship of For-itself to In-itself. Thinking of objective reality and of how it is known, he writes: 'my objectivity cannot itself derive *for me* from the objectivity of the world since I am precisely the one by whom *there is* a world'; and he elucidates further: 'not only am I unable to *know* myself, but my very being escapes – although I am that very escape from my being – and I am absolutely nothing'; and the world is that which I, the For-itself, project as my possibilities, in both my intentional ideas and my intentional willing, upon the In-itself (pp. 345, 349). In sum, he seems to say that the objectivity of both myself and my world is inaccessible to me myself in isolation. For the 'I' of his text is now speaking from the point of view of For-itself or, in terms of our impressions of Sartre's absolute, from the god's-eye point of view.

However, enter the other, and I experience her look. Immediately and without further ado, I am an object. But that means, Sartre hastens to add, that neither the look nor the one who looks at me is thereby experienced as an object. The look is not identifiable with the eyes that are instrumental in seeing me; and an object of the nature of the In-itself cannot as such, in any case, make another its object; it is incapable of that kind of presence to another thing which Sartre attributes to consciousness alone. In the look, then, I encounter the seer. And the relationship is symmetrical, in that I similarly make an object of the other person. I locate the other person in the world of things, on a chair in a room, as the other person simultaneously locates me, standing by the window. Sartre expresses this reciprocity as follows: 'In a word, my apprehension of the Other in the world as *probably being* a man refers to my permanent possibility of *being-seen-by-him*; that is, to the permanent possibility that a subject who sees me may be substituted for the object seen by me. *Being-seen-by-the-Other* is the truth of *seeing-the-Other*' (p. 345). But notice two things. The permanent possibility of being seen by another person is substituted in that quotation for an actual person looking at me; and the word 'probably' qualifies my apprehension of the other person as being in actual fact a person. Ask, then: Why do the terms 'possibility' and 'probability' qualify significant elements of this account of encountering another person?

The answers, whether satisfactory or not, are straightforward enough in any case. For Sartre notes, quite rightly, that this encounter with the other is far from being confined to instances in which I notice someone actually looking at me. Being the object of another's look is a permanently possible feature of my existential status – as I pass a window, for instance, or hear a twig snap in a wood. I am thus constantly the one who is the object of another's look, possibly; and across that possibility I grasp my own objectivity in the world, permanently. And by saying that on the occasion of any particular look, it is probably a person who is looking, I simply mean to convey the fact that I cannot apprehend the object there in the world looking at me simply and directly as a self-consciousness, as a pure consciousness (of) self. Very well, then. That is fine as an explanation of the terms 'possible' and 'probable'. But must we then conclude that these same terms remain in effect, to the point of qualifying this topic of the chapter itself, the *existence* of others; and if so, which is it to be, possible or probable? And in either case, what is the foundation of the possibility or probability?

Consciousness is, strictly speaking, contentless. It relates to the In-itself by simple 'nihilation' – Sartre went to the trouble of coining that term in order to connote a particularly absolute kind of pure and simple negating. Hence consciousness is a black hole into which things disappear. That is as true of myself as an object in the world as it is true of anything else. I continuously escape myself, as Sartre put it. And in the look of another I experience myself escaping into another black hole; not in such a way that I can be conscious of that black hole as I am conscious of the black hole which is my own For-itself; but simply in that in the look of another I experience my escaping towards a nihilating entity of which I am not (self-)conscious, and in *that* experience of my escaping I get a sense of my objectivity in the world that I do not have in my own nihilating consciousness of myself. Correspondingly I see the other seeing me by being a nihilating of her objective dimension in which she can then grasp her objectivity as she could not as a solitary For-itself. Being-seen-by-the-other is the truth of seeing-the-other. Hence the terms 'possibly' and 'probably' in their separate contexts make the same point. As I cannot be certain that this object now looking at me is a woman – it could be a very realistic hologram – the probability I express in each concrete instance refers to there being a subject *there*, that is, actually located in the object which appears in the world as anything from an unfeathered biped within my range of vision to the sound of breaking twigs. The probability does not refer to the subject, the consciousness to which the looking belongs. Correspondingly, when I refer to my being seen as a permanent possibility, I am simply repeating the truism that the look is not to be identified with eyes or indeed with any other configuration of things in the world. Which leaves intact, Sartre thinks, his certainty of the existence of other persons, and our encounter in the looks that mutually objectify. In short, I am certain of the existence of other persons: it is their location, it is the existence of others-as-objects amongst the other In-itself objects in the world, that remains uncertain, possible or probable, for these are all in any case and of their nature subject to nihilation, transient, forever fleeing from me (pp. 368ff).

The problem with accepting this means of securing my certainty of the existence of and encounter with another person – by confining the qualities of probability or possibility to my apprehension of persons merely as objects-in-the-world – is that it reinstates in the solution the precise form of dualism which causes there to be a problem about explaining encounter with other persons in the first place. This is the dualism of the person defined strictly in terms of pure consciousness, in terms of Sartre's For-itself which simply nihilates or entirely separates itself (the terms are equivalent) from the In-itself, the reality of the material universe. Indeed the manner in which this dualism is reintroduced into the solution to the problem of the encounter with another person serves to create, and to increase the impression of, an allegedly Aristotelian God serenely detached from all worldly entities and events. For the look, being of its nature consciousness, is constantly distinguished from eyes, from persons-as-objects-in-the-world; it is as little present in or as these, as little involved with them as it is with windows and the sound of twigs breaking in the forest. Therefore, for all his intricate logical wriggling, and for all the persuasiveness of his imaginative insight into the emotions of shame and pride and so on with which I respond to another's look, Sartre in this matter of the existence of others has but two options open to him. Either I know of another person's existence because I, as a subject, encounter the other as a subject without the mediation of any thing in the world (and this Sartre declares to be impossible); or my knowledge of the existence of another person would have to take the form of inference from the appearance of unfeathered bipeds, their looks and other observable states and behaviours, on some analogy with my own experience of such observable states and behaviours in me. Then indeed I would have to talk in terms of probability or possibility; but probability and possibility can only be measured against actual knowledge of, encounter with, another subject in some instances of states or behaviours, so that I could at least have the possibility of detecting the instances in which I was mistaken. Probability and possibility, in short, are only intelligible within some system of verification and falsification. But in the kind of dualism which character- ised both the beginning and end of Sartre's argument, no encounter with another person in any observable state or behaviour is possible; and so this second option for knowledge of the existence of the other is also unavailable to Sartre.

When Sartre at similarly great analytic length discusses the human body, a similar problem emerges. What he wants to conclude, he cannot conclude successfully, because of the permanent presence of the dichotomous dualism of his opening definitions of For-itself and In- itself. The body which my doctor deals with is an In-itself, obviously, and in so far as I can look at it and see what the doctor sees, it remains such for me also. But the same body is in my consciousness as my possibilities of dancing, eating, working on wood and so forth: it is For-itself. Sartre wants to say simultaneously that 'since these two aspects of the body are on *different* and *incommunicable levels of being*, they cannot be reduced to one another'; yet that 'Being-for-itself must be *wholly* body [as object in the world, I presume] and it must be *wholly* consciousness' (p. 404; all italics are mine). Sartre wants to say these two things simultaneously; and particularly in the case of my body, for that is the obvious candidate for allowing me to understand how I can be a For-itself/For-others. But the crude dualism with which he begins the argument of the book and from which he refuses to the end to resile, prevents me from ever understanding what I see he wants to say. To that extent his philosophy continues to fail.

It does not appear that Sartre has succeeded any better than have the others in the phenomenological tradition whom he criticised for various shortcomings. It might be worth-while, then, to offer at this point a brief summary analysis of this phenomenological tradition which reaches a kind of closure with Sartre. At worst it can serve as a kind of account- taking of the contents of this tradition as it reached the boundaries of postmodernism.

THE PHILOSOPHICAL PROGENY OF THE PHENOMENOLOGICAL APPROACH

In a phenomenological tradition of philosophy, the philosophising be- gins with or from the phenomenon. That goes without saying; it says no more than what the name, phenomenology suggests. The differences between the philosophers in this tradition consist in the way in which this beginning with or from the phenomenon is understood by each. In Sartre's case – to take our selection of philosophers now in reverse order – the philosophising begins at the most transcendental dimension of the subject, at a point of (self-)conscious being at which consciousness is as yet contentless. For this it is that is described as a separate region of being, and, as a presence to, a relationship to, any other kind of being must originate with it, so too the account of that relationship must begin with it. Sartre, then, begins with the phenomenon that is constituted by that self-appearing entity, and with its transcendence glossed as initial separation. But it appears, if the analysis conducted above has any virtue, that from this beginning Sartre cannot explain how any relationship, and least of all a relationship of knowing, can be constructed as a bridge to any other subject or thing. To speak from my own point of view: unless I am this Sartrian (self-)consciousness, it does not exist; or in theological terms, either I am this allegedly Aristotelian godlike being or this god does not exist. And even if I am and it does, then to my knowledge no thing and no other self exists. Is this in effect the philosophy of Advaita Vedanta, in which pure absolute Self alone exists and all else is illusion? But what, then, is the origin and existential status of the illusions? Perhaps the illusions result from that negating which seems essential to consciousness in its empirical relational mode; in Sartre's case, for his For-itself, this would take the form of nihilation. It would have to be conceived, that is to say, in terms of the absolute Self imagining some thing other than itself in order to secure itself by nihilating this thing, by seeing it as a (Self-created) illusion. Difficulties remain with this kind of explanation; but they are difficulties which only a good Advaita Vedantist could overcome.[9] But the result would then be too theological in content for a convinced atheist like Sartre to be expected to stomach. In any case, when Sartre begins with this most transcendent dimension of consciousness, and takes transcendent to connote separation, all of reality other than his For-itself is forever lost from view.

The phenomenon with which Husserl begins would appear to be a much more substantial phenomenon than Sartre's. Husserl's subject has the transcendental dimension that Sartre separates off as the very definition of the For-itself, but it also has all the intentional content which we identify with the more empirical ego; concerning which, as we saw, Sartre was sometimes clear about its exclusion from the nature of

[9] For a very clear and persuasive account of this kind of Indian philosophy, see the two books by Ananda Wood, *From the Upanishads* and *Interpreting the Upanishads* (New Delhi: Full Circle, 1997).

his For-itself, sometimes bordering on self-contradiction. From such a beginning it would surely be possible to understand the existential relationship between such a mind full of determinate intentional ideas, and other such minds, and the material world of which we all are such a bodily part. And as a consequence it would be possible to understand how this more empirical subject – empirical in the sense that it now has determinate thought content included in its reality – could know other subjects and the material world of which we are such a bodily part. Perhaps that would be possible if Husserl had not insisted on the initial *epoche*, for that insistence has the effect of treating the transcendence of the world of this, now more empirical, subject as in effect a separation; and from such a separate original existence, it is again difficult to explain how this Husserlian subject can know any other subject or thing. That was the point that Sartre made in criticism of Husserl when he considered this plurality of separated minds, each containing the configurations of (parts of) an allegedly common material world, and said that he still saw no way in which any one of these could be conscious of any one of the others; especially since the further transcendental dimension of this still separated mind appeared to have no other function than to unify the manifold of intentional ideas in this mind, in the role of the Kantian unifying apperceptive ego. Because of this original separation by the *epoche*, this further transcendental dimension of the mind, by which it transcends each intentional content towards a unity that made them into a 'world', could still not be seen to transcend itself beyond and towards any subject or thing other than itself. Solipsism, and the threat of the loss of the material world, together with its other embodied subjects, still appears the only sure result. The only significant difference between Sartre and Husserl, then, consists in the fact that, though both take transcendence to mean separation, Husserl places the separation between the material world and the ego, as Sartre would call it, whereas Sartre when he is being clear about the matter places the separation between material world and its embodied egos, on the one hand, and a pure, contentless consciousness, on the other.

There is in fact a theological counterpart to this Husserlian subject also. And since practically all of the philosophers in this chapter insist on making theological points, and since the overriding interest of this philosophical essay is in theology, it is worth describing it briefly. The Husserlian subject, first seen in separation from the material world, resembles nothing so much as a traditional divinity that appeared on the scene when Christianity baptised Middle Platonism. For in Middle

Platonism the Platonic Forms or Ideals came to be seen as Ideas in the mind of the still self-contemplating (Aristotelian) God, there to function as exemplar ideas according to which the world was created.[10] It is worth remarking also that this account of God, if left at that, would not explain how God could know the material world. For this God's transcendence is still thought of as original separation, and the highest dimension of this divinity's transcendence is thus no greater than the transcendence of a Kantian apperceptive ego unifying the mind's contents. So, even if it is said that God created the world, it would still not follow that this God could know the world simply by focussing on her own exemplar ideas in her *Logos*. The material world is, as Plato well understood, a very different thing from any set of ideal forms. And a creator God could only know the world if she transcended herself further towards or, better, became immanent in the material world, no longer separated from it. Once again it can be said: I would only know this godlike entity of Husserl's if I were this God, and even then I would not necessarily know any other subject or thing.

There is a very real sense in which Heidegger begins with a similar, and similarly separate, idea of a phenomenal subject, in that he intentionally sets up a philosophy that is designed to get rid of it. Thus the presence of a 'Cartesian' dualism continues to be influential throughout Heidegger's philosophy. 'Cartesian dualism' can be deemed to be present and effective in any thought sequence in which transcendence connotes separation, 'outside of' or, as the Scots say, 'outwith'; and also where negation means simple nihilation, for that is the ultimate process of putting something out. The presence and influence of such 'Cartesian' dualism is in the form of absence and opposition, that is to say, in the form of something which one so consistently tries to avoid that it shapes the account of reality which then results almost as much as if it had been positively used for purposes of shaping that account. Reference has already been made to a kind of crude materialist view of reality that can only be expressed and understood on the basis of a mind–matter dualist conception, for the materiality of reality is secured by the denial of the incidence of mind. In a somewhat analogous manner, so persistent is Heidegger's determination to rid us of a transcendent subject in the crude sense of transcendence which yields what he too

---

[10] Early Christian theologians, including the great Athanasius, envisaged God at first in separation from creation, then creating consecutively the *cosmos noetos*, the idea-world that was contained in God's *Logos* or Word, and then through this the *cosmos aesthetos*, the tangible world of bodies and embodied souls.

designated as these godlike subjects, that his philosophy swings to the extreme of an increasingly dominant, virtually exclusive, focus on the world of the fourfold as the creative agency responsible for our human world. This tends to leave us rather too embodied in the world, with little or no transcendence of any kind. In the end, we are just the poets in which the 'worlding' process by which world comes to be, comes to expression; and even an individual poet tends to fade behind the text. Outside of that effectively supererogatory role, even the concrete, embodied human subjects find little opportunity to transcend the 'worlding' that forges through them. One drifts towards impressions of reality as a process without a subject, unless Heidegger's ambiguous but very immanent god/divinities as part of his fourfold structuring can be construed as subjects. And one can almost anticipate, before they actually appear on the horizon, the dismissal of the subject in Barthes, Foucault and, last but by no means least, Derrida, who did after all abandon a doctoral dissertation on Husserl, and then took off from Heidegger in the course of embarking on his own characteristic postmodernist philosophy.

The 'Cartesian' dualism of two entirely different and initially separate substances continued to wield a dominant influence throughout this tradition of philosophy called phenomenology; and its influence seems undiminished at the historical point now reached even, if not indeed especially, in the case of those who wish most adamantly to get rid of it once and for all. The major results of this influence can be tabulated briefly, and they can be seen to confirm and develop a little further the schematic anticipations set out at the beginning of this chapter.

The more unquestioned remains the sway of 'Cartesian' dualism, the more persistent the simultaneous tendency of these philosophies to begin always from the phenomenal world of mind, the more difficult it becomes to establish the relationship with the rest of reality; and in particular the relationship in this respect of knower to known. The loss of reality is imminent.

The more this effect of this combination of 'Cartesian' dualism and the phenomenological method in philosophy is noticed, but the more redress is attempted by seeking to remove the admittedly godlike mind-substance which almost inevitably results from this combination, the more difficult it becomes to maintain a real and identifying role in the onward progress of this material world for the real embodied subjects we otherwise seem to ourselves to be. The loss of the subject is threatened.

INTERMEZZO: SUBJECT AND REALITY IN SOME PERSONALIST
PHILOSOPHIES OF THIS CENTURY

It is perhaps worth pausing at this point to observe what happened to
our general topic of the (loss of the) subject, in the predominantly
personalist philosophies which have emerged in the course of this
century; philosophies which it would be difficult to include within the
stricter phenomenological tradition. The overriding theological interest
of this philosophical essay would encourage this interlude, for these
philosophies were welcomed with a mixture of relief and gratitude, and
as much by Christian theologians as by moralists, who felt that prevailing philosophies of the kind that more obviously attract the attention of
this chapter left little or no ground on which to cultivate either of their
disciplines. It would not be possible, of course, to survey all the philosophies of this century which could claim the soubriquet personalist. But
it is certainly of interest to note that from a sample of two of these
philosophies, the earlier philosophy of Macmurray and the more recent
philosophy of Levinas, a strong impression is gained which is of direct
relevance at this stage of the essay. It is an impression of instability here
in these personalist philosophies also; and an instability, moreover,
which bears remarkable similarities to the one we have just seen, in
which the broad phenomenological tradition of recent philosophy left us
teetering between a questionable kind of subject, on the one hand, and
on the other, a world process from which the subject had all but
vanished.

Certainly when taken together, Macmurray and Levinas, and in that
order, the impression emerges once more of a pendulum swing. The
swing begins from a philosophical point at which the subject is certainly
secured, but in a manner in which the existence of other subjects can
only be inferential – and it is now clear how such a subject of its nature
tends towards solipsism, and to a doubt about the very existence both of
other persons and other things. The swing ends at the other philosophical point at which what appear at first to be the existence and inter-
relationships of persons seem to be submerged, or as close as dammit to
submerged, in structures and processes in being which are of such
general ontic dimensions that they neither yield nor require any application of the adjective personal. If this is so, the influence of phenomenology upon the emergence of a postmodernism in which both mind and
reality seem lost to view can scarcely be reduced by recourse to the most
determinedly personalist of recent philosophies.

John Macmurray, 'Persons in Relation'

In his most celebrated work[11] Macmurray set out to secure, against some very impersonal philosophies and psychologies of the behaviourist kind, not merely the fact that there were persons in the world, but the fact that they were essentially intersubjective or relational entities, in defiance of some impressions of persons as rational monads which could then, of course, fashion relationships with others – an idea too close for comfort to that of the solipsist. And he very wisely devotes a good deal of the early analysis and argument of the book to the human infant from the moment of birth. For if what he has to say about the essence of personhood is true, it must be verifiable at each and every point of human existence. This, then, in brief is what he has to say.

Whereas the newborn animal is directed by instinct to fashion its earliest behaviour in such a way that, with some initial and necessary help from its parents – feeding it and keeping it warm and safe, and so on – and an inevitable amount of trial and error, it can secure its existence in the ecological niche it comes to occupy; the newborn person, though requiring the same kinds of initial helps from the parents, and conditioned to express distress when these are not forthcoming, appears from the outset to be motivated to seek the presence of the parent, the parent's company, one might say, as a necessary boon never quite reducible to the occasional presences of the parent in order to supply the necessary helps already noted. Hence, where the governing motivation of the newborn animal – if we can speak of motivation at all, rather than of instinct – is to acquire the strategies for survival, with help from the parent, including perhaps demonstrations of certain skills, the governing motivation of the human infant is for the companionship of the parent. This is the positive side of the total and prolonged dependence of human newborn on parent, in which again it differs very significantly from the animal newborn; and it goes its own way to establish the fact that persons are persons-in-relationship from birth to death, and hence essentially so. Furthermore, the infant communicates this governing motivation to have the parent present as companion both by crying for the parent when it does not need food, for instance, and by the usual expressions of satisfaction in the mere presence of the parent. In fact these expressed emotions in presence and absence of the parent are the germs of love and fear, the twin governing emotions of adult

[11] John Macmurray, *Persons in Relation* (1955) (London: Faber and Faber, 1961).

relationships: fear of loneliness and implicitly of death, and the love of the loved one that says 'thou shalt not die'. 'He can live only through other people and in dynamic relations with them', Macmurray then concludes of the human infant. 'In virtue of this fact he is a person, for the personal is constituted by the relationship of persons. His rationality is already present, though only germinally, in the fact that he lives and can only live by communication. His essential natural endowment is the impulse to communicate with another human being.'[12]

Macmurray then gives a detailed account of the development during its early years of the human neonate, and he continues to contrast it with the development of the animal. At first the motivation of which Macmurray spoke, both in its governing and in its more specific forms, is but consciousness itself, and consciousness moreover in its most elementary form: in the form of the most elementary kinds of feeling that distinguish between discomfort and comfort in response to stimuli, including the negative stimuli such as hunger or, specifically in the case of the human neonate, loneliness. So whether it is the governing motivation towards the companionship of the parent or a more specific motivation towards food that is in question, the human neonate cannot be said to *know*, strictly speaking, that that is what it is all about; it does not have the explicit intentionality, one might say, towards that state or end. It does not yet understand, it is not yet rational about, all of this. It is the parent who, for quite a long time in the case of humans, supplies the intentionality, the rationality; it is she who knows and understands and intends the successful outcome of the infant's 'random' movements and trial-and-error behaviour in general. The human neonate, one might say, is rational during these earliest years, but only potentially so, only by proxy. That human pattern continues to be clarified by a continued contrast of the human with the relatively early independence of the animal neonate, and in particular by means of the contrast of habit, which must be learned, with instinct, which cannot be.[13]

The animal's behaviour is regulated by instinct from the outset, so that, with the inevitable amount of trial and error, it adapts to its environment, discriminates between things and their uses and effects, and so survives. No rational process, strictly speaking, emerges now or later in the animal's life. With the human person, on the contrary, everything has to be learned. Even perceptual discrimination must be

---

[12] Ibid. p. 51.
[13] Ibid. p. 57: 'In the absence of intention and knowledge, consciousness is motive'; 'in human activity, habit takes the place of instinct in animals'.

learned at the beginning and throughout the long process of learning to deal with things and persons. The human infant is endowed with imagination, of course; but at the outset the imagination merely serves to perform the elementary function of coordinating visual, tactual and auditory input, and so on. It is the parent who knows that each particular discrimination, each pattern of behaviour towards things or persons, is the correct or right one. The infant behaves according to its original, in-built motivation *as if* it understood quite rationally that, being a person rather than an animal, it must learn the truth of perceptions and the rightness of behaviour in interpersonal relationship. It cries for the presence of the parent, experiences the satisfaction of that mutual presence become mutual and then, as it were, double in intensity, with the particular satisfactions expressed by the one who *knows* when its particular perceptions are correct and its particular behaviours towards other things and persons are right. In this way it acquires the habit of correct perceptions and right behaviours and, simultaneously, it achieves that awareness of the reality of the world and of its affordances which secure its adaptation, its survival, its prospects of life and life more abundant. By learning, by habit, and not by instinct.

There is a point in the early development of the child, Macmurray notices, when its behaviour takes the form of play in which an element of fantasy is clearly present. The child repeats behavioural skills learned already, but with signs of imagination in a more creative role; for the behavioural skills are repeated for their own sake now, and they thus demonstrate the presence of a certain reflective role for the imagination. The parent's presence is still required for these 'displays', yet at this stage there is already evidence that the child is developing that reflective pattern of consciousness which inevitably develops into full-blown reasoning. That final stage comes about with the acquisition of language, for with that comes the more complete acquisition of the knowledge of truth about things and rightness of action thus far accumulated in the human community in the world; a knowledge of scientific, practical and moral truth to which the new member of the human race will be expected to contribute in its own time, and to instil in its own offspring in turn.

Now, this account of Macmurray's seems at first sight to be a totally intelligible and convincing explanation of the reality of personhood through the essential processes of encounter with persons in the very coming-to-be of persons. And yet on deeper reflection it is fairly seriously flawed; and flawed, moreover, in ways that are of interest at the present stage of this essay. The principal flaw can be detected when one notices, again, that for all his talk about human persons being in relation with other persons from the outset, and for all his frequent use of the term communication to describe that process, both the knowledge of what is going on in these processes which initiate and maintain parent and child in a relation of companionship, and the whole of the intentionality which rationalises these processes, is for a considerable length of time attributed entirely to the parent. Hence the child for all of that time is relating as a consciousness which is no more than a complex of very elementary feelings, some of which are admittedly predisposed by some biological process to seek and maintain the very presence – but again, to it, a very elementary physical and emotional presence – of a parent. Furthermore, in describing these feelings Macmurray has resiled, if he ever knew of this, from the far more substantial account which Descartes offered of the original emotions and of their status as means of actually knowing the other, and particularly the personal other of the parent. Notice also that the look, which for Sartre is itself the very paradigm of the conscious, knowing encounter with another person, falls for Macmurray amongst these random movements of the infant which of themselves achieve no knowledge of anything.

The suspicion then begins to grow in strength that for Macmurray the person is really equivalent to the rational mind. His statement to the effect that rationality is only germinal in the newborn, since it reduces in his text to the statement that the newborn is rational by proxy, means that the newborn is still only potentially a person. Something similar must be said of his statement that personal relationships are of the essence of personhood. Since the initial relationship of newborn to parent is constituted of some biological predisposition for the presence of a parent, in the absence of instinctive equipment for survival, *that* relationship, in the form of a motivation expressed in very elementary feelings, contains within itself the potentiality for the relationship in which, some considerable length of time later, a person now equipped with rational mind and explicit intentionality will relate to another such person. The initial relationship, once again, is one which contains but the potentiality for a truly personal relationship; it represents potential personhood. The actual personhood, on these terms, will then consist in a process in which rational intentionality – in short, knowledge about things and persons and how to behave towards them – is transferred from a person who has much of this to a (potential) person who has initially none of it. But since the initial motivation of the neonate constitutes at most a relationship of proximity in which such transference can take place, it does not of itself explain how it takes place, and it can be considered a flaw in Macmurray's argument that thereafter he merely describes the stages in which it takes place. At the very least he leaves a very deep ambiguity in his pivotal contention to the effect that persons are constituted in relationship, and that the relationhip in which they are constituted is present from the very outset of their existence.

The flaw in his philosophy, or, if one prefers to take the milder view, the deep ambiguity at the centre of his argument, surely shows that he is haunted by the still dominant mind–body dualism, in which the former is a mental substance replete with scientific truths and moral principles, and the latter is an extended substance, part of the extended substance of the world, which has to be understood scientifically in its needs and processes, and regulated morally in its activities. But the problem with this dualist model, to repeat in other words what has been said perhaps too often already, can be put in the following terms: how can I know that another person is transmitting knowledge to me unless I already know within myself not only that I know, but what a sign or symbol is? How would I ever, at any stage of my development, recognise a word spoken or written as a word unless I could speak words, or at least unless I could already deploy preverbal symbolism? I have to be a knowing, intentional being myself, already knowingly 'signing' or symbolising through the structures of my body and through those physical features of the world that are affordances to me through my body, before I can recognise and thus encounter signs as signs, signs which can transmit intuitive, theoretical, practical and moral truths; and thus know, encounter, in and through these signs, the embodied personal other.

So, by depriving the neonate of all 'intention which rationalises', Macmurray makes it impossible to understand how human neonates come to be rational-intentional agents, persons in their own right, given that in the earliest nurturing relationships rational intentionality seems restricted to the parental mind. Indeed, Macmurray's account of human neonate development may reveal a still haunting presence of a 'Cartesian' dualism. It would, of course, be quite an unjustified exaggeration to accuse him of subscribing to such a dichotomous dualism in any explicit fashion. So much that he has said about the nature of persons in relation is so obviously heading in the right direction. But it would be fair to say, nevertheless, that in the unstable philosophy of the time, his work shows the pendulum still swinging towards the extreme of the solipsistic mind, unwelcome in its likeness to certain traditional gods,[14] and described in such a manner that one is unable to understand how it could secure an encounter with other minds, or indeed in the end with other things.

Levinas: persons are For-Others

In the case of Levinas the pendulum swings in the opposite direction. Levinas took a somewhat dim view of Heidegger, particularly when he focussed upon the ethical implications of the latter's work. He is thinking more perhaps of the 'earlier' Heidegger of *Sein und Zeit*; thinking more of *homo faber*, of human beings making their own little worlds within Being from the things, the *pragmata*, at their disposal. He is not thinking so much of Heidegger's later image of the human being as poet more than artisan, the one now who occupies a pivotal position in the 'clearing in the forest' in which Being, through the worlding of the world, comes to an always individual and temporary expression, different from every other one. Thinking mostly it would seem, then, of Heidegger's *homo faber*, Levinas pictures the 'being with' of persons in the world as a scene of mutual violence. At least each successive artisan must work over the traces left upon the world by the artisan who went before, stamping her own projects upon the world, and in this way appropriating at least that small part of the world to her self. This is the For-itself in a quite sinister meaning of the term; and unless a substantial corrective is added, there will inevitably ensue an ethic of plundering the world for booty in the interests of securing each separate, bounded, individual self; each trying, vainly as Sartre would say, but still inevitably trying to make itself into an In-itself. The corrective applied by Levinas, as Levinas would say, consists in a simple recognition of a relationship between persons which should condition my choices, and determine at least their proper direction, because it exists before any individual choice is ever made.

Levinas's central conviction and foundational insight, then, is this: the person is essentially and originally, and quite literally originally, For-the-Other. Sartre, of course, described the subject as being also For-another, but the subject in Sartre was already constituted as a For-itself (and, we might add, because of his definition of the For-itself his attempt to explain how it could then be for another was fatally compromised);

---

[14] The theological dimension of his work was clearly within the intention of Macmurray himself. Indeed he seems to have thought of his major work as a kind of natural theology, in which the relation of infant to parent presaged a personal universe in which God is the ultimate reality.

hence, he was unable to understand the original and originating status of the For-the-Other. This original structure of the For-the-Other can already be seen, according to Levinas, from animate beings, with their triple endowment of movement, ingestion and sensibility. An animate being's movement upon a surface is always preceded by the resistance to be offered to the movement by that surface; its ingestion is preceded by that gestation by another which gave it origin. Or it might, perhaps, be better to put that point the other way round: gestation by an animal is preceded by its being 'ingested', by the other taking from it the substance of its body. And its sensing of an other is always preceded by its being an object of sensing by another. In short, the animate being is always already vulnerable to another in all distinctive aspects of its being. But it is the self-conscious, rational, intellectual being that offers the instance *par excellence* of this most indigenous structure of reality. The intellectual act of apprehension seems at first sight to be the most complete act of mastery of all objects which come within its imperial purview; but it is in fact the most impressive example of something which is obsessed by objects, in Levinas's etymological use of the term obsession as a laying siege to something. In short, then, the one who would think of itself as For-itself is always already vulnerable to another, such that in fact its being a self is constituted by that vulnerability, that fundamental passivity as Levinas thinks of it, rather than by anything that that one might be or do on one's own account.

Levinas goes on then to give his most convincing account of the structure of this For-an-Other in the course of his analysis of human subjects; even though the structure evidently applies in the case of all animate beings and, as we must note shortly in a critique of Levinas, his general analysis of the structure would appear to be applicable to anything, animate or inanimate. In passages reminiscent of Sartre's thoughts on the look, Levinas writes of the face of another person as constituting a kind of epiphany in which I am actually exposed to, offered up to, another, measured one might say by another. And it is not as if I or any other person could suddenly assume some neutral, third-party position from which a measurement of one against the other could be accomplished. Persons are not things; they are not fully defined by what they already have achieved. They are self-transcending entities and as such are containable within no known limits. Therefore, in another's face, when she looks at me, I am exposed, offered up to, measured against an entity which cannot itself be defined and thus delimited. That then for me is an experience of infinity; for however

88 *Historical–critical*

unusedbusy I may make myself in trying to, well, make something of myself, as if I could ever be fulfilled and finally defined by whatever I had thereby done or acquired, in my encounter with the face, the look of another person, I realise that, since I cannot appropriate that other to be simply another acquisition and extension of my self, I am measured against infinity.[15] I truly am the forever undefined self I try to ignore in forever acting as a For-itself trying to make itself into an In-itself. It is in the encounter with the other, then, and in the ensuing vulnerability to the other's siege and claim, in the ensuing exposure, measuring, accountability, responsibility, that I *realise* my true nature and being as a person. Persons are in essence, in origin, For-Others.

So far the account seems both intelligible and persuasive. But soon a problem arises. It arises from the uncompromising insistence of Levinas on the originating and hence preceding efficacy of the other in constituting me, any 'me', the vulnerable one, the one already under the claim of the other, the accountable, the responsible one, and hence the truly (moral) personal being that in fact I am. For this insistence on this originating precedence makes Levinas talk of 'passivity beyond passivity', in one of his most characteristic phrases. The phrase means that I am to think of myself as vulnerable to, passive with respect to, the siege the other lays to me, the claim of the other upon me, before I myself do anything to lay myself open to such constitutive vulnerability. As he himself puts it: 'It is a having been offered . . . and not the generosity of offering oneself, which would already be an act . . . This non-initiative is older than any present, and is not a passivity contemporaneous with and counterpart of an act.'[16] Now, in view of the sheer reciprocity of others in this particular version of the very constitution of selfhood, I am bound to think of this kind of originating efficacy as one which is exercised by no currently active person. Like Sartre's look, this other by whose initiative my true selfhood is constituted cannot coincide with any individual person *act*ually laying siege and claim to me in this world that we both share. However, the case is worse for Levinas than it was with Sartre. For at least Sartre could be taken to imply that an entirely other-worldly being might be looking at me (as in fact it was pointed out that his For-itself in its original separateness looked very like someone squatting outside the world). But Levinas has described passivity in a manner that makes the description equally applicable to animate, impersonal beings. Furthermore, since he gives movement as one of the

---

[15] E. Levinas, *Collected Philosophical Papers* (The Hague: Nijhoff, 1987), p. 54.
[16] E. Levinas, *Otherwise Than Being or Beyond Essence* (The Hague: Nijhoff, 1981), p. 75.

examples of this passivity, there is no reason to suppose that the description would not equally apply to inanimate beings. All beings then, on his account of the matter, could be thought to suffer the 'prior' vulnerability, the passivity beyond passivity, which he thinks constitutive of persons. And then the preceding other would take the form of some impersonal and general structure of being, something perhaps like Heidegger's structural and ever operative distinction between Being and beings. In which case, since an impersonal structure cannot easily be thought to account for the origin of persons, personhood is really being submerged in the impersonal structures of being; the subject is being lost, really, and the pendulum swing of recent philosophy is rapidly approaching the other extreme of its course. This logical process in which the person who actually gestures to me (and thus makes me response-ible, and so on), ceases to be a person waving at me, and comes to assume instead the reality of personhood drowning altogether in some encompassing impersonal stuff, is noticed by Gillian Rose, of course, but also cleverly illustrated by her in a reference to Stevie Smith's poem, *Not Waving but Drowning*:

> Nobody heard him the dead man
> But still he lay moaning
>
> I was much further out than you thought
> And not waving but drowning.[17]

Now, it might be objected that it is wide of the mark to criticise Levinas for submerging the otherness in which personhood consists in a general structure of being. The very title of his major work, *Otherwise Than Being*, surely suggests that otherness consists in some kind of entity that is transcendental with respect to Being, even if that then turns out to be a kind of nothingness, as in Sartre's depiction of the For-itself? But then the same criticism would simply recur through the kind of critical attention already turned towards the term transcendence in this kind of context. For transcendent is now taken in the sense of entirely separate, separate from the being I encounter in and as the empirical world of things and other persons. And that is either a very self-contained personal entity, in which case it would be difficult to understand how it could relate at all to empirical persons, much less besiege them, lay claim to them, render them vulnerable in what must prove on Levinas's ontology to be a reciprocal enterprise. Or it would have to be

[17] Gillian Rose, *Mourning Becomes the Law* (Cambridge University Press, 1966), p. 37.

a very absolute kind of nothingness. Or perhaps both? A kind of transcendent, that is absolutely separate, wholly other being, whose very nature and ethos it would then be to negate, simply and utterly negate, any being other than itself as having the possibility of contributing anything at all to its being, particularly its being as knowing. Indeed this seems like the being-as-nothingness that we actually encounter as the infinity in and of others in Levinas's account of the latter; and in particular in those theological parts of his work in which he talks of this in terms of my being accountable before (Infinity) God, but without understanding God as any entity that could ever be represented or conceptualised.[18]

In summary, then, we really do encounter in Levinas just those questionable usages of the terms transcendent and nothingness or negating, which, far from enabling us to understand the encounter, the knowledge of, and thence the nature of other persons, whether human or divine, and their relationship to each other and to the rest of reality, positively frustrates such understanding. The transcendence I do experience is always a determinate transcendence; that is to say, a transcendence of this particular, empirical self, which coincides with a determinate negation; that is to say, a negation of this particular self that is part of the process of its emergence in a higher form to which it is driven or called. A transcendence which goes beyond, in the sense of utterly separating from, the whole of being of and in the world, and the corresponding kind of nothingness or nothing I neither encounter, nor can I even begin to know or understand it. Hence the other which is utterly other than being, which is in no way immanent in and encounterable in the others I do encounter in all our reciprocal and active presence to each other, embodied and active in this world, is either a God with whom I can never form a real personal, that is reciprocal, relationship, or a general nothingness that is some kind of counterpart of the general structure of being. In the case of Levinas, for reasons just stated, it looks more like the latter. And as such, of course, it submerges rather than founds the personhood of the persons that actually exist. *A fortiori* it cannot found the fundamental relationships between these that constitute the nature and existence of morality. But that is another matter.[19]

[18] Levinas, *Otherwise Than Being*, p. 149.
[19] Gillian Rose offers a fine critique of the way in which nothingness in Heidegger (where it occurs empirically as death) and in Levinas fails entirely to play the foundational role with respect to the human (moral) person which they appear to expect from it: *Mourning Becomes the Law*, pp. 133ff.

If we can generalise at all from these two cases, then, the most determined of personalist philosophies in recent times have themselves been disturbed by the ghostly presence of a 'Cartesian' dualism. Its distorting effect is seen in the manner in which the terms transcendence and negation are simplified to the point of crudity in actual usage. But most of all the distorting effect is seen in the corresponding manner in which philosophy is pushed either to envisage an extreme form of subject which is increasingly difficult to relate in any intelligible fashion to the reality of the empirical world, or to envisage the co-relative extreme of a form of structures or processes in reality which are increasingly intolerant of the inclusion of subjects and which, *a fortiori*, make it increasingly difficult to understand how anything which could reasonably be called a subject could ever derive from them. All that remains, then, in this thematic introduction of postmodernism to the argument of this essay is to describe the event of the encounter of this phenomenological tradition of philosophy with the Marxism of, say, Althusser, in which the second extreme encountered above, in the form of a view of reality as a historical process without a subject, seems to finally see off the subject from any philosophy, or indeed from any science or other form of discourse it comes to influence.

THE RECENT GENESIS OF POSTMODERNISM
FROM THE MORE MATERIALIST APPROACH

However, this last part of the thematic introduction of postmodernism cannot take the form of a simple story of the encounter of the holy trinity of postmodernism, Barthes–Foucault–Derrida, already destabilised by phenomenology in their attitude to the subject, with Althusser-type Marxism; with the consequent and obvious result, not just of the death of the subject, but of the conviction that the subject had never existed at all. For it is not as if, shortly after Marx himself died, some Engels-type materialism took over the connotation of that programmatic phrase historical materialism, and from that day to this Marxism simply connotes a view of reality as a historical process without a subject. An account of the progress of Marxism through this century, of the different people it influenced, and of the different results of this influence, requires an analysis and explanation much more complex than such a simple story could possibly encompass. Furthermore, it must prove to be an account that is beset at every point by a characteristic difficulty: this is the difficulty of continuing to identify clearly any 'ism' that survives for more than one generation beyond the alleged originating author of the 'ism'. For example, if we were to define Marxism quite strictly as 'the sum total of views and theories of the historical Karl Marx', even then we should quickly discover, first, that not all of the views, methods and theories of Karl Marx were distinctively and exclusively his; second, that some of his methodology in particular soon passed into the general practice of social-scientific inquiry and so ceased to be identifiable as Marxist; and, finally, that his views were inevitably interpreted by those who declared themselves his followers in their different times and circumstances, in addition to being used to produce differing interpretations of apparently similar features and events in the world.[20] Despite all of this, though, it is possible for our more restricted purposes to propose a brief account of the progressive influence of Marxism up to the point of the emergence of the postmodernists.

'Radical rationalism in thinking; steadfast resistance of any invasion of myth into science; an entirely secular view of the world; criticism pushed to its utmost limits; distrust of all closed doctrines and systems' – if these are not particular to Marx in his time – and they are not – what is? Kolakowski suggests, in general, the ability 'to look at human affairs through the prism of universal history; to see, on the one hand, how man in society is formed by the struggle against nature and, on the other hand, the simultaneous process by which man's work humanises nature; to consider thinking as a product of practical activity'.[21] He points out that the influence of these Marxist principles is to be found in the development of the social sciences, as much if not more than it is to be found in developing philosophy. And he adds that the application of these principles can prove them to be ambiguous. For we can take the principles to refer to a 'specific concept of determinism: the requirement that in a genetic analysis of political institutions and various forms of social consciousness we should look for the relationships that link them with social divisions arising from the system of ownership, or more generally, from the system of production'; and then the more material system of production will determine the content of social consciousness, without needing the intervention of any subject whose mind can transcend imaginatively and creatively that given content.

---

[20] By far the best account of what can count as Marxism during the course of this century is that by the renegade Marxist philosopher Leszek Kolakowski in *Marxism and Beyond* (London: Paladin, 1971), esp. the chapter 'Permanent vs Transitory Aspects of Marxism'.

[21] Kolakowski, *Marxism and Beyond*, p. 205.

Or we can take the principle to refer to

a certain type of historicism which not only rejects attempts to evaluate historical phenomena from the viewpoint of a moralistic keeper of eternal values, but which is based on the general principles of the historical relativity of the subjects under study, and also on the conviction that . . . our entire conception of the world is *socially subjective*. This means it is a product of collective activity, which creatively organises reality to adapt it to man's biological and social orientation in the world, and only thus formed does it remain in our minds. In this sense, then, the whole extra-human world is created by man.[22]

And, then, there be subjects indeed; subjects consciously creating the world, and thus knowing it, in all the relativity of historical progress and change. In the first case, to say that thinking is a product of practical activity means that the content of any thought or expression, however recorded, is fully determined by the physical systems of production and the subsequent structures of society; in the second case, it means that thinking is the envisaging and planning of a world to be created for the practical purposes of meeting human biological (and) social needs.

Now it is true to say both that Marxist influence found its way especially into the development of the social sciences – and, it might be added, from there to some of the leading postmodernists – and that this influence remained ambiguous as far as the status of the subject is concerned. And it is this line of investigation we must briefly follow, rather than simply bring on Althusser and his very subjectless Marxist philosophy of history as a process without a subject.

When Mary Douglas, the noted British anthropologist, delivered the Gifford Lectures at Edinburgh in 1989, she entitled the first lecture 'Mythology Demoted'.[23] If we take the term mythology in this title to be a cipher for those mental constructs, expressed at first orally and later in literary form, in which a people gives an account of the world and of its own place and prospects within it, we shall find in the brief story of social science which she then told a neat introduction to the unfolding dynamic between the structures of the world of the human being and the practical images and ideas that the human being constructs. We shall find an evolving social-scientific account of the dynamic between structures of reality and subjects, and that is sufficient for our purposes at this point.

22 Ibid. pp. 197–8.
23 In what follows I am indebted to the first draft of the first lecture, which I have by courtesy of Mary Douglas, and to subsequent conversation and correspondence.

Mary Douglas's story began with Max Muller, who had delivered his Gifford Lectures a century before hers. Now, Muller, Mary Douglas allowed, did in fact have a somewhat precocious understanding of the social importance of knowledge, and of the consequent need for those who would rule of gaining some control both of its repositories (the traditional poet in a non-literate society or the text in a literate one), and over its dissemination. Yet, for all of that, he still did not understand the deeper connections between the structures, the social structures in particular, and the oral or written deposits of wisdom. His principal way of dealing with myths was to interpret them as primitive anticipations of the more rational analyses of reality beloved of the Enlightenment. Thus Kronos eating and vomiting up his children became sanitised as a striking metaphor for night ending and beginning the sequence of our days. And the ridicule to which Muller's work was increasingly subjected in the intervening decades was in part due, according to Mary Douglas, to the corresponding failure on Muller's part to see more deeply into the relationship between structures and myths which his insight into the related control mechanisms should have revealed to him.

Indeed, she maintains, that deeper insight, and with it a more scientific anthropology, was available to Muller. For in the year in which Muller's Gifford Lectures were first published,[24] a noted Scottish scholar, William Robertson Smith, whose work influenced Durkheim, was painting a far more credible picture of the relationship between structures and subject-constructions in the human world, a picture which simultaneously made more sense of the persistent attempt of would-be rulers to control the deposit and dissemination of myths and philosophies, and allowed social science to become much more scientific than Muller's kind of rationalising could ever promise to be. Briefly, Robertson Smith contended, the reality of the world of our ancestors consisted in the 'institutions and practices' by which that world was constructed and formed. If we concentrated on the content of the surviving myths, we would learn nothing of the reality of these past worlds; for that content is confusing, self-contradictory or merely mystifying. But if we concentrate on the *structures* of the surviving myths, then we may well be able to see the corresponding 'structures and activities' of the real world that, then and now, lie behind and are revealed in the structures of the myths. Then we shall simultaneously understand the determination of those who held the dominant social

---

[24] Max Muller, *Contributions to the Science of Mythology* (London: Longmans Green, 1897).

roles in that world, or in any world for that matter, to control the deposit and dissemination of the myth or philosophy, the structures of which express the structures of the social world in which their dominance is so far secure.

In Mary Douglas's view of the turn that is seen in the work of Robertson Smith, it was that turn that made anthropology into the truly scientific discipline that it is to this day. It resulted in what can in general terms be called structuralism. Was its development due to the influence of a parallel development in Marxism? From what has already been said above concerning the presence in Marx's work of elements not exclusively his, and concerning the way in which successful innovative elements then tend to 'disappear' into the general methodology of investigative disciplines, it is better to ask that question in these terms, rather than to ask: Bluntly, Is this Marxism? And the answer would then appear to be in the affirmative. The similarities are so close, whether one considers the beginnings or the more recent forms of Marxist thought. At the beginning there was the characteristic Marxist philosophy of the intrinsic relationship between the structures of productive practices and ensuing social institutions, on the one hand, and human 'socially subjective' constructions, on the other. And this bears a striking resemblance to the relation between Robertson Smith's 'institutions and practices' and the oral and literary constructs they leave behind. At the more recent stage of development there is the striking resemblance between, on the one hand, the Marxism of Althusser, in which subjectless processes and structures sufficiently accounted for reality as a historical process without a subject, and on the other hand, the social-scientific philosophy of Lévi-Strauss, who roundly concluded that the goal of the human sciences is not to constitute man but to dissolve him.[25] Of course, one cannot conclude at this point of this development, its origins and influences, that the subject is already lost before the main postmodernists are even heard. For this development, because of the Marxist influence within it, still contains the ambiguity noted at the outset concerning the determining influence of structural process or subject. And we cannot then conclude that we are finally rid of the subject, and that Barthes–Foucault–Derrida were rid of the subject before their joint race was run. In actual fact, the subject (and reality with it) does not entirely disappear with Barthes, and only, if at all, at a certain extreme of the Foucault–Derrida run.

[25] Claude Lévi-Strauss's *The Savage Mind* (London: Weidenfeld and Nicolson, 1966) is most particularly engaged in the dismissal of the human subject in the form of the Sartrian For-itself.

Besides, there is another feature of this development as it emerges in Lévi-Strauss that goes some distance towards understanding the distinctive approach of the principal postmodernists and, as it happens, the precise means by which the subject (and the rest of reality) is finally made to disappear from view. This feature can be described either as the extension of the influence of 'Marxist' philosophy through the social sciences into the study of literature, or as the foundational decision of the modern social sciences to treat culture as a text.[26] It is not easy to relate these two descriptions causally, and to come up with a single explanation of the fact that Lévi-Strauss did decide that the best way to analyse patterns of social relationships was to analyse the structures of people's language – such that, in his memorable phrase, incest is bad grammar.[27] The process by which a dominant philosophy wields extensive influence over allegedly independent sciences and over the most ostentatiously critical of literary criticism is perhaps too common to call for much explanation. But that does not quite explain the reverse process by which social sciences take the written text as the paradigm of the subject matter of their discipline. Perhaps it is just that anthropologists in particular are especially dependent upon written accounts from obsolete or obsolescent cultures?

Whatever the explanation, the fact is that the text became the paradigm of the subject matter that one studies in disciplines devoted to explaining our world. That, then, in part at least, accounts for the distinctive approach of the principal postmodernists in that the material on which they mainly work consists of bodies of literature. And it probably helps to account also for their penchant for conceiving of that which lies behind the published works as itself something in the nature of a linguistic composition, a text-behind-the-texts, forever incomplete. Finally, the fact that the text became the paradigm of the subject matter that one studies in disciplines devoted to explaining our world might also account for the intrusion at the point of emergence of postmodernism of the semiology of Saussure; for we are dealing now with a 'Marxist' philosophy working through social-scientific and literary critical categories which it had itself done much to fashion. Certainly the intrusion of this version of semiology had a major part to play in turning

---

[26] For Lévi-Strauss and the anthropology of his era in particular, as Clifford Geertz puts it, 'the culture of a people is an ensemble of texts, themselves ensembles, which the anthropologist strains to read over the shoulders of those to whom they properly belong': *The Interpretation of Cultures* (London: Fontana, 1993), p. 452.

[27] Claude Lévi-Strauss, *Structural Anthropology* (London: Allen Lane, 1967), pp. 33ff.

a hitherto structuralist investigation into a deconstructionist one.[28] And it was probably not possible, in a context in which the paradigm of one's subject matter was now a text, to keep out of the investigative discussion for much longer[29] work on semiology that was so central to the study of language.

Whatever account we may give of the accidental or logical influences which brought the development of the philosophical investigation of the world to this point, it is in any case this stage of development of modern philosophy, with just these factors intertwined in it, that prepares for the final performance so far of the principal postmodernists – Barthes, Foucault, Derrida.

POSTMODERNISM AND THE (GRADUAL) LOSS OF THE SUBJECT (AND OF REALITY)

For those who see postmodernism as the funeral oration for the subject or author rather than as the final encomium for relativism, Roland Barthes's 'The Death of the Author', published in France in 1968, fills as well as anything else might fill the role of manifesto for the movement. One can include 'subject' with 'author', because although Barthes is mainly focussed upon literary texts, like the other postmodernists he goes far beyond the current critique of that style of literary criticism that practically reduced itself to discovering the intentions and meanings of the original authors of texts; and thus he drives beyond the pale of human discourse a more generally conceived subject or self than that of the author of a literary text. As he puts the matter: 'writing is the destruction of every voice, of every point of origin. Writing is that neutral, composite, oblique space where our subject slips away, the negative where all identity is lost, starting with the very identity of the body writing.' Nor must we read such sentences with the reservation intact: yes, but there surely is an original writing out of which all partial and relative human scripts are composed, behind which we might conjecture a more-than-human author. 'The text is a place where . . . a

---

[28] It is sometimes suggested that it was the influence of the view that it was structures of practice and institutions that found expression in structures of language, that gave rise to Saussure's idea of arbitrariness in signification, where previously signs had been thought to represent in some way the reality of the structured world. But this cannot be so. For even though in the structuralist view the immediate connotation of the signs (words, sentences) of the myth may be merely mystifying, the structure of the language-composition or text can still be thought to represent in some way the reality of the structured world-and-society.

[29] Ferdinand de Saussure's *Course in General Linguistics* was available in France from 1915 but remained without noticeable influence for almost half a century.

variety of writings, none of them original, blend and clash'; 'the writer can only imitate a gesture that is always anterior, never original'.[30] All subjects seem to be definitively declared lost from view.

Yet for well over a decade before this manifesto appeared with such uncompromising dismissals, Barthes had worked within general structuralist categories. Furthermore, the structuralist categories within which he worked were of Marxist influence, if not origin: he was a confessedly left-wing social philosopher or, as he would no doubt prefer to say, a social scientist intentionally ethical in purpose and intent. Correspondingly, he was a major influence on certain Marxist revisionists of the 1950s. These, however, were people who took a very clear line on what has otherwise been described as the inherent ambiguity of Marxist-dominant structuralist philosophy. Asked whether it was the structures of the material world that determined in some mindless manner the representations of it that then appeared as philosophy, art and so on; or whether it was the conscious, wilful and continuously creative activity of the human community in the world that made it a (human) world, and hence knowable and expressible in the first place, they would unquestionably lean towards the latter. And so would he. However, he would warn of the permanent temptation and constant practice of those who write or read any accounts of the human world, philosophical or fictional, to treat these after the fashion of naive realism, that is to say, to see them as the former option sees them, as expressions of nature (as in *Deus sive Natura*) which pass through a human being without any contribution, much less control, from the latter. But, then, of course, the subject is not lost to sight in Barthes's thought, at least not yet?

That is correct; and it is very clear in Barthes's *Mythologies*, still one of his best-known works, written a decade before 'The Death of the Author', and despite his use in that work of Saussure's semiology, presumably in pursuit of the scientific image. Suffice it to say here that Saussure in his study of the sign, and in a move remarkably reminiscent of Husserl's initial *epoche*, begins by breaking that synthetic unity of sign and signified – the sign expresses the signified – which is essential to all forms of representationalism, no matter how sophisticated, no matter how innocent of naive realism. Saussure replaces this with the trio signifier–signified–sign. In the case of speech, the signifier is an 'acoustic image of the psychic order', that is, something heard by a psychophysi-

---

[30] Roland Barthes, 'The Death of the Author', in *Image–Music–Text* (London: Fontana, 1977), pp. 142, 146.

cal entity; the signified is something of the order of an idea; the sign then consists in the 'associative totality', the *rapport*, of the signifier and the signified. The *epoche*, the breaking of the original unity of sign-expresses-signified, now prevents us from asking at this point: 'The sign of what?' Furthermore, we are told that the signifier is in itself empty; that is to say, it has in itself no meaning. It can be differentiated from other signifiers only by its insertion in a system of signifiers, by its subsequent difference from other signifiers in the system, each of which is itself without meaning, so that the system is in a real sense arbitrary. The example of the signifier 'the 12.15 train from Edinburgh to London King's Cross' is used to explain this. That signifier cannot 'mean' any actual train. The one now standing at this platform has different carriages, driver, passengers from the one yesterday; and it hardly ever leaves at 12.15. It signifies an idea in someone's mind, and can be differentiated from other signifiers only by its place in a timetable, underneath 'the 11.30 from Edinburgh to Aberdeen'.

Whatever one may think of the necessity of these initial definitions in the interests, presumably, of turning semiology into a science which, like the paradigmatic physical sciences, liked to see the subject(ivity) removed from their subject matter, this newer science is surely as prone as was Husserl's phenomenology to lose sight of both subject and reality. Barthes, however, prevents such loss of either subject or (the rest of) reality, but not by attempting to show how to make one's way back to either from such a Husserlian–Saussurean premise. In effect, he simply makes use of Saussure to put out of play the naive realist view of the linguistic productions of the race. He then replaces this with a view of language briefly described as 'speaking things', 'designed to *do* things'; a view of language suitable for the discourse of revisionist Marxism, of left-wing revolutionaries; a discourse from which neither the subjects nor the world they create can really disappear; in which both are then really present, and can be expressed, re-presented in language. He appeals to Marx to say that the most natural thing in the world retains a 'political' trace, however faint and dispersed, a 'presence' more or less recoverable of a human act that produced, managed, used, subsumed or even rejected that thing. There is, he then insists, what he calls an 'object-language', a language which 'speaks things' rather than speaks about them, which can thus bring these traces to light, can manifest them. For this language is designed to 'do' things (*dressé . . . à les agir;* like Heidegger's *pragmata* (things), with which we have to do in the world of *homo faber*). Hence it is designed, and enabled, to express people doing things, and to represent the world as done, made or in the making by people.

Most of the linguistic productions of the race, however, are used in such a way as if they constituted what he calls a meta-language. This usage, though it is most obviously instanced in myths recognisable as such, is also insidiously and widely present in the general languages of all peoples. It is characterised precisely by that naive realism in which the signs are signs of things, of their structures and processes, which simply are as they are, and will be as they will be, and which are represented as such in all of our otherwise inactive and obedient little minds.[31] This meta-language, as Barthes describes it, this view and use of language, corresponds exactly to Marx's view of the role of law, philosophy (science, theology), literature and so on, acting as the *vis inertiae* of history, keeping the status quo secure in the interests of those who currently govern and get the most out of it.

At the time of writing his *Mythologies*, then, Barthes had made use of a philosophy that throws out the baby with the bath water. As the similarity to a Husserlian starting point suggests, Saussure's starting point in the name of science leaves little chance of ever recovering sight of either subject or reality again. But then Barthes had simultaneously introduced, with little comment and even less philosophical analysis, a more enterprising baby in a far more ecologically friendly bath water; a 'Marxist' subject creating a world and succeeding at some level in giving it expression. Had he changed his mind a decade later? Do the uncompromising quotes which introduced his 'Death of the Author' above signal his acceptance at that stage of the final dismissal of the subject? Not quite. In fact, as a patient reading of his whole corpus would show, his recourse to the language of subjects slipping away and getting lost, language so reminiscent of Saussure's programme and its intended or unintended result, has the effect here also of getting rid of only a certain kind of subject, while constantly reintroducing a more acceptable subject in a more realistic role. The subject of which the manifesto seeks to rid us is described in the manifesto itself as a godlike subject-author which really consists in no more than the hypostasising of 'reason, science, law'.[32] That is to say, this subject is the precise counterpart of

---

[31] Roland Barthes, *Mythologies* (Paris: Editions du Seuil, 1957), esp. p. 23. This naive realist view is sometimes referred to as representationalism, or the instrumental view of language, thus obscuring the fact that mental constructs and signs can be thought to represent or express the world and entities within it, yet not incur the faults of naive realism.

[32] Barthes, *Image–Music–Text*, p. 147.

the naive realist view of mental construct and language rejected in the earlier work: a subject that virtually consists in the idea system of which it appears to be the mere container. Its description as godlike strikes a note of recognition in our minds, for there was a traditional divinity, a *Logos* or Word divinity, a mind containing the exemplar ideas by which the world was constructed and run. And it is particularly threatened with disappearance when faced with a Saussurean or Husserlian system. These systems begin simply with idea clusters or sign clusters on their own, and can never really make their way again to an encounter with either subjects or (the rest of) reality. But having dismissed this subject in this way, Barthes then as before proceeds to introduce a more accept-able subject. Hence he is still using Saussure as a disposable bouncer, hired to eject only a particularly undesirable subject.

It would not be worth while to try to reconstruct in detail from Barthes's corpus the more acceptable subject whose constant return accompanies the death of the godlike one. We should be quite unlikely to arrive at such a clear, consistent and substantial portrait of this subject as would enable us to make progress towards answers to the questions that concern us in this essay. This is partly because Barthes is more interested in the subject as literary author than in the human subject in general, and partly because his persistent use of a Saussurean semiology which would rid us of all subjects reduces us to the problematic posture of trying to see the acceptable subject through a veritable thicket of negatives, qualifications and hesitations. Suffice it to say, then, that the acceptable subject appears as both embodied and mortal; not the mind-container of ideas of a 'Cartesian' dualism, but a subject truly immanent in the physical world; and destined to leave but a trace in the world, a far from totalising impact that may be taken up by others. In words which reveal the predominantly literary context in which this subject is described:

were I a writer, and dead, how I would love it if my life, through the pains of some friendly and detached biographer, were to reduce itself to a few details, a few preferences, a few inflections, let us say: to *biographemes* whose distinction and mobility might go beyond any fate and come to touch, like Epicurean atoms, some future body, destined to the same dispersion.[33]

This portrait, or rather this barest of sketches of an empirical ego, does allow us to see a subject that is not too transcendent, that does not enjoy, to be more precise, the wrong kind of transcendence-as-separation, like

[33] Quoted in Burke, *The Death and Return of the Author*, p. 60.

the dismissed subject. But the assembled sketch still does not allow us to decide if its subject is transcendent enough to become mutually immanent with others, rather than remain, as in the case of Heidegger's subjects, merely physically *with* each other in the world in the mode of predators of each other's traces, possibly not even recognising them as traces ('like Epicurean atoms'). For that in the end would leave us unable to explain the creation of a *world*, even in the Marxist sense of that project.

Foucault by contrast is very determined about the total disappearance of the subject. The subject – now certainly the human subject in general and not merely the literary author – is made to doubly disappear. The first disappearance occurs in the course of an account of historical periods in terms of structured patterns, each of which gives rise in fully deterministic fashion to its characteristic philosophies, sciences, literatures and so on without any influence or control on the part of individuals, who are merely scribes or mouthpieces. The second disappearance will take the form of the end of the current historical period, a period which, as it happens, threw up for the first time in history discourse which actually described the human subject as a reality in its world. When this period comes to an end, as every period must, even that appearance of the human subject will be at an end also. That will then constitute the disappearance of the very appearance of the human subject, or of any other subject for that matter.

In order to illustrate these points as briefly as possible, it is necessary here to refer only to the two most recent periods in the history which Foucault traces in his monumental work *The Order of Things,* the Classical period, which he dates roughly from Descartes to 1800, and the Modern period, which is still running its course. The Classical period, he proposes, is characterised by representationalism. Read that term as it is so often used these days to convey an epistemology of naive realism, and the period is then characterised as one which lived by the conception of idea systems which simply and straightforwardly mirrored the things and processes that make up the world. These idea systems were no doubt contained in minds, but minds were not responsible for their shape or content; individual subjects had no real role as such. In the Modern period, with Kant in particular as the father of phenomenology, the human subject as subject of knowledge emerged out of nothing, as a real if problematic factor on the scene: 'man is only a recent invention, a figure not yet two centuries old, a new wrinkle in our knowledge, and he will disappear again as soon as that knowledge has discovered a new form'.[34] This problematic human subject who appears in this period Foucault describes in the by now familiar terms of the simultaneously transcendent and empirical ego: 'a strange empirico-transcendental doublet . . . a being such that knowledge will be attained by him of what renders all knowledge possible'.[35] This is no longer the container mind of the simple representationalist or naive-realist period; this is rather the active subject that both knows and is yet always transcending towards the unknown that always faces it: in the resolutely In-itself, in the determining structures of the material world, in the unconscious. It is at once the knower and the possibility of knowing that is always faced with the unknown. Promises have been held out to this subject by others of its kind, promises of total transparency and total presence in absolute knowledge, but none of them have been redeemed.

There is not much that can or, for present purposes, need be said about this magisterial explanatory project of Foucault's. It does bear a certain overall resemblance to that Althusser-type Marxism which looks to certain structures in the empirical world and thinks these to be entirely determinative of all forms of what we call culture. But there are some profound differences also. First, the underlying structures or substrates which, according to Foucault, determine the cultural forms of the successive periods do not seem to coincide with the ones that Marxists clearly and intelligibly describe: that is, those material resources and patterns that sustain human life, and the patterns of production and of reproduction that follow on from these. Instead, in Foucault's case, the determinative substrates seem to be things already in the order of knowledge: his word for such a substrate is *episteme*. But it is very difficult to understand what kind of things these *epistemi* might be. Do they consist of some form of text? Perhaps not necessarily a physical, written (or electronic) text, but its immaterial equivalent? It is worth remarking that there is a similar problem with 'the unconscious', and it would appear in this essay if Lacan were included in this brief survey of the postmodernists. 'The unconscious' is an inherently ambiguous term. It clearly refers to something of which a subject is not consciously aware at a particular time, but is that something itself of the order of mind? In which case we are talking about the mind's temporary unawareness of some of its own contents and dimensions. And if not that, does the phrase not then simply refer to the kind of material structures of which

[34] Michel Foucault, *The Order of Things: An Archaeology of the Human Sciences* (London: Tavistock, 1970), p. xxiii.
[35] Ibid. p. 318.

Marxists speak, but of which we can and do become successively conscious? Or is some more mutually immanent status of mind and matter hidden behind the phrase, of the kind that would quickly bring Hegel to mind? With Foucault in any case it is probable that he is thinking of some patterns of thought in some original and originating linguistic form, a very mysterious kind of pre-text. That probability arises from the prominence of language as the focus of analysis in Foucault's other works; and it facilitates the usual bracketing of Foucault with Derrida in so many accounts of postmodernism.

The second difference between Foucault and Marxist theory is even more significant. It consists in this: that the relationship between the periods of history is no longer in Foucault, as it remains in all Hegelian–Marxist theory, a dialectical relationship. These contrasting conceptions of the relationships between successive periods of history can be stated most simply in terms of the by now familiar contrast between definitions of negation. In Hegelian–Marxist theory negation consists in a determinate nothingness or nothinging; that is to say, it is an intrinsic part of the transcendence of each subsequent period in taking up into a higher form the content and patterns of the previous period thus and to that extent said to be negated. In terms of this kind of negation, even the subjectless history of Althusser looks nevertheless like the product of a continuously creative agent capable of directing things to an end – usually a hallmark of knowledgeable, intelligent agency – albeit not the (self-)conscious agent more usually called a subject. But in Foucault's scheme of things, negation is more like Sartre's nihilating. It is a simple and absolute nothinging of what went before. It is as if each succeeding period entirely and completely cancelled the previous incumbent *epi-steme*, the preceding tenant of time. 'As if', because no causal operation, not even a destructive one, can be allowed to link these periods and their *epistemi*.

It is not necessary for our present purposes either to include a critique of Foucault's reading of the history of philosophy since Descartes, or to suspect the return of the subject in Foucault's own work, despite all his advertising and prophesying the subject's double disappearance. It will be obvious from this essay up to this point that Foucault's reading of modern philosophy is not an agreed one. And on the second issue, one need do no more than ask: Who is writing – indeed who is capable of writing? – this magnificent meta-narrative entitled *The Order of Things*? Who knows, who could know, these utterly discontinuous periods, and how? Seán Burke answers that question: 'the subject who announces the disappearance of subjectivity does so only at the risk of becoming – inferentially at least – the sole subject, the Last and Absolute Subject, left to face his subjecthood in the face of an otherwise subjectless terrain, ever captive to a mirror of solipsism'.[36] It is necessary only to retain from Foucault the impressions that the substrate *epistemi* which govern all explicit formulations of thought and imagination are somewhat in the nature of texts; and that the *difference* that separates them is of the nature of a simple nothingness; but that it is *epistemi* that are thus the subject of *difference*, rather than signifiers. With such similarities and subordinate differences of application in mind, it is then possible to pass on to the final dismisser of the subject in postmodernism. Finally, then, to Derrida.

It is the case with Derrida, as it is with Foucault, that the argument by which he means to arrive at his characteristic position serves to obscure rather than to clarify it in the mind of the reader. As in the case of Foucault also, this feature of his work is particularly illustrated by his quite questionable reading of all previous Western philosophy, and most particularly in Derrida's case by his insistence that philosophy hitherto has privileged speech over writing and, furthermore, that that unwarranted privilege was the cause of the stultifying logocentricism we have inherited. Happily, however, Derrida's position becomes clear, and more rapidly so, to the reader who ignores all that and begins to read Derrida's work, as indeed he himself sees it, as a radical rewriting of Heidegger. Heidegger famously accused virtually the whole of Western philosophy of the oblivion of Being, and he expanded slightly on this when he wrote, 'the oblivion of Being is the oblivion of the distinction between Being and beings'.[37] For *distinction* there, read *difference* or, better still, in order to signal the presence of a technical term, the French *différance*, and the pathway to clarity on Derrida begins to widen perceptively.

The oblivion of Being that Heidegger writes about is, if this is not too crude or mystifying a manner of putting the matter, the oblivion of the Be*ing* of Being, the oblivion of that essential feature of Being which consists in that it is always coming to be. And it constantly comes to be precisely in particular beings, in those manifold entities that come into being and, of course, pass away and – here is the *différance* – are distinct from each other in the spatiotemporal continuum that simultaneously

[36] Burke, *The Death and Return of the Author*, p. 103.
[37] Quoted by Derrida in the course of his piece *'Différance'* in *Margins of Philosophy* (Brighton, Sussex: Harvester, 1982), p. 23.

comes into being. Or, to view the matter from the other side of the same coin, oblivion of Be*ing* consists in our belief that what we see is *Be*ing, that is to say, something that is always already fully and statically in being, in existence; a kind of Parmenidean totality from which all becoming has always been and will forever be foreign. A belief, then, that we do, or in any case can comprehend, Being in some simple and undifferentiated consciousness (of) it – like Sartre's prereflective cogito – or in some Logos-type idea system which contains only one Idea; a consciousness/Logos once more transcendent in the sense of (a) separate (region of being) from the changing empirical world, and which simply negates all of that world as unreal, illusory, because it is the totally adequate expression or re-presentation of all that truly is. From such a Parmenidean totality the differences between those empirical entities that come and go must quickly fade, and the corresponding consciousness/idea system must then take the form of an other-worldly, eternal Consciousness/*Logos* innocent of all transience. What is rejected, then, as logocentricism is in reality that simplistic representationalism already met with and rejected, a theory of truth as simple mutual presence or adequation of mind-idea and object; and this is done in the name of the reality of *différance*: oblivion of Being is oblivion of the difference between Being and beings and, *a fortiori*, oblivion of the differences between beings. Now, it is in his account of this ubiquitous *différance* that Derrida attempts to radicalise Heidegger.

This attempt is best understood through attention to the concept of *traces*. For Heidegger, Being in the course of its Be*ing* or, later in his writings, world in the course of its worlding, leaves traces. Now, traces, to put the matter in the epistemological terms used already, imply a self-presenting of something which still remains in a sense absent. In reading Heidegger's philosophy the traces that come primarily to mind are those that occur as Be*ing* comes through *homo faber* or, later, as Being comes to expression through the human poet. But to leave the matter there would be to restrict the idea of traces to the wilful productions of human subjects, or even to the actual compositions by human writers. And that would not suit Derrida; nor would it do full justice to Heidegger himself, in whose later work at least the constant worlding of the world in the form of our empirical life-world takes the clear initiative over wilful compositions of any kind. Derrida certainly wants to talk about traces, and indeed about a system of traces, or a *writing*, that precedes and conditions all specific human compositions. In fact, he wants to talk about a system of traces that is already 'beyond' that left by

Be*ing* in its emergence in the form of different beings, in the form, in shorthand, of *différance*.

There may be a difference still more unthought than the difference between Being and beings. We certainly can go further toward naming it in our language. Beyond Being and beings, this difference, ceaselessly differing from and deferring (itself), would trace (itself) (by itself) – this *différance* would be the first or last trace if one could still speak, here, of origin and end.[38]

There is, as it happens, a rather simple way of understanding that last, rather bombastic and mystifying claim. If for Be*ing*, by which all the different beings come into existence, one were to read 'the evolution of reality', which in our specific written (scientific) compositions we try to retrace, then it is easy to understand that there are what might well be called information systems always already 'written into' the reality which proceeds in this fashion to give rise to all the pullulating entities, species and individuals that come to occupy their different niches in space and time. The simplest example is that of genetic codes, but much more elaborate examples are also to hand. In the very next chapter of this essay the universe will be considered as a great computer (or the multiverse as a computer network?). Computers are run by or run programs. It does not much matter which way one says that. There is an information system written into evolving reality from the outset; there is a 'script' for the Be*ing* which gives rise to beings, and which it did not itself first 'write' and only then follow, nor is anyone outside the universe seen to have written it. This, or something very like this, is what Derrida must mean by his reference to a *différance* that is beyond Being and beings. He is certainly not talking about a verbal or lettered script that is in existence before the only reality we know to be comes to be. And nor, when he issued his most memorable statement, *'il n'y a pas de hors texte'* (nothing is outside the text), was he suggesting that there exists this utterly original script, all by itself, and that nothing else exists. The 'script' is not beyond Being in any temporal, much less spatial, sense; the 'script' by which beings and their *différance* simultaneously come into existence is always already there with Be*ing*, and so neither is there any being which is either before or outside of the 'script'. However, as Frederick Turner has noticed,

this insight would correspond to a rejection of any naïve deconstruction that reduced a text to a hot soup of traces, of 'differances', to use Derrida's word-play: what is of far more significance is that those differences collapse

---

[38] Derrida, *Margins of Philosophy*, p. 66.

together into meanings that make possible further meanings and further meanings still, in an evolutionary ecology of meaning which does not merely erase but subsumes its predecessors.[39]

And then we should have to wonder if Derrida had gone beyond Heidegger at all, as he promised he would. For on this evolutionary analogy he would have done no more than Heidegger set out to do, namely, to rid reality of some extra-mundane, disembedded self or subject. And this would threaten the human subject only if the script or evolving information factor was deemed to be itself some mechanistic, deterministic-type entity which altogether nullified human creativity, rather than give rise to the latter in the course of its evolutionary elan, thereafter to make most of its future progress in and through human creativity. Similarly of course, Heidegger's 'worlding' of the world is corrosive of the human subject only as long as his account of god/divinities and their role in the 'worlding' of the world remains as vague as he (presumably) deliberately left it. For the fact that a universe (and even a multiverse) forms a unity of interactive entities must give rise to the suspicion that any script or evolving information system itself reveals an entity or factor immanent in the universe which gives rise to one script, even if that is to be a script forever unfinished. And that entirely immanent entity or factor, were it possible to describe it more fully, could as easily qualify for the position of Heidegger's god/divinities as it could account for the empirically obvious and growing creativity of the human subject in the evolution process as we know it.

But Derrida does go beyond Heidegger in attempting to rid the world not merely of a godlike subject squatting disembedded outside it, but of a human subject also. And it appears on a close reading of his argument that he does this by making a more radical use of Saussure's semiology – a more radical use, for instance, than Barthes had made of it. For Barthes has used that particular semiology in order to usher out the front door in ostentatious fashion a subject too transcendent in the crude, 'separate' sense of the word; only later to sneak in by the back door a more acceptable left-wing, revolutionary subject of the kind that Barthes fancied himself to be. But Derrida makes a much more radical and subject-destructive use of that same semiology; and he does so precisely by fastening first on the signifier, and insisting that the consideration of the signifier must predominate or, as he puts it, that the signifier must be privileged, particularly over the signified, in the course

---

[39] Frederick Turner, *Rebirth of Value* (Albany: State University of New York Press, 1991), p. x.

of assessing the explanatory power and the results of Saussurean semiology.

The very use of Saussure, signalled in the terminology of signifier–signified–sign and in any case always freely acknowledged by Derrida, already detaches the 'script' from the reality in which it is inscribed. Now this manoeuvre in itself might be considered a temporary *epoche* in the name of the desired objectivity of science; and one which would not deter us later from seeing the 'script' inscribed once more in reality or, rather, one which would not deter us from being the benificiaries of a process by which that original 'script' enabled admittedly poor and very partial 'copies' to emerge in our proliferating accounts of the world. But this possibility of our seeing, however provisionally, imperfectly and partially, the script inscribed in the world; this possibility of the world making itself present at all and in however provisional, imperfect and partial a fashion, is predicated on the privileging of the signified over the signifier. This is because it is of the signifiers, the sound sequence emitted or the sequence of ink-marks on a page, that it can be said both that they are arbitrary and that they are differentiated from each other simply by the one not being the other; differentiated, that is to say, by simple negation. For as long, therefore, as we privilege the signifier, for as long as we allow to any set of signifiers the primary role in conditioning our understanding of discourse, we shall deprive ourselves of the possibility of encountering anything we could count as discourse at all. Derrida's dissemination will not then result in relativity; it will result quite literally in nonsense. A sequence of arbitrary sounds or ink marks, distinguished primarily by their occupation of different locations or moments with respect to each other, are thus far meaningless. Correspondingly, a world seen primarily from the point of view of *différance*, seen then as a collection or sequence – if even these categories are as yet possible – of entities differing from each other by nothing, literally, and hence entirely unrelated, is not yet a world. For as long as we privilege the signifier, then, we shall not get back again either to a subject – even to the unacceptable kind of subject that consists in no more than a container-mind of idea-signifieds – or to a world.

The privileging of the signified, on the other hand, while giving the signifier an essential role, allows for the possibility of getting back at least to a world. For the signified is an idea, an image, better still a judgement. The content of these is essentially relational; that is to say, they always refer to patterns of entities – remember Hegel's treatment of the 'this' that could not be 'said' – that differ from each other in the very process

that assimilates them to each other. The paradigm here once more is
Be*ing* that emerges in beings, or evolving reality: patterns ever coming
together to form other patterns, Being always already 'scripted' and
'scripting', and each different being at once negating the form of
another but only by bringing it to another stage of development. That is
why most, if not indeed all, of our signifiers are polysemic; they already
relate to a number of possible entities or processes; and they are
therefore designed, however arbitrary the choice of sound or mark may
be in each individual case, to designate difference-in-assimilation, or a
mutual negation that is always part of a positive transcendence. By
privileging the signified over the signifier, then, without in the least
reducing the essential role of the latter, we can at least get back to the
world, to the 'script' that is always already inscribed in Being and
conditioning all our specific and impoverished attempts to rewrite it.
Therefore, Derrida's radicalising of Heidegger really took the form of
bringing to bear a version or usage of Saussure's semiology, which may
not be the only version of Saussure that is possible on the latter's
premises.

The result of Derrida's radical move, whatever we may think of
Saussure's own system, was a stranding in an eternally self-deconstructing set of signifiers, full of sounds and scribbles and signifying nothing,
by and to no one. There is no point in asking Derrida: But who
produced this archi-text, this utterly original script? It is not sufficiently
like the patterned structures of Althusser-type Marxism, and not even
sufficiently like the *epistemi* of Foucault's system, so that an answer in
terms of a rational agent or subject of some kind could be suggested.
And there is little point even in showing, as can be done, that in
Derrida's own corpus, as in his study of the corpus of Rousseau, spectres
of author-subjects continue to appear. The result of Derrida's labours
still remains the realisation of Eco's nightmare, the final loss of both
mind and reality, a loss that is then widely attributed by commentators
like Eco to postmodernism in general.

ASSESSMENT AND PROSPECT

The upshot of this last section, then, which was centred upon the more
Marxist-influenced traditions of philosophy in this century, is distress-
ingly similar to the upshot of the previous section, in which the mainline
phenomenological tradition was subject to a lengthy analysis. Indeed,
as these traditions are seen to merge, the features that cause philosophi-

cal distress appear in their most extreme forms. It is necessary, there-fore, at this point to recall these features only in summary form; and perhaps to end this chapter of the essay with a brief attempt to envisage the kind of philosophy which would have to emerge if the distressing features of the combined traditions of philosophy so far analysed were to be avoided.

The basic premise of the most materialist versions of Marxism, and of philosophies influenced by these versions, is that of reality as a process without a subject. Yet the traditions of philosophy analysed in this last section are haunted by subjects constantly denied, yet continually re-turning like spectres of differing shapes and sizes, within and around the discourse that cannot admit them. If, for instance, the account of the process-without-a-subject makes it look very like a purposeful, teleologi-cal kind of process, or indeed like any kind of orderly, and therefore intelligible process, one can resist the suggestion that it is itself a subject only by insisting that, although it seems to be a knowledgeable agent, it is not a *(self-)conscious* agent. It does not have that kind of transcendence that makes a subject in the full and proper sense of a self. If one's interlocutor accepts that answer, if only for the sake of argument – for it is not at all obvious that a truly orderly and therefore intelligible process must not be such as to transcend itself towards ever further dimensions of reality, and thus comply with the basic qualifications for conscious-ness – she can still ask: But who then is writing the account of this process? The answer to this further question could of course be: Well, yes, there can be a self-conscious entity, a subject in your sense of the word, a subject that merely contemplates the reality process, a con-sciousness entirely (in)formed as to its contents by the (re)present(ations) of this reality process, but this subject would not be real in my sense of the term, for it would have no real effect in or on the reality project which in my philosophy is alone truly real. That same answer would probably suffice for those smaller, even less transcendent subjects that creep back into the writings of Barthes after he has used Saussure to evacuate the transcendent subject who transcends the world process in the crude sense of remaining separate and separable from it. These smaller, even less transcendent subjects who leave their traces on things could, on second thoughts, be described as also unreal in the operative sense. That is to say, it is the subjectless process that makes traces in and through them, and they contribute nothing effective to the process. In this way the little subjects that come back to haunt Barthes can be dismissed, in the same way as the much greater subject that haunts

Foucault can be dismissed, without any significant loss to the reality process.

But is this kind of answer acceptable? Is it even intelligible? How would I recognise the *human* traces in things that Barthes writes about, and express these in the language that then 'speaks things', unless I could recognise these traces as the result of the effects of human subjects on the reality process? And how would I write an account of the periods of this history like the account Foucault wrote, unless I in all my temporal and spatial conditioning, in my mortality, confined as I am to my little time and space, could yet understand myself to be an intrinsic part of a stream of consciousness that always goes beyond or transcends me and my individual consciousness in this world? The point is not simply that this is a *historical* reality process that I am dealing with, and I need to be able to commune with those who recorded past historical periods as contemporaries in order to compose accounts of the reality process; for history already requires the effective presence of subjects like me to make it history; and in this respect I simply return to the question as addressed to Barthes. The point is, rather, that that broader and larger aspect of the reality process in which it is a cosmic, evolutionary process rather than a purely historical process requires that I in my constricted circumstances am required to be part of a community of investigative subjects in order to make progress in understanding and to be able to write up even those partial and imperfect accounts of the reality process that continue to proliferate. The investigative community is constantly engaged in composing accounts of the reality process that try to comprehend its past and present, and to project future effect. And the more this particular tradition of philosophy attempts to depict me as a materially circumscribed part of this material reality process, the more and not the less I need to be able to hypothesise, and then to verify and understand, an intrinsic transcendence of my own consciousness towards the consciousness of others similarly inset in this material reality process. And what kind of transcendent structure of consciousness must then emerge? Some kind of communal consciousness that unites somehow all human individuals, and which is immanent in the reality process only to the extent that they are immanent in it? Or some kind of consciousness more general still that is immanent in the whole of the reality process? That last might not be verifiable in retrospect, as it were. But suppose our communal human efforts to become conscious of the whole fabric of reality process some day achieved complete success, and such success as then enabled us to reproduce the reality process indefinitely thereafter, would we not then be able to speak in prospect if not in retrospect of the entire reality process as itself consisting in the status of (self-)conscious subject? That is a prospect we shall meet, in full scientific seriousness, in the next chapter of this essay. It is anticipated at this point merely to show that the more the materialist philosophy tries to incarcerate individual subjects in a material reality process; the more it tries to write accounts of these as utterly immanent there, the more it requires to investigate and explain consciousness in all the dimensions of transcendence that have been already indicated.

The strategies for avoiding such recourse to conscious subjects linked intrinsically in a structure of consciousness that is at one and the same time utterly transcendent and utterly immanent in the reality process – the strategies, that is to say, for getting rid of the subject in this tradition of philosophy – are twofold as we have just seen them, and neither version is persuasive.

First, there is Derrida's final solution. The archi-script which not even Being precedes is constructed of dominant signifiers, eternally negating each other so as to postpone indefinitely any intelligible structure; an original and 'last' self-deconstructing entity – if, as he rather unnecessarily adds, one can speak of either originality or finality in this context. For in order to deconstruct, there has to be something already construed or constructed. What Derrida offers us, then, is something that cannot be either real or mindful (that is, understood). The subject is really dismissed then by Derrida and without remainder, replaced by a permanently self-deconstructing script, but at the simultaneous cost of the loss of the whole of the reality process.

The others whose philosophies, unlike Derrida's, continue to be haunted by the spectre of the subject achieve the goal of an account of reality as a process without a subject by the joint manoeuvre of loudly dismissing the subject while at the same time construing in terms of simple separateness that transcendence that is of the essence of subjecthood; so that the dismissal may not appear to deprive the reality process of anything necessarily immanent to it. In this manner, both the subject as bearer of ideas, and the subject that constantly transcends these ideas – both of which, incidentally, we know from our experience to be simultaneously dimensions of one and the same embodied subject – is separated from the embodied human being, and from each other. This can be done, of course, only on the basis of that kind of dualism we continue to call 'Cartesian'. So that we see once more how a deconstruction can only proceed on the strength of a previous construction. In this case these dismissers of subjects construct a 'Cartesian' dualism of mind/consciousness–body/matter, and submit their account of subject-less reality process which in the end consists in, and is only intelligible as, the denial of consciousness substance in one or both of the forms of this already mentioned. Correspondingly, these authors make use of the same questionable ideas of transcendence and negation which, we have already seen, advertise the continuing, formative influence of 'Cartesian' dualism.

Seeing the same failed features recur, then, in the philosophies that begin with the mind alone, the phenomenological ones, and in the philosophies that begin with a subjectless reality process, a certain kind of Marxist-influenced ones; and seeing the failures increase when these two traditions merge, is it possible to hazard an initial guess at a kind of philosophical approach which, taking all that was best in the analysis of these combined philosophical traditions, might promise a better out-come?

The simplest suggestion would appear to be that the most promising approach should now consist in ridding ourselves at the outset of the most characteristic and most compromising features of the ubiquitous and insidious 'Cartesian' dualism, namely, the strict separations (and the consequently indeterminate negations) that were introduced, in turn, between the structured, evolving bodily world of which we are so very bodily a part and the more empirical mind which transcends it; and then between this mind, replete with intentional ideas and images, and the yet more transcendent dimension of that mind at which it is continually driven to go beyond all of these intentional ideas and images. Put more positively, the suggestion would be to put back together again the elements that both the phenomenological and the Marxist-influenced traditions of philosophy conspired to set asunder, if only in the process of concentrating exclusively, or originally privileging, the one at the expense of postponing or even nihilating the others: the structured, dynamic bodily world (the bias of 'materialist' Marxism), the more empirical ego (the bias of Husserl and of part of Barthes), and the most transcendent subject (the bias of Sartre). The suggested approach would then begin with consciousness incarnate, subjectivity thoroughly embodied, thoroughly embedded in bodies and, through these, in the body of the material world. We can surely do this on the basis of our own immediate human experience, without the need (or licence?) at the outset to envisage either a subject separate from this world or, *pace* Hume, a world in which a subject or self is merely the result of 'relations of ideas', a purely notional entity. Such an approach really ought to appeal at one and the same time to the phenomenological tradition as it was first conceived in Hegel's *Phenomenology*, and to the Marxist-influenced tradition as that was conceived by Marx himself.

With this approach and this beginning we should soon enough have an account of worldly reality immanent in mind while transcending it, and as the other side of the same coin, a simultaneous account of subject immanent in worldly reality while transcending it. The least of our gains at this point would take the form of a far more sophisticated account of transcendence and, incidentally, a more intelligible idea of negation than that extremely simplistic, not to say crude, idea for which Sartre went to the quite unnecessary trouble to coin the term nihilation.

Transcendence, seen from the point of view of the subjective or personal pole of this incarnate consciousness – seen, in other words, from the conscious dimension of this entity – would connote that feature of its existence and action whereby, because of a certain reflectivity in its structure, it projects beyond the range of reality that is already immanent in and so constitutive of it. Beyond that range, one might well ask: And then towards what? The usual answer, based on everyday experience, would be: Towards a greater extent or depth of the reality than that which is at any moment within the subject's active awareness. And it is at this point that the more sophisticated notion of negation comes to light, the Hegelian notion of negation as 'a determinate nothingness, one which has content'; an idea of a negation which is a constitutive part of a positive process of transcendence. For as the subject goes beyond its present connotable quotient of worldly reality towards a more ample reality now coming-to-be(-known), there occurs a kind of negation of the (form of) reality which existed at each prior stage. For an example of this process it is necessary only to recall Hegel's opening treatment of immediate or sense intuition. In such intuition each this-here-now appears to come to consciousness with an immediacy and a fullness that exhibits the final and absolute state of being-known. *On reflection*, however, it appears as a this amongst thises, and so as a that; a here amongst heres, and so as a there; and so on. But *it* re-emerges from that process in a more extensive, deeper or higher form of being-known. Its first negation is thus part of the process of a positive transcendence.

A similar question could be asked, of course, from the point of view of worldly reality which at any moment appears to range beyond what is immanent in a subject's mind. Its further putative range as reality-beyond-mind reveals it to be transcendent also with respect to its immanence in mind. Hence the question: From its point of view, towards what does this transcending now take place? I can certainly pose that question. To do so I need no more than a version of Marx's play on the German word *Bewusstsein*, as *das bewusste Sein*, the Being Conscious. I have asked, and answered the question from the point of view of the Being *Conscious*; from the pole of consciousness, one might say. Correspondingly, could I not ask the same question from the point of view of *Being* Conscious; from the pole of reality, could one say? But even if I can ask that second question, it does not necessarily follow that *I* can answer it. I know the answer I would like to give, namely, that that (dimension, part of) reality that currently transcends my consciousness of reality is ever transcending this towards (my) consciousness of itself. I bracketed the second 'my' in that preceding sentence because, if the preferred answer turned out to be true, that might entail a considerable expansion, or some considerable change at any rate, in the manner in which I am currently constituted. For that answer could entail a continuance of limitless or infinite character of the correspondence I currently experience between *Conscious* Being's transcendence of Conscious *Being* towards greater Conscious *Being*, and Conscious *Being*'s transcendence of *Conscious* Being towards higher *Conscious* Being.

I cannot, in any case, simply give this answer. I, the essayist who shall otherwise be anonymous, cannot now simply give it. I can only express it as a kind of Hegelian hope. By that I do not mean a hope based on the fact – if it is a fact – that Hegel experienced the end result of the process by which Reality, full and entire, from its inchoate immanence in (his) consciousness, transcended itself towards (his) full and entire consciousness of It, and that his saying so and his description of that culminated process gives me hope. Philosophy does not prove anything to happen or to exist. It simply offers an analysis and an explanation which each one can only confirm, or fail to confirm, in each one's own active experience. It is a Hegelian kind of hope, then, in that it arises in my developing experience from an account of Conscious Being and transcendence which Hegel correctly analysed. Yet there is one thing I can say with confidence of this process by which *Being* Conscious progressively transcends itself towards my Being *Conscious* – for that correspondence holds currently in my experience – namely, that I am constantly negated, in the positive connotation of negation as a negation in which I, myself, re-emerge in altered form. That is to say, as worldly reality beyond (a current) consciousness of it transcends itself towards that consciousness, it transforms the consciousness in question by a process of negating the current form or status of the consciousness so that *it* may arise in a higher form or status – precisely corresponding to the process by which reality is negated in a process known as 'determinate nothingness', so that a greater depth or extent of reality emerges. The process of transcendence looked at from the point of view of Conscious *Being* can be represented as the continual dying, or rather the putting to death, of a self so that it may rise in higher form. Some philosophers such as Spinoza and Simone Weil, as different in approach and method from Hegel as they are from each other, envisage the final, the ideal, stage of that process as a kind of final death (though not an annihilation?) of the individual 'I', self or subject, and the consequent emergence of an Absolute Self which is then all-*in-all*. [40]

A far more sophisticated account of immanence, then, could correspondingly emerge from a philosophical approach that begins from consciousness incarnate, from worldly embodied subject. Immanence would now connote a mutual existential co-inherence of consciousness and worldly reality, of the kind that is in fact actually experienced by individual subjects. Hence one would say of the mutual transcendence of subject and worldly reality that subject transcends worldly reality from within that reality, and that worldly reality transcends subject from within subject. There is a mutual going-beyond from within what is gone beyond and, so far as experience goes, ending in what is gone beyond in some further form of the latter. But this 'within' must not be taken in its spatial connotation, as is usual with the ghost-in-the-machine metaphor, but rather in the connotation of a kind of co-inherence which appears to be *sui generis*. Subject and worldly reality which go beyond are each, at beginning and end of each process of going beyond, co-inherent in the other. It follows that transcendence and immanence, in their properly sophisticated senses, turn out to be correlative terms rather than contraries; each calling for the other, rather than replacing each other, as happens when transcendence is taken in the crude sense of separation. In corresponding ontic terminology, subject and worldly reality could be described as correlative poles of the one inclusive being, rather than entirely separate regions of being. And as all of this emerged from a philosophical investigation which began with incarnate consciousness, with subject embodied in world, a real possibility of under-

---

[40] A remarkable article by David Cockburn, 'Self, World and God in Spinoza and Weil', *Studies in World Christianity* 4 (1998), 173–86, shows how the very different philosophies of the Jew Spinoza and the Christian Simone Weil converge on this ideal from what appear to be two quite opposite philosophical approaches.

standing the relation of incarnate consciousness(es) to worldly reality
and, if only through worldly reality, to other incarnate consciousness(es),
might also emerge more easily. Perhaps even the possibility of envisaging some absolute *Conscious Being*, if only as something to be encountered
in the course of a 'journey' (as the on-going process of transcendence-in-
immanence is sometimes described)? The very fact that most, if not
indeed all, of those who were seen so far to conspire to rid philosophy of
the subject expressly designate that subject as godlike leaves open the
possibility, once the subject returns through an investigation that takes
all that was positive in their analysis and explanation after the distorting
elements already criticised have been removed, that amongst the re-
turning subjects there may emerge one that merits the epithet divine.

But all of that must remain, at this point, speculative. For it is never
enough, although it is initially useful, to try to envisage a better philosophical approach and outcome simply by seeing what might emerge if
the shortcomings of received philosophical traditions were left behind.
There still remains the whole task of doing philosophy, of carrying
forward all that was best and positive in the analysis and explanations of
the received traditions, and working these patiently through all the
processes and dimensions of the world-embodied subject from which
one must begin. The first step on this road must be to seek out
contemporary emergent systems which already begin to illustrate Umberto Eco's 'cognitive revolution'. And the best place to look for these is
in the halls of science. Physics was the seedbed of metaphysics at the
origins of Western philosophy. Science was the inspiration of the pion-
eers of modern philosophy. And it is therefore likely to give us the lead
we need into the post-postmodern era. For, as it was in the beginning,
the true scientist focusses on the things that are (*ta onta*), and tries to
discover their nature, oblivious to those who would suggest that reality
has disappeared from view; and never more than provisionally persuaded by those who add that, whatever about reality, something that
can seriously be called self or subject will never be found. As it happens,
the two scientific examples chosen for illustrative purposes in this essay –
one which begins from the psychological side, the other from the
physical side, if only to keep the symmetry with the phenomenological/
materialist division of the previous chapter – both find ample room for
self or subject in reality. The first, from the physical side, sees the
creative role of very human-like rational subjects increase exponentially
as the present universe approaches its eschaton. The second, from the
psychological side, finds true subjectivity at the beginning and, intrigu-

ingly, a kind or level of subjectivity, inter-subjectivity in fact, which carries us already well beyond the solitary rational mind so redolent of 'Cartesian'dualism, so beloved of the Age of Reason, and so vulnerable to the sustained efforts we have seen in this chapter to get rid of it entirely.

CHAPTER 3

Beginnings: old and new

However momentarily deluded one might be while in the powerful grip
of nostalgia, it is never really possible to reinstate past forms effectively
in present circumstances, and that is as true of philosophy as it is of any
other form of life. Yet, as the search commences for new beginnings in
contemporary thought that take with the fullest initial seriousness the
material world and human flesh – if not indeed also the palpable devils –
it is surely worth casting a quick look backwards to the origins of
Western philosophy some two and a half millennia ago; to the so-called
'physicists' of Asia Minor with whom that philosophy is deemed to have
begun. This is not simply because the appeal to antiquity which wielded
such authority in the ancient world still today seems to play its role –
notice the number of atheistic or agnostic humanists who appeal to
Aristotle, or Confucius – but because growth in philosophical wisdom,
like growth in other forms of knowledge, does reveal a certain cumulative aspect, despite all the quantum leaps, relatively successful or relatively failed, that regularly break the lines of smooth traditional developments. At the very least, then, the quick look back to first beginnings
could help detect lines of development, so that we and our contemporaries might not look like the first people in history to have caught a
glimpse of the right approach to the most extensive truth, and in
addition so that some prevailing interpretations-in-hindsight of those
ancient authorities might be properly challenged.

THE RETURN TO SCIENCE

It is sometimes said that Western philosophy was born in the course of a
move from *mythos* to *logos*. It is certainly true that the mythic mind,
whose guiding spirit takes the form of that powerful investigative and
envisaging faculty known as the imagination, tends to overrun the
imaginative into the imaginary. At that point it becomes self-serving,

both by envisaging entities that are thought to fulfil without more ado our deepest desires, and by having waking nightmares about threatening entities that increase exponentially and in a most debilitating, if not self-destructive, fashion our native *Angst*. So much for the attempt to describe the origin of philosophy from the perspective of that from which it tried to move away; though it never moved entirely away from imagination's inevitable service and irreplaceable role. But to attempt to complete the description of newborn philosophy by a brief, complementary account of the *logos* towards which the move was directed would be a futile task. The fact of the matter is that the understanding of *logos* itself changed and developed throughout the succeeding centuries, in a manner which would take at least a separate volume to describe. In any case, it suits our present context better to concentrate instead on the first concrete formula for philosophy which the earliest pre-Socratics, as they are called, offered in their move away from myth, because of the latter's alleged epistemological and moral drawbacks. The first rule of the (new) discipline, they believed, should be a severe concentration on *ta onta*, on *the things that are*, before our eyes, above our heads and under our feet; no more imaginary entities, powers or persons; only what we actually encounter. Even if we have to do something or go on some kind of journey in order to experience the encounter; for philosophy from its origins was thought to be a 'way' as much as a *theoria*.

It is not this rule alone which recommends the brief recall at this point of these earliest philosophers, nor is it this that explains why some now call them 'physicists' in the misleading manner in which this epithet is often used. They were not interested simply in an inventory of the things that are; quite to the contrary, their dominant interest was in what they would term the *physis ton onton*, the nature of things, and so the key to their distinctive approach resides in an understanding of the term *physis* (from which the term physics, amongst many others, derives). The term *physis*, of course, just like the term *logos*, has its own long and complex history, but it also reveals a kind of core meaning which it carries with it through the long history of Greek-inspired Western philosophy. Aristotle probably expressed this core meaning most succinctly when in the *Physics* (193b, 3–4) he defined *physis* as 'the shape or form of things which have in themselves the source of their motion'. Once one remembers that form (*morphe*) for Aristotle really refers to a mode of being, that is to say, a modality of the continuous process in which Being (*ousia*), as Heidegger would describe it, is the event of Be*ing*, then *physis* carries the core meaning of, or connotes, Being or reality as a process moving by immanent dynamism from source to goal.[1]

The quest for the *physis ton onton*, therefore, comprises not merely the investigation of these dynamic and evolving forms or modes of being through which the rich fabric of reality can be progressively understood, but also, and without any gap between these aspects of the matter, the investigation of the most original and comprehensive source that may be detected, as well as the furthest goal or destiny that may come, however dimly, within the range of human vision. If this was physics, then – and the similarity of its range of investigation with that embraced by some contemporary physicists will soon be obvious – it was also theology, and it was explicitly recognised to be such by all of its practitioners from Thales onward.[2]

The reason why this physics is also theology, clearly, is because the word *theos*, or God, is taken to connote the most comprehensive and original source, immanent in the world, of 'the things that are', and as such is most influential in, if not determinative of, the ultimate goal of our empirical universe. In other words, philosophy from its birth can also be called, with equal accuracy, physics or theology. And the reason why so many scholars in ancient philosophy or ancient classics call the early philosophers physicists, with the intention of denying that they were theologians, and sometimes even with the intention of denying that they were yet even philosophers, is that these scholars – the philosophers first, and the classicists who then uncritically suffer their influence – are victims of distinctions that have been driven between science, philosophy and theology either by accident or design in the course of history, and some of them victims simultaneously of the rather crude ideas of transcendence as separation and the opposite of imma-nence, and of the accompanying dualism which has undermined vir-tually all of modern philosophy. Unwilling to use a more sophisticated connotation of the word transcendence, in which it is the correlate rather than the contrary of immanence, and equally unwilling to use physics in the effort to understand the ultimate fabric of reality in other than the most reductionist sense, these scholars engage in the entirely anachronistic enterprise of describing at least the pre-Socratics as physi-cists as a means of insisting that they were not (either philosophers or) theologians.

[1] See Joseph O'Leary, 'Heidegger and Indian Philosophy', *Poznan Studies in the Philosophy of the Sciences and the Humanities* 59 (1997), 174.
[2] See Werner Jaeger, *The Theology of the Early Greek Philosophers* (Oxford University Press, 1947).

It is true, of course, that by the time Socrates came on the scene Western philosophy had developed agnostic and perhaps even atheistic positions – it is difficult to be sure of the latter, if only because the term atheist was then most commonly used for what we would nowadays call idolatry; an atheist is someone who worships a different god from mine. The agnosticism of a Protagoras, who was quoted as saying that in the end he did not know whether the gods existed or not, is perhaps not too serious, if only in view of the fact that the tradition had long advertised the difficulty for the tiny human mind of coming to know the most comprehensive and original source of all. More serious were the Sophists, with their very anthropocentric approach to the investigation into the nature of things. Their era did cast up explanations of religious beliefs which, like a distant echo of some modern psychological and sociological systems, could be deemed to throw considerable doubt on the truth of these beliefs in the gods: the linking of belief in the gods with dreams, by Democritus for instance, or with the social benefits of having an invisible lawgiver-cum-policeman to back up the efforts of his very human and limited counterparts, as in Critias' *Sisyphus*. God as the projection of psychic propensities or human needs?

However, the most common ground for the charge of atheism as it was levelled, not just at the pre-Socratics but at Socrates himself, was the dominant tendency of this philosophy to see the truly transcendent, continuously creating or 'forming' divinity to be fully immanent in its creation. And the charge, as we can see from the case of Socrates, was levelled by devotees of political theology, the *theologia politikon*. The term *theologia* had by this time been coined for this dimension of philosophy and for the triple kind of theology recognised: *mythikon* for the theology of Hesiod's *Theogony*, for instance; *physikon*, 'natural theology', for the philosophical theology described above; and *politikon* for the official theology – whether civic or ecclesiastical or both – which every established, institutional religion must have. And the guardians of the *theologia politikon* are too often prepared to authorise only an external, separate, interventionist divinity, one which could, and would, intervene when called upon in order to guarantee their good life and prosperity, both here and hereafter, and their defence and vindication against their enemies. The authorised guardians of institutional religion, and its authentic theological interpreters, as they took themselves to be, were not reluctant to press a charge of atheism (idolatry) against the *physiologoi*, as they called our philosophical theologians, and, as the case of Socrates proves, to apply the penalty.

And it is absolutely fascinating to find contemporary scholars concur in sustaining the charge of atheism (albeit now in the modern sense of the word) against these same ancient *physiologoi*. As examples of such contemporary scholars, Mark McPherran, in his book on the religion of Socrates, introduces Martha Nussbaum, who insists on interpreting Socrates' references to his *daimonion* and so on as no more than a *façon de parler*, a surreptitious reference, phrased in a manner that would please popular opinion, to the 'inner promptings of his utterly secular, completely human power of ratiocination'. He also introduces Gregory Vlastos, who reads the *physiologoi* pretty well from Thales onward as proponents of 'the concept of a nature that encompasses all there is, even divinity' and thus as people who created 'a new conception of the universe as a cosmos, a realm of all-encompassing, *necessary* order, whose regularities cannot be breached by interventionist entities outside it because outside it there is nothing'; a concept of nature elsewhere described as 'mechanistic' and regarded as a 'precondition of the progress of science'.[3] Indeed one would not have to look very far to find another contemporary scholar, but now one who shares a belief in an outside and separate (transcendent in that sense) interventionist God, and who repeats the ancient view that Anaxagoras was most typical of the *physiologoi*, describing the resulting cosmos as a 'machine universe', a world of 'mindless, mechanical occurrences (of the type Anaxagoras described)'.[4] Despite all the evidence that Anaxagoras' divine creative Mind clearly had a cosmic *ergon*, a task to which a profoundly moral philosopher like Socrates could also call us in co-creative responsibility, albeit in Socrates' view we could never fully comprehend that task in our tiny and error-prone human minds.

What lesson can be drawn from this odd collusion between ancient judges of Socrates and contemporary scholars? First, that we should suspect the prejudicial presence of an insidious dualism, of a correspondingly unsophisticated understanding of transcendence and immanence, and of an attendant presumption that investigations that begin and are destined, at least while we live, to remain with us within this evolving and historical reality we call our world, must run counter to any prospect of a theological dimension to our physics and its derivative philosophies. Second, that we should rid ourselves of the unscholarly

[3] Mark L. McPherran, *The Religion of Socrates* (University Park: Pennsylvania State University Press, 1996), esp. pp. 6, 102.
[4] Robert J. O'Connell, *Plato and the Human Paradox* (New York: Fordham University Press, 1997), p. 103.

anachronisms that read back into innocent sources in the classical era both atheistic and agnostic positions that are based on such dualisms (remember the number of godlike subjects rejected on this basis in the course of modern philosophy) and some that are based also on theological dismissals of the sufficiency of 'natural' theologies, dismissals that are predicated on official pronouncements from institutional religion. And, finally, that we should reinstate this other tradition of philosophy (a philosophy that could range from physics to theology), if only as an inspiration to investigate the more recent cognitive revolutions that begin in and with this world, with minds unprejudiced as to how deep or how high these might lead us once again.

The central failure of these contemporary scholars of antiquity consists in their blindness to the sheer range and potentiality of the core meaning of the term *physis*. Such was its range and power, and its longevity, that the great medieval Irish philosopher John Scotus Eriugena could entitle his systematic account of everything from matter to God *Periphysion*. 'Nature' during all that time and in the sheer extent of its core connotation could encompass all that we know as mind. And despite the hostility of the political theologians of institutional religion, whose key concept of morality was theocratic, this 'nature' could encompass morality, the reality of truly moral activity or, as we might now say, the objectivity of moral values. It could even relate such moral value and obligation to God, as Socrates shows, without identifying morality with the raw will of God, or with God's enforced justice or implied favouritism. It could then, of course, encompass God, though not as another thing amongst things, but *epekeina tes ousias* (to take a phrase of Plato's which his successors applied to God), transcending the category of substance (from within). Does the contemporary scene offer an example of a naturalist philosophy that encompasses some or all of this? Certainly there are contemporary *physiologoi*, and there is a range of self-styled naturalist philosophies from which to choose. There is even a movement, not to say a school, of self-styled naturalist theology, including an allegedly Christian, and even an Evangelical Protestant naturalist theology. The most ancient, distinctive, scientific approach of Western philosophy is once again alive and well, and today we are certainly not strapped for choice.

The distinguishing feature of naturalist systems is the wish to see every thing and agent that may be encountered, and in particular human beings, to be wholly involved, if not indeed entirely enmeshed, within the natural world the structure of which the various natural sciences seek to describe. Amongst the most popular of these systems is the work of Richard Dawkins, particularly since the publication of *The Selfish Gene* in 1976. This new *Gene*sis consists in a simple combination of two key concepts: the information-carrying gene and its mutations, and the ingenious engineer of survival-optimising devices, Darwin's natural selection. Turning the pages of the new Book of Genesis, we read of discoveries of genes 'designed for' everything from intelligence to inferiority complexes, from altruism to alcoholism. The dominant human science is now sociobiology. The genes now take the place of Aristotle's unmoved movers, rigorously rational and purposeful, with the sole aim of survival. Individual human beings begin to look like little more than the genes' way of reproducing themselves. This particular philosophy, despite Dawkins's almost religious (anti-religious? – it is much the same thing) fervour in promoting and popularising it, is increasingly accused by fellow scientists of a vast oversimplification of the evolving world. In addition, it is interesting to note, some of its critics see in Dawkins's genes the dark shadow of a post-Enlightenment male-rational, competitive-individualist, *Logos*-type deity, with the unenviable added attribute of Calvinist predestinationism. The spectre of a theology once again haunting its most avid enemy.[5]

If the question is pressed – but can any of these new naturalist philosophies accommodate what we experience as mind? – the answer is likely to be found in the perhaps even newer science known as evolutionary psychology; and from its most fervent prophet and preacher, Steven Pinker, the answer is a resounding no![6] Pinker makes use of the same simple set of concepts, the gene and natural selection, but his specific focus is on the brain as an information-processing machine – the mind conceived as anything additional to what the brain does in the most physicochemical of terms is an obsolete fiction (like the tooth-fairy, Pinker adds helpfully) – and the engineering prowess of natural selection maximising the reproductive fitness of its various 'modules'. Much the same criticism as that applied to Dawkins, then, applies to Pinker also.

And morality? Can any of the new naturalist philosophies encompass it? The freedom of the will, in some sense of these terms, is often thought to be crucial to the reality of true moral action. And Robert Kane has recently sought to model human behavioural autonomy on a combination of, on the one hand, the indeterminacy that is characteristic of the quantum level of physics and its effects upon chaotic processes, that is to

[5] See for example Steven Rose, *Lifelines: Biology, Freedom, Determinism* (London: Penguin, 1997).
[6] Steven Pinker, *How the Mind Works* (London: Penguin, 1997).

say, processes that are influenced by minute changes in initial conditions, and, on the other hand, comprehensive networks of neural connections, forming synchronised patterns of wave activity, that represent
the usual motivational patterns of human agents, which he calls 'self-
networks'.[7] It is a sophisticated and in many ways a quite persuasive
piece of analysis and explanation. But once again, though to a lesser
degree than that which applies to the others above, critics wonder at the
need to be so reductionist in the service of a simplicity that must seem
oversimplified when compared to our actual experience of ourselves in
our rich and varied world.

This kind of criticism usually sees its more positive suggestions cluster
round the concept of 'emergence'. While we have every reason to
believe that what happens at the macrocosmic level of mountains and
human beings is sustained by what happens at the microcosmic level
investigated by modern physics, and at the slightly less microcosmic
level of chemistry, we have also good reason to think that at all critical
junctures of natural evolution there 'emerge' holistic features that then
exert a non-derivative form of causality or influence upon the cosmic
level from which they emerged. Once this pattern of emergence is taken
into account, it is claimed, there can result a thoroughly naturalist
philosophy that can encompass quite easily mind as we know it and, as
David Deutsch puts it, the objectivity of moral, and even of aesthetic,
values as real attributes of processes in this remorselessly material
world.[8]

The idea of emergence, a central though not always fully explained
idea in the naturalist philosophies now under consideration, can be
clarified somewhat by attention to the opposing idea, dear to real
reductionists, the idea of reverse engineering. Whereas engineers
commonly devise structures in order to bring about certain practical
results, reductionists, whether they be physicists, sociobiologists or evolutionary psychologists, on the contrary, deduce the 'pre-existence' of
structures in order to explain processes in practice now observed – a
kind of secularised version of Paley's Argument from Design. It is worth
quoting Barbara Herrenstein Smith's comment on reverse engineering,
from her review of Pinker:

for the programme of reverse engineering to make sense, every mental organ
thereby deduced would have to be the end-product of a series of genetic

---

[7] Robert Kane, *The Significance of Free Will* (Oxford University Press, 1997).
[8] David Deutsch, *The Fabric of Reality* (London: Penguin, 1997), pp. 362–3.

variants, each of which had conferred a reproductive advantage on members of the species possessing it. It is, however, difficult at best to reconstruct, and in the case of such highly specific or complex traits as the ability to form the past tense of verbs (one of the myriad innate mental modules posited by evolutionary psychologists) impossible even to hypothesize, evolutionary sequences of that kind that are simultaneously genetically, neuro-physiologically and ecologically plausible. Thus, as a number of evolutionary biologists point out, many of the explanatory accounts of evolutionary psychology – like those of its most immediate ancestor, sociobiology – require the assumption of evolutionary scenarios that range from the speculative to the unimaginable.[9]

And, finally, religion, divinity, theology? Can this be accommodated within any contemporary naturalist philosophy? There are those who say so. Frank Tipler, as a scientist, gives an account of the universe, and particularly of its end or omega point, which he argues coincides in substance with the content of traditional Christian doctrines.[10] Charley Hardwick, coming at the matter from the opposite direction, as a believing Christian of the Evangelical Protestant persuasion, believes he can give an entirely rational and persuasive account even of original sin, Calvinist-style, in the terms provided by some of these naturalist philosophies.[11] However, it would be best to take as dialogue partner at this point of the essay, David Deutsch and his thoroughly naturalist account of the fabric of reality, for although it is an account that boasts as much of eschaton as of origin, Deutsch is highly critical of Tipler's Christian-compatible conclusions, and so the choice of his work does not prejudice in advance the critical question of a continuing place for a theological dimension of Western philosophy. At the same time, Deutsch deliberately and significantly advances upon the more reductionist of naturalist philosophies; hence the rejection of a theological dimension is no longer, as it was in so many of the modern philosophies so far surveyed, implicated in any case in flawed features of these philosophies.

DAVID DEUTSCH'S THEORY OF EVERYTHING – PHYSICS OR METAPHYSICS?

David Deutsch's *The Fabric of Reality* is metaphysics. This is true not merely in the elementary sense that he sets his face against the reductionists who have recently proliferated within the practice of physics; he

[9] *Times Literary Supplement*, 20 February 1998.
[10] Frank Tipler, *The Physics of Immortality* (New York: Doubleday, 1995).
[11] Charley D. Hardwick, *Events of Grace: Naturalism, Existentialism and Theology* (Cambridge University Press, 1996).

does set his face against these, naming Stephen Hawking in particular, and he clearly distinguishes his 'theory of everything' from theirs, in that their much-sought-after theory of everything remains within the boundaries of physics, while his theory of everything requires the mutual engagement of theory of computation, quantum theory, evolutionary theory and theory of knowledge, on the grounds that computation, quantum events, evolution and knowledge are the combined processes by which reality is and comes to be. But Deutsch's work is metaphysics also in the more expansive sense of the term: its explanation and understanding of the fabric of reality ranges from origin to omega point, from alpha to eschaton; it encompasses the presence and purposes of intelligent and free agents, their cosmic influence and significance, and the intertwining of their destinies with that of the universe(s). These intelligent agents are human in our present experience, and though they must be vastly different at omega point from our present form and status, they may well prove to be our evolutionary successors. Deutsch is a humanist, then, although his humanism is not as restricted and, literally, pathetic as is, say, Martha Nussbaum's in her sustained efforts to make us weep, but bravely and still lovingly of course, at the inevitable continuance for all time of our present bodiliness, mortality and attendant ills. And, as already remarked, Deutsch's humanism therefore includes the moral and even the aesthetic dimensions as real and objective dimensions of reality. Deutsch's study of reality as such, so comprehensively conceived, whatever its ensuing successes or failures, is metaphysics on any traditional and defensible connotation of the term. And the point is worth repeating, particularly in the presence of philosophers and others who still wish to rid us of what they call metaphysical baggage.

At the same time, it is a resolutely non-dualist form of metaphysics. This is true once again in the merely elementary sense that Deutsch will have no truck with the crude concept of transcendence-as-separation which serves those visions of godlike beings squatting beyond the material universe(s); he is critical of Tipler's image of an eschatological divinity, not on the ground that it looks more like a society than an individual – for so, as a matter of fact, do some recent Christian theologies of the Trinity – but on the ground that it is described in terms of uncontextualised omniscience and omnipotence, as if one could ever see it or know it out of relationship with the material universe of which we are so essentially a part. And although there are, in Deutsch's view, innumerable other universes parallel to the one in which he writes and we read his book, all of these are physical universes that may interact physically with ours, and none takes the form of that purely spiritual other world that has existed and may still exist according to some Platonist and some Christian theologians. Consequently, Deutsch's non-dualism is true also in the stronger sense that, although he maintains clear distinctions between mind and physical brain, for instance, or between consciousness and preceding processes in biological evolution, he always considers the former to be emergent features of the latter, and destined moreover to be forever inscribed in whatever bodily universes that continue to exist. Everything that is ever known by us, therefore, even at omega point, at which our knowledge may indeed achieve limitless potential, will be known to be, and continue to be known as, immanent in the material universe(s); and though we or our distant successors, if that is what some of the intelligences turn out to be, may no longer have bodies in any way like ours, they will still be entities according to some analogy with programs running, or running on, some physical systems. Deutsch, then, is a true successor to the ancient *physiologoi*, and just as determined as they were to investigate only 'the things that are', and to parade as discoveries only what could be seen *in* the things that are, at whatever depth of origin or height of prospect these visions of reality might be achieved then, or now, or in the future. One can imagine that a reading of these ancient *physiologoi* by someone like Deutsch would be a welcome relief from the readings we currently get from philosophical and literary scholars of these ancient Western sources, skewered as these are by a kind of empiricist dogma that is crude in comparison with Deutsch's empiricism, and far from innocent of an accompanying *ersatz* dualism.[12]

A central theme of *The Fabric of Reality*, then, is this: 'The fabric of reality does not consist only . . . of time, space and sub-atomic particles, but also, for example, of life, thought and computation.' Deutsch accepts that quantum theory is the most successful explanation of the time, space and subatomic dimension of the fabric of reality, and appears to believe that, although the theory is as yet in its infancy and

---

[12] If any doubt remains about Deutsch's regarding himself as a philosopher, in contradistinction to being a scientist – although his principal professional work has been in quantum physics and in the pioneering of the new quantum computers – the pages of *The Fabric of Reality* (pp. 84–5) in which he places the device of ranging mathematics, physics and philosophy according to decreasing degrees of possible certainty, alongside the physicist reductionism he has already rejected (on pp. 24ff) should remove that doubt. He insists in fact that purely mathematical arguments derive their reliability from the physical and philosophical arguments that underpin them.

has yet to be successfully applied to some basic features of physical reality – a quantum theory of gravitation? – it will never again be displaced, as Newtonian physics has been displaced. Quantum theory as a fundamental theory in physics takes its name from quantisation, the property of having a discrete (rather than continuous) set of possible values. 'There are no measurable continuous quantities in physics' (p. 36), just discrete particles interacting or interfering. Deutsch rejects the 'Copenhagen' view of quantum theory, namely, that the equations of quantum physics apply only to unobserved aspects of physical reality; that different processes take over as human observation interacts with the subatomic realm – he rightly sees this as evasion rather than acceptance of quantum theory. Nor does he see any reason to accept Bohm's elaboration on the basics of quantum theory, when the latter supposes that particles are associated with waves and in this way explains some observed phenomena, such as the shadow patterns that photons make when fired through holes in barriers.

The present essayist would not feel safe saying anything more concerning quantum physics nor, *a fortiori*, in offering any overall assessment of Deutsch's theory of everything. There is, for example, Deutsch's conviction that we deal not with a single universe, but with a multiverse. Experiments such as those that yield the shadow patterns mentioned above show a 'tangible' or 'visible' photon being interfered with by something, presumably another quantum particle, but now a kind of invisible, intangible *Doppelgänger*. Deutsch is amongst those physicists who conclude from these and many other experimental results that there exists what they call a multiverse; that is to say, a system containing a vast number of parallel universes that can interact, albeit weakly and occasionally, with each other. So parallel indeed are these universes as described that David Deutsch talks about numbers of other Davids writing *The Fabric of Reality* in some of them, about some of these doing rather better with this part of the book than he is doing, and some perhaps taking a coffee break from the job. Now, one can only hope that a dialogue with Deutsch on the matter that is of concern to this essay can be conducted without the need to attempt any final assessment of a multiverse metaphysics.

It is true that Deutsch uses the multiverse hypothesis in order to explain the phenomenon of moral freedom, which must turn out to be of central importance in this essay. He offers the following breakdown of a moral decision and offers the ensuing explanation of each step in that process in terms of multiverse theory. 'After careful thought I chose to do X' = 'After careful thought some copies of me, including the one speaking, chose to do X'; 'I could have chosen otherwise' = 'Other copies of me chose otherwise'; 'It was the right decision' = 'Representations of the moral or aesthetic values that are reflected in my choice of option X are repeated much more widely in the multiverse than representations of rival values'; 'I am good at making such decisions' = 'The copies of me who chose X, and who chose rightly in other such situations, greatly outnumber those who did not' (p. 339). Now, it may well be, as Deutsch claims, that free will is notoriously difficult to explain in classical physics, with its rather deterministic laws of motion operating in a 'spacetime block', but it does not seem to be any easier with this use of the multiverse theory. To put the point perhaps too harshly, the criterion of good moral decision-making used here seems to consist in a sophisticated form of the 'survival of the fittest' concept: there are greater numbers of those who chose particular values (options) than of those who did not. But that in itself does not show how the choice was a moral and hence a free one; for the use of that kind of criterion is quite compatible with a theory that requires no more than the ideas of genes mutating and something called 'nature' selecting certain of these mutations for survival. Correspondingly, there is no reason to suppose that such an explanation of free will would not be as successful in one universe only, the tangible one, or that a multiverse would make it any more persuasive, apart of course from adding greater numbers to the equations. And in any case, as we shall shortly see, David Deutsch's account of knowledge and of the role it plays in reality provides ample opportunity for an adequate understanding of freedom, and of moral and aesthetic value.

And one must of course generalise somewhat from this point about the multiverse hypothesis. One must admit that not only is the present essayist incapable of a critical account of Deutsch's theory as a whole, but that the more reflective members of the scientific community are always amongst the first to warn of the foolishness of thinking that any general theory of the universe(s) is likely to be the final one. Deutsch's theory is chosen as dialogue partner, then, because, although he may possibly be wrong about the multiverse, and although it may be more than probable that his whole theory will be superseded in the future – despite what he says about quantum physics (what if, as some physicists now suspect, *all* particle physics is about to come to the end of its useful life?) – Deutsch does represent what looks like the best overall theory available to our current stage of studying the things that are. More particularly he does incorporate fully the advances upon the most reductionist models for theories of everything which until recently tended to dominate the minds of reflective (i.e. philosophical) scientists; and this at least seems like a reversal that will not in turn be reversed. For the rest, it is now as it was in the beginning with the *physiologoi* (and also with the author(s) of the Book of Genesis), and as it will be to the end: metaphysical and theological levels of investigation begin, and end, in the categories in which the physics, the quest for the *physis ton onton*, is currently conducted.

THE FOUR ELEMENTS OF CONTEMPORARY (META)PHYSICS
FIRST AMONGST THEM, KNOWLEDGE

Of the four elements that go into the make-up of the fabric of reality, it is indeed best to take, as Deutsch does, knowledge next, immediately after the quantum phenomena, but to include in this account much that he has to say about knowledge in later chapters of the book. This is because knowledge turns out to be a very pivotal aspect of the analysis of the two remaining elements that go into the make-up of the fabric of reality, evolution and computation.

That is the first point, then, to be noted about his analysis of knowledge, namely, that knowledge is considered to be part of the very fabric of reality, that is to say, that it is an intrinsic element in the being and coming-to-be of reality itself, and not merely a reflection of reality that might be thought to occupy some notional rather than some existential realm. For this reason he rejects at the outset the claims of the theory of induction, the theory of knowledge thought to be most apposite for the understanding of the scientific process itself, and urged upon us as a consequence by empiricist philosophies of the early Linguistic Analytic kind in the mistaken belief that it is supported by the very existence and success of science. It is impossible – and so it has never been done in science – to derive a hypothesis from a sequence of observations without a logically prior theory or tentative explanation which already binds observations into sequences. A hypothesis is really a tentative explanation, occasioned not by a simple series of observations, but by a problem which emerges from previous explanations and understandings of the world, and which will be tested not merely by its way of meeting the problem, but also by its ability to enable an understanding of a greater range of reality. Deutsch is equally dismissive of what he calls the instrumentalist theory of knowledge which is often advanced by scien-

tists. This is the view that even the most successful of scientific theories
do not necessarily tell us anything about the nature of objective reality,
but they nevertheless *work*, particularly in the sense that they enable us
to make predictions concerning effects or phenomena, and thereby
enable us to manage, or manage with, a reality that remains mysterious
and virtually unknown. Thus he arrives at the first, and paradigmatic,
form of knowledge, to which any adequate theory of knowledge must do
full justice. It is knowledge in the form of explanation or, better,
understanding (for understanding is proportionate to the success of
explanations); and he quite clearly states that understanding is a unique
function of the human mind – although knowledge in general, as we
shall see, is predicated also of biological processes and of computers.

It is hard, he writes, to give a precise definition of explanation and
understanding, as distinct from mere description and prediction:
'Roughly speaking, they are about *why* rather than *what*; about the inner
working of things; about how things really are, not just how they appear
to be; about what must be so, rather than what happens to be so; about
laws of nature rather than rules of thumb' (p. 11). One senses here, as
indeed throughout the book, that he is after a concept of understanding
that culminates in as deep and comprehensive and true a knowledge of
the whole of reality as it is possible for an intelligent being to achieve – a
philosophy in the oldest sense of the term. But even more than this is
entailed in his concept of understanding.

Part of this additional connotation has been touched on already in the
course of pointing to his continued insistence that the only intelligences
we shall ever know will be those immanent in physical systems, or, as he
puts it more tersely, the knowers and their knowledge are no less
physical than that which is known. He does at times write of mind and
matter as if he were still harbouring the remnants of a cruder dualism;
he writes about body being external to mind (p. 111), or about hunger,
and so on, being internal to body but external to mind (p. 106); and even
when he declares himself roundly to be a realist, in contrast to induc-
tionists and instrumentalists, he occasionally gives the impression that
he is a very 'indirect' realist indeed. For example, 'our external experience is never direct; nor do we even experience the signals in our nerves
directly – we would not know what to make of the streams of electrical
crackles that they carry. What we experience directly is a virtual-reality
rendering, conveniently generated for us by our unconscious minds
from sensory data plus complex inborn and acquired theories (i.e.
programs) about how to interpret them' (pp. 120–1). There he sounds

very like Kant; and even his use of the idea of virtual reality in this context would appear to serve to separate further the virtual from the reality.

On the whole, however, and in the main thrust of his analysis, he is consistently better than this. He dismisses solipsism (or idealism, it might be better to say) by simply pointing out that in addition to its total content which coincides with that of the mind of the realist, the solipsistic mind has to come up with additional explanations as to why it appears to advance in knowledge in ways that are either surprising or frustrating, or both. He disagrees with Popper's view that 'no theory of knowledge should attempt to explain why we are successful in our attempts to explain things' (p. 341). That view would hold only if on some crude dualist basis we began our theory of knowledge from within knowledge itself in isolation from (the rest of) reality. But of course, Deutsch never tires of repeating, that knowledge is part of the fabric of reality, and that goes for understanding also as the unique form of knowledge enjoyed by human, intelligent beings; and so we should be able to explain and understand the why and the what of understanding just as well, or as badly, as we can explain any of the other three elements that make up the fabric of reality. This point can be developed by reference to Deutsch's much-used idea of virtual reality.

'The ecological niche that human beings occupy depends on virtual reality as directly and as absolutely as the ecological niche that Koala bears occupy depends on eucalyptus leaves' (p. 121). Now, although virtual reality at first 'refers to any situation in which a person is artificially given the experience of being in a specific environment' (p. 98), the note of artificiality is successively modified as Deutsch applies the term virtual reality, first to all living processes, for these are physical processes that embody general theories about the environment, and then to intelligent agents. 'Every last scrap of our external experience is of virtual reality. And every last scrap of our knowledge – including our knowledge of the non-physical worlds of logic, mathematics and philosophy, and of imagination, fiction, art and fantasy – is encoded in the form of programs for the rendering of these worlds on our brain's own virtual-reality generator' (p. 121). In fact, he invites us 'to think of all our knowledge-generating processes, our whole culture and civilization, and all the thought processes in the minds of every individual, and indeed the entire evolving biosphere as well, as being . . . a virtual-reality program in the process of rendering, with ever-increasing accuracy, the whole of existence' (pp. 317–18).

In sum, what we can glean from his ever more extended use of the idea of virtual reality is this: knowledge refers to a kind of self-similarity of reality. The processes that we refer to as knowledge processes at all levels both reflect and create the reality of which they are so integral a part. At the genetic level, the process is one of replicating certain coded elements in interaction with an environment, and creating further such elements through the adaptive use of mutations. At the level of intelligence, there is a replication of features of reality likewise, and likewise also a creative dimension that takes the form of envisaging and engaging with its future prospects on the basis of the current levels of understanding of what is, after all, an evolving entity. The former process is slow; it is comparatively blind in that it depends in part on random events, and it is comparatively localised in the individual effectiveness of the individual species. The latter is swift, with a swiftness that can only increase as it masters better modes of computation and has increasing powers of the material universe in its control. It is exponentially more comprehensive in its replication of the fabric of reality (including itself). Its ecological niche can be as extensive as the universe itself, and its creativity is correspondingly and simultaneously both its own responsibility and increasingly crucial for the destiny of the whole universe, as we shall shortly see Deutsch explain. But for the moment, all of this is simply to illustrate the contention that knowledge, even in the highest form of understanding, is to be described as the self-similarity of reality in all of its past and present evolutionary processes and future prospects. This description is certainly to be preferred to that found in more dualistic theories of knowledge, where knowledge names a separable set of symbols of various kinds that somehow replicate (the rest of) reality. Then we must give both terms of the phrase 'virtual reality' equal weight when using it to describe knowledge, even at the level of explanation and understanding; just as we must give the accompanying phrase 'rendering reality' its correspondingly double meaning as both a simulation and an actual creation by which certain states of reality are sustained or come to be. And we can explain how explanation and understanding can in turn be explained by a replication which expresses that process also as an integral part of the fabric of reality which is crucial for its final continuance and its eschatological forms, as we shall shortly see from Deutsch's account of omega point.

We must certainly look to Deutsch's account of omega point, for, however much like science fiction it might seem at first blush, it is in fact an extrapolation which offers a powerful means of assessing his large claim for his philosophy to the effect that 'Far from denying free will, far from placing human values in a context where they are trivial and insignificant, far from being pessimistic, it is a fundamentally optimistic worldview that places human minds at the centre of the physical universe, and explanation and understanding at the centre of human purposes' (p. 342). But it is sufficient for the moment to note how very mutually immanent are mind and knowledge in Deutsch's physical universe, and his physical universe in mind and knowledge. All of this does become clearest in Deutsch's eschatology, but in order to assess fairly that eschatology, it is necessary to visit briefly his account of the other two elements that, in addition to quantum events, go to make up the fabric of reality: evolution and computation.

His account of the reality process known as biological evolution follows the basic lines of Richard Dawkins's Darwinism. At its base are those replicators known as molecules, for they cause the environment to make copies of them; then genes, which are made up of four kinds of molecule, which are adapted to the environment, and which Deutsch is already talking about in terms of computer programs; and finally cells, the mechanisms of which he then describes as the computers, for they execute the genetic programs. The execution takes the form of manufacturing molecules in and from the material afforded by the environment, and in accordance with the programs provided for and by adaptation. Natural selection then favours the better adapted over the more poorly adapted.

But then Deutsch makes a significant advance upon Dawkins, in two connected steps. First, he takes knowledge to be the prime focus of the description of this evolutionary process: what is primarily at issue, and crucially so for the continued being and becoming in which reality consists, is not the survival of the genes, as the matter is so often and far too simply expressed, but the survival and creation of *knowledge*; 'Genes embody knowledge about their niches' (p. 179). This interactive process by which cell mechanisms cause environments to replicate them is 'more than just computing. It is virtual-reality rendering' (p. 178). That is to say, in an explanation that takes both terms, virtual and reality, with equal weight and uses both senses of the word rendering, the self-similarity involved in this evolutionary process makes it an engine for the transmission of the knowledge involved; and at the same time, by facing up to the 'problems' implicit in its present status, by trying out changed 'codes', so to say, it creates knowledge, at least when a successful 'becoming' ensues. In both cases, knowledge occurs in the course of *doing*; in maintaining in existence the reality that is, and in evolving it.

At this point, incidentally, Deutsch has to criticise Dawkins's assertions to the effect that these complex adaptations come together spontaneously and that we should not be surprised at this. These are assertions, Deutsch points out; and what science needs is explanation and understanding. For explanation of this reality-rendering process known as biological evolution, it is not sufficient to point to the quantum phenomena which account both for the regular interaction of the physical variables that store information and for the myriad of minute variations at the DNA level. Nor is it sufficient to add a reference to the presumptuously named natural selection – in itself no more than an assertion once again that some variations in the codes fail to solve the problems entailed in sustaining or evolving their niches and themselves in the ever developing fabric of reality. For *explanation* here it is necessary to note the actual presence and operation of something that can only be called knowledge or, as Deutsch puts it, virtual-reality generation *and* its potential universality. Only that latter can explain the existence and operation of those highly adapted replicators.

And the reference just now to universality? This is the second step that Deutsch takes in his advance on Dawkins's Darwinian position. It might seem at first blush that life, confined as it today appears to be to an entirely insignificant speck in the universe, could hardly then be conferred with anything even vaguely approaching universal significance. Yet the moment we see these biological processes which the term life connotes as constituting *knowledge* – and irrespective, once again, of the matter of the incidence of life in the other universes that make up Deutsch's multiverse – its universal significance becomes clear. For as a form of knowledge, despite the drawbacks we noted in this form when compared with the intelligent form, it participates in one of the most basic constitutive elements of the fabric of universal reality. Hence its universal significance. It is possible to note already at this point the co-involvement of the four strands of which the fabric of reality and our understanding of it consists and, incidentally, to note also the altered connotation this confers on the term emergence. None of the strands is prior or privileged with respect to the others. If the biological-evolutionary strand emerges from the quantum-physical strand this means that it is non-reductively influenced by the latter; and the emergence of intelligent or conscious knowing processes from genetic-biological ones is also a case of non-reductive influence. That means, more positively, that the knowledge strand also non-reductively influences the quantum-physical strand; just as the intelligent level of knowing also non-reductively influences the genetic-biological level of knowing, for example in the case of genetic engineering. Emergence then comes to connote a mutual influence of each strand on the others – for it is the positive influence that one has on another that gives meaning to the statement that that other emerged from that one – and the necessary mutuality of the influence prevents any possibility of reducing any one strand to any other strand and, *a fortiori*, the reduction of all to just one strand. This becomes clearer still on a brief consideration of the final strand, computation.

Deutsch invites us

to think of all our knowledge-generating processes, our whole culture and civilization, and all the thought processes in the minds of every individual, and indeed the entire evolving biosphere as well, as being a gigantic *computation*. The whole thing is executing a self-motivated, self-generating computer program. More specifically it is, as I have mentioned, a virtual-reality program in the process of rendering, with ever increasing accuracy, the whole of existence. [Pp. 317–18)

One might register a passing point of puzzlement here, in anticipation of a more substantial critique to be offered in the course of a final assessment of this philosophy: why is there explicit mention only of the biosphere? Why is there no explicit inclusion of the physical realm (still) beyond the influence of biological processes? Or is this implicitly contained in the reference to the *entire* biosphere, on some view of the unity of the universe (multiverse)? Deutsch does come quite quickly, after all, to favour quantum computers – our brains, he suspects, are at this stage of our evolution computers of the more classical kind – when describing computation as one of the basic strands in the fabric of reality as a whole. And he does describe as computers – albeit special quantum computers – things like interferometers, which plot the paths of two or more versions of a photon, and therefore have to do with the physical level of reality outwith biological influences.

However that may be, there are two features of Deutsch's account of this final strand in the fabric of reality, and of our understanding of it, on which we can concentrate and which suffice for our purposes. The first concerns the possibility of constructing a universal quantum computer; and the second concerns the prospect that intelligence of the kind we experience, or any evolved stage of it, will not find itself to be merely a program run by some other entity on 'its' universal computer – as some of the reductionist views of our world as a computer seem to envisage – but will find itself in the creative driving seat both as regards the emergence of this universal quantum computer and in its uses in order to maintain and further develop the whole fabric of reality.

A quantum computer, then, is one that makes use of quantum mechanical processes, especially interference. As presented in the popularising literature on which so many of us are dependent in these matters, it is said to imitate the physical processes of evolution itself, and therefore it is described as the most potent instrument yet devised for the investigation of the universe. A universal quantum computer is one that can render any finite, physically possible environment in virtual reality. As it would thus enable us, or some intelligent beings who might be our successors, to understand the whole physical universe and to plot all of its further possibilities, it would correspondingly enable us to manipulate it, to take our part in creating its future states. 'The laws of physics', Deutsch explains, 'permit computers that can render every physically possible environment' (p. 221). Or, as he puts another version of that claim in a similar context: 'If the laws of physics as they apply to any physical object or process are to be comprehensible, they must be capable of being embodied in another physical object – the knower' (p. 135). Or, stronger still, 'the laws of physics may be said to mandate their own comprehensibility' (ibid.). This must be understood in terms of the mutual emergence, the co-inherence, of the strands of the fabric of reality mentioned already. In this case, knowledge (the laws of physics) emerges from quantum-physical phenomena as they in turn emerge from it. And that is why a universal quantum computer must be possible. There are practical problems about a universal quantum computer, Deutsch tells us. It would need unlimited memory capacity (in the form of suitable states of particles and of the gravitational field), an unlimited running time (in order to be able to complete an unlimited number of computation steps) and an unlimited energy supply. If we ignore once again Deutsch's use of his multiverse hypothesis in order to assert that what is possible actually exists in some universe(s); and if we ignore for the present also other indications that, on Deutsch's own principles, this universal quantum computer might, and perhaps must, be thought to exist in our own tangible universe – taking into account its incalculable complement of that 'shadow' matter which Deutsch attributes to other universes, we are then directed to Deutsch's omega-point scenario in order to see how the possibility of a universal quantum computer becomes an actuality in our universe.

On the other feature of this final strand in the fabric of reality, computation; on the issue of the role of intelligent agents within it, there are two relevant points from Deutsch to consider. The first concerns the fact that at omega point the physical conditions are most likely to be of a kind that no bodies such as we now experience as our own could survive. Therefore, if the construction of the universal quantum computer is to be attributed at that time to some evolutionary successors of ours, their intelligence would need to be embodied in some vastly different physical configurations. The second concerns his contention that there is no difficulty in principle in this universe as it is currently fabricated in envisaging the creation or emergence of genuinely artificial intelligence. For he defines artificial intelligence as 'a computer program that possesses properties of the human mind including intelligence, consciousness, free will and emotions, but runs on hardware other than the human brain' (p. 331). For intelligence, after all, simply refers to a knowledge which exhibits a further level of replication (a reflective process) that emerges in this material universe over and above the replication that occurs at the level of biological evolution, and by which the intricate and interactive structures of the universe are replicated in anticipation, or in the process of (re-)fashioning them. Indeed, the correspondence of these two points makes it difficult to understand why the latter instance has to be called artificial. If in the former instance the operative intelligence can be called human, even though it will be vastly evolved from the stage and state of intelligence we currently experience as human beings, what is the difference from that which is envisaged in the latter instance, namely, an intelligence run on hardware other than the human brain? There are some hidden assumptions here that concern the nature and extent of that form of knowledge known as intelligence within the fabric of universal reality. But, once again, these can only be brought to light by looking at Deutsch's eschatology, his account of omega point, and by submitting the whole picture to some final philosophical assessment.

A CONTEMPORARY (META)PHYSICAL VIEW OF THE ESCHATON
THE INTELLIGENCE OPERATIVE IN THE END TIME

Omega-point scenarios are increasingly frequent in contemporary physics. Deutsch's would rival anything to be found in ancient apocalyptic, and the following brief paraphrase can do little justice to its evocative power.

At the Big Crunch, the shape of the universe would change, and the degree of deformation would reflect a series of exponentially rapid increases and decreases. The amplitude and frequency of these oscillations would also increase without limit as the final singularity was approached. 'Matter as we know it would not survive: all matter, even the atoms themselves, would be wrenched apart by the gravitational shearing forces generated by the deformed spacetime' (p. 349). However, provided that elementary particles and a gravitational field in some relevant state did continue to exist, the utter violence of these final seconds of the universe would secure just that unlimited memory capacity, and an unlimited running time and energy supply, that are required for a universal quantum computer, a universal virtual-reality generator. And Deutsch feels safe in assuming that intelligence will survive and will then have the power to build and run the omega-point quantum computer. He says that he infers this from the Turing Principle – which states that it is possible to create a universal virtual-reality generator – and from 'some other independently justifiable assumptions' (p. 351); but it is clear from the larger argument in this chapter, 'The Ends of the Universe', that this assumption of the continued presence of intelligence to the very end finds its furthest basis on all the evidence we have always had to the effect that knowledge is one of the integral elements in the fabric of reality.

The intelligence operative in the end time will be an intelligence very like ours, working creatively at the problem of creating and maintaining its life and its necessary environment; noting, in its mode of critique, the ever changing forms of that permanent problem, and fashioning in its more creative mode the tentative 'solutions' which may then be verified, at worst by survival and at best by enhancement of existence and life; doing all of this by dint of its high level of replicative (reflective) processing, and all in the context of concrete experience and creatively active response. Except of course that, in the dying seconds of the universe as we know it, this characteristic task of intelligent entities will increase exponentially in difficulty. As it happens, the oscillations of spacetime on the approach of omega point would be highly unstable, and thus would threaten the conditions for the continuing computation in which our end-time intelligent successors, if that is what they turn out to be, will need to engage: 'the technology used for the stabilizing mechanisms, and for storing information, would have to be continually improved – indeed improved an infinite number of times – as the density and stresses became ever higher without limit. This would require the continual creation of knowledge' (p. 352), improving also, one must assume, an infinite number of times. But, as we saw, the resources would be there to do all of this. The only question that remains then is this: would these successors of ours(?) decide to do it, and to continue to do it to the last second of the universe. 'If you have only one second left to live, why not just sit back and take it easy at last?' (p. 352). That is surely the most exotic image in the whole of Deutsch's eschatology: after all the frantic millennia of pullulating life forms jostling for space and fighting for a little more time, here is this group of intelligent beings, with only a second to make the decision, opting for taking it easy . . . for a second.

However, as Deutsch quickly points out, this image radically misrepresents the situation. For, although it does represent quite accurately the inevitably and intrinsically moral, and possibly the equally inevitably aesthetic, dimensions of intelligent knowledge in operation – and only later in the essay will there be opportunity to attempt a more expansive account of these dimensions – it quite misrepresents the nature of time. It envisages time on the obsolete 'spacetime block' model of classical physics; but according to quantum physics, time itself is a quantum concept: it comes into existence and remains and changes in existence after the manner in which quantum physics describes the fabric of reality. Of these omega point successors of ours, then, Deutsch can say:

these people's minds will be running as computer programs in computers whose physical speed is increasing without limit. Their thoughts will, like ours, be virtual-reality renderings performed by these computers. It is true that at the end of that final second the whole sophisticated mechanism will be destroyed. But we know that the subjective duration of a virtual-reality experience is determined not by the elapsed time, but by the computations that are performed in that time. In an infinite number of computational steps there is time for an infinite number of thoughts – plenty of time for the thinkers to place themselves into any virtual-reality environment they like, and to experience it for however long they like. If they tire of it, they can switch to any other environment, or to any other number of environments they care to design. Subjectively, they will not be at the final stages of their lives but at the very beginning. They will be in no hurry, for subjectively they will live forever. (P. 352)

If the sheer wonder which this picture naturally evokes in our minds were to be broken for a moment by the intrusion of some rather more selfish interests, we might be inclined to ask: What's in this optimistic picture for us? Would these end-time creators – for that is what they are;

using the material of the universe as the quantum hardware with which to create eternal life in new heavens and a new earth; 'virtual' now becomes an unnecessary prefix to reality – would they do anything for us who do now daily face suffering, uncertainty and death? Deutsch asserts that they certainly could, if they wanted to (there's the moral dimension of knowledge as know-how again). Had sufficient information been retained about the initial conditions of the universe the final stage of which they now control, or equivalent information about its evolutionary trajectory, they would certainly have it in their power to reproduce the forms of matter now represented by us in our present environment. They could even reproduce us and our environment while divesting both of their least acceptable features – a kind of heaven on earth – although Deutsch himself would prefer it if in their good will they opted instead to bring us up to their infinitely more advanced level of life and intelligence.

In much of this, Deutsch is in some agreement with Frank Tipler's eschatology. But he takes issue with Tipler when the latter considers that this society of intelligent beings of the end time is the equivalent of the Christian God – omnipotent, omniscient, omnipresent. Although there is certainly a sense in which these end-time intelligences will be omnipresent in the universe – our successors will have to begin this process of extending their presence in the universe before the sun fails us – there is no obvious sense in which they can be said to be either omnipotent or omniscient. The power to create (virtual) reality will always be constrained by the physical laws which must obtain at any stage of existence of a physical universe; and the knowledge which is intrinsic to the 'problem-solving' of continuing and developing life and existence, even into eternity, will still always be knowledge of what is, or is to be. It has been pointed out already in this essay, however, that these abstract ways of defining God – and particular mention was made of omnipotence and omniscience – although they are common in the practice of the philosophy of religion, and in particular as critical fodder for its atheistic or agnostic forms, are themselves of highly questionable value as a conceptual basis for any argument in philosophy of religion. The question as to whether there are possible theological dimensions to the kind of naturalist metaphysics that Deutsch has produced cannot be decided, then, by simple manipulation of these abstract concepts. It must await a more ample assessment of this thoroughgoing naturalism, of a kind that one can only summarise at this point.

AN OPEN OR CLOSED METAPHYSIC?

The principal query that grows in the mind of the reader of *The Fabric of Reality* has to do with a perception of a distance – which itself seems to grow as the argument of the book reaches its conclusion – between, on the one hand, Deutsch's metaphysical system of the co-inherence of the four strands of the fabric of reality, and consequently of the four theories that together form his Theory of Everything, and, on the other hand, the story he tells of the history of our tangible universe. For in the story of our universe knowledge would appear to come into being with the remote origins of life, and knowledge in its intelligent form only some considerable time after that. In addition, knowledge in its intelligible form would seem to achieve the degree and level at which it can truly look like a constituent element of the whole fabric of reality in the very last seconds of the history of our universe. The query can then be construed as follows.

Deutsch's understanding of emergence allows us to start with any of the four strands, for in the model of co-inherence none is privileged over the others. Suppose, then, that we start from the computation strand, if only because this does seem to be the strand from which, more than from any of the other three, we can see the co-inherence of all four. Deutsch would seem to endorse that choice when he quotes Tomasso Toffoli's remark 'We never perform a computation ourselves, we just hitch a ride on the great Computation that is going on already'; and he appears to approve of the remark, with the proviso that we do not see ourselves *just* as 'someone else's program running on someone else's computer', as some sociobiologists and evolutionary psychologists see the matter (p. 346).

Quantum particle-events and their interferences then give rise to this physical universe, but only because they already run a program. For otherwise the regularities – the intelligible 'laws' of physics that 'mandate' their own understanding, in Deutsch's phraseology – otherwise these entities that make a universe rather than a chaos would not be the result of quantum events ever, at any stage or level of reality. Knowledge, then, does not appear first at, or with the level of, biological evolution; it is simply the case that we can see it more clearly there in its essentially and simultaneously replicative and experimental-progressive or 'problem-solving' modes, and we can then experience it most clearly in these essential modes in our own case as intelligent and free contributors to its cosmogenic processes. But if that is the case, and that is what

Deutsch's metaphysical system entails, then the truth of the matter must be that the universal quantum computer, the universal virtual-reality generator, must have been there always. And what Deutsch's *story* of our tangible universe tells us is that we, *Homo sapiens sapiens*, come to be more and more reflectively aware of this cosmically intelligent (virtual-)reality generator, and more and more capable of free cooperation with it until, in the eschaton, some of our successors (and perhaps all of us, if the totality of this cosmic intelligence benevolently so wishes) will actually grow towards the stature of the cosmic creative intelligence itself.

Having emerged from the *original* creativity of that cosmic intelligence as intelligent and hence consciously co-creative entities, we shall at the eschaton reach the fullest stature possible as 'sons' of this 'god', presumably by participating as fully as possible in its creative activity for all eternity. We – our evolutionary successors, that is – shall certainly not replace the original cosmic creative intelligence, even in Deutsch's account of the eschaton. That is an implication of his insistence that quantum physics will never be replaced. For that in turn implies the belief, which Deutsch also holds, that the particles are eternal. When the inconceivably violent turbulence of the end time shears the very atoms, particles will remain. But of course particles have properties; that is to say, they are already formed matter, and as it is form which facilitates those interactions which allow creative evolution to take place according to the laws of physics, that form itself is part of the design originating in the knowledge element that we come to see as the creative intelligence working through the whole fabric of reality. So our successors at the end time will be creating for all eternity within the limits of the formed particles and the ensuing laws of physics which the original, utterly immanent and creative intelligence has designed. Co-creators, then, freely and creatively participating in the original creation with the cosmic intelligence, and thus knowing that cosmic creator and the creation as fully as it is possible for derivative entities to do.

It is difficult to see how that could be deemed an unfair reading of Deutsch's philosophy. In fact, if one were to take into account all that he has to say about his multiverse, one would find much more support than one would encounter reservations for this reading. At one point, when Deutsch is writing about genetic algorithm computation – the most striking function, it would appear, which the new quantum computers could achieve – and he is calculating the resources it would take to factorise an algorithm known as Shor's algorithm, he tells us that this could not be done if we were dependent on the resources of our tangible universe. For the factorisation of Shor's algorithm would require computational resources vastly in excess of the number of atoms which can at present be calculated to exist in this visible universe. 'So if the visible universe were the extent of physical reality, physical reality would not even remotely contain the resources required to factorize such a large number. Who did factorize it, then? How, and where, was the computation performed?' (p. 217). The 'Who' in that penultimate question might just represent a slip of the pen. On the other hand, it might be no less than an honest expression of the reasonable view that an intelligent agency operating in this kind of manner must be spoken of in personal terms.

Apart from that particular context, Deutsch does regularly invoke his multiverse hypothesis in ways that support the reading of his system given above. For as he regularly takes the possibility of an entity or a process to entail its actual existence in some of the vast numbers of universes that make up the multiverse, so it is with the universal quantum computer, the universal virtual-reality generator. And if we then take into account his admittedly tentative suggestions for understanding the processes by which knowledge is transmitted between universes in their interactions, then it is possible to see him support the view that a universal creative, computing agency is always operative in what is, after all, whether multiverse or just a tangible universe that somehow includes 'shadow' matter of currently incalculable quantity, a unified (fabric of) reality. This might, then, of course, appear, in his terms, more like a 'multiversal' virtual-reality generator, to be conceived as bringing into eventual existence the more developed, intelligent entities like us, who could in different universes at different times and stages, perhaps, aspire to the status of participant intelligences in the eternal generation of reality; that or a society of universal virtual-reality generators, each operating in its own universe, but all bound together by some means which produces a society rather than a plurality of simple diversity.

When all allowances are made for the infinitely more sophisticated science involved, this is now reminiscent of yet another ancient and intrinsically theological philosophy: the Stoic philosophy, some of the central themes of which – in particular the very immanent creator divinity it named *Logos*, and the consequent 'natural law' morality – were to prove a central influence on developing Christian theology some centuries later.[13] The Stoicism of which Deutsch can remind us is,

---

[13] In a recent article entitled 'Recombination, Rationality, Reductionism and Romantic Reactions: Culture, Computers and the Genetic Algorithm', for *Social Studies of Science* 28 (1998), of which I had the privilege of a preview, Stefan Helmreich argues, from fieldwork among

however, Stoicism before it was co-opted by a dominant Platonism during that eclectic period in the history of Western philosophy known as Middle Platonism. It is the original Stoicism of Zeno that was born of a deliberate rejection of an increasingly dualistic separation of mind and matter in developing Platonism. In that original Stoicism, reality consists of *Logos* and matter; not a bad way of summarising Deutsch's four-strand fabric of reality, since after quantum physics knowledge, knowledge creation and creative intelligence dominate the accounts of the remaining three co-inherent strands. *Logos* was totally immanent in matter, not yet elevated above and outside the world as happened in the course of a co-opting Middle Platonism. Yet *Logos* was simultaneously totally transcendent within the material universe, for the *Logos* was as yet not virtually defined as the Mind-container of exemplar ideas for the world, at first separate from the world – that too came later with a dominating influence from developing Platonism. *Logos*, rather, was a dynamic, creative intelligence, a *pur technikon*, a craftsman-like fire that created by (trans)forming everything, a *physis* (the *physiologoi* are back with a vengeance) – and these two represent two of its other divine names; it is also Zeus – a virtual-reality generator progressively rendering all possible physical environments to any required degree of accuracy, as Deutsch might put it, and thus transcending each and all of these.

Indeed there is a case to be made for claiming that Deutsch's metaphysics is quite compatible with a Christian theology of creation, which was also centred upon an incarnate creative *Logos*. Humanity was brought forth in the image of that creator; Jesus, according to Christians, was the definitive incarnation of this creative 'Reason', with the purpose that all human beings should grow to the stature of such 'sonship' of God. Hence the main reasons given by Deutsch in order to distance his eschatological metaphysics from Christian belief – namely, the fact that a community is involved in creation of eternal life, and that our successors will remain bound by the laws of physics – are not altogether effective.

If *Logos* (Knowledge-Intelligence in creative action), then, is taken in its original Stoic (and Christian) meaning, not as the fully formed and

genetic-algorithm workers and analysis of genetic-algorithm texts, that the picture of 'nature' embedded in genetic-algorithm computing theory and practice is resonant with the values of secularised Judeo-Christian white middle-class U.S.-American and European heterosexual culture! The theological resonances and reminiscences are, then, perhaps not altogether figments in the mind of a philosophically trained theologian.

separate Idea System squatting outside the world that appeared in Middle Platonism, but as an Intelligence-type entity which forms matter in creative and evolutionary fashion into a universe – the Christian story of creation has its creator form the universe out of something described as empty, void and dark – what then is matter? Deutsch assumes that it consists of subatomic particles. But these exist at a level which already reveals the formative influence of Intelligence. Hence they cannot account for matter as the co-ordinate pole in the fabric of reality of a forming Intelligence. They cannot, then, substitute for an account of 'prime matter', as Aristotle named the correlate of intelligible, dynamic form. Perhaps as something that is in some sense the substrate of formed things and that is not itself at bottom already formed, matter is not so far apart from Intelligence/Mind in some respects that we could never understand either their co-inherence or the emergence of the former from the latter. Some beginnings may already be made in Kant's case for space and time as constructs of consciousness. But perhaps we shall never fully understand matter, and how it originates from mind. Or perhaps we shall only understand this when, as in Deutsch's eschaton, we too participate in the creative running of the ultimate universal virtual-reality generator.

It is best then to return at this point to some further analysis of the other co-ordinate entity in Deutsch's metaphysics: the knowledge-intelligence which is the dominant feature in those elements operative in and as the fabric of reality named as life (evolution understood as the survival and development of knowledge) and computation. If only to ascertain more fully if the larger and possibly theological implications of his thought which have just been suggested are at all fair and defensible.

For it does appear fair to say that Deutsch's frequent references, both explicit and implicit, to what he calls knowledge leave an unfinished, if not an unclear, picture behind. Because of the distance between his metaphysical system and the story of our universe, his account of knowledge agency in the story of our universe raises more questions than it answers. Although at times he sounds suitably uncertain as to whether the end-time knowledge-bearers running computer programs on the universal virtual-reality generator will or will not turn out to be our freely creative successors, he mostly seems to assume that they will be. At the head of his chapter 'The Ends of the Universe' he quotes Popper: 'Although history has no meaning, we can give it a meaning' (p. 344). A fine secular humanist manifesto in miniature, but of little enough help if it is designed to foreclose on questions that, despite its defiant human self-reliance, still remain very open.

For, to repeat a point already made, but in a different form: if in the end time the continuous and eternal creation of the universe with surviving particles of the present one, is the possibility and privilege of humanity, albeit a vastly developed humanity compared to us who live here and now, it must follow that the knowledge entity which continually creates the universe before or outwith the historic agency of this particular human species, is somewhat in the image of human intelligence, though probably of an incalculably higher order. For it is originating of all intelligible and evolving form, and this particular human species remains derivative, and must continue to be so, no matter how fully it comes in the end time to participate in that more original creative process.

It is time, then, to research some further samples of contemporary science, and in particular those which study the human intelligence, mind or psyche. For although this human intelligence seems to be paradigmatic for Deutsch in his quest for the primary element in the continuously creative fabric of reality, he would hardly be expected as a physicist to advance our knowledge of it as much as would those who professionally study it. Turn then to the psychologists who continue to study the human psyche as it is embedded and active in our very physical universe.

A SCIENTIFIC APPROACH FROM THE SIDE OF
(EMBODIED) PSYCHE

The turn at this point to the more psychological approach, it is no harm to repeat, in no way signals any persistence of allegiance to any of the cruder kinds of dualism; it signals no more than an interest in a correlative kind of investigative strength to that of Deutsch's. In actual fact, the leading lights in the rather new movement in developmental psychology which is now about to be considered for our purposes are professional exponents of a number of different specialist approaches to the overall subject; ranging as they do from those who could be called psychologists simply, or social psychologists, to those like Colwyn Trevarthen who profess psychobiology, and to others whose disciplines fall within neuroscience – neuropsychology, neurobiology, neurophysiology. The sheer fact that such a range of disciplines or subdisciplines is so evenly represented within the cooperative group at the heart of the new movement in developmental psychology is, apart altogether from express statements from some of the group, sufficient guarantee that not even the mildest and most insidious presence of dichotomous dualism can hold sway here. But the final guarantee consists of course in the manner in which, in the following account of it, this movement in developmental psychology analyses and describes the elements and processes of its subject matter as clearly, and often simultaneously, in neurological as in psychological terms.

References to this movement in developmental psychology as new, or even newest, can certainly cause their own forms of hesitation in the mind of a reader. Is it sufficiently well known by practising philosophers, or (even less likely?) by practising theologians, to make a constructive contribution to the theme of this essay? Some of the anonymous readers of the proposal for this book made much of this question. The short answer is that if it is not better known, it ought to be, for reasons which should shortly emerge; and certainly such an answer would be valid for any who understand how prevailing philosophies do, and ought to, influence relevant theologies; and indeed how prevailing philosophies ought to pay the closest attention to the most insightful scientific investigations into the fabric of reality.[14] Correspondingly, it is one's responsibility, when conducting a philosophico-theological investigation like the present one, to seek to identify the most insightful investigations into the fabric of reality that appear on the scene; and to put these forward purely on the merits of the overall philosophical view to which they can then be seen to contribute.

Further, there is one feature of the new movement in developmental psychology which at once aligns it with a similar feature to be found elsewhere in contemporary psychology[15] and makes it an almost automatic choice in the present context. It contains a consistent critique – and a critique moreover which stems from its own most central experimental results – of the kind of 'Cartesian' mind–body dualism that has

---

[14] For those who wish for an introduction to the movement, a short history of it and its international body of contributors and promoters can be found in Colwyn Trevarthen, 'The Concept and Foundation of Infant Intersubjectivity', in S. Bräten (ed.), *Intersubjective Communication and Emotion in Early Ontogeny* (Cambridge University Press, 1998); and a brief account of the movement, together with a defence against the 'extreme scepticism' with which it is still viewed in some quarters of the discipline, can be found in Vasudevi Reddy et al., 'Communication in Infancy: Mutual Regulation of Affect and Attention', in Gavin Bremner et al. (eds.), *Infant Development: Recent Advances* (Hove, Sussex: Psychology Press, 1997), pp. 247–72.

[15] For example, the feminist critique of the classical developmental psychology of Piaget, Kohlberg and so on, spearheaded by Carol Gilligan's *In Another Voice* (1982), does and can find in the movement under review here not merely a supportive critical voice, but a positive alternative to the classical dominance of a 'male' individualist rationalism in previous developmental psychology.

featured so largely so far in these pages; and, in consequence, of the kind of classical developmental psychologies which can now be seen all too clearly to have been overinfluenced by that dominant philosophical mood. As Reddy, Murray and Trevarthen put the matter, scepticism of their new movement is 'also due in part to continuing acceptance of the proposition that things mental, being invisible, are graspable only conceptually and with difficulty'.[16] There *in nuce* is the 'Cartesian' dualism that has dominated so much of classical psychology also. And the account of human development which results? Briefly, human minds, separate from their bodies and from other minds, seek rational clarity. In infancy they take in information concerning reality and behaviour through early stimuli, at a stage when they are governed by biological instinct and self-serving emotions, and when they are aware of other persons more or less as objects that have particular properties and affordances. On being taught a language, their acquisition of knowledge increases exponentially; both knowledge of the nature and structures of reality and, perhaps even more crucially, of the conventional rules of socially acceptable behaviour. Thereafter, 'with good management of education and social government, individuals learn how to negotiate with social partners, and converge in awareness of transcendental universals in their individual consciousness and purposes, to their mutual benefit'.[17]

It is not that this account of how the Piagetian child privately and logically solves its epistemological problems is simply wrong. The processes it describes do also occur. The problem, rather, is that in its bias, its partiality, literally, towards an individualist, rationalist cognitivism, it fails to explain and to allow us to understand the very elements and processes it so confidently evokes; and that is very poor science. First, as previous critique of dualist models in this essay constantly concluded, it fails to explain how any individual person actually comes to know another person – there is hardly any need to expand on that point any further. But second, and as a consequence, it actually fails to explain how language, so pivotal for this whole theory of development, is acquired, or indeed how it functions. For linguistic symbols actually function as such, only *are* such, within what Habermas called a 'structure of subjectivity', or, as Wittgenstein would say, there is no such thing as a private language. Sounds made by my vocal chords, conventional

[16] Reddy et al., 'Communication in Infancy', p. 247.
[17] Colwyn Trevarthen, 'Intersubjectivity', in Rob Wilson and Frank Keil (eds.), *The MIT Encyclopedia of Cognitive Science* (Cambridge, MA: MIT Press, 1988).

squiggles on a page, are not as such language; language exists only in the process of intersubjective communication. It requires for its explanation, then, a theory of personhood or subjectivity; and the explanation of its acquisition and use, as a consequence, requires a prior knowledge, encounter, awareness of another subject as person.

Now, it is just this kind of explanation of the acquisition/use of language/knowledge that the new movement provides from the experimental observation of human neonates. First, in terms of the trio – knowledge, intelligence, consciousness – consciousness of another person emerges as that which is, in the strictest sense of the word, original in the neonate. Trevarthen refers to this feature of this explanatory model as the 'Intersubjective First' (or 'Intrinsic Subjectivity') position, in clear contrast to the 'Subjective First' position (or 'Extrinsic Intersubjectivity' – immediate awareness-knowledge of one's own individual self only, and of other selves through inference from extrinsic evidence) that seems to be entailed in 'Cartesian' dualism. This corresponds to Bräten's theory of the virtual other,[18] in which he hypothesises that intersubjective communication depends upon a dual motive system in each communicating subject, which generates a representation (or virtual self) of the expressive subject's body, in dynamic emotional relation with respect to a cerebral representation (or virtual other) of the experienced other subject's expressive body. And it is relevant to this point to mention the consistent experimental finding that infants demonstrate that they perceive persons as essentially different 'objects' from anything non-living and non-human; they exhibit such different patterns of behaviour to persons than they do to objects that there simply is no evidence to suggest that they ever have to learn what another person is, or to infer the existence of other persons by some possibly difficult rational process.

Second, the references just now to 'the expressive subject's body' and 'the experienced other subject's expressive body', both of which are simultaneously always already present as cerebral representation in the human neonate (diagramatically represented as a dynamic relationship between virtual self and virtual other already inscribed in the operative features of the human brain and central nervous system)[19] – these references confirm the farewell to 'Cartesian' dualism as the hitherto all

---

[18] S. Bräten, 'Dialogical Mind: The Infant and Adult in Protoconversation', in M. Carvallo (ed.), *Nature, Cognition and System* (Dordrecht: Reidel, 1987).

[19] See Kenneth J. Aitken and Colwyn Trevarthen, 'Self–Other Organization in Human Psychological Development', *Development and Pathology* 9 (1997), 656.

too common starting point for a truly scientific investigation of the genesis of the human person and of the human person's characteristic attributes. And as this makes one wonder once more at the power of received philosophical impressions, by whatever accidents of thought and history these may be seen, usually with critical hindsight, to have developed; and indeed at the power of such received impressions to influence the most determined of the practitioners of conspicuously entitled empirical science, it advertises, by happy contrast, the persistent prospects held out by the recurrent determination to pay the closest attention to the nature, that is, to the genesis and goal, of *the things that are*; and in this case in particular, it presages the return to a more sophisticated mind–body monism, or a more sophisticated mind–body dualism of co-inherent features, than either the 'Cartesian' dualists or the crude materialists could ever manage.

Third, by taking note of the centrality in even the briefest of advertisements for the new movement of such phrases, already used above, as 'motive system' and 'dynamic emotional relation', one can appreciate how original and determinative is motive and emotion in (and of course the consequent bodiliness of) the original and originating intersubjectivity of human consciousness, and for the whole communal doing-learning, in all of its growing complexity and apparently limitless developments, that comprises human life and destiny in its extended body, the universe. In 'Cartesian' dualism and in the cruder kinds of Platonism which preceded it, the (e)motive feature of human existence was too frequently associated with spiritual perturbance to allow sight of the essential contribution it makes to effective human awareness and increasing knowledge of reality. The Stoic philosophers were exceptional in giving 'judgement' a central role in their treatment of the emotions. Descartes, for those who take the trouble to read him without 'Cartesian' blinkers, had much that was positive to say about the emotions in his quest for an explanation of mind–body unity, and even, as we already observed, a little on infant emotions that could with generosity be deemed to anticipate the current theory. But it is rare indeed to encounter an acceptably adequate account of emotions in any philosopher up to the present day, and in particular of their fundamental role in the conjoint processes of interpersonal relationships and the concomitant communal knowledgeable dealings with the fabric of reality.

Max Scheler, interestingly enough in an article on suffering, provides an exception. 'Our emotional life', he wrote, 'is a highly differentiated system of natural revelations and signs, by means of which we are made aware of ourselves. A certain kind of emotion presents *itself* in experience as something of a *meaning*, a *sense*, in which the emotion presents certain (objective) evaluations of states of affairs, of an activity, of a fate that befalls us.' And he goes on to observe that it is not sufficient to regard emotions as simple states of our existence and experience to which the personal centre is relatively passive. On the contrary, as the reference to evaluation suggests, the emotions, like motives in this also, are far more integral to the functioning of the (inter)subjective centre of the human being. They are central to our investigation of the world and our evaluation of it, but they are also central to our expression of our understandings and intentions with regard to it, and indeed – although Scheler does not make much of this – to the two-way communications of such understandings and intentions which go to the make-up of our social construal and construction of our world.[20]

All of this, and more, emerges from the new movement in developmental psychology: the originality – in every sense of the word: beginning as well as source of what follows – of the (e)motive feature in the already intersubjective and very bodily investigative dealings with reality and its concomitant communicative expressions. This third feature of the current theory, then, ties together all three. These three have been identified, admittedly, for the purposes of the present essay, but not, one hopes, in such a way as to distort the theory in any way. It remains only to put some flesh on these bare bones, and to draw such conclusions as one may for the prospects of a more adequate philosophy for this time; one which will at least not continue to lose sight of both subject and reality, and which may allow a reasonable assessment of the possibility of a religious depth to reality, and of a theological dimension to philosophy, of which the still dominant traditions of philosophy have been so suspiciously persistent in their explicit rejection.

THE PRIMACY OF EMOTION IN ACTIVE, EMBODIED INTERSUBJECTIVITY
THE EMERGENCE OF PERSONHOOD

Motives and emotions, motivating and emoting, are clearly cousins under the skin, if not indeed siblings, as their common connotation in 'what moves or is found moving' so easily suggests; and they certainly go together in this psychological theory of the genesis of the knowledgeable agent known as a person. But it is best to begin with motive, if only to

[20] Max Scheler, *Centennial Essays* (The Hague: Nijhof, 1974), pp. 121–3.

156 *Historical–critical*

stress from the outset the initiative that even neonates take in the developmental process that is now described.

What a person perceives and does depends on motives as well as on contingencies of stimulation from the environment. Motives can be conceived as patterned states of interneuronal systems in the brain that initiate movements or behaviour, and that interact with perception in the generation of experiences. The strength, morphology and timing of every movement in the muscles and joints of the body depend on a combination of bio-mechanical effects generated in the periphery and the pattern and timing of an excitatory neuromotor impulse from the brain. Motives also change the sensitivity, coordination and discriminative biases of sensory systems; orienting, opening and closing avenues of awareness. Acting between neural systems in the brain in the form of neurochemical transmissions, motives also determine the accumulation, accessing and combining of memories . . . In all these activities motives have the additional power to produce emotional expressions that have emotive effects in sympathetic subjects.[21]

The ability of motive so conceived to initiate movements of all kinds, and to influence so powerfully and in such a variety of ways both perception–awareness–memory and expression–communication, leads Trevarthen to talk of an Intrinsic Motive Formation, and he describes its first and principal function as follows: 'an Intrinsic Motive Formation (IMF) is ready at birth to engage with the expressed emotions of adult companions in a mutual guidance of infant brain development and sociocultural learning'; it forms the biological substrate for social behaviour, and it generates what Bräten has called a virtual other, or an organismically provided need for a partner.[22]

Trevarthen and Aitken then offer the following description of the functioning of the IMF in a manner that brings out the three skeletal themes which still need some flesh put on them: the primacy of intersubjective consciousness of others as the first 'objects'; the primacy in this of the emotional forms in the course of perception–expression; and the consequently derivative and secondary status of the more conceptual, inferential, abstract or contemplative knowledge of objects.

Neurons, tracts, and chemical messengers of an *intrinsic motive formation* (IMF) pattern the psychological mechanism of the embryo and fetal brain and after birth the same formation animates the child's consciousness and understanding as he or she learns to fit within a society and a culture. The IMF does so by

[21] Colwyn Trevarthen and K. J. Aitken, 'La fonction des émotions dans la compréhension des autres', in R. Pry (ed.), *Autisme et regulation de l'action* (Montpellier: Université Paul Valery, 1996), p. 11.
[22] Aitken and Trevarthen, 'Self–Other Organization', p. 654.

constraining or directing the infant's brain emotionally – in exploratory activity, in attention, in the identification and intentional use of objects, and in the formation of habits and memories – especially while the infant is communicating with the emotions and interests of other people . . . the infant brain is not only seeking emotional regulation and *self control*, but also has well-formed motives for cooperation in intelligence in order to learn through understanding the thoughts, purposes, and feelings of caregivers as other subjects . . . The newborn infant is conspicuously adapted to seek intersubjective or interpersonal support through transfer of feelings, not only in consistent, tender *attachment* with nurturing and protective care, but also by starting to build human *companionship* with a widening circle of partners who are happy to be both playmates and teachers. At first, the IMF participated in the *closed* morphogenesis of cerebral cortical tissues in human form and their integration with the rest of the brain in the embryo and fetus. After birth, the emotions the IMF generates and expresses to one or a few significant others, with the emotions received from them, guide the infant's assimilation of experience and the formation of *dynamic representations* or *working models*, in psychologically *open* brain development and learning. Humans, whether young or old, can get into one another's minds in a unique way, and this gives critical advantages for communication of ideas and learning.[23]

The primacy of intersubjective awareness, and the primacy within that of emotional encounter, can best be understood through explanation of the expressive or communicative power of emotions or, in other words, by explaining how emotions are themselves ways of knowing. Much that is said at this point, of course, applies to motives also; because of the connotative affinity that binds them, it is normally my manifest emotions that make my motives known: the fear in my eyes 'explains' my motives in ignominious retreat.

The intrinsic motivating system is connected with the most complex expressive organs to be found anywhere amongst the primates – the facial organs, the vocal organs and the gesturing organs, especially the hands. At the same time as the infant brain, in addition to 'mapping' and coordinating its body and other bodies and their relationships in a single body-related spatiotemporal frame of reference, is construing its own range of motives and emotions and their expressions, it is recognising, 'mapping' and coordinating with these, the similar motives, emotions and their expressions that it encounters in other persons. Long before the use of language in the normal sense of the spoken (or, later, written) words is mastered, the neonate is already communicating intention and inquiry, and hence sense and meaning, through highly

[23] C. Trevarthen and K. J. Aitken, 'Brain Development, Infant Communication, and Empathy Disorders: Intrinsic Factors in Child Mental Health', *Development and Psychopathology* 6 (1994), 598.

coordinated facial expression, gesture and prelinguistic vocalisation, which are coordinated with similar expressions from attendant significant others. One need only consider the enormous range of meaning the human face alone can encompass. A look can connote an invitation to attend to one, and to intimacies of a deeper kind; or it can express fear or dislike and thus connote a concomitant avoidance or rejection; together with a complex of other facial expressions and with gestures such as turning the face away temporarily, it can express shyness, which connotes a highly sophisticated, tempered invitation to intimacy, but an intimacy not too persistent or invasive; combined with yet other gestures, of reaching with the hands for instance, it can connote the invitation to cooperation in investigation and manipulation of the common world of these intentional companions.

Intermittent vocalisation can connote approval or disapproval of what is being expressed or achieved; and indeed the alternation of vocalisation with a significant adult, even if the one is still prelinguistic, connotes the intent to hold conversation. There is scarcely any need to elaborate further; the reader can be referred to the literature noted in this section for the most extensive and captivating of experimental exemplification. The point, for present purposes, is this: this very open, if not limitless, range of facial expression, gesture and vocalisation is in fact a fully fledged semiotic system; on the analogy of a sign language used by mutes, which is as truly a language in respect of its epigenesis and evolution as verbal languages, it is a true language, which, in deference only to its eventual development into the further and most significant dimension of a verbal language, may be termed a proto-language. It is called the language of (e)motion, simply because the heuristic and informative motives and emotions of the human beings involved supply both its source and its mode of being.

These emotion-laden expressions or, rather, these expressive emotions are intentional, then, in the basic sense of intentionality which epistemologists of the various pragmatic or practicalist theories of knowledge favour. That is to say, knowledge is born and grows in integral and active engagement with others and objects in our common world, in the (e)motive sphere, that is to say, and its truth is forever bound up with evaluation of that engagement, however that evaluation is to be construed. Indeed it is necessary to say at this point, if only to preserve the unbroken developmental continuity with the later stage of verbal language and communication: would-be dichotomous distinctions between (e)motive knowledge and conceptual, inferential, 'objective' knowledge are always in the end more notional than real. The infant is already intelligent, as we must shortly see in a comparison with other primates. But it is more apposite to observe, in the case of the more abstract semiotic systems represented by common languages, even when supplemented by scientific notation, that neither the investigations conducted nor the results expressed by means of these are ever without an integral underpinning of motivation and an equally integral emotional overtone, nor can the use-in-practice of the alleged knowledge so acquired and expressed be forever postponed in the process of its verification. These conclusions are rendered all the more secure when one concentrates again on the concomitant primacy of knowledge of other persons within the persisting primacy of the (e)motive matrix of knowledge and its expression.

Implicit in the account so far, and coming closer to explicitness all the time, is the question: What then, if anything, is distinctive about those human subjects we call persons? It has been claimed in experiments with captive apes, for instance, that these primates actually demonstrate conversational intelligence, because they repeat for various cooperative purposes the arbitrarily coded gestures or symbol manipulations of the humans involved in the experimental game-like exchanges. And it is clear in any case from observation of the natural behaviour of such species that they do indeed imitate intentions and share purposes together. Yet, although there is clear evolutionary relationship between the primates and *Homo sapiens sapiens*, there is still a difference, and not just one of degree but of kind, between the two. The task is simply to find the significant difference for the present context, which seeks to put some flesh on that primacy of the intersubjective and (e)motive features of knowledge in cases to which the term person is conventionally and commonly applied.

When other species observe and imitate intentions, demonstrating what has been called *theory of mind*, they show limitations in curiosity and goal selection. They acquire stereotyped action sequences deploying a limited repertoire of signs to accomplish defined social functions, or they learn, by imitating, how to manipulate environmental resources for immediate consumption. Human toddlers and older children, in contrast, observe, learn and re-enact social mannerisms, ethical principles, cognitive interests and investigative, problem-solving behaviour. Before they walk, they pick up, and represent to themselves in imaginative play, elaborate routines of execution for technical and artistic use of environmental affordances for goals that are remote in time and space.[24]

---

[24] Colwyn Trevarthen, Theano Kokkinaki and Geraldo A. Fiamenghi, 'What Infants' Imitations Communicate: With Mothers, with Fathers and with Peers', in J. Nadel and G. Butterworth (eds.), *Imitation in Infancy* (Cambridge University Press, 1997), p. 7.

Significant difference is certainly expressed in that paragraph from an essay by Trevarthen, Kokkinaki and Fiamenghi. Dare one say it could be expressed even better? There is the clear impression that the human infant is already capable of representations – signs or symbols – that signify ranges of reality far beyond those concretely encountered in the immediate environment; and that, it has been said before, is symptomatic of a level of knowledge that Deutsch would call intelligence; or it is symptomatic of a significantly different level of intelligence from that possessed by other species. In addition, there are the references to ethical principles and cognitive interests – we must note at greater length later the coincidence of moral and theoretical knowing in this developmental model – and to investigative, problem-solving behaviour, and to artistic use, which introduces the element of creativity. But then the infant is said to learn these, and that opens a tiny crack for some possible misunderstanding to enter once more. For it is then not entirely clear that the human neonate is itself already capable of cognitive interest, investigative behaviour and, as a consequence, meaningful (prelinguistic) conversation; and that it is simply learning to deploy these more extensively in practice. The paragraph might just possibly be read as an endorsement of the view that the human neonate, perhaps with some innate biological preparedness for this, receives as input, and then learns by repeated imitation sets of techniques and signs that have, as it happens, a far greater range of applicability than those received from significant others by other primates.

This comment, one hopes, is not nit-picking. It is designed to acknowledge the finesse of analysis that must be brought to bear if the significant difference that makes for what we conventionally call persons is to be clearly seen and adequately expressed. And it leads to the suggestion that Trevarthen puts the same matter much more succinctly and unambiguously in a set of passages from another context, which are again worth quoting in full.

Symbols are created by combination of ideas generated by *both* intersubjective and pragmatic motives. Study of infant communication on the threshold of language has led some investigators to concentrate on pragmatics; the activities and intentional basis for cooperation in the prevailing circumstances. These psychologists interpret the initiatives of infants and their responses in terms of the philosophy of Speech Acts. We need to enrich this insight with appreciation of the dynamic interpersonal motives that allow human minds to sense one another's impulses and preferences *directly*, as well as by way of orientations to a shared reality.

What is peculiarly human about infants and about us is the need to become involved, from time to time, in the continuous emergence of the thoughts of others; to be willing to make, or receive, a story of the mind being active; to cooperate in a generation of fictive reality for its own sake; to join in the rhythm and poetry of invention, or the work of construction. Human empathy is an involvement in the emergent makings of thought seeking referents, in the possibilities of thinking fantasies while doing real things.

The lesson that our empiricist and rationalist Psychology has to learn, and to teach its novices, is that the simplest human state of mind is one of unrealistic and to-be-worked-out empathy, seeking fulfilment in company. No knowledge has value, or meaning, unless it has been explored in intermental territory.[25]

Conversation, then, is the key: the key simultaneously to the difference in kind between human and other primates, the key to the definition of personhood, and to the fleshing out of our understanding of human consciousness, intelligence, knowledge. In Trevarthen's words again, but now with a dog for comparison: 'We perceive our pets to have human attributes and human understanding, but there is an absolute limit to their real grasp of what we hope to share with them. A dog, while a rewarding companion, quick to follow our interest and actions and capable of devoted loyalty, makes a puzzled conversation partner'; whereas 'a newborn searches for conversation with a partner'. 'Being part of that dynamic intensity of psychological exchange is what makes a baby a person.'[26] And that means, of course, that the human neonate is always already a person. For the very idea of conversation entails not just the ability to sign and to be directed by signs, but the awareness that what one is doing is signing. Conversation simply means the offering of a sign as invitation of a return sign; it is quite distinguishable from the use of biologically determined initiatives designed to elicit directions for pragmatic achievements necessary for the intentional purposes of physical and social survival. This exchange of signs intended as such, rather than sequences of their uses for immediate pragmatic purposes, entails in turn a certain reflectivity of consciousness, in that one is simultaneously aware that the look, expression, gesture, vocalisation (even preverbal vocalisation) signifies in a manner not limited by, in a manner that transcends, immediately present objects or goals; for that entails a reflective awareness of the awareness expressed in the sign. Here is the relevance of Trevarthen's terms fictive, fantasy, unrealistic – though

[25] Colwyn Trevarthen, 'Contracts of Mutual Understanding: Negotiating Meanings and Moral Sentiments with Infants', *Journal of Contemporary Legal Issues* 6 (1995), 392, 395; italics are mine.
[26] Ibid. pp. 375–6.

some would prefer the use here, together with the term fictive, of the cognate term imaginative – and the inevitable introduction of reference to inventiveness or creativity with which, as we shall later see, the moral dimension of human knowing and acting is essentially related. And, finally, this reflectivity of consciousness, evidenced in the conscious deployment of signs in order to elicit other signs, entails a level of consciousness that can be called self-consciousness. This is the most obvious reason for calling this level of conscious being a self, subject or person; yet it is a deeply mysterious feature of our commonest experience of what we are.

In our actual experience, as indeed in the results of both the neurobiological and the more psychological investigations conducted by this new movement in developmental psychology, self-consciousness appears inextricably bound up with a virtual other, and, from analysis of our earliest experiences, with consciousness of real other persons. Does this mean that we can only be self-conscious (persons) in the course of being conscious of other selves (persons); that consciousness at this personal level is socially constructed from origin through all exercise to end? (We are back with Hegel again, and light years ahead of Sartre.) That would appear to be the case for humans, at any rate, and it is the import of the published work of Trevarthen and his international cohort of colleagues in the Intersubjectivity First movement, from their talk about the primacy of the human neonate's seeking companionship, through references to the inevitably intermental territory of meaning, to the insistence on the direct encounter of human minds. For if we see bodily movement, especially in the forms of facial expression, vocalisation (preverbal and, later, verbal) and gestures of all kinds, as signs self-consciously known by the user and perceived by the recipient as signs, then this self-consciousness is so embodied that only some remnants in our brainwashed minds of a 'Cartesian' dualism could prevent us from agreeing that persons, however mysterious they may remain, do indeed, as even Descartes knew, encounter each other directly in the street.

It is unnecessary for present purposes, although it is in itself increasingly revealing and instructive, to follow the pattern by which the infant, already competent in prelinguistic expression or proto-conversation, acquires a language conventionally so called. In some ways it is simply a matter of adding a highly complex system of arbitrarily or, rather, conventionally chosen vocalisations and, later still, of squiggles on pages and screens, to the stock of bodily movements and effects already used as knowledge-bearing (knowledge-acquiring and knowledge-expressing) signs. Suffice it to say that this conventional extension to the original semiotic system provides for a potentially limitless range of signification, and hence for a potentially limitless accumulation of explanation, understanding, invention and creation. It is also unnecessary for present purposes to plot the relationship between the more emotive–imaginative form of intelligence which dominates the original system of bodily expressions, vocalisations and gestures, and the more abstract–analytic, logical–inferential forms of intelligence and its expression which can be added to this in the course of using the vastly extended repertoire of received conventional verbal signs.

Suffice it to say once more that the developmental psychology to which this essay is here so heavily indebted provides the details which can yield a genetic account of this relationship also. It describes in captivating detail the manner in which the rhythm, time and pitch of music, together with the rhyme and rhythm of poetry, and, partly as an effect of participating in these, the turn-taking that characterises proto-conversations in the mutual signings of infant and adult, sets the stage for the introduction of these polysemous vocalisations called words, the systems of which form the conventional languages of the world. These are first, then, acquired and used in the story-telling format, or the dramatic-dialogue format, itself a part of playing; in the formats, in short, which characterise the proto-conversations. That is how poly-semous vocalisations can be manipulated to carry and extend the precise meaning which the conversation partners intend at any one time. (The sentence, the basic unit of narrative, is the essential context in which the polysemy of words is managed towards the passing precision of intended meaning.) And it is in the course of this continual process of forging precision of meaning from 'the mud and slime of verbal impreci-sion' that the vastly extended repertoire of verbal signs enables a focussing on finer and finer features or details of things in an infinitely rich and complex world; and which eventually yields those technical languages characteristic of disciplines in science and philosophy (and theology) that are thought of, legitimately, as the abstract–analytic, logical–inferential processes of knowing *par excellence*, though sometimes also thought of, this time illegitimately, as the only processes that can be called rational or intelligent.

It remains only to outline the contribution made by this developmental psychology, characterised by its 'Intersubjective First' position, to the understanding of the human being in its world, and to assess its advantages, and in particular its relevance, to the current topic.

A person (self, or subject in that sense of the word) known to and as a human person is a highly complex organism, with a particularly complex brain and central nervous system, that enjoys a certain kind or level of consciousness. 'Every conscious entity is conscious of being conscious.' That is simply, as Sartre said, a simple acknowledgement of the essential nature of consciousness as such. In the case of consciousness embedded, as Heidegger would say, in mundane body – and this is the only condition of conscious being that we humans directly know – there would appear to be a range of possible levels of consciousness. At one extreme, that of animals and perhaps of some plants and other living things, conscious entities are conscious of the states and acts of their very live, interactive being in its worldly environment, and of the corresponding states and acts of the entities with which they interact. At a 'higher' level this basic level of consciousness arrives at a (yet more) reduplicative stage, which can be conveniently called, again after Sartre, a level of reflectivity. At this stage and level, in addition to just being conscious events, the conscious entity reflects, or 'is bent back over', the now determinate contents of (its own) consciousness, and thus becomes reflectively conscious, simultaneously, of these determinate contents and of its 'self' reflectively aware of these. There is here a more transcendent (level of) consciousness with respect to the empirical (content of) consciousness and to the basic level of consciousness which is always evident. It is at this level of consciousness that we can talk of selves in the sense of subjects or persons. And it immediately entails the properties of persons, such as their use of language in the widest sense of the term, the ability to use signs, to signify; as well as their moral and artistic attributes.

But take language first, for that is essentially bound up with another and quintessential dimension of personhood, namely, its interpersonal structure. The (self-)consciousness of this person 'is bent back over', overlaps, transcends any and every current content of its consciousness. It is aware of a hand grasping for something, for example; but by being reflectively aware of being aware of this hand, it is concomitantly aware of the possible cessation of the grasping, the absence of the hand, or a possibly different action, or a possibly different hand. Its most concrete images, in short, are suffused by a kind of awareness already beyond them towards other possible forms and other possibilities. But this means that this kind of conscious entity is capable of re-presenting the contents of its consciousness. Not in the simplistic sense of representationalism found in dualist systems, in which images in the mind are pictures of what exists outside the mind. No, the image is capable of presenting this grasping hand that currently monopolises my attention simultaneously with indefinite other possibilities, precisely because of the reflectively self-conscious image it is. And so I can 'sign' or signify (the) grasping hand; by etching the form of a hand on the wall of a cave, for instance, or by any of a number of natural or conventional gestures or effects which can be used to (re)present a hand, and all that it can accomplish. So it is with all the states and acts of a person's interactive being and all the things with which the person interacts. The self-conscious self is capable from the outset of signifying some, and eventually all, of this.

Now, the capacity to signify entails the existence of another (self-conscious) self who can be signed to, and can therefore also signify. This is what is meant by talk of the human neonate being psycho-physically constructed and functioning as if in relationship to another person; the idea of the virtual other. And certainly as far as all our experience goes, the whole of our signifying activity from beginning to end is a signifying to and from real other persons; that is to say, it is essentially an interpersonal, cooperative, communal or social enterprise. At the beginning of life the neonate requests and receives vastly more signified content than it can contribute; but all through life the very structures of personal, self-conscious selves, with their characteristic and inevitable signifying, expressive or communicating properties, are realised in direct interpersonal encounter and its consequent exchange. Direct, because it is embodied self-conscious selves that are in question; because the signs that emanate from them are then essentially bodily, consisting in acts and gestures of the signifier's body. So that I cannot prevent you from being conscious of my embodied consciousness even if I wanted to. Of course, the larger my repertoire of signs becomes with the use, say, of conventional languages, the more of the content of my self-consciousness I can conceal from you if I so wish. I could best effect that concealment, significantly, by refusing to talk to you – lying would be another option, but that raises other, moral, issues, to which we must

shortly come. But then concealment runs counter to the essentially
intersubjective, communal structuring of conscious beings at the personal level – and the revelation of this intersubjective, social structure of
personhood is perhaps the major contribution of the new movement in
science – as it also counteracts the highest prospects of persons-in-
communion reaching the highest goals afforded them in the universe as
we know it.

This endemic intersubjectivity of the process by which humans know
and express what they know of reality was one of Husserl's central
themes: we saw it summarised by Sartre in the words 'whether I
consider this table or this tree or this bare wall in solitude or with
companions, the Other is always there as a layer of constitutive meanings which belong to the very object which I consider; in short, he is the
veritable guarantee of the object's objectivity'. (Interesting, is it not, that
a profound insight can find sufficient support in a sophisticated monism,
a support which is entirely absent in a crude dualism?) The reference to
objectivity is easily understood. The other person of which I am directly
conscious, since it is itself a conscious entity that transcends all current
content of consciousness, and shows itself to be such in the constant and
characteristic signifyings in which it engages, cannot even be imagined
by me to be no more than a subjective image or idea of my mind. It is the
primary 'object' of my awareness which of its nature resists any subjectivist, solipsistic reduction. Just as a good deal of philosophical anthropology is doomed to failure by the presence of dichotomously distinct, if
not contrary, notions of mind and matter, so a good deal of epistemology is doomed by similar distinctions and oppositions between subjectivity and objectivity. These also are in reality correlates rather than
contraries. All knowledge is both subjective and objective; and the
relevant task of epistemology is to investigate the ratios and respects in
which it is both.

I know the other person to be, and I know what it is, and never from
the time I was born could I confuse it with any *thing* else; and I am
inextricably co-involved with it in all the investigation and expression of
that relationship itself and of our common world which I shall ever
achieve. But it is the exponentially increased creativity of our knowledge
of reality and of our expressions of this, rather than the issue of the
objectivity of knowledge acquired and expressed, that must be brought
into focus as one continues to outline this scientific account of the
human person's attributes, this time as artist. The process in which I
gradually and increasingly come to know reality, in which I am increas-

ingly informed by the ever developing forms of the fabric of reality, is also the process in which, through the transcendence of my kind of consciousness of reality, I continually re-form received impressions of it. This yields both Deutsch's deeper and more extensive explanatory hypotheses on which science proceeds; and it also yields the activities characteristic of persons as artisans and artists – quite naturally envisioning reality, in the promises held out by its own evolving forms, as it might yet be and might be made to be. It is this process which is exponentially increased by the intersubjective or social structure of personhood. Not merely in the case of infants being taught a verbal language and thus rapidly gaining access to vast accumulations of formulated knowledge and creative vision, but in the case of communities of scientists, philosophers, artisans, poets, writers and other artists, and indeed the whole community of the race; for this intersubjective dimension of personhood is co-extensive with (at least) the race, the species-being of Marx and Feuerbach. Consciousness, then, at this level of persons, is not, as Sartre's crude dualistic distinctions between For-itself and In-itself suggested, a nothingness into which all formed meaning continuously disappears; but rather the dynamic intersubjective matrix within which meaning is at once received, exchanged and continuously created. And that characteristic of human language in which its terms are continuously modified without closure and without limit is not due, as Derrida suggests, to differences between terms which act as simple negations of each other – with the result, again as in Sartre, of meaning forever escaping towards nothingness. It is due, rather, to the positive and continuous creativity with which persons-in-communion receive and deploy their knowledge of reality.

Finally, the moral attributes of persons come clear from the Intersubjective First position. To see this it is necessary only to concentrate once more on the (e)motive features of human life. We are, as Heidegger rightly observed, little projects thrown into a world of projects, everyone and everything driven towards its own developmental goals (the Platonic Eros, in short); in our case the goal consists in the kind of life we live and that life ever more abundant. Further, the whole pullulating world of entities and their eventful interactions, from the very first moment and through the whole course of our interaction with it, in the course of informing us incessantly and increasingly of its own dynamic forms, formations and reformations, exercises upon us various forces of attraction and repulsion. And as active engagement with reality is confirmed as the prime and permanent matrix and source of all our knowledge of it, simultaneously the emotive is found to be inextricably intertwined with the motive force of the native Eros. The primacy and pervasiveness of motive and emotion which the new movement so clearly reveals in human life's beginnings continues throughout the whole life of the person – in actual fact, the range and power of emotion, too, is increased by the acquisition of a language.

Add, then, the primacy of the intersubjective dimension in this co-inherence of knowing and interactive engagement; realise once more that the other person is the first 'object' of interactive awareness, and thereafter persistently involved in it; and the lineaments of an adequate definition of moral agency and of morality in general are already in place. For if a conscious entity at this personal level engages in motivated (inter)action that has an element of creativity in it (a self-transcending conscious entity is not only informed by the evolving formations of reality; it can also envisage further interactive formations originating in itself); and if its primary and permanent interactive partnership is with other persons throughout the whole course of its knowledgeable interaction with reality, thus increasing creativity exponentially; then there is access to as adequate and defensible an account of morality as could be formulated in a short sentence. Morality consists in an informed, active and creative responsiveness to other persons, and through and with these to the whole evolving fabric of reality.[27] But it is sufficient to note at this point the way in which the Intersubjective First position in developmental psychology offers an explanation and secures an understanding of morality (and of art also) as a native property of persons and, in so far as personal beings are creatively and increasingly involved in the whole fabric of reality, secures also a growing understanding of that evolving, continuously created reality as itself a moral process – a growing understanding which should be increasingly important to ecologists.

The assessment of this contemporary advance in science, and in particular of its possible contribution to a more adequate philosophy for this time, can begin with an endorsement of the claims made by its principal protagonist, Colwyn Trevarthen. For although his claims are extensive – as Deutsch's were for his version of a Theory of Everything – they do appear to be justified. He claims that the Intersubjective First

---

[27] The Intersubjective First position gives a demonstrably better account of the nature of morality than that which derives more directly from the Subjective First position which is so endemic in Kantian-type dualism, and which thinks of morality in terms of freedom to obey, or not to obey, internal or internalised, but in any case already formulated, laws – the legal(ist) model of morality, as it is called. And it also succeeds better than Macmurray and Levinas, because its personalist approach is more sophisticated and less dualistic than theirs.

approach, and its increasing crop of impressive results, explains and
enables us to understand ever better not just the human psyche, brain
and central nervous system, but the origin of language, the nature of
morality, the world of science and technology and of international
economy, politics, law and social institutions of many kinds.

Instead of asking what developing cognition gives to human purposes, we can
ask what effect innate human communicative competence has on learning,
imitation, or instinctive growth of a *language acquisition device*, we can ask in what
ways language enriches the infant's already competent non-verbal, pre-seman-
tic expressions of alert purposiveness and human-sensing emotion, and why the
adult finds this rewarding. We can begin to understand what it is that gives our
actions moral value, and our words metaphorical meanings with infinite future
significance and narrative power. We can develop a theory of how natural
motives for cooperation in gaining sense of the world and performing
cooperative tasks can lead to scientific, technical and economic activities in our
elaborately organised and institutionalised adult society, with its politics and
laws.[28]

Is the absence of religion from this list of human activities and
institutions significant? Does the assessment of this scientific movement
include any prospect for a theological dimension to the more adequate
philosophy it undoubtedly facilitates? Trevarthen at times refers to
philosophies of religious experience when seeking to show that a primacy of intersubjectivity, though absent in a still dominant classical
psychology, is adopted and promoted to good and wide-ranging effect
elsewhere. 'The concept of intersubjectivity has a natural place in
certain philosophical debates on the social context of human consciousness of reality, especially those concerned with moral and religious
impulses', he writes.[29] 'A different conception of human consciousness,
exhibiting affinity with some philosophies of religious experience, perceives interpersonal awareness, cooperative action in society and cultural learning as manifestations of innate motives for sympathy in
purpose, interests and feelings.'[30] However, even though, as we have so
often seen, these persistent references to identifiable theological themes
raise suspicions that theology does in fact continue to have something to
say to the matter in hand, so that one suspects it is a better theology that
is required, rather than none at all, there is far too little to go on, in the
case of Trevarthen's references to philosophies of religious experience,
than would enable us to make an assessment for greater or lesser

[28] Trevarthen, 'The Concept and Foundation of Infant Intersubjectivity', p. 2.
[29] Ibid. p. 1. [30] Trevarthen, 'Intersubjectivity', *MIT Encyclopedia.*

prospects for theology than we have so far seen. No more need be implied in Trevarthen's remarks than might be allowed by Marx, for instance; namely, that some theologies got some features of the fabric of reality right – in this case a certain primacy of intersubjectivity – but then mistakenly thought they were talking about divine and human reality, rather than the human only.

Yet an assessment can be made of the prospects for a theological dimension to philosophy, whether greater or lesser, as a result of the distinctive contributions of the current psychobiology. It can be made by critically appreciative recipients as much as by proponents; and it can best be made in the context of the present essay by asking what the current psychobiology adds to the picture of the fabric of reality painted by David Deutsch. Deutsch's picture left some prospects for theological investigations. Have these been strengthened or weakened?

Much of the meaning-in-use of key terms such as knowledge, intelligence, consciousness coincides with Deutsch's while being fleshed out in ways that should command consent. Thus intelligence occurs at the stage and level of consciousness at which it is constituted as a reflective awareness (or knowledge) of its own contents and of itself. This feature of 'bent back over' transcendence of all its present content allows it to project itself in a limitless fashion onto all actual and possible ranges of reality. And to do this in a mixture of imagination (hypothesis) and creative engagement with reality. At the animal level there is a consciousness, awareness, knowledge of reality and of its affordances, of which other animals are part. Elements and features of this reality can be expressed, indicated, signed. But though the signs are used and effective in stimulating response, the animals are not aware that 'signing' is what they are doing. Hence they cannot converse, cannot invent and use a language; and they are correspondingly not self-conscious in the reflective sense that constitutes intelligence proper. They can properly be said to have and to deploy knowledge; but only in a reductive or analogical sense should they be said to be intelligent. At the 'lower' biological levels (and the physical), where we have no evidence(?) of consciousness, we can say that there is a process of forming, informing and reforming going on which makes the whole reality process highly intelligible to us (and rather more locally known to animals); so we can conceive of reality at this level not only interacting with us but 'informing' our minds, and passing on 'information' within itself. We can then talk about knowledge at this level, but apparently, once again, only in an analogous or reductive sense.

Now, what the most advanced developmental psychology does is to highlight and prioritise in this account of intelligence – and hence of personhood, subjecthood, selfhood: epithets properly applied to intelligent beings – an element which is mentioned above but is scarcely visible or operative in further deployments of this kind of argument.

This is the element of reflective consciousness. It is the consciousness (of) consciousness which we know occurs at this reflective level. It is that which Sartre identified; but then Sartre, on the basis of naming it the prereflective Cogito, mistakenly described it as a separate region of being. For in our case and from our worm's-eye point of view, from the only point of view we can occupy, it only occurs in the process of reflection upon the empirical (contents of) consciousness. Which Sartre rightly, if incongruously, admitted when he said that the prereflective Cogito needed the reflective or thetic, positional consciousness in order to exist – and then went through the contortions of explaining that it existed by nihilating the latter, and so on. Not that we can say with any certainty that such a consciousness does not exist in separation (in the misleading meaning of transcendence) from empirical, embedded consciousness. But if and while it does so exist, we do not know it. Yet this reflective consciousness, consciousness of a self that perdures (*pace* Hume) through all the vagaries of an ever transcended empirical consciousness, does occur in our case, still more transcendent than, if always utterly immanent in, the latter. And it is the source – here is the prioritising – of that transcendence of consciousness as a whole which raises it to the intelligent, personal level which we actually experience.

Furthermore, this especially transcendent consciousness, or factor or element within consciousness as we directly know it, always occurs in contact with another such similarly transcendent and driven consciousness. There might be question here of a virtual other; but virtual connotes what is possible and could be generated and made real. And in all our experience this intrinsic and apparently constitutive contact is with real others, of indeterminate number and kind. This defining insight of the Intersubjective First position means that the experience of a driven, immanent transcendence is reduplicated, as Levinas's exposition of our experience in face of the other so well explained. Indeed it is reduplicated and intensified in a limitlessly extended fashion, for it is intrinsically indifferent to the issue of the number and status of actual and possible other subjects. It is in some way in its common world in contact with (traces of) them all. Feuerbach's exposition of this feature of the Intersubjective First position yielded his talk of the limitless dimensions and prospects of the species-being of humanity, together with the suspicion that this now approached the status of divinity; a suspicion that much in Marxist ideas of humanity as true creator of itself and its world served only to solidify. For, before we come to the creation issue as such, the sheer mystery of this intrinsic encounter of subjects, to apparently limitless extent, urges us to ask: What could it be, what further level of universally transcendent, yet utterly immanent, consciousness could come to light that would explain this inherently com-m*unity* status of an entity of such inherently limitless range, which the Intersubjectivity-First position presents? The question was put to Hegel; and it is answered by him in terms of the Spirit that is absolutely transcendent while remaining immanent in the whole of reality, and particularly in all finite subjects who gradually make their way towards their birthright participation in it.

But finally it must come to the creation issue, for it is on this issue that the Intersubjective First position is most crucial to Deutsch's metaphysics. In simple terms, the Intersubjective First position which privileges the transcendent consciousness over the empirical can better explain the continuous creativity which characterises the inherently evolving universe that we know. In the Subjective First position characteristic of Enlightenment philosophy and psychology, the empirical consciousness, with its system of idea-contents, was privileged over the more transcendent consciousness; the latter then playing little more part than that of providing the unity in the system attributable to any apperceptive ego. And that, both at the microcosmic level of moral action in the world, and at the cosmic level at which a divine creator could be envisaged, yielded ideas of a mechanistic universe governed by immutable laws. And it yielded also an individual morality which consisted in imposition and acceptance of equally immutable divine precepts. This Subjective First position left an ever diminishing place for either a cosmic creator of any continuing effectiveness, or for genuine initiative, creativity and hence moral responsibility on the part of individual subjects within that cosmos. Correspondingly, when Deutsch was accused of modelling his quantum-computer–creator of (virtual) reality upon a Judeo-Christian (male) enlightenment type of divinity, it was this particular version of a Logos-type divinity which his accusers had in mind: a mind-container of a system of exemplar ideas unified by the apperceptive ego of the mind whose ideas they were.

The validity of that criticism is interestingly illustrated when Deutsch imagines our much-evolved successors at the end time re-creating us for eternal life. If they had enough relevant information about our world, he says, they could certainly do so. But on this kind of account of the matter – minds informed of an idea-system representing what we were – what kind of creatures would we then be? No more than just programs running on someone else's computer? Certainly not the kind of creatures in which knowledge of the world, like all knowledge in the world, is simultaneously acquired and applied through creative engagement-agency in and with it. For it would take an intelligent agency character-ised by the primacy and predominance of the most transcendent con-sciousness to create, re-create or generate creatures like ourselves, endowed with the free creativity of true moral agency, and to create the world of which we are so obviously and increasingly co-creators. This kind of criticism of Deutsch and his fellow quantum-computer cosmolo-gists is accepted to this extent, then, that he himself did not develop his analysis and understanding of human intelligent being and agency to the point to which the Intersubjectivity First position developed it; and that that development is necessary in order to give intelligent agency the cosmic role in an evolutionary, or continuously creative, universe that is the only kind we know to exist.

Last, is the other point of the criticism levelled at Deutsch's kind of (meta)physics also endorsed? The point, namely, of the likeness to divinity of his intelligently produced universal (virtual-)reality gener-ator? That depends in part on the perceived strength of the argument, already presented, to the effect that this universal virtual-reality gener-ator, which Deutsch envisages our much-evolved successors developing in the dying seconds of this universe, must have existed before the human race existed. Or, if we are deprived by quantum physics of the linear-flow image of time, the argument that it must exist far and away beyond purely human agency. If that argument has force – and it certainly enjoys a great deal of support from Deutsch's own principles and assertions – then the creation of eternal life in which our successors could possibly engage, but transposed now to the categories of the Intersubjective First position, could of course serve as an analogue for that more original creation of our world and ourselves in which it would then be seen to participate as fully as this is possible for derivative beings.

Then we should indeed be in the position of gaining an insight, courtesy of the analogical imagination, into the absolutely transcendent, though utterly immanent, creative agency which accounts for the emergence of reality as a whole. By the reverse dynamism of the image which derivative creators of end-time eternal life project, we might then have an image of the original creator of all. Then too we might have a better understanding of that mysterious comm*unity* feature of Intersubjectivity, courtesy of the predominance within intersubjective consciousness of the most transcendent consciousness. An inkling perhaps of our predominantly transcendent consciousnesses participating in the most universally transcendent consciousness (like Hegel's Spirit), which is ever immanent in all of those transcendent–empirical consciousnesses that, after all, creatively derive from it, as does all else that exists.

Then, finally, Trevarthen's references to theological or religious themes as those which clearly illustrate the Intersubjectivity First position and its furthest consequences, could be seen to be the result of a real analogy of being, rather than the outcome of some accidental similarities with the products of an overheated religious imagination. But any or all of this would be far too strong a set of conclusions to draw at the end of a long historical–critical account of the origins of (post)modernity. It, or any of it, could only emerge, if at all, from the more systematic analysis in the critical–constructive part of this essay, which seeks to build upon the best insights of past philosophy and present science.

PART TWO

Critical–constructive

Prologue

The prologue to Part One ended with the prospect held out of wedding the best of what postmodernism has inherited and promoted to the best that current scientific questers after truth have found, so as to come to as clear a view as possible of the nature, function and truth value, in short, of the prospects of theology today; for that is the end goal of this essay.

Now, of course postmodernism inherited a great deal that is good. The product of an eventual coming together of the two main streams of modern philosophy, the phenomenological and the 'Marxist', it inherited the best features, as well as the worst, of its parents. And as for that which postmodernism itself then distinctively promotes, there is also in this respect much that is good, and some that is bad. Indubitably the best example of the worst that postmodernism has distinctively produced is found in that scene from Derrida in which writing (like knowledge, and language, its bearer) is stranded between a 'disappeared' subject and a 'disappeared' reality. This left language as a play of signifiers amongst themselves, with a simple mutual negating, or what Sartre called nihilating, dominating the relationships between these ever dominant signifiers. So that meaning was permanently deconstructed, and truth infinitely postponed.

However, beneath this kind of excess, and when the mistake that led to it has been unmasked, there is visible a feature of postmodernism, in the form of its proposals concerning knowledge and language, which resonates particularly with our current and predominantly evolutionary experience of our world; and which lends to postmodernism a value that can surely survive the increasingly cliched use of its terms and the mindless name-dropping which characterise its overpopularity amongst the general literati and the media commentators of the age. This feature of knowledge and of language can be said to consist in its continual reconstruction; provided only that one realises that reconstruction always involves deconstruction also. But the deconstruction is now, like

Hegel's 'patient labour of the negative' in the evolution of Spirit-Reality to its absolute status, a necessary part of the evolution of other, if not always better, species of being. Something is deconstructed in the process of reconstruction, provided the negative effects of the deconstruction can themselves be negated so that something creatively new comes out of the process – corresponding to Hegel's own account of this dialectic of reality in terms of the stages of that process: affirmation, negation, negation of the negation. This is something that the scientist sees in every instance of evolution; when the first negative effects of a mutation in a hitherto stable species are in turn overcome by the adaptation of that very mutation in the course of those positive adaptation processes that continue to predominate.

The reason why this is no transient account of the nature of knowledge and of language, its bearer, is because knowledge is perpetually applied and achieved by creative interaction of all knowledge-bearing agents in and with the evolving universe. In this respect one sees once more the coming together of the main evolutionary phenomenology, refined and authoritatively defined by modern scientists, with the practicalist understanding of knowledge of which the 'Marxist' tradition has been the dominant representative. And one understands how truth itself is a gradual acquisition, and one also appreciates the fact that final truth, if and when such is achieved, cannot take the form of a comprehensive and perfect idea system either already possessed or eventually achievable by some subject – for such is the claim and the darling of all would-be dictators, civic or ecclesiastical.

Correspondingly, it is not the case that one must discuss the nature, function and prospects for theology today in a postmodern context from which the very presence and possibility of theology has already been made to disappear. Gods and godlike agents, explicitly so named, have continued to haunt philosophical discourse from Descartes to the present day, and that includes the discourse of the most recent postmodernists and the most contemporary scientist-metaphysicians. God was clearly in evidence from Descartes to Hegel, and evident in the different theological portraits, and in combinations of these, already painted in the course of the long Christian tradition of the West. But even after Hegel, when for the first time in the history of the West gods were either ostentatiously routed, or given notice to quit, or simply declared absent, they still continued to haunt philosophical discourse, and those that did so looked still suspiciously like the portraits painted when they were deemed present. Furthermore they continued to haunt the discourse in such a way as to direct its development with almost as much efficacy as if they were still deemed to be alive and present. So that the discourse is still to that extent theological, or at least such as to require the admixture of theological analysis and argument in order to secure its results.

Feuerbach's powerful exposition of the infinite nature of the consciousness manifest in and as the defining feature of the human species being, looked alarmingly like the Christian creator God, and indeed was intended to do so. Marx therefore complained that Feuerbach was really reintroducing such a divinity, but since Marx thought that anything called divinity had to be transcendent in the crude separate, 'squatting beyond the world', sense of that word, his criticism took the form of accusing Feuerbach of leaving us with a creative humanity squatting outside the real world of praxis and historical process. But that left the question as to whether or not the human species being, which for Marx was the ultimate creator in and of the world as its extended body, was any less like the Christian creator for being entirely immanent in that same world, and whether, therefore, the much trumpeted replacement of the Christian creator was very much more successful. Deutsch's Omega-point humans, creators of eternal life, like other quantum-computer construction of evolving universes, have had their likeness to the Judeo-Christian creator God duly noted by commentators from the more erudite and philosophically minded members of the scientific community. As has indeed even Dawkins's gene, that rigorously rational and purposeful agent, continuously creating the universe we know in all of its most significant evolving features, from all the affordances of its matter, and with the goal in view of its own indefinite survival.

Sartre has a prereflective Cogito, which he calls an absolute, belonging to a separate region of being from the empirical world, and resembling nothing so much as the traditional Aristotelian or better, the Neoplatonic One, utterly inconceivable because devoid in its own proper being of any determinate mental content. Foucault's *The Order of Things* positively invites those who finish reading it to cry: 'Author, author' and to anticipate the appearance of 'the Last and Absolute Subject left to face his subjecthood in the face of an otherwise subjectless terrain, ever captive to a mirror of solipsism'. The eradication of such otherworldly subjects, these *Geistdingen* that occur through 'Cartesian' influence in writers like Husserl also, Heidegger set as a guiding aim of his philosophy, and there is no doubt about the fact that, as a result, the subsequently embedded humanity in the overwhelming 'worlding' in and of the world itself bears little resemblance to the creative power and place of knowledge-bearers in our world, even as Deutsch's more modest accounts describe these; and that it is in any case but poorly balanced by ambiguous references to gods/divinity operative in the course of that 'worlding'. The sheer determination to get rid of traditional intelligent creators, and the fear of the return of immanent doppelgangers, undoubtedly shapes this unsatisfactory result. Similarly Derrida's determination to rid us of Logocentricism, the understanding of reality as the creation of a Logos source-container of a comprehensive system of exemplar ideas (since that was the only model of creative knowledge or intelligence he worked with), inevitably drove him to a philosophy from which all constructive meaning and real, even if partial, truth was indefinitely postponed. In Levinas also, if we look at this matter from a slightly different angle, we can sense that the passivity-beyond-passivity could only support personhood and yet achieve the metaphysical generality and originality it enjoys in his analysis, if some infinite subject were creative in all the universe and to a degree passive in its responsibility for that very process; so that it is no longer described, as God is described in his few direct references, in purely negative terms. In short, his systematic analysis of reality requires for cohesion and conviction a Subject operative at the requisite level of metaphysical originality and universality; and we are once again in the presence of an absence, whether assumed or declared, which explains a relative failure.

There is no need to go further in rehearsing such features of the history of thought in Part One in order to secure the point that theology – the *logos* of *theos* – had never gone away; and that the task of investigating the nature, function and prospects of theology today is one that must take the form of revision rather than reinstatement. Now, the whole thrust of the development of modern philosophy to the present day, and of the coming together of its tributary sources, has conspired to set the initial focus on the cosmic agency attributable to humanity. Humanism, atheistic or at least agnostic, has come to provide the most prevailing climate of philosophical thought. The initial investigative focus in a constructive–critical part, therefore, should be on the creative role of humanity in the evolution or continuous creation of the universe. And since creativity at the human level is, as we must see, the essence of what is called morality, the first area of investigation is morality. As an apparently and increasingly pivotal part of the evolution of the universe, human moral behaviour must raise two related questions: first, the question of the objectivity of what is called moral value in the universe, as part of the very fabric of reality, and, second, the extent to which the fabric of reality may be deemed to be itself a moral process. These two questions and the investigation that they initiate may be succinctly indexed under the title 'Morality and Metaphysics'. The second of these questions is really a question concerning what is revealed to us in the course of our (moral) interaction with reality; whether, for instance, there is revealed a moral agency more original and comprehensive than ours alone; so that we should be, to ourselves at least, a paradigm of such creative agency always already operative in the universe, much as was argued should be the case in Deutsch's metaphysics. Since much of the most recent moral philosophy invokes art as source of a sense of an objectivity of moral value that transcends our individual or communal human interests; since the artist is the visionary who sees with particular power and penetration what is being unveiled from the greater depths and ranges of reality itself, the further pursuit of that second question can be succinctly suggested in the title 'Art and the Role of Revelation'. Finally, before one can come to a conclusion, whatever it is of the nature of creative agency that is deemed to be revealed from the greatest depths and most comprehensive ranges of reality itself must be compared with the definitive theological conceptions, mainly the ideas of revealed gods, of some impressive religious traditions. In this way a further critical revision can be accomplished of the portraits of divinity which are still operative, in continuity with those whose explicit or implicit presence, or indeed whose declared or enforced absence, so influenced modern philosophy and contemporary (meta)physics.

CHAPTER 4

Morality and metaphysics

Modern philosophy from its inception with Descartes has been characterised by a dominant interest in knowledge itself, in epistemology, phenomenology, semiology, linguistic analysis. An adequate theory of the nature of knowledge and of its role in the continuously creative fabric of reality must understand and explain the knower and the known, for it is by their interaction that knowledge is produced, if not constituted. This insight points towards pragmatism in general or the practicalist theory of knowledge. And it simultaneously suggests a moral dimension to all knowing (and a corresponding cognitivist–realist dimension to all moral valuing). This is certainly so in so far as some of the interactive agents involved are capable of some creativity, and hence some degree of freedom from strict determinacy. But such freedom from strict determinacy is precisely what the theory of emergence guarantees. Provided only that emergence is properly evidenced, as increasingly it appears to be, and that it is fully outlined and understood, so that it coincides with the key evolutionary concept of continuous mutual adaptation of individuals, of species, and of the different defined levels in the fabric of reality.

Emergence was defined above in terms of aspects or features which 'emerge' at certain levels of the continuous fabric of reality, and which then can be seen to exercise a non-derivative influence upon other levels. The purpose of the adjective non-derivative is to protect the full implications of the idea of emergence from reductionist–imperialist moves by any particular discipline when dealing with its own chosen and abstracted elements or aspects of reality. More positively put, features which emerge in one analytically abstracted area of the elements, processes and aspects that make up the continuous fabric of reality, are found to wield an influence in other areas. Yet the emergence of the features in question could not be accounted for, fully or causally, by simple straightforward reference to features found in any of these other areas. In other words, instead of a linear, unidirectional influence between elements and processes operative between levels or areas of reality – of the kind that allow for reductionist–imperialist claims – everywhere reciprocal influence is at work. Such that the phenomena to be explained always require for adequacy accounts which can accommodate two-directional, if not multi-directional, influences. Unsurprisingly, the best model for this fully understood idea of emergence is that process of mutual adaptation which the study of evolution shows to hold both in the microcosm of individual mutations and in the macrocosm of interacting species or 'levels' of reality (physical, chemical, biological, psychological, sociobiological and so on).

The way forward from this point must, then, be through an investigation of the nature of morality and of its role in evolving, continuously creative reality. An investigation which should reveal the extent of moral agency in the universe; and in this way lead to the further investigation of the prospects of a religious dimension to it, depending upon some perceived depth and comprehensiveness of moral agency in the universe as a whole.[1]

---

[1] Colwyn Trevarthen, having read the first draft of this essay, lent me Frederick Turner's *Rebirth of Value* (Albany: State University of New York Press, 1991), and I was intrigued to find that Turner had plotted a similar path, though it took him through different disciplines, like literature, aesthetics, ecology, education. Already in the introduction Turner is pointing out that 'Everywhere the nonlinear, reflexive, iterative, self-organising, dissipative, period-doubling, turbulent, open-ended, or fractal systems that are associated with feedback have appeared at the heart of nature's mysteries.' 'Evolution now appears to be central not only to the content and form of knowledge, but also to its growth and development. A new evolutionary epistemology and dialectic of discourse seems to be coming into focus. Between single absolutist hegemonic worldviews, which generate a certainty of truth at the expense of its richness and variety, and relativist and pluralist worldviews, whose claim to certainty is so diffident that it enfeebles and thus corrupts and trivialises the mind that entertains them, we see appear an evolving ecology of worldviews, competing or cooperating, but always tending towards the production of more comprehensive and thus concrete ideas.' 'The new scientific view of the universe is that it is a living machine: an organic mechanism which generates and is nurtured by freedom, creativity, and self-transcendence – and which may, as we do, have a wholeness that is greater than the sum of its parts, a Soul which has been the inner goal of all religions.' He even takes time in the same introduction, in parentheses, to put Derrida in his place: 'On the level of literary critical theory this insight would correspond to a rejection of any naïve doconstruction that reduced a text to a hot soup of traces, of "differances", to use Derrida's wordplay: what is of far more significance is that those differences collapse together into meanings that make possible further meanings and further meanings still, in an evolutionary ecology of meaning which does not merely erase but subsumes its predecessors.'

MORAL REALISM
THE OBJECTIVITY OF MORAL VALUE IN THE FABRIC OF
REALITY IN FACE OF THE FACT–VALUE DICHOTOMY

There are, then, two sides to the philosophical coinage that is being proffered for analysis and assessment under the description 'Morality and Metaphysics'. On the one side of it, the investigation must arrive at a view of moral discourse as referring to reality; on the other side, it must appear in the course of the investigation that reality, to some extent at least, is itself a moral enterprise. It is best to begin this phase of the investigation by attending first to moral discourse, if only as a means of giving Anglophone philosophy, and particularly its still dominant Analytic tradition, a degree of attention in some reasonable ratio to the degree of attention accorded to Continental traditions of philosophy in Part One. For Anglophone philosophy has contributed the lion's share of moral philosophy in this century. In addition, despite a continuing indebtedness to Hume in many instances, it is now responsible for many important and promising insights into the relationship between morality and metaphysics.

At the beginning of this century moral philosophy in Britain, and indeed most Anglophone moral philosophy, underwent what proved to be the sustained influence of G. E. Moore's *Principia Ethica*. According to Moore's central thesis the primary moral term, good, cannot be defined either in terms of a natural object or in terms of a non-natural object. The latter referred, apparently, to those objects which philosophers of a metaphysical turn of mind were wont to talk about. Good, Moore said, was indefinable; and any who would attempt to define it in either set of terms would incur the naturalist fallacy. It is not quite clear what Moore meant by defining the term good; nor is it clear what 'naturalistic' connotes if the fallacy so named is committed by defining 'good' in terms of non-natural objects. But despite such confusion concerning pivotal ideas in Moore's argument, the crucial conviction does emerge: some things possess intrinsically this indefinable characteristic or property called good, and we can certainly recognise these, and so recognise good. Some examples of such things: 'No one probably, who has asked himself the question, has ever doubted that personal affection and the appreciation of what is beautiful in Art or Nature, are good in themselves.'[2] Furthermore, because we can recognise good, though we may

---

[2] G. E. Moore, *Principia Ethica* (Oxford University Press, 1903), p. 188.

not define it, we can also calculate which acts of ours are best designed to bring it about and in what measure they may do so. We are thus capable of deciding what we ought to do, and a second key idea in moral philosophy, the idea of moral obligation, falls into place.

Whether or not it follows logically that, good being indefinable, ought is also indefinable, that conclusion was in fact subsequently drawn by H. A. Prichard, who may be included with Moore in the general ranks of intuitionists in ethics. Ought, he said, or the quality of being a duty, is not definable in terms of any thing or any (other) characteristic of any thing. And when W. D. Ross said something quite similar about right or rightness, it seemed as if the central ethical vocabulary was all to be included in the embargo on definition. This state of the vocabulary of moral philosophy changed little, if at all, with the advent of Linguistic Analysis. When Ayer divided all genuine propositions, into two classes, the main ethical propositions in which we attempt to say what is good or what we ought to do, did not seem to fit easily into either of them. Ayer himself appeared to adopt one of the more elementary emotivist theories of ethics. Ethical judgements, on this view, combine an expression of personal feeling with an exhortation – or at least they can be so interpreted once their occasional density is properly, linguistically, unpacked. It follows that, although that part of the moral judgement which contained at least an implied reference to actual feelings could be included in Ayer's second class – of propositions concerning empirical matters of fact – the properly ethical element in the judgement could not. Hence the properly ethical element continued in its status of being indefinable in terms of natural objects and their natural properties. And since metaphysics for Ayer was, strictly speaking, nonsense, neither could the moral term good be defined in terms of the metaphysician's non-natural objects. As Ayer himself put it, statements concerning moral values are 'simply expressions of emotion which are neither true nor false'; or 'the only information we can legitimately derive from the study of our aesthetic and moral experiences is information about our own mental and physical make-up'.[3]

The more developed forms of the emotivist theory of ethics did not interrupt the continuance of the central conviction classically expressed by Moore. When Stevenson, for example, added that emotive ethical language produces, as well as expresses, feeling, and by doing so is influential upon others in their choice of behaviour, as indeed it is meant

---

[3] See Ayer's 'Critique of Ethics and Theology', in Geoffrey Sayre-McCord (ed.), *Essays on Moral Realism* (Ithaca, NY: Cornell University Press, 1988), p. 35.

to be, we are no further from non-naturalism than Ayer had left us. It is even possible for Mary Warnock to include representative American pragmatists, as influences upon Stevenson, within this uninterrupted saga of non-naturalism in ethical theory. Dewey is quoted as follows: 'Moral science is not something with a separate province. It is physical, biological and historic knowledge placed in a human context where it will illuminate and guide the activities of men.' Now, although the first impression here may be the polar opposite of non-naturalism, it is possible to interpret the 'human context where it will guide activities' in emotivist terms and to imply, then, as Stevenson and other emotivists did, that the properly ethical element in all ethical judgement is still indefinable in naturalistic terms. (It is possible, but whether it is persuasive is another matter.) All naturalistic descriptions of the activities of persons, from physical, biological and historical knowledge, would still, it was argued, leave open the question: Ought I to perform these? Or are these good or productive of good?[4]

The upshot of this development in any case must surely be a substantial degree of uncertainty concerning the referential status of key moral terms, in particular the good, and a corresponding uncertainty concerning the ontic status of whatever it is to which these might refer. The good in Moore's classical statement of an essentially Humean position – and this would seem to apply to cognate moral terms and to their negative correlates, such as evil and so on – would seem to refer to certain characteristics or features of real things. For Moore does, after all, speak of things which are 'good in themselves', and that should certainly suggest a bespoke realism of some kind in moral discourse. That the examples of things which he asks us to agree are undoubtedly good in themselves is not crucial at this point. Personal affection or love is seldom missing from a list of such examples, though it may not be clear whether it is beauty in art or nature that is good in itself, or our appreciation of this. What is crucial is that good does apparently refer to some real characteristics of the fabric of reality which we recognise rather than construe in some quite subjective fashion. Only we are warned not to define the term. And that seems to mean that we are not to act as if its connotation were coterminous with that of any other term or set of terms which referred to natural entities, or with any term or set of terms which referred to those entities of the kind that traditional Western metaphysicians talked about, and in particular the Supreme Being, God.

---

[4] For a much fuller analysis of the whole development of Anglophone moral philosophy in this century, see Mary Warnock, *Ethics since 1900* (Oxford University Press, 1978).

Now, the question as to whether traditional metaphysics had committed the naturalistic fallacy in this particular manner is quite a complex one and cannot be answered satisfactorily here. Certainly Plato had included in the *Republic* (508d–509e) the view that the Good is the cause of knowledge and of truth. Yet when telling the story of creation in the *Timaeus* (29d–30a), for instance, the impression given is that the Creator God (*demiourgos*) is good, certainly, but striving to realise a level of goodness which is not simply identifiable with the creator's own being. The creator strives to make everything as good as can be. The impression is given, then, that the creator looks to an ideal (Form) of goodness, and is good in being and so doing. Later in the developing Platonic tradition after Plato, when the Forms came to be established as Idea(l)s in the divine mind, and the Good emerged, in line with hints in Plato's dialogues, as the highest of the Forms (though occasionally challenged by Beauty for this position), the tendency to use the term the Good synonymously with God inevitably increased, until the terms became virtually interchangeable with Plotinus and Neoplatonism: Plotinus' Ennead vi, 9, is entitled 'On the Good, or the One'. And yet in the Ninth Tractate of the Sixth Ennead, Plotinus virtually repeats Plato's 'beyond being – *epekeina tes ousias*' formula. Writing now of the One, he says it 'is no being but precedent to all Being', and 'it cannot be a being' (vi, 9.3). In the same tractate, although he may at one point say bluntly of the One, 'This is the Good', he is soon careful to explain that the Good is not therefore defined as the One. 'This Principle (the One) is not, therefore, to be identified with the good of which it is the source; it is good in the unique mode of being the Good above all that is good' (vi, 9.6).[5] Clearly the good(ness) of the One is as much beyond human power to define as is the Supreme One itself, if only because it is the ultimate source of all that is good, that is to say, of all that responds to our real needs ('whatever may be said to be in need is needing a good', vi, 9.6). Such finite good as this latter we may of course recognise and at the very least denote. The Good that is the One we may also hope to encounter at the end of a journey which takes the form of a pilgrim's progress through the inscape of the soul. But that supreme good we cannot by definition define; not least because, as has been said already, it is not a being amongst others or in addition to other (de)finite and hence definable entities.

It seems fair to say, then, that the more sophisticated proponents of traditional Western metaphysics did not commit Moore's naturalistic fallacy by defining good in terms of non-natural objects. Good, to them

[5] I use Stephen McKenna's translation of *The Enneads*, edited and introduced by John Dillon (London: Penguin, 1991).

as to Moore, certainly referred to a characteristic or feature of reality, both natural and, as they no doubt would prefer to say, supernatural realities; and to both together only by highly sophisticated uses of language which require the simultaneous application of the 'three ways'. These are the way of analogy, the way of eminence and the way of negation. Good, or any other predicate of divinity, is applied only in a highly analogous manner, and its connotation is then so eminently beyond the connotation of the same predicate when applied to finite entities, that a simple denial of the predicate in the case of divinity would prove a necessary step on the journey to the final truth of the matter. Of course there were less sophisticated exponents and more simple re-ceivers of this metaphysical tradition, for whom the divinity did appear as a being in addition to all other beings, and who – or whose will at least – was uniquely, if not exclusively, defined as the good. On such lower levels of the Christianised Platonism of the West, not only was Moore's naturalistic fallacy committed, but most of those damaging effects upon the very nature and understanding of morality were incurred which keep atheistic humanist critics of religion in good business to the present day. At this stage, though, it is necessary only to remark that it appears no more inevitable that Moore's naturalistic fallacy be committed at a theological level than it is at the level of the natural – whatever that must be taken to mean in Moore's philosophy and in the Hume-influenced philosophies which both preceded and succeeded him.

It is in any case at this natural level that the implications of Moore's fact–value dichotomy, as it is so often called, now need to be calculated, especially at this stage of the inquiry, where the concern is with a view of moral discourse as a description of reality. It appears, then, both from Moore's language about something that can be called good in itself, and from his talk of recognising an indefinable character or property called good, that it is dangerously misleading to paraphrase the fact–value dichotomy in terms of the distinction between discourse which tells us about the way the world is and discourse which tells us about moral values, about the good and so on. The fact–value dichotomy, to repeat that all-too-common phrase, can only be paraphrased as follows if Moore is to remain our guide: moral discourse, value language, is not reducible to connotations that coincide with the connotation of words that denote natural objects, that is to say, things, elements or properties of things studied by the empirical sciences. And that paraphrase holds true only on the inductivist theory of the *modus operandi* of these sciences (a theory which coincides, incidentally, with Humean empiricism, if one

takes the view that Hume really was a proto-empiricist). For, as
Deutsch's work clearly demonstrates – however questionable his own
account of moral agency and hence moral value may have been – once
one takes a larger view of the progress of science and technology; and in
particular once one takes fully into account the role of knowledge and at
least of certain kinds of knowledge-bearers in a more broadly conceived
fabric of reality, then discourse which tells us about the way the world is
and discourse which tells us about moral values no longer fall apart into
dichotomously distinct categories such as the unadorned fact–value
dichotomy suggests.

A Humean-type empiricism implies its own type of metaphysics.
Discrete entities, things, elements, properties in the world to which
correspond clusters and sequences of sensations, perceptions, passions
and the ideas that arise from these according to the mechanisms described; of these and only of these is the fabric of reality constructed.
Some who would remain empiricist within some form of such a view of
reality, though one perhaps vastly more sophisticated than Hume could
have dreamt of (simple views of random mutation plus natural selection,
for example), would perhaps resent the suggestion that they were metaphysicians, or even that their world-view implied metaphysics. Metaphysics to such people might always entail the postulating of additional
entities, additional that is to say to the discrete 'natural' entities that the
empirical sciences study. Despite the fact that the metaphysicians of the
Western tradition saw metaphysics as the study of the most comprehensive structures of reality, which were just as real as elements that would
otherwise seem discrete and chaotic in themselves. So be it, then. But
instead of getting involved in either a semantic argument or, worse still,
in a debate about natural/non-natural(supernatural) distinctions – distinctions which, incidentally, some Christian theologians have questioned as severely as hard dualisms have been questioned in the course
of this essay – it is necessary at this point to concentrate on those who do
now realise and indeed argue, that moral discourse does have reference
to features of reality; that it does tell us about the way the world is; that it
does tell us about fact, even if fact has to be taken in a more sophisticated
sense than empiricist-inductivists of the young Ayer's ilk would like to
countenance. In other words, and to continue with Moore's language, if
some entities are good in themselves; if we can recognise good as a real
characteristic of such entities, then fact must include real features of the
fabric of reality to which moral discourse refers. And indeed, just as
some of the older proponents and interpreters of the fact–value dichot-

omy resisted the very name of metaphysics, others of their more recent
following in Anglophone philosophy feel no need to do so.[6]

The picture that emerges, then, from the first half or more of the
present century of Anglophone moral philosophy is one which reveals a
certain confusion that underlies some persistent assumptions. And it
may be important to recognise the fact that some of that confusion
carries over into the contemporary debate between realists or cognitivists (objectivists?) and non-realists or non-cognitivists (subjectivists?).
The assumption is the (metaphysical) one about reality consisting of
initially discrete entities or particles of some kind; the assumption that
seems common to the empiricist-inductivist persuasion. The attending
confusion is contained in the concomitant insistence that moral value
cannot be defined in terms of natural fact; yet things are good in
themselves, and we can recognise moral value in the world – rather than
invent it, presumably.

A brief illustration of this kind of confusion from the recent debate
amongst Anglophone philosophers must suffice for present purposes.
J. L. Mackie must surely be placed amongst the non-cognitivists or non-
realists: 'there are no objective moral values'.[7] And he himself accepts
the description of subjectivist, though not quite in the sense in which a
simple emotivist theory would use that term. On the first issue, his
non-realism, he uses the argument from queerness, as it has been called.
Moral values 'would be entities or qualities or relations of a very strange
sort, utterly different from anything else in the universe'.[8] On the second
issue, his advance over a simple emotivism, he argues that both moral
values and the obligation to act upon them come about, not as a result of
individual feelings or emotions seeking satisfaction, but rather as a result
of societal moves to limit the individualistic, self-seeking war of all
against all; and, more positively put, as a result of societal moves to
enhance by cooperative action the prospects of a better human life for
all. The content of our moral values, then, takes the form of 'a system of
law from which the legislator has been removed'.[9] He is not proposing

[6] It is worth noting that many writers in the recent debates within Anglophone moral philosophy
do expressly acknowledge that metaphysics is at issue. Michael Smith, for instance, in 'Realism',
in Peter Singer (ed.), *A Companion to Ethics* (Oxford: Blackwell, 1991), p. 402, describes realist views
of morality as metaphysical or ontological views. David Brink, *Moral Realism and the Foundation of
Ethics* (Cambridge University Press, 1989), p. 278, writes of the plausible metaphysical and
epistemological commitments of moral realists. Even Simon Blackburn, with his quasi-realism, in
'Errors and the Phenomenology of Value', in Ted Honderich (ed.), *Morality and Objectivity: A
Tribute to J. L. Mackie* (London: Routledge and Kegan Paul, 1985), p. 19, calls it a metaphysical
view.
[7] J. L. Mackie, *Ethics: Inventing Right and Wrong* (London: Penguin, 1977), p. 15.
[8] Ibid. p. 38.   [9] Ibid. p. 45.

some utopian future in which humankind will not need government with legislative, executive and coercive powers. No; he is simply saying, in what appears to be a mixture of utilitarian and social-contract moods, that human beings in their inevitably social settings create their moral values rather than discover or recognise them. And that the same social imperatives account for the obligatory nature of these values, even if they have not been enshrined in positive law, and no policeman is watching you just now, and may not detect your crime later. The aim of such social making of moral values is, of course, the good life which Mackie describes as being 'made up largely of the effective pursuit of activities that [he] finds worthwhile, either intrinsically, or because they are directly beneficial to others about whom [he] cares, or because [he] knows them to be instrumental in providing the means of well-being for [himself] and those closely connected with [him]'.[10]

It must suffice for present purposes to mention briefly one more non-cognitivist at this point in order to illustrate further the cumulative confusion concerning realism and the emotions, and to help towards a clearer view of the matter. Simon Blackburn, who has perhaps the best claim to being considered as a contemporary Humean, would prefer to call himself a quasi-realist in the matter of the philosophy of morals. He is less wary than was Mackie about describing moral values as made or projected from the basis of our sentiments; although he does also stress that it is not simply the individual's passing sentiments and consequent approvals and commitments that fashion moral values and supply moral imperatives. There are also the sentiments of others, including for instance animals, to be taken into account. And there is a corresponding sensibility on each individual's part which, if it should turn out to be defective, may lead to wrongdoing in the form, for instance, of causing suffering of various kinds to others. Moral values, approvals, imperatives are projected on the basis of such sentiment and sensibility; they are not discovered as features of objective reality are discovered. Nevertheless, the common assumption of ordinary people that moral values are objective in some manner analogous to the way in which objects studied by empirical science are objective, is not to be simply deemed an error, according to Blackburn. This is basically because the conviction that moral values are objective – recognised rather than made – is not so much a false theory as an expression of an attitude to moral values, an attitude that rightly considers them to be really obligatory; even though they are projected rather than discovered.[11] Blackburn, then, if he has to

10 Ibid. p. 170.
11 Blackburn, 'Errors and the Phenomenology of Value', pp. 5–11, 124.

be labelled, would prefer the label quasi-realist. And he repeats a form of Mackie's contention to the effect that the aim of all our busy moralising is the very real aim of the enhancement of human (and other) life.

Correspondingly, it will speed the analysis at this stage if the chosen representatives of the realist or cognitivist position are those who afford least place to emotion in their account of the discovery of moral values and of the recognised authority of these values over our lives. In John McDowell's realist moral philosophy, moral values are a real part of the real world, discovered, not invented. In fact, they are more like secondary qualities, such as colour, sound and so on, than like the primary qualities which the most physical sciences investigate. But if a subjective structure must then be considered an intrinsic part of the process of the recognition or discovery of moral values – and of what piece of objective knowledge of reality by human investigation is this not the case? – we must not thereby be lured towards the impression that the emotions have any essential part to play in the matter. Neither in the discovery of the details of our moral values and obligations, nor in the mechanism of our motivation to pursue these does emotion, our particular desires, play an independent role. Although it is common experience that desire does of course play a part in motivating moral agents, the reasoning faculty in its investigative and logical modes is the sufficient cause of the discovery of value and obligation, and to it our particular desires are secondary, and should be subject.[12] Jonathan Dancey in similar mood denies that 'desire must be part of what motivates the agent'.[13] For we discover moral values and feel them obliging us to act in particular ways by representing the world to ourselves; sometimes by a kind of double representation, of the world before and after the act contemplated; but always from our own particular perspective, and most particularly from a perspective constituted by consideration of 'thick' moral properties, that is, representations of wellbeing secured or damage done by the act contemplated, according to which the 'thin' moral properties of goodness or badness are then constituted. But in all of this there is question of discovery of moral value in the world as a source of moral obligation, by reason rather than emotion. Implications for emotional wellbeing may be part of a reasoned discovery or recogniton of such objective moral

[12] John McDowell, 'Are Moral Requirements Hypothetical Imperatives?' *Proceedings of the Aristotelian Society* 52 (1978), 15.

[13] Jonathan Dancey, *Moral Reasons* (Oxford: Blackwell, 1993), p. 30. Dancey regards McDowell as a weak realist because of the latter's analogy between moral values and secondary qualities: see Dancey, 'Two Conceptions of Moral Realism', *Proceedings of the Aristotelian Society* 60 (1986), 168.

values, but that is an entirely different case from the view of moral values as projections from emotions, and from a consequent view of emotions as themselves necessary sources of our obligation or impulsion to act.

Has the confusion which remained in Moore – where something could be good in itself and good could be recognised, yet good could not be defined in terms of natural of supernatural things – has this confusion now given way to a clear-cut choice between realism and non-realism? It would seem so at first blush. And yet there is a case to be made that, because of the alignment of non-naturalism with emotivist theory in ethics, the old confusion has simply been compounded by the addition of a new confusion. For the emotions are thought by both sides of the contemporary debate to be non-cognitivist, subjectivist. That is why realists are as anxious to keep them out of moral motivation, despite all experience to the contrary, as non-realists are to attribute to them the invention of moral value. Yet any contention to the effect that the emotions are not cognitive is highly questionable; and to that extent the old confusion in Anglophone moral philosophy is indeed merely compounded by a newer confusion.

As far back as the analysis of Descartes's position it was noted that he wrote of the emotions in terms of perceptions or 'knowings'. As short a distance back as the attention to a contemporary development in psychology there was reference to Max Scheler's account of certain emotions carrying meaning or sense and, in addition, presenting us with evaluations of actual states of affairs in the world; evaluations which are likely to be as objective as the aforementioned meaning and sense. But it is in the course of the attention to the contemporary movement in developmental psychology, more particularly to its pivotal Intersubjective First position, and most particularly of all in its advance upon the still admirably personalist philosophy of Macmurray, that the essential role of the emotions as heuristic, cognitive devices comes most empirically, most fully and most persuasively into view. From these contexts only the following elements of what can be learned of the best of past and present need now be brought to bear.

Descartes's six foundational emotions were admiration, desire, love, hate, joy and sadness. All other analytically identified emotions in our variegated emotional experience could be deemed derivatives or combinations of these. And they are all, of course, heuristic or cognitive after their fashion. Descartes has something similar to say concerning appetites, or affections, as he calls them: hunger and thirst, pain and so on; and he has something quite similar to say also about the higher and

clearer 'interior emotions' (also named love, desire and so on) which
follow more closely upon the exercise of reason upon experience and are
correspondingly more clear, less confused and obscure in their heuristic
and cognitive charge. The overall impression which survives the analyti-
cal rigour of Descartes's work is surely that of a kind of seamless robe of
affection and appetite, perturbed and perturbing emotion, interior and
more rational emotion; a robe that is as seamless as the *one person* ('une
seule personne') is a natural unity that, on analytic reflection, proves to
be a unity of soul and body. Or, to mix metaphors rather drastically, the
overall impression is of a highly complex mechanism which plays its full
part in a process, as bodily as it is mental, in which we come to know our
world, and ourselves as integral parts of it. The impression is not one of
emotions as 'mere' feelings, let alone whims, which are to be dubbed
subjective, in clear distinction from those cognitive mechanisms and
their results, which may be deemed objective. Certainly allowance is
amply made for the occasional strength and narrowly focussed nature of
some appetites and emotions, and for the manner in which, unless they
can be quickly brought back within the more comprehensive remit of
reflective memory and experience, they perturb us and distort the
picture of reality and of our place and prospects within it. Fear, for
example, while undoubtedly informing me of some agent or element in
reality which threatens me with loss or even destruction, can also cause
me to run away and to hide from something which, if not dealt with
somehow, can certainly cause even greater destruction later on. And if
that means that emotions must be educated, as the saying sometimes
goes, it may not be forgotten that the reason or intellect in ever
developing persons needs to be educated also, by all accounts. An
exclusively logical and highly abstract use of reason, and in particular
such use of reason as is indifferent at best to people's emotions, can
result in programmes for people which prove far more destructive in
their social enactment than can any amount of indulgence in purely
passionate response.

The impression, then, is of a unified bodily–mental human being
coming to know reality, ideally speaking, in and through a well-integ-
rated range of appetitive, affective and ratiocinative procedures. And
this, even in Descartes, does little to suggest ideas of emotions and
reason on opposite sides of the subjective–objective divide. If that is true,
then the realists or cognitivists in the modern debate need not be so
anxious to rule out emotion from the sources either of our knowledge of
the details of moral value, or of our sense of moral obligation. In

addition a quite different assessment of emotivist theories of ethics is made possible; and, in the end, an assessment which would challenge the need for proponents of these to feel that they need to remain on the subjectivist or non-cognitive side of the contemporary Anglophone debate. Now, of course the contenders on both sides of the contemporary debate about realism and moral value might well resent the suggestion that an old confusion stemming from the naturalistic-fallacy movement and accompanying emotivist theory of ethics was still at large. But the game begins to be given away by Mackie when he writes of the good life, the goal of ethical action, consisting of that which the agent '*finds worthwhile*, either *intrinsically*, or because they are directly *bene*ficial to others about whom he cares, or because he *knows* them to be instrumental in providing the means of *well-being* for himself and those closely connected with him'.[14] The italics are added here in what may well be a superfluous effort to bring to the reader's attention the combination in that sentence of words which refer to value ('worth' and 'well'; *bene* is related to *bonum*, the good) and words which are clearly cousins to recognition and discovery ('finds', ('intrinsically'), 'knows') rather than being related to making or inventing. So very little linguistic analysis is necessary to see this that an apology is perhaps in order for pausing to point it out. And only some strange inversion of the already questionable efforts by some legal theorists to keep law and morality dichotomously distinct could allow Mackie to say in response that socially constructed rules and their observance alone constituted moralising and morality, but not the recognition of the good, as in the good life.

Here, then, a self-declared subjectivist provides a clear instance of the survival of an old confusion, by use of language that clearly connotes a realist position. The game is given away further by Blackburn, and now with particular reference to the compounding of the confusion by explicit inclusion of the role of emotion. For Blackburn, unlike Mackie, accounts for moral values by direct invocation of the role of sentiment and sensibility. He too talks of the enhancement of human life as the goal of moral striving. This is surely, then, a value, a good, if not the good; and, therefore, either it is recognised by those sentiments and sensibilities which give rise to moral value, or it is recognised by, say, reason, and reason must then guide sentiment in sentiment's invention of moral value. Blackburn's preference for the label quasi-realist may

---

[14] Mackie, *Ethics*, p. 170.

take us beyond his own reasons for adopting it, and towards a suspicion that it is more of an admisssion both of the falsity of the assumption of the subjectivity of the emotions, and of the concomitantly increasing strength of the case for moral realism.

But the game is finally given away – and again with specific reference to compounding confusion by their account of the role of the emotions – by the realists who oppose Mackie and Blackburn. For these, while having to recognise our common experience of the role of desire and other emotions in all our moral motivation, feel bound to deny that emotion has any necessary or constitutive part either in identifying moral value and the detail of moral duty for us, or in motivating us to realise these values and to comply with the accompanying obligation (the two distinguishable yet scarcely separable features of the moral life). Hence the realists find themselves in the rather compromised position, surely, of admitting the presence and power of emotion, which they too consider to be an inherently subjectivist process in our moral life, while denying that emotion then generally renders moral valuation subjective. Little wonder if the contemporary debate is still so inconclusive. It could hardly be otherwise if there is, as there appears to be, confusion concerning the full realism of the realist position and the non-realism of the non-realist position. The shortest cut to a conclusion on moral realism or non-realism would then appear to be a cut through the lingering confusion and, to take the two concomitant forms in reverse order, first, the confusion associated with the assumption of the subjectivity of the emotions and, second, the confusion associated with the assumption of a Humean-empiricist metaphysics (or, as its assumers might well prefer it to be called, an anti-metaphysics).

MORAL REALISM
THE ROLE OF EMOTION OR PASSION IN KNOWING
(WHAT IS) VALUE(D)

The theme now broached is older than Western philosophy; and it would be foolish to assume that all that is worthwhile has been written about it in modern times. It is the theme of Eros, passion, a theme that is at the heart of Plato's philosophy and of Platonism, but which came to Plato from the mythic past. In its philosophical form Eros retained the comprehensiveness of its mythic presence and role. Despite the efforts of some of the more dualist-minded Platonists, or of particular groups of

Platonists such as the early Christian theologians, to split Eros in two, to distinguish a more sensual from a more spiritual Eros (following Pausanias' speech in Plato's *Symposium*), or to contrast eros with agape – a more subjective desire, erotic in the modern meaning of the word, with a more objective love of others – Eros to the more discerning minds has always retained its most comprehensive connotation. Equally translatable as either love or passion, Eros refers to every form or instance of desire. Its parents are Need and Plenty, as Plato's *Symposium* myth recalls, and so it names every emotion by which a human being is driven and drawn to fulfil a need from the rich affordances of the fabric of that reality of which the human being is so integral a part. It names all of these together, ensemble, and so signifies the unity of the human being in its own way, a unity which only the processes of analysis–abstraction conceals, and that only temporarily, for its own artificial, scientific purposes. In addition, in its original and Platonic contexts, Eros names the need of every thing in the whole universe, and its ensuing drivenness; it is a universal phenomenon.

Now, each need is particular, specific or generic. That is to say, it takes its shape or, to use the more traditional term, its form from the individual, the species and the genus of which it is a need. And that form carries over into an element of desire or drivenness which operates within need. In this way Eros is heuristic and cognitive in that it is always driving towards, drawn to and thus searching for whatever it is that will satisfy a particular, specific or generic, but always already formed, need. Furthermore, in this process it inevitably encounters and recognises others in need. Whatever it is that will satisfy the particular need that is driving desire in any particular instance, it will satisfy it only if it is a good example of its kind, one which has had its own needs for fulfilment allowed. I had a hazel tree in my garden in San Francisco. I never saw a squirrel near it until the day the hazelnuts ripened. And since the squirrels knew more accurately than I did just when the hazel nuts' needs for sun and nutrition had been adequately fulfilled, they usually managed to take most of them, apart from the relatively inedible ones I had picked too soon in a vain attempt to secure my fair share. There seems to be a universal law according to which self-interest and altruism are correlates, for all things live at others' expense, yet for that very reason have a vested interest in the good of the other. Eros, in any case, as a cosmic process plays an intrinsic role in enabling knowers to know the world, and to know the needs and consequent goods each of the other.

In the microcosm that is human nature a similar picture emerges of unity in diversity of heuristic-cognitive and conative function. The inherent unity of Eros or passion is at the very least implied in Descartes, in so far as the emotions are consigned to the unity of the *one person* ('une seule personne') and so, by implication at least, the appetites and affections of the body are united with the interior emotions which are triggered by ideas of the mind. The appearance of the separation of the emotions into apparently watertight compartments, is then due to the needs of the analytic-abstractive method of studying them, while in reality all are integral to the holistic Eros of the human being as it searches for the good and is drawn to it, and seeks to avoid the bad. Admittedly this image of unity is compromised in Descartes, in general by the surviving impressions of a dualist way of talking which was still dominant, despite his work on the passions, or because of its late and incomplete state at his death. But it is still there, and probably less affected by the surviving imbalance in his *Oeuvres*, than is that unity of Eros and reason which remains more deeply damaged, as the symptoms of his thoughts on the 'interior' emotions suggests.

Nevertheless, a quite cohesive kind of unity between passion and reason must surely emerge as strongly as that between the passions, affections and appetites themselves, from any analysis that succeeds in extricating itself at the outset from the influences of hard dualism. Eros – to revert to the comprehensive name for the cohesive whole of our appetites, affections and passions – not only drives the senses, the imagination and even the active memory; it drives the intelligence, the reasoning faculty, as well.[15] Indeed, there is already a possible fault in that way of putting the matter: it yields too much to the results of the analytic-abstractive method in studying the knowing process, just as

---

[15] It is Eros that makes us look instead of just seeing, that makes our memory so focussed, if not selective. Its role in imagination is either entirely obvious or it needs a tractate to itself. And there is an interesting analysis of its role vis-à-vis reason or, as he calls it, understanding in Augustine's *De Trinitate* when, seeking traces of the Trinity in creation, he offers the example of the way in which Eros, now named 'will' as in the old faculty psychology, directs intelligence to the storehouse Augustine calls *memoria*, in order that it should seek and ultimately find Wisdom (see especially books x and xiv). In more general terms, Martha Nussbaum describes well the heuristic properties of the appetitive, desiring part of human nature. She highlights its inherent intentionality, and she then has this to say about its relationship to reason: 'It is our nature to be animal, the sort of animal that is rational. If we do not give a debased account of the animal or a puffed-up account of the rational, we will be in a position to see how well suited the one is to contribute to the flourishing of the other' (*The Fragility of Goodness* (Cambridge University Press, 1986), p. 287). It is a pity, though, that, like others who adopt the more superficial habit of contrasting Aristotle with Plato, she fails to see how much master and pupil still have in common and, in particular, how close Plato's fuller treatment of Eros is to what she thinks she finds only in Aristotle.

happens so often in studying emotion. The fact of the matter is that all levels of knowing or seeking to know, from raw sense perception onward, are shot through with intelligence, with the attempt at least to 'read inside' (*intus legere*), to see into, to understand. Hence one should be talking of the interactive unity of emotion and the human knowing process as a whole.

Hegel, it will be remembered, in writing of consciousness and of its inherently reflective nature in which it constantly transcends all determinate content, commented upon the manner in which its repose is always troubled by its inability to rest replete with any finite, determinate content. But left at this level of analysis, reflective consciousness, self-consciousness exhibits the mere possibility of constantly receiving yet other content. It is not yet seen as the real and positive potency for infinite content – the agent intellect, as the Medievals would call it – which we experience. So Hegel wrote too of a kind of violence it suffered, and the suggestion was made that this might be analogous to the drivenness that is reminiscent of the role of Eros according to Plato. Hegel then argued that this engine of transcendence, this Eros-driven openness and restlessness of spirit, would draw us until we reached some infinite, no longer finite or limited, fulfilment. Not in the sense of some endless trek through finite contents and achievements – the *perennierendes Sollen*, *perenniendes Jenseits* of the posturing Romantics he so heartily despised – but in the form of such final unity of knower and known that no fissure could ever again creep in to create a limitation: the state and status of Absolute Spirit. But the point can be put in terms that have more resonance in the present context; and that would, incidentally, reverberate more closely with the writings of critical followers of Hegel, such as Feuerbach and even Marx.

Eros is not a shapeless, formless force. It takes form from that within which it drives to fulfilment, and it seeks corresponding form in the affordances to which it is drawn throughout the broad fabric of reality.[16] This is called adaptation in evolutionary terms. In addition, though the precise process involved varies from the human species to other species, the Eros that drives through a particular species fashions or should fashion such behaviour as would be calculated to respect the wellbeing of the interdependent species in the relevant environment that make up a single universe. That, so far, is merely a restatement of the general heuristic-cognitive function of emotion; and an attempt at an appreci-

---

[16] One recalls once more Aristotle's definition of *physis*, in *Physics* 193b, as 'the shape or form of things which have in themselves the source of their motion'.

ation of the fact – for it very much appears to be the fact – that the integrality of emotion to the knowing process at all levels is designed not to detract from but rather to enhance the objectivity, the realism, of the knowing processes as such. Attending, then, to the specifically human dimension of universal Eros, what becomes clear is the unity of appetite–affection–emotion–will, on the one side, and, on the other side, sense–imagination–memory–intellect, all of which, together with the two corresponding and comprehensive categories of desiring and knowing, are separable only by analysis and abstraction. And what becomes clear in this dimension of reality also is the fully surviving prospect of the objectivity of knowledge which is here in question.

Instead of setting reason over against emotion, as even some realists or cognitivists in the contemporary debate tend to do; and instead of seeing reason regularly as a common Platonist tradition is wont to do, as a control and corrective of emotional arbitrariness and whim-like subjectivity, reason, which is equally Eros-driven, is to be seen as a further dimension of the cognitive processes operative at the level of the senses. Reason, furthermore, is to be seen as a dimension which, though it undoubtedly can control and correct the waywardness of appetites and sensual affections, is more positively engaged in extending their participative purchase upon reality. Further still, reason itself is in need of control and correction through its own self-critical functions, on these occasions when its indwelling Eros tends to add to its own occasional blindness or inadvertence a further distortion of reality. As indeed when its native pride in its most elaborate schemes causes a failure in its own self-critical functioning, it may well need control and correction from some well-honed sensitivities of its finer emotions.

Now, if it is an implication of this analysis of an intrinsically Eros-driven human knowing process that the possibility of objective knowledge remains fully intact, is there a corresponding implication to the effect that moral values are not at all queer entities, as certain non-cognitivists claim they would be if they were thought to exist objectively in the real world? Paradoxically perhaps, it is by attending to the role of passion within the knowing process, rather than in attending to the role of an artificially abstracted reason, as some realists do, that a view of moral value as an objective part of the fabric of reality is secured. Eros is the offspring of need: a mythic way of saying that need is experienced as the driving–drawing force of a particular shape or form of reality. Often the shape or form is a quite complex one, of many dimensions, particularly in the case of those psychosomatic beings called humans. Now need is an objective feature of finite and contingent entities, as of course is that which, were it available, would fulfil the need. Both can be recognised or discovered by the usual processes of perceiving, under-standing, hypothesis and verifying, rather than being invented, as that term might suggest, in some arbitrary or entirely subjective fashion. As a recent quotation from Plotinus hinted, that can be defined as a good which fulfils a need and thus enables any entity or group of entities to realise real potential. Of course emotion can outstrip the need of which it is born, and drive both the needy entity and its equally needy co-dependants to destruction. That, too, is unfortunately a common experience. But all it proves is the need for constant critical attention, or other forms of learning from experience which even pests subjected to pesticides exhibit after their fashion. It does nothing to lessen the conviction that both needs and the details of the good which are such because they fulfil these, are objective features of reality. Quite to the contrary, a mistake is only recognisable as such if the truth can be known.

Good, then, refers to structures of need and fulfilment that actually exist or can be brought into existence in the actual fabric of reality. The phrase 'can be brought into existence' would seem to imply that moral value can after all be said to be invented or made, as much as it may be recognised or discovered. And in so far as the needy are themselves, as they usually are, active in the effort to fulfil their needs, that is surely true. Yet recognition or discovery remains the dominant note, since each agent must wait to see if that which it has acquired, invented or made really results in its fulfilment rather than resulting in mutual diminishment. Best say, then, that good refers to relational structures in reality; and these are as objective and real as, and may be known as well as any other features of reality.

Motivation or, as it is more correctly called, the sense of obligation, which also concerns moral philosophers, and which is part of the experience of moral valuation which realists wished also to keep clear of any constitutive influence from emotion – that too, as it turns out, can be as clearly identified as an objective element in the fabric of reality, by concentrating on the Eros element as much as by concentrating on some allegedly apathetic reason. Passion is after all as much a feature of the fabric of reality as is anything else; and passion it is that drives us to maintain, acquire or create whatever entities or states of affairs we see as the fulfilment of our real needs, our fullest potentialities. Some would prefer to change the metaphor here, from Eros driving to Eros drawing, in deference to the experienced fact that it is Eros-originated recognition of those entities or elements in reality which truly fulfil our needs and potentialities that motivates us towards these. But whichever metaphor is used, driving or drawing – and, as with all metaphor, it is better to use more than one – the sense of being actively, practically bound to or for some real entity or state of affairs, either present or to come or to be brought about – in short, the sense of obligation, as it is most commonly called – is shown by attention to passion to be as much an objective feature of the fabric of reality as are those relational structures that are connoted by the term good and other value terms.[17]

Since this initial approach to the theme of morality and metaphysics is through Anglophone moral philosophy and in particular its analytic tradition, this section concerning emotion or passion might well be closed with a quotation from Denis de Rougement's book *Passion in Society*, one of the most comprehensive and perceptive studies of the presence of Eros in the history of Western thought from before Plato to the present century. In the context he is concentrating upon the relationship between language, in particular literature, and passion. Literature, he comments, can be shown historically 'to have bestowed its vocabulary upon passion'; and by so doing it actually fosters the development of emotions which might otherwise lie latent, inchoate or distorted. But then he moves to a much, much deeper relationship between the two. 'Passion', he writes, 'comes to birth in that powerful impetus of the mind which also brings language into existence.'[18] Since he had previously glossed Eros as 'infinite transcendence', there can be little doubt but that the powerful impetus of the mind which sees the

[17] Richard Garner, 'On the Genuine Queerness of Moral Properties and Facts', *Australian Journal of Philosophy* 68 (1990), 137–46, would concede the case made here against the non-realists, to the effect that good as the fulfilment of need is an objective feature of reality. He makes this concession in conversation with some moral realists who argue for a similarity between human need-fulfilling evolution towards human goals in the world, and other entities which the evolution sciences see engaged in quite similar projects. (See, for example, Richard Boyd, 'How to Be a Moral Realist', in Sayre-McCord, *Essays on Moral Realism*; and Brink, *Moral Realism and the Foundation of Ethics*, who argues for continuity of supervention of moral properties with that of biological, psychological and sociological properties upon physical properties.) But his concession stops short of including what he calls the 'prescriptive feature' of moral values. This, he insists, remains queer when compared with other entities in the world and the ways in which they evolve creatively. Perhaps he has been answered in what has just been said about the ought or prescriptive factor, about the sense of obligation naturally explained in terms of the impulsive–attractive force of formed and in-formed Eros. Such an answer he should accept, unless of course he is obsessed by a rule model of ethics and can only conceive of obligation, of being bound to or for, in terms of social engineering. In any case, the fuller form of this answer will come when we consider Eros as a universal force, driving and drawing all things.

[18] Denis de Rougement, *Passion in Society* (London: Faber and Faber, 1956), p. 173.

simultaneous birth of passion and language refers to just that dynamic structure of the human mind which Hegel so accurately analysed in terms of reflective consciousness, itself driven by the inherent unrest which passion provides.

Because no determinate content derived from awareness of finite reality can ever leave my consciousness replete; because, in and through consciousness of any determinate content, I am (self-)conscious of mind and spirit not yet filled, much less fulfilled, I can envisage any particular determinate content – a woman, for instance – as absent, or duplicated, or different; in short, as one of at least a possible class of such objects. And as soon as I can do that I can sign and be signed to. I am no longer reduced to pointing, in any of the possible forms of that indicative process. In such signing, language of any and every kind consists, and sign is on (as has been said already) – language exists only in – the active commerce of self-conscious minds investigating and contemplating reality together after their own quite distinctive fashion. Literature simply allows this essential cooperation to bridge space and time elapsed.

But, it will be remembered, there is more to be said about this transcendence of the mind. It is no mere possibility; it is an active potentiality, driven and drawn by its inherent Eros. Thus it envisages, say, the woman as she is, and as she might or might not be, changed or replaced perhaps, but in any case fitting into a larger relational structure than the knowledge faculty, which needs more and more content, could alone and of itself account for. And the language will then refer to the reality conceived as it is, and as it ought to be, if it is not already as it ought to be in this particular relational structure with this woman, and only needing to be so maintained. 'Words', as the poet Auden once put it, 'are for those with promises to keep.' In more prosaic terms, language bears a double relationship to morality. It is born of the same reflective mind, the inherent passion of which enables it, first, to recognise and to create moral value in the fabric of reality, and again to recognise it once it is really and truly created; and second and simultaneously, to send out signs the native openness of which to further and different instances is positively forged by passion into a creative act of envisioning – a point to be developed in a later section of this essay, on the relationship of art to morality. Analysis, then, of all philosophical methods and processes, ought to be convinced of the cognitive or realist status of moral discourse. Blackburn's quasi realism could really drop the 'quasi' without detriment to his perceptive analysis of sentiment and sensitivity. Like most moral philosophers of a generally emotivist kind, he too needed little more than a more sustained analysis of the nature and function of the emotions; and he had already argued quite specifically that language which conveyed the objectivity of moral value in fact secured the reality of moral obligation.

MORAL REALISM

THE COINCIDENCE OF KNOWING WITH PASSION-DRIVEN

NEED-FULFILMENT AND VALUE-CREATING PRAXIS

It is possible, and profitable, to pursue further this case for the objectivity of moral value, and for the coincidence of morality and metaphysics, by looking briefly to some of the more practicalist theories of knowledge, to those, that is, that emphasise the interpenetration of knowing and doing, or of 'knowing how' and 'knowing that', and, more generally stated, to philosophies of a more pragmatist turn of mind. This may entail a turn from the side of the 'morality and metaphysics' coin which sets in relief the capacity of moral discourse to refer to constitutive features of the fabric of reality, to that other side of the same coin which now sets in relief the character of reality as a moral enterprise. But the turn of the coin will be gradual, and far from a simple flip. For it begins with a brief visit to Wittgenstein, whose major work was produced within Anglophone philosophy and is still influential in that milieu.

The focus here is upon the later Wittgenstein, as Wittgensteinian scholarship would have it, and upon the theme developed there of the relationship between language and practice. Here practice is taken to refer not simply to what we do, as in some of the cruder expressions of pragmatist philosophy in which truth seems almost identified with certain forms of success or even effectiveness. Practice is taken to refer rather more broadly to what we experience, to what we undergo in life in every process of effecting something, to the passivity as well as to the activity it always accompanies. Furthermore, as far as Wittgenstein was concerned, if we must talk about meaning before talking about truth – truth would then be meaning that is verified according to some acceptable method of verification – we need to say more about the conditions under which the meanings of terms arise and are established; more than simply saying that meaning and truth come about in and from practice, even in the wide sense of practice which Wittgenstein preferred. When Wittgenstein talks about language, about any particular piece of speech or writing as 'a description of what actually takes place in human life',[19] he is thinking of two further features of the conditions under which the meanings of terms are established and accepted as true, additional to the mere occurrence of life experience in individual cases. Both features are communal in nature and structure: they are conversation and interaction – for meaning does not consist in, or derive from, a single and initially solitary mental activity.[20] Fergus Kerr mentions Wittgenstein in the same breath as Heidegger when tracing the philosophical assault of the 1930s upon the idea of the distinct and self-enclosed mental substance then identified as a certain godlike self.[21] Both Wittgenstein and Heidegger sought in their different ways to re-embody the self in this world. Wittgenstein in tracing the conditions under which the meanings of language come to be established in use – since meanings do not first exist in a solitary godlike mind, only later to be attached to words and things – pointed to the mutually educational interaction of life experiences in human society and to the conversation that grows out of and accompanies this. Set words back in such a social interactive context, he suggested, and you will at one and the same time discover meaning and find out whether you can yourself accept what is being conveyed.

The most striking examples used by Wittgenstein which relate most closely to the concerns of this essay are examples of religious, and in particular Christian language. Yet the language that Wittgenstein chooses, language of sin and salvation, carries such substantial moral import that it may be quite legitimately used at this point, while the possibility of verifying its purely religious connotation may once again be left for later investigation. In the context in question, then, Wittgenstein quotes Paul's statement in 1 Corinthians 12:3, 'no one can say Jesus is Lord except by the Holy Spirit'.[22] His comment is to the effect that he himself could not say 'Jesus is Lord.' He could not accept that as true for his own case; for in order to do so he would have to be living a very different kind of life from the life he in fact lives. Only if he were living this very different kind of life would it mean something to him to say that Jesus is Lord, and only then could he give assent to that proposition. There is, then, this language suggests, a kind of life made up of distinctive experiences and actions which is shared by a community and to which this community gives expression in its shared language or conver-

[19] L. Wittgenstein, *Culture and Value* (Oxford: Blackwell, 1980), p. 28.
[20] L. Wittgenstein, *Philosophical Investigations* (Oxford: Blackwell, 1953), pt I, paras. 692–3.
[21] In a lecture to the Graduate School in Divinity, University of Edinburgh, February 1998.
[22] Wittgenstein, *Culture and Value*, p. 33.

sation; depicting it as being controlled and judged by Jesus. In that interactive life and conversation the proposition Jesus is Lord gains meaning and truth for those for whom it is meaningful and true. But for Wittgenstein himself it is neither.

On the other hand, the statement to the effect that 'the Lord is risen' Wittgenstein can treat somewhat differently. It is as if he has access to the meaning of that particular piece of Christian conversation, and can at least consider the possibility of assent to it, in ways that elude him when he is asked to repeat the statement Jesus is Lord. As he meditates briefly on the matter, he reckons that claims concerning Jesus' resurrection seem to take their meaning from Christians' life experience of some presence that saves them from the destructive practices they call sin, and liberates them instead for a life lived in the power of redeeming love. And that is something that means or signifies more than the life of a man, now long dead, who left behind some highly insightful and inspirational teachings. In the latter case, then, it is as if a minimum interaction with a particular community, while remaining essentially outside of it, and a corresponding overhearing of the community's conversation, can allow Wittgenstein to perceive the meaning of the language 'the Lord is risen', and even to consider the possibility of assent as he witnesses the life experience to which the language refers.

That, of course, may be to read too much into brief notes which Wittgenstein wrote for himself, but it does at least illustrate the view that is developing at this stage of the essay; the view, namely, that the fact–value dichotomy is even less secure in the later Wittgenstein than it is in the rest of Anglophone philosophy. For as we move towards philosophies of a more pragmatist turn of mind, we learn already from the later Wittgenstein that language refers first and foremost to human communal living, to the inextricable mixture of what we do and what happens to us; in short, to all that is comprised under the heading of morality: discovering–creating–discovering reality that is of value, in the course of successively fulfilling mutual needs. (Corroborating, incidentally, what has been said above about language having a double reference to this reality: in that it both envisages and expresses what both ought to be and is.) Correspondingly, we learn that it is the practical processes that make up the structure of reality, experienced from the point of view of communities of human beings active–passive within these, that yield the meanings of words, within the conversations that accompany and participate in these creative, evolutionary processes themselves. It is this praxis, this life–experience, that yields all the knowledge we may ever have of the whole fabric of reality, ever active towards the fulfilment of needs and potentialities which we may ever enjoy; and that yields all its concomitant and creative expression, principally in words. Thus is the realism of moral discourse made even more secure, and with it the coincidence of morality and metaphysics.

As one looks to the other side of the coin that is issued in the name of 'Morality and Metaphysics'; as one turns it over from the side on which is engraved the cognitivist, realist status of moral discourse to the side that begins to set in relief the extent to which reality is itself a moral enterprise; as one then attempts to comprehend the coin as a single entity; and as one seeks the most empirical and persuasive evidence for the corresponding kind of metaphysical picture of reality, one cannot but call to mind once more the findings of the kind of developmental psychology which concluded the investigations of the historical part of this essay. At the very least the parts of that metaphysical portrait which have appeared sequentially so far in the analysis of this current section come together in that contemporary and still-developing version of modern psychology, and do so in such a manner as to allow one to assess the resulting metaphysical portrait as a whole.

The pivotal nature and function of emotion, operative from the very beginning of the process of getting to know the world, is there related most intimately to the experience of motivation. The originary and essentially intersubjective nature of the combination of heuristic emotion and motivation to solicit experience and to act, simultaneously satisfies the need to account for the constant communal dimension of this person-centred view of the world, and sets in relief the origin and inevitability in the whole process of language and conversation. And of course the essential integrality of knowing or learning to communal doing and conversing is then revealed to the presumed satisfaction of all but the most grudging of pragmatist philosophers. And all of this over the influential signature of empirical science; in such a way as to bring joy to the heart of a pre-Socratic, if we could bring one back to life. For he would still be urging the closest and most permanent of attention to *ta onta*, the things that are, and to the *physis ton onton*, the nature and dynamic, Eros-driven form of all the things that are. And he would still be expecting from this the revelation of a 'way' rather than restriction to the formation of a theory artificially purified of any vision of better prospect for us in our common world. For he would see no need to segregate the physical, empirical sciences from philosophy, for anything other than some rather artificial and temporary practical purposes; the kind of purposes, for instance, which drive all of us these days towards ever increasing specialisation while we call more and more desperately for interdisciplinarity.

MORAL REALISM
REALITY ITSELF AS A MORAL ENTERPRISE
THROUGH THE ACTIVITY OF VALUE-CONSERVING AND
VALUE-CREATING AGENTS

In order to turn the coin further from the side on which is engraved the real referential status of moral discourse to the side that correspondingly sets in relief the status of reality as a moral enterprise, it is only necessary to recall briefly some of the salient features of the Intersubjective First position in contemporary psychology, and to focus particularly on some further refinements to be found there, concerning the pivotal concept of motivation. For the concept of motivation (setting in motion, *kinesis*) is at the heart of the broader concept of praxis, which in turn provides the substance of practicalist theories of knowledge and of pragmatist philosophies in general. Simultaneously, this contemporary psychology shows how pivotal is motivation in the provenance of passion or emotion and, consequently, in our fuller understanding of the part that passion plays in the continuous creation of the world and in the progress of our accompanying knowledge of it.

The presence and functioning of an Intrinsic Motive Formation (IMF), it will be remembered, is studied at every level, from that of neurophysiology to the psychology of neonate behaviour. Located, in so far as such things can be, at the core or limbus of the brain, from where it interacts with the later-developing neocortical system to which more abstract, conceptual knowledge, logical inference and so on are thought to belong, this motivating process, as its name suggests, already has a distinctive form; it is not an initially formless impetus. Quite to the contrary, it simultaneously shapes, if only by being selective or discriminatory, both what the person perceives or, in broader terms, experiences and what the person does. It is probably preferable to say that what we call (e)motive(s) or passions is an intrinsic part of its operative being, or is at the very least the expression of its presence and functioning. It is better to say something like this than to think of emotion as a separable entity upon which the motive formation also exercises its formative function. The IMF is, after all, what moves us to desire or revulsion in all their various forms, combinations and derivatives. It is what moves us

simultaneously to action and to openness to active experience of a form
that corresponds to and can therefore satisfy its form.

This feature of the analysis at the human level, it is worth remarking,
corresponds to the more general analysis of the evolutionary process in
our universe; especially at that point at which the all-too-common
account of that process simply in terms of genetic mutation and natural
selection becomes questionable. The myriad of minute variations at the
DNA level, as already remarked, does not provide an explanation of an
evolving universe simply by adding a reference to something named
natural selection. For natural selection might then prove to be no more
than an empty name for the brute facts that certain combinations
survived and others did not. What is missing, what is needed for
explanation and understanding of our evolving universe, is the added
reference to adaptive and adaptable functions of the replicators involved. Now, on a little analysis, the terms adaptation and emergence
reveal a similar connotation to that of the term IMF, for in all these cases
there are in-built and formed structures which guide an active receptivity to the formed affordances of surrounding entities.

Indeed, as an earlier passing remark might suggest, this current
analysis corresponds to a much earlier metaphysical position. When
Aristotle, in pursuit of the traditional Greek concept of *physis* as something dynamic, defined it as 'the shape or form of things which have in
themselves the source of their motion', he was virtually attributing to
everything which exists, and to the whole physical universe, a feature
which could without distortion be termed an Intrinsic Motive Formation. There are substantial forms, as he would call them, in all of the
material universe, and these serve both to define the entities of which
they are the substantial forms, and to guide these in the further development of their formed potentialities in the context of the surrounding
forms that make up the whole physical universe. However, the more this
analysis of the human agent has its denotation stretched to cover what
are now claimed to be similar processes over the whole pullulating
physical universe, the more difficult it would seem to be to think that the
processes so described could fulfil the criteria for calling them knowledge. Yet this is the least that would be demanded under the heading of
cognitivist, realist theories of moral discourse. Correspondingly, on this
analysis so widely applied, it is difficult to see how the same processes
could be included in the connotation of the term moral, even in the case
of quite advanced replicators called human beings.

The resolution to the first apparent difficulty is found in the realisation that a preformed impetus towards the universe of formed entities is no more an obstacle to some apprehension of these as they truly are than would be some formless impetus towards them. This realisation, admittedly, is more likely to dawn on someone who holds to a practicalist theory of knowledge than it is on one who holds to, say, a rather hard dualist theory of knowledge, such as Kant's, or indeed to any theory which would undertake to study knowledge in abstraction from knower and known, signifier and signified. It is in such systems that the preformed structures of the former seem to militate against any apprehension of the forms of things as they are in themselves. In practicalist theories of knowledge, on the other hand, the clue to success in the enterprise is perhaps best given in the examples offered by students of evolution, and their talk or emergence, of mutual adaptation. For there, as the name suggests, the process is of formed entities coming to practical grips with each other, and apprehending simultaneously themselves and each other as the evolving entities they in reality are, in and by that very process. Even where the process involves an attempt at straightforward assimilation, appropriation or consumption of one by the other, there is question of quest and recognition; for not all forms can be consumed by a particular form. That is why Deutsch names the central operative factor in evolution as knowledge, thus extending the denotation of the term far beyond the range of self-conscious, or even conscious, beings. The fuller implications, as well as justification, of quite that extension of the denotation of the term knowledge must exercise us later.

But for now, naturally, our own human (form of) nature shows most clearly how a substantial species-specific preformed impetus which, as motivating and hence moving, always exhibits the dimension of emotion in its act and expression thereby seeks and recognises a compatible entity which has its own preformed impetus. Endowed with reflective consciousness before it is born, capable therefore of signing and of knowing that it is signing, the principal form of the human being's IMF which infuses and informs all other forms of its IMF (the impetus towards food, sex and so on) is the special form of cooperative impetus which consists in the impetus towards communication or conversation. The earliest forms of human behaviour, therefore, as the Intersubjective First school of psychology insists, are characterised by the search for, and the consequent recognition of and interaction with, those other substantial forms in nature which can also sign, and thus enter into conversation with it, even if these conversations must initially consist of the requisitely

emotionally charged gestures: preverbal vocalisations, the organising
and coordinating of facial expression, the look and the eye movement
and so on. From then onward, from these earliest forms of conversation
concomitant with active exploration of the environment, the self-same
pattern of inherently socialised existence continues as the human IMF,
far from hindering knowledge of other dynamic forms of existence, in
effect enables such knowledge of human, personal forms to come about
and, through such mutual knowing, enables increase of knowledge of all
other interactive substantial forms in a shared universe.

In this way the Intersubjective First position provides adequate support for practicalist theory of knowledge and broader pragmatist philosophy, in securing an account of the objectivity of knowledge. Needless to
say, the objectivity of knowledge is always vulnerable to the presence of
subjective factors such as prejudice, inordinate emotion, inattentiveness,
credulity and so on, and indeed to the presence of objective factors also,
ranging from aspects of light and perspective to the mendacity of others.
True knowledge is never guaranteed at any level, but it is always
available. For human beings it is available in and through that emotionally charged kinetic process in which the particular form which Aristotle
named rational animality, and which is later defined as a reflectively
(self-)conscious animate body, seeks out and engages with a similarly
intrinsically formed kinetic substance, which it thereby knows, and
initiates with this a combined cooperation of acting and signing by
which the interactive forms of the world are engaged and, in and
through that self-same process, known.

And the justification for calling this knowing process a moral process
also? It has already been claimed that the Intersubjective First position
in psychology provides a better understanding of morality than do those
hard dualist systems which envisage the content of our moral duties and
precepts coming to us from a godlike reason or rational will.[23] In such
systems the moral dimension of behaviour tends to be consigned to the
very thin concept of the freedom of the will to obey or not to obey the
emergent maxims; a phenomenon difficult to ascertain, and even more
difficult to measure, especially when the critical mass of emotional life is
displaced from the role of motivating to that of distracting or disruptive
disturbance. Now, however, the very processes by which entities are
known are seen to be the very same processes by which entities are
continually, mutually and creatively evolved, and thereby valued. For

[23] Shades of this are still surely detectable in those proponents of cognitivism in moral discourse
who try to keep reason pure of emotion in their accounts of both moral value and motivation.

the intrinsic forms of things which are the sources of (e)motion – the
motivating forces, the IMF's – these set in motion an already (in)formed
quest for and mutual adaptation to similarly formed and moved entities
in the highly integrated fabric of reality. And since this is all in aid of
being and living as long and as much as the entity desires to be and to
live, it involves an assessment of the interacting entities in terms of the
fulfilment of their potentialities, the satisfaction of their needs. It involves, in short, value judgement; it consists in action informed by such
assessment or judgement. And this need not be, though it always can be,
a totally self-centred judgement by one formed and motivated entity
which has in it not even a hint of valuing in its own right the sought-after
and equally needy other. Even such totally self-centred behaviour and
judgement would be moral in the generic sense of the term, destructive
rather than creative of life; and it would bear its own ersatz witness to
the mutual dependence of all in the conservation and creation of what is
good for each.[24] Thus the process of coming to know reality and the
process of valuing are scarcely separable sides of the same features of
nature as process, where nature is taken in an ancient Greek philosophical sense, as coterminous with reality. Thus, too, the objectivity of
knowledge is secured at the same time as is the realist theory of moral
discourse. For morality as such is now thought of in terms not of law and
obedience but of the formed and informed *kinesis*, the behaviour of
things through which they maintain and develop themselves in that
essentially interactive process which evolution scientists call adaptation–
emergence.[25]

In the case of human beings, the case in which analysis is naturally
easiest, morality names that complex process in which an agent, now in
the form of a reflexively (self-)conscious bodily being, is equipped at

[24] These profound metaphysical–moral insights seem already anticipated in the earliest extant
quotation from the beginnings of Western philosophy, namely, Anaximander's statement that
'from whatever things is the genesis of the things that are (*ta onta*), into these they must pass away
according to necessity; for they must pay the penalty and make atonement to one another for
their injustice, according to time's decree'. And there are also the aphorisms of Heraclitus to the
effect that all entities live each other's deaths and die each other's lives. See John Burnet, *Early
Greek Philosophy* (New York: Meridian, 1957), pp. 135, 138.

[25] In adopting the evolutionary formula of emergence–adaptation as the model for what is called
morality here, there is no intention to endorse a linear teleological account of evolution,
unidirectional towards a single goal, ever onward and upward. On the contrary, the formula is
just as well fitted to the conviction of many scientists that evolution does not appear to be going
anywhere in particular; well fitted too to the conviction of some historians that things are not
getting better, just different; and well fitted to the conviction of some religious believers to the
effect that the ultimate goal they envisage is achievable and achieved, as it has always been, in
this world and its life, and not in any other world or life yet to come.

every analysable level with a virtual other and, being so formed, is actively engaged from the outset in a passionate quest for, and encounter with, another agent of similar form. This active encounter then consists in the essentially cooperative behaviour of signing, and the extension of this cooperative behaviour to the simultaneous exploration of, and adaptation to and of, the widest common environment. To say that this behaviour is cooperative, to say that it is sign accompanied, and to add also that it is adaptive of the widest environment as well as being adapted to it, is to suggest that a combination of responsibility and creativity provides the connotation and the denotation of the term morality; rather than the thin concept of the freedom of the will, which is preferred in legalist or rule-model construals of the nature of morality. Morality is, then, the common name for all those active encounters of form-driven agents which, being reflectively conscious, can envisage (imagine) not just how states of affairs at any momentary content of consciousness appear to be, but how they might be or not be, so that the combined needs of the form-driven agents involved might be further satisfied.

But is not freedom the more commonly identified hallmark and criterion of morality? Yes, and it still can be, provided that freedom is understood as the quality of not being bound in deterministic fashion either by the intrinsic forms of the agent or by the received forms of the stimuli from its world; provided that freedom is understood as the quality of being driven–drawn yet relatively open to ever further envisaging and mutual adaptation. Freedom, understood now as this precise element of indeterminacy that is part and parcel of any true act of creation, can then continue to be named as the hallmark of morality. But that freedom of the will which is represented by the thin concept of the ability to obey or disobey a law, is as secondary and derivative a concept of freedom as the definition of morality in terms of laws, precepts, maxims and so on is a secondary and derivative definition of morality. Morality consists, first and foremost, in the cooperative (co-responsive) creativity of agents engaged in passionate and informed attempts to satisfy their mutual needs and thus to realise the good. It is principally for purposes of cooperation in larger communities of persons and, in prominent part, in order to secure the communal moral enterprise from disruptive elements, that the need arises to try to classify moral behaviour – in the generic sense of the term used in this context, to cover morally good and morally evil behaviour – and to that end to construct moral codes, legal systems and so on. The authors of such codes, and the authorities on them, are then some particular persons or groups chosen or accepted by society for this purpose. But this kind of authorship in the matter of morality is always derivative and secondary, and, as a consequence, both the elements which make it up – the content of the codes and the authority of those who provide these in society – are always subject to change. As morality consists, then, in the cooperative, formed, informed and passionate interaction of agents satisfying their mutual needs and so realising the good, all of these agents are the primary authors of morality, and the principal authorities in the matter of morality.[26]

THE EXTENT TO WHICH REALITY IS A MORAL ENTERPRISE ONLY TO THE EXTENT THAT HUMANITY IS INVOLVED?

All of this continues to secure the inseparability of knowing how (as things interact, both between themselves and with the quester after knowledge, in pursuit of being over non-being) and knowing that; the coincidence of knowing and valuing; and the subsequent claim of moral discourse to be as cognitivist or realist as is so-called scientific discourse. A value is as much a real feature of what is and what comes to be as is any other feature of the fabric of reality.[27] A value *is* a mutual need-fulfilment; mutual because of the interdependence of all things in an emergent (i.e. mutually adaptive) universe of things. An 'ought' *is* that

[26] The nature of morality is much more fully analysed along these lines in my *Power and Christian Ethics* (Cambridge University Press, 1994), especially in the chapter 'The Anatomy of Morals'.

[27] Of relevance to this question as to the extent to which the whole of reality is a moral enterprise, is the work of moral realists like Boyd and Brink – see n. 17 above – who argue for moral realism either by comparing moral propositions with scientific propositions on the ground that both have reference to processes in which existential potentialities or needs and the goods which satisfy these can be described in terms of open-ended, flexible entities interacting in an evolving universe; or by seeing the superventionist theory of moral properties in strict continuity with the way in which emergence theory envisages the mutual supervention of biological, psychological, sociological and physical properties. And are there then further implications for the extent to which the practising scientist needs to be simultaneously a practising moralist? Or can the scientist, as some do, continue to say: I simply discover what is the case (with nuclear fission, for example); morality comes into the equation only when I or someone else decides what to do with the knowledge I gain; science and technology are distinct, no matter how closely they are related? Perhaps scientists say this kind of thing only because they think of morality on the legalist model, and want to insist on some kind of independence from interference, as they would see it, from less knowledgeable legislators; or, worse, from church leaders pretending to know God's will on such matters. In that case, what is said above about moral authorship and authority belonging primarily to the practitioners involved might persuade scientists also to abandon a position of professional amorality which few outside the profession would accept; and to take on instead the greater challenge of a greater truth, while still maintaining, for practical purposes, the analytic abstraction of a narrow focus on relevant elements or aspects of reality.

same need-fulfilment named after the aspect of the drive–attraction which is an intrinsic part of it. A right *is* the same need-fulfilment named after the fittingness of the forms mutually adapting. The act of writing in which I am currently engaged satisfies simultaneously the criterion for an ought and an is; it *is* both. Hence there is simultaneously secured the view of reality as we know it as itself a moral enterprise. The process by which entities interact to satisfy their needs and the process by which all entities are and continue to come to be are one and the same; the universe is an evolving, continuously creative unity. Yet this set of coincidences – the coincidence of ought and is, and of knowing and valuing – may simply serve to hide an ambiguity in the analysis so far, and a correspondingly unanswered question. In terms of the ambiguity: morality has been defined as cooperative or interactive need-fulfilment behaviour, on the model of evolutionary emergence–adaptation, between all the entities that make up the unified fabric of reality. Yet the finer details of the definition of morality have been worked out in what must surely seem rather distinctively human terms: reflective conscious-ness overseeing its contents towards mutual adaptations that ought to be, and thereby giving rise to that responsive creativity in which the essence of morality consists. Is morality a specifically human phenom-enon, then? That is the unanswered question. And is morality a feature of the whole of reality only to the (still quite restricted) extent to which human beings interact with the whole? Is reality itself a moral enter-prise, and does the coincidence of morality and metaphysics hold only to that quite specifically restricted extent?

The question is a crucial one in any case, but it is likely to prove even more crucial in the wider context of this essay. For, to put the matter in very provisional terms at this point: if the whole of reality were to be found to be wholly a moral enterprise, one would certainly feel closer to some, though by no means all, religious views, and to the corresponding prospect of a theological dimension to philosophy. As crucial as the question is, however, a secure answer does not seem to be easily available. This is partly because most moral philosophy has up to quite recently proceeded upon the simple and unquestioned assumption that ethical categories were confined to human beings – with the possible addition, if one believed in these, of persons on an even higher scale of rationality – so that morality referred to action and interaction of which these and these alone were the subjects. And partly because common and sustained attempts by philosophers to extend moral categories to other than human agents, at least within our common biosphere, seem to be still some way from fully securing their ground, and sometimes indeed unsure, or not quite in agreement, as to how much ground can be secured. It would not be wise to survey the relevant literature at this point.[28] It is better to be content with a brief analysis of the issue in continuity with the ideas already adopted in defining morality in the present context.

The basic definition of moral good and evil which results from these ideas is quite a complex one. That is good which actually satisfies existential need, and behaviour which secures that good is correspondingly good. Evil is that which frustrates the fulfilment of existential need, and behaviour which causes such frustration is evil. Add the inevitable interdependence of all agents within the unified fabric of reality, and there is the added requirement for each agent to fulfil another's need as well as its own.[29] And then, since it seems to be the case that agents in this universe exist and thrive at each other's expense, it would seem to be necessary to gloss the primordial moral principle, do good and avoid evil, somewhat as follows: every agent is obliged to ask of other agents in the common environment for, or to enforce upon these, the least sacrifice necessary for the fulfilment sought, and if possible to make compensation for the loss of need-fulfilment which the others thereby suffered.[30]

The point of commenting upon the complexity of moral behaviour and concomitant moral judgement, in the context of the current question concerning the extent to which reality as a whole is a moral enterprise, is this: good moral behaviour would seem to require a quite complex and extensive knowledge of interactive and co-dependent agencies, at least within the immediate spatial environment of the behaviour in question. The only candidates for this kind of knowledge which we directly encounter would seem to be members of our own species, *homo sapiens*. And even these, despite their possession of reflective consciousness, with its powers to comprehend quite complex combinations of interdependent agencies, actions and effects; despite their

[28] For a brief discussion of the issues involved here, and in a theological context, see Ruth Page, 'God, Natural Evil and the Ecological Crisis', *Studies in World Christianity* 3 (1977), 68–86.
[29] That altruism and self-interest are correlates rather than contraries can be seen from a close reading of evolution as we know it; and this fact further supports the use of evolutionary adaptation as a model for morality. See, for example, Stephen Clark, 'The Goals of Goodness', *Studies in World Christianity* 4 (1998), 228–44.
[30] The morality of satisfying the human need to eat adopted by vegetarians and vegans is a fine example of morality in this realistically complex understanding of it; although human carnivores do argue that they are responsible for conserving species which might otherwise become extinct. The idea of atonement is contained in the quote from Anaximander in n. 24 above.

powers to creatively envision even more of these combinations, and their concomitant powers to communicate this exponentially increasing knowledge – even these seem to have taken a long time to comprehend the complex interactivity and interdependence which characterises the fabric of reality. And even still each major advance in knowledge is accompanied by surprise at depths of reality revealed, and by a realisation of the extent of the still unknown. If these are the best candidates for application of the definition of moral agency, what can be said for other species which cohabit our common universe?

Animals are consciously aware of a lesser but still real area of environmental space, with its combinations of affordances and demands upon them; and they achieve this awareness through the same process that humans use, the process of formed and informed passionate interaction with that environment. Yet they do not seem to be reflectively aware of the fact that their environment is a combination of affordances and demands. It is difficult, then, to say that they know that they know; and so that they know that their knowledge is a driven valuing. And, not being aware of valuing, it is difficult to say that they are subjects of moral obligation; that they have moral duties or, at least, that they transgress moral duties; that they are guilty when, for instance, they kill beyond their need for food. Yet they do seem to fulfil the basic criterion for moral behaviour, in that they do consciously, and indeed sometimes quite creatively, interact with others for the fulfilment of existential need, in pursuit of the good. Is it possible, then, that there are degrees of being moral? That, for example, animals are subjects of moral rights, but not of moral obligations? Where a moral right connotes that which actually corresponds to existential needs, and a moral duty or obligation connotes one's awareness of being drawn or driven to that which corresponds to existential needs, but drawn or driven at a level of creativity that entails a degree of freedom, and not coercively as happens in the case of those agents who act only on instinct?

And could something analogous be said of plant and other less complex forms of life, and even of the myriad interactive agencies that make up the inorganic sector? If I were to say that, because carbon is necessary for the origins of life and carbon is created by the death of stars, stars die so that I should live, would that be a piece of pure poetic licence? Or could it possibly pass for an admittedly inflated instance of the attribution of moral behaviour to inorganic bodies? Certainly the evolutionary processes from which the model for morality – the model of emergence or evolutionary adaptation – was taken are normally seen to belong to the biosphere. Yet the biosphere also evolves; and so the evolutionary model must be sufficiently flexible to extend into the inorganic sector, the agents of which also adapt, and adapt to each other and to the agencies which operate at the biological level. Emergence properly understood, in a non-hierarchical or mutually adaptive sense, applies to the whole fabric of reality, and equally and simultaneously to all its levels. Are we back, then, to the suggestion of degrees of morality, and to an extension throughout all levels of reality of the case made for animals? The case made for animals hinged upon the presence of knowledge in their interactive behaviour with their effective environment. But can one talk of knowing in the case of agencies operative at lower levels of the biosphere, and even at the inorganic level? Deutsch has done so, and in the process has included knowledge as one of the four constituent elements in the fabric of reality as a whole. More generally, people do talk of genes carrying information; and more generally still, there is much talk about formed entities mutually adapting to their environments in a general process that involves a mutual transformation that can just as easily be represented as implying some mutual in-formation, some mutual apprehension of agent and interactive environment. Clearly at this point knowledge is being talked about in very analogous ways indeed; covering a range of phenomena, from reflective consciousness, through 'mere' consciousness, to information-carrying and information-acquiring which is, or at the very least appears to be, unconscious. So one could say that the whole of reality is a moral enterprise, because it is entirely made up of mutually adapting knowledgeable agencies, all together seeking the fulfilment of their existential needs and potentialities. The term moral, then, is used analogously; just as the terms knowledge and knowledgeable are.

But that, it must be said, is an answer to a question that hides as many difficulties as it solves. For first, the analogous use of a term is predicated upon its application to a number of different objects or object areas; and it presupposes a kind of normative, minimal connotation of the term so used, so that the same term can be seen to be genuinely applicable, albeit in different ways, to these different areas or objects. And in a philosophical atmosphere in which knowledge, at the very minimum of its connotation, is thought to be coterminous in connotation with consciousness, to use the term 'knowledge', of the mutual in-formation which takes place between genetic structures is quite problematic, to say the least. It would seem preferable to say that such mutual in-formation at that level is available as knowledge only to agents who can be consciously aware of it. But second, and more seriously perhaps, the resort to analogy in order to explain how the whole fabric of reality can be seen as a moral enterprise entails the logical dissolution of the same fabric of reality into distinct levels or areas – the human, the animal, the rest of the living, the inorganic, and perhaps many other quite feasible subdivisions within these. For analogical predication requires a distribution of the predicate across different objects of predication, where there is difference yet similarity of connotation as between these objects. But this invites us to ignore the fact, in the case of the current question, that these distinctions of levels or areas of reality are analytic distinctions denoting what are in reality inseparable levels or areas within a thoroughly unified fabric of reality as a whole. Hence the question as to whether reality as a whole is a moral enterprise, the question as to the extent of the coincidence of morality and metaphysics, must be asked and answered from the perspective of the whole fabric of reality rather than from the sequential perspectives of distinctive levels or parts of it. Correspondingly, the question will have to be answered by use of whatever we decide is the normative connotation of the term moral, and only then will there be room for an analogous deployment of the term at different levels of reality. At this stage of the investigation, then, the answer to the question which heads this section hinges upon what is revealed when one attends to the fabric of reality as a whole. So it is now necessary to turn to art and its open attentiveness, and to the consequent role of revelation. But before doing so it is worth calling to mind the sequence of modern philosophies which ended in the view that the fabric of reality is a moral enterprise only to the extent that humankind is operative within it.

Hegel, who is at the source of these philosophies, understood the power or process that makes the whole of reality a moral enterprise, to be an entirely immanent *Geist*, God or Absolute in continuous evolutionary-creative action. And he then described the corresponding process by which the human spirit made its evolutionary-creative journey from inchoate to full union with that Absolute. With Feuerbach, although the identity of the power or subject that makes or will make the whole of reality a moral enterprise is clearly said to be that of the human species-being, its status is ambiguous. That is to say, the distinction between divinity immanent in humanity and 'mere' humanity is never quite secure in Feuerbach. Indeed it would seem, both from some of the quotations reproduced in a previous section, and from some features of the logic of Feuerbach's argument already referred to, that such a distinction may not have been fully intended. Feuerbach began his most celebrated work with an analysis of the inherently limitless self-transcendence of which human nature is aware in the innermost reaches of itself. When that insight is put together with his later analysis of the concept of creation and providence, it fits well the image of an evolving universe, within which operates a self-transcending consciousness that is at the centre of the universe, and co-extensive with the whole of humanity, past, present and future. Feuerbach does, then, remain ambiguous at best as to the status of the power and process which makes the whole fabric of reality a moral enterprise. Something similar could be said of Deutsch's picture of the end game of our universe. Deutsch goes to quite explicit trouble to point out that the creators of the universal (virtual-) reality machine of the end time differ in quite substantial respects from a Christian creator god as commonly understood. Yet there do exist in fact, even in the Christian tradition, much more sophisticated concepts of a more immanent deity, and more immanent in and operative through humanity in particular, to which his contrasts would not so easily apply.

Finally, in Marx's version of pragmatist philosophy – 'philosophy hitherto has interpreted the world; the point however is to change it' – the agency which is to make the whole of reality a moral enterprise is very definitely the species-being known as humanity, and divine agency is distinctly excluded. This is done largely by Marx's criticism of Feuerbach's definition of the human species-being, and his corresponding insistence on defining humanity in terms of the ensemble of practical relationships which bind its members together and to this lean earth. Yet Marx described the universe as the extended body of the human race; and he believed that humanity could create by its labour a world in which not only its own existential needs, but also those of its extended body, would be understood and fulfilled. In a sentence which anticipates a key concept of the next chapter, on art, he asserted that humanity knew how to create everywhere in accordance with beauty.[31] And this leaves us once more with a question as to the status of this species-being from which this cosmic responsibility is required; and indeed with a question as to the revelation of the beauty which appears to be some criterion of its conduct of that responsibility.

[31] D. McLellan, *Karl Marx: Selected Writings* (Oxford University Press, 1977), p. 82.

CHAPTER 5

Art and the role of revelation

The centrality of knowing how to knowing that or, more revealingly, the coincidence of knowing and valuing, of seeing and envisioning, led simultaneously to the cognitivist status of moral discourse, and to the sense of the universe as, in part at least, a moral enterprise.[1] The recovery of the sense of formed (e)motion as the universal engine of evolving, ever creative being, and as the concomitant knowing, the mutual in-formation and continuous re-formation that binds all the entities in the universe together – this, then raised the question as to the full extent to which reality as a whole, as a universe, is a moral enterprise.

Traditional theological metaphysics in the West answered that latter question most fulsomely. A personal God creatively at work throughout the whole universe and all of its history, in cooperation of course with the other moral agents that we know of, made of it all a wholly moral enterprise. And the same theological metaphysics simultaneously se-cured the fullest objectivity of moral value. More recently, however, the educated observer of contemporary Anglophone moral philosophy, and particularly one who has in mind our current question concerning the extent to which reality as a whole is a moral enterprise, cannot but notice the following two features of that philosophy. First, these moral philosophers have recourse to art in order to secure the objectivity of moral value and the realist status of moral valuation; and, second, they express a clear preference for art in this essential role in moral philos-ophy, in lieu of lost religious conviction, and indeed over some forms of that religious conviction which have traditionally existed and still do exist. It is worth pursuing our current question, then, in dialogue with some of these philosophers.

---

[1] In other words, as Levinas would say, moral philosophy is first philosophy; or in terms used above, moral philosophy and metaphysics coincide.

ART AND THE HUMANISING OF THE REAL

Anthony O'Hear, for instance, combines quite succinctly both of the features mentioned, in a programmatic piece of analysis and argument concerning values in society, and particularly in the education process that is so central to any society's concerns. He does this by using the term transcendent as the cipher for what is otherwise called the objectivity of moral values, and for a corresponding status of at least a range of reality as itself a moral enterprise. 'On pain of distorting our understanding of our values and of our lives', he writes, 'we cannot see our values as projections of our desires, or as no more than devices for the smooth running of society.' And that means that, in his words, 'it is hard to think about our moral experience without being drawn to think of the transcendent'. When allowance is made for his negative assumptions about desire here; and when the second part of his sentence is taken to refer to a particularly legalist understanding of morality, in which it is reduced to the means of achieving specific desiderata of particular societies, it is clear that he is asserting the requirement for moral value to transcend and to be known to transcend both individual whim and the particular desiderata of certain collectives.

How, though, is this requirement for moral value to transcend such individual and social subjectivities to be secured, and secured to the satisfaction of those who see this requirement to be central to the very possibility of any moral enterprise properly so called? In the somewhat constrained context from which the quotations above have been taken, he simply refers to those religious intimations of transcendence supplied by what he calls, somewhat special-pleadingly, dogmatic religion; and he quickly moves away from these. For himself and so many others they have ceased to provide moral value with its required transcendence, if indeed they ever truly managed to do so; and so he searches briefly for 'non-religious intimations of the transcendent'. First he refers to 'our lived sense of the sacredness of human life and of something approaching awe in matters to do with the creation, beginning, nurturing and ending of specifically human life'. But second, and almost as if this sense of the sacred, this awe with which we contemplate creation – and not simply the creation of human life – were still a little too redolent of traditional religious intimations of the transcendent, he refers us to art. With acknowledgement of Iris Murdoch, who has made the most persuasive contemporary case for this, he proposes art, or in any case good art, as that which in an irreligious age may give people their clearest experience of true transcendence, and with this a transcendent locus or source of moral value.[2]

In a paper entitled 'The real or the Real: Chardin or Rothko?'[3] O'Hear puts much more flesh on both sides of this philosophical equation: the role of art in securing the transcendent basis of moral value, and the subsequent displacement from this role of religious belief and conviction. Rothko provides O'Hear with his example of an artist who, in an age that saw the decline of natural theology and the collapse of creedal religion, solved the problem of devising still a way of presenting the essence of religion. He did so by painting canvases that 'produce an experience of engulfing the perceiver, . . . by their working from a ragged, indeterminate edge to quasi-rectangular expanses of deep colour'. 'In Rothko's work', he continues, 'there is no trace of the concrete, nothing appears; we are overwhelmed by hazy, empty sublimity.' Then he asks, '[Is] engulfment, the wiping away of all determinations and horizons, what life – and art – is all about?' And he concludes, '[If] it is, then human effort and perception and perspective are, in the final analysis, mocked' (pp. 50–1).

Chardin, on the contrary, fills his canvases with the most ordinary things: pots and other utensils of kitchen and table, food and drink. Thus is revealed the real beauty of the ordinary things of the natural world, freed now from 'a false ideal of beauty, one constrained by grandiosity and sublimity'. O'Hear quotes Proust on Chardin: 'from Chardin we had learnt that a pear is as alive as a woman, that common crockery is as beautiful as a precious stone. The painter had proclaimed the divine equality of all things before the mind that contemplates them, before the light that beautifies them.' And he is then well on his way to intimating the relationship between art and morality, as follows.

He quotes Cézanne: 'Le paysage se reflète, s'humanise, se pense en moi' (p. 48). He refers then to our practices in the world and the associated sensory apparatus; the latter, he quickly adds, are shot through with self-conscious intelligence. Hence – if there is no distortion in translating his thought into terms already in use in this essay – we, on the one hand, (in)form our natural world and are (in)formed by it, and on the other hand, (emotion-in-action recollected in tranquillity) we can reflectively and simultaneously enjoy and appreciate (evaluate) the

[2] See Anthony O'Hear's chapter in John Haldane (ed.), *Education, Values and Culture* (University of St Andrews, 1992), pp. 47ff.

[3] In Michael McGhee (ed.), *Philosophy, Religion and the Spiritual Life* (Cambridge University Press, 1992), pp. 47–58. Page numbers in the text refer to this paper.

forms that then correspond to our active human interests and human perspectives. In this way an artist – at least one like Chardin – can enable us to see the forms that reveal themselves in a world within which human beings have evolved and interacted, and have developed the ability to perceive these forms, and the interest to appreciate them.[4] Finally, in contrast to Rothko and the admittedly artistic, yet purportedly religious, intimations of the transcendent which he attempts, human effort and perceptions and perspective are not now mocked when it is Chardin who opens our eyes to the real. Quite to the contrary in fact, human effort and perception and perspective are both necessary and sufficient for an adequate aesthetic, a workable morality and an acceptable metaphysic. And yet that does not mean that there is no emptiness in Chardin's world, that all is light and the forms it reveals, forms which both embody and reflect it. Rather 'the objects [which Chardin paints] emerge shyly, from a soft and indeterminate background, against which they quiver in the light almost on the edge of invisibility'. And O'Hear quotes Proust once more, to the effect that these objects seem to be summoned 'out from the everlasting darkness in which they had been interred' (p. 48). But this is not the sublime emptiness which Rothko wants to evoke, in which we are engulfed, so as to render all human passion and project nugatory. It is, in Chardin's work, an absence of light and of form which serves to enhance the role of human effort and human perspective in bringing form to light and to being, while implying also perhaps the contingency, the frailty of both the forms and of those who bring them to light.

Yet in this important affair of the securing of the necessary transcendence for moral value, even in this short piece O'Hear does not leave the replacement of religion as a mere entailment of the preference for one painter over another. He includes in his argument a very modern theological position proposed by John Hick, whose work in the philosophy of religion has recently aimed to salvage some credible account of the essence of a religious view of reality from the confusing and usually quite dogmatic claims of the plurality of religious faiths still active today. By considering this theological position, O'Hear clearly feels, the contrasting cases for religious and artistic intimations of transcendence so necessary for true morality can be assessed, and the displacement of the

[4] O'Hear takes a dim view of science in this respect: by adopting a 'view from nowhere' it cannot admit the human perspective; and in any case he writes as if science still entails a reductivist process of the most physical kind so that, once again, it could handle neither the idea of goodness nor that of beauty.

former by the latter can be made more secure than if we were confined to comparing two artists and their work. So Hick argues that there is a Real behind the different religious traditions, and that each of these offers a different but genuine insight into the Real. Leaving aside Hick's and indeed O'Hear's supporting stories – the former about the Axial Age and the tendency of reflective reason to seek universal absolutes beyond local phenomenological imagery, the latter about Socrates' (alleged) replacement of myth and Spengler's analysis of civilisation's hostility to culture – the outcome of Hick's discovery of a Real hidden behind the phenomenal deities of the many religions is this: a noumenal entity in a Kantian sense, quite devoid of phenomenal content, the kind of utterly unknown and unknowable in which the traditional *via negativa*, if taken by itself, would be bound to result. And with this, O'Hear observes, not only is belief in it indistinguishable from agnosticism; but it would be scarcely possible to detect any intelligible or appreciable effects which worshipping such an inherently indeterminate entity could ever have, in the form of a shaping source or motivating direction for our moral values and our moral efforts.

At this point the comparison with Rothko becomes clear. It is the comparison of Hick's Real, which is empty of all humanly conceivable content, with the engulfing emptiness into which the eye is drawn from ragged empirical edges on a Rothko canvas. And O'Hear's conclusion is worth quoting.

Against such a background the emptiness – at its worst, the rhetoric – of Rothko would be vindicated against the painstaking and human modesty of Chardin, and what Chardin presents to us as an all-too-fragile achievement will be swallowed up in the abyss of the divine. At the same time, it is doubtless true that we come to see Chardin's achievement as the achievement it is just when we begin to understand that we are standing above an abyss, cosmically speaking, and that human domesticity and human perception rest on no secure foundation. In terms of my illustrative analogy, then, Rothko's Real might be seen to serve as the background from which Chardin's reality – and ours – emerges and is perceived. (Pp. 57–8)

In answer to the current question, then, concerning the extent to which reality is itself a moral enterprise, O'Hear seems to be arguing for a restriction of that extent to purely and distinctively human involvement. Indeed, in addition, and in contrast to suspicions we might entertain about, for example, Feuerbach's infinity of human nature, O'Hear's humanity is very human indeed. Cézanne's conviction that the world comes to thoughtful reflection and is humanised in and by

humanity is wholeheartedly endorsed by O'Hear, to the point of stress-
ing that disembodied beings and *a fortiori* divine Emptinesses could not
interact with this concrete world at all, and certainly could not perceive
and appreciate this world as we humans do. It is very much human
practices, human and very embodied perception and reflection, human
appreciation or valuing, that thus recognise value in the world, and
make of the universe a very human place. This in lieu of the divine
creation hitherto invoked. At the same time, there is full recognition of
the fragility of this cosmic achievement, captured so powerfully on a
Chardin canvas, when human *pragmata*, as Heidegger would call them,
'quiver in the light almost on the edge of invisibility', ever threatened
with engulfment again in the surrounding abyss.

Now, there is no gainsaying the power of this picture, and the
persuasiveness of the accompanying analysis. It is a picture quite often
painted in modern times by atheistic humanists. It is a philosophy of life
which can congratulate itself on the ring of truth that recommends it,
and can take pride in the courage it asks of those who would live as
human beings without illusions. And yet it must be asked if it does not in
the end make at once too much and too little of humanity in humanity's
one and only universe? Too much in this way: a certain recourse to art
for intimations of the transcendent status of moral value may focus too
exclusively, if only by default of wider vision, on humanity, and on too
much talk of *humanising* reality. We may well be left with the impression,
if not of an elitism which intimates that only those who create or
appreciate fine art achieve the highest purpose detectable in this universe, then of an assumption that everything else in our common
universe exists, or at least is valued, only by and for human beings. In
that case, the intimations of the transcendent which art is said here to
supply, would presumably get our moral valuing beyond the whimsical
desires of the individual, and perhaps also beyond the communal
necessities of individual societies as each individual society happens to
see these. But it would not get us beyond what might be called the
perceived interests of the human race, in the actual numbers and states
of development in which the whole human race at any time consists.

At the same time, perhaps, too little, and in this way: a certain
recourse to art for intimations of the transcendent may, like certain
other forms of modern humanism, focus too much on the fragility, the
sheer contingency, the permanent existential threatenedness both of
humanity and of all that it recognises to be of value (to it). There is, then,
a dismissal, in such atheistic humanist philosophies of life, of illusions

about the transcendent. Usually where the transcendent refers to a being who, we hope, will somehow recreate us after death in a world from which death and its harbingers, illness and pain, fear and its ensuing violence, are forever banished. Now, such dismissal is indeed often based upon a solid ground of objections to the damage these kinds of alleged illusion are seen to do to the very texture of human morality in this life and world. But the dismissal of these kinds of alleged illusion, and of the kind of transcendent which operates in them to the alleged detriment of human morality, often serves to hide from view very real dimensions both of human spiritual depths and heights, and of humanity's realistic prospects despite or even in death. The human spirit, be it as embodied as the most fervent atheistic humanist wishes to see it, is clearly capable of envisaging its contribution towards immortal effect in quite a variety of ways. And the hope that is thereby born is nurtured upon experience of past and present. But, significantly, that vision, experience and hope is always predicated upon the status and role of the race as an integral part of a wider agency and process, which is thereby reciprocally immanent to humanity, rather than transcendent in the sense of something extrinsic to and separate from the universe of which the human race is so integral a part.

Something along these lines is what is meant by saying that some versions of secular humanism make at once too much and too little of humanity. What we are witnessing today, after all, is ecological disaster caused in great part by an increasingly common interest across the whole of humanity as a global marketplace rules the whole planet in a rather overly materialistic ideal of human wellbeing. This illustrates at one and the same time the way in which humanity as a whole, and not just individuals or separately organised societies, can act on what is then seen as a self-serving whim, and the way in which that same global humanity can take a view of its prospects within the integral fabric of reality which actually diminish it in exact proportion to the degree in which its view of itself as the sole source and goal of value aggrandises it. It is not now being suggested that this rather dismal result is the necessary outcome of O'Hear's attempt to enlist art in aid of the transcendence of moral value. He himself suggests, though briefly, that a humanist art like Chardin's, in contrast to a religious art like Rothko's, enables us to replace a conspicuous consumerist ethic of instant disposability of all that the world affords us, with an aesthetic of true beauty of form and content, and a corresponding ethic of the appreciation and humanising of things (p. 48). But that, it might well seem, is still not

enough to lure us beyond, say, making our artifacts more aesthetically
pleasing and having a reason then for cherishing them that is additional
to purely functional use. Not enough has yet been said here, it might
seem, to prevent us from making at once too much and too little of
humanity in our search for the transcendent source or locus of value.
And that suspicion is only strengthened by those aesthetic theorists who
seek to secure the objectivity of aesthetic value – either as an analogy to,
or in relationship with, a similar objectivity of moral value – by confining attention to properties of works of art themselves, which transcend
the subjective views of those who appreciate them. For all of this then
remains within the closed circle of artists, their works of art and those
who appreciate these; with no reference which might transcend that
circle towards a wider reality.

O'Hear refers to Iris Murdoch in the course of his own recommenda-
tion of art as that which, in lieu of religion, is now to provide such
intimations of the transcendent as we need in order to secure and
understand true moral value. And it is well to turn to Iris Murdoch's
mature philosophical work, not merely to see a more sustained analysis
of these suggested relationships between art and morality, but to allay
any suspicions which may still remain in our heads concerning the
effectiveness so far of the corresponding attempt, as a result of these
relationships, to finally displace religion. For it is probably fair to say at
this point that suspicions of this kind do still remain. So much that has
been said so far concerning art and religion and morality is simply too
reminiscent of scenes from history, of the putative dismissal or replacement of divinity which proved to be ineffective. This suspicion of
ineffectiveness could arise because denial, in this case, of divinity could
be seen to be logically necessary to the understanding of what was then
asserted. In O'Hear's case one could well ask: Is the emptiness of the
threatening abyss intelligible only through the evacuation of divinity?
Emptiness usually connotes the absence of something from some thing
or place where one would expect it to be. Or the suspicion of ineffectiveness could arise because the divinity, which in this case is denied, could
quite easily be said to be divinity misconceived, or malconceived. We
have already encountered in modern philosophy the idea of a divinity,
initially quite separate from the world, defined in terms of an infinite
consciousness with no determinate content, like Hick's Noumenal Reality. But that may not be, or may not be all, that people have understood
as a creative divinity immanently operative in the universe. In both
cases, then, the remaining suspicion serves to keep open the prospect of

an argument for the reintroduction of a genuine and true theological dimension.

Put in more general terms, and with particular reference to the contention that some humanist philosophers appear to make at once too much and too little of humanity:[5] some suspicion remains at this point that, while art does indeed provide for morality the necessary intimations of the transcendent, it is still not quite clear that the said transcendent cannot be seen to have a genuinely religious dimension. Hegel, after all, thought art, religion and philosophy to be equally ways, if not in his own view equal ways, of access to the Absolute, which was also in his view the God of Christianity. Many others of course, like William Blake, offer a similar choice of access, although Blake, unlike Hegel, would rate art above philosophy. There is nothing inevitably atheistic or even agnostic about a transcendent as a result of its being intimated in art.

IRIS MURDOCH
ART, MORALITY AND THE TRANSCENDENCE OF THE HUMAN

Iris Murdoch, it might be said, enlarges in two connected ways the view that is here developing of the manner in which art secures the transcendence of moral value; and secures this beyond any limits still vulnerable to suspicions of an overly humanised and correspondingly human-centred perspective on moral value. In the first of these, she highlights the attentiveness which she insists is an essential characteristic of all great art; in the second she argues for a degree of transcendence for the fundamental moral value, the good, which without questioning its permanent immanence in our empirical world, clearly resists any tendency to restrict it to the range of human presence and human achievement. Iris Murdoch is very much in agreement with those who see a central role for art in securing the transcendence or objectivity of moral value. Significantly, she attributes that same role to emotion, and in particular to the fundamental and most comprehensive emotion of love, in line with the Platonic Eros. And it is obvious from the way she writes about religion that the good transcends the human also, while remain-

---

[5] Martha Nussbaum is a good example of a humanist operating with too small a vision of bodily, finite humanity, recommended by far too emotional a sensitivity to its inevitable suffering and mortality. In addition, in support of such a view, she is one of those who read a profoundly religious thinker like Plato's Socrates in such a wholly anachronistic fashion as to present him as the equivalent of a modern secular humanist.

ing immanent in all our activity and experience. For she argues that the decline of traditional Christian religion is to be greeted with qualified regret. Its support for the transcendence of moral value did, and where it survives can still do, much good despite the harm it has also done. Hence she is prepared to talk of a demythologised religious dimension in a world in which The (impersonal) Good is now Sovereign; and to welcome also the continuity of some correspondingly and suitably demythologised practices that retain a certain religious quality, practices such as prayer and contemplation.

First, then, the act of attention, the task of attending, according to Iris Murdoch in *The Sovereignty of Good*, is common to both art and morality.[6] Attention connotes 'the idea of a just and loving gaze directed upon an individual reality'.[7] Twenty years later art and love come together again in *Metaphysics as a Guide to Morals*, as sources and supports for the act of attention which she considers to be crucial to our appropriation of real, that is to say adequately transcendent, moral value.[8] Much has already been said about emotion as a cognitive enterprise in a context in which doing (movement, *kinesis*, interaction) and knowing, and then knowing and valuing and knowing (recognising) value, all coincide. So, the part of the act of attention in the role that art plays in securing the transcendence of moral value, according to Iris Murdoch, is quickly and easily stated. Transcendence is still understood in the sense of going beyond individual whim, whether that refers to an individual simply, or an individual group, however large a particular grouping might be. A whim refers to a desire, a(n) (e)motion driven and shaped by a need, but one which is exclusively focussed upon the need of the individual moved by it, and exclusively also upon some element in the world as nothing other than the immediate fulfilment of that felt need. Such inordinate self-centredness produces what Iris Murdoch calls false images; in religious language, idols. And it is this that art enables us to transcend. So she pictures the artist as the one who 'attends to the dark something out of which he feels he can, if he concentrates and waits, elicit his poem, picture, music'. As one poet, Seamus Heaney, put it:

> Strange how things in the offing, once they're sensed,
> Convert to things foreknown;
> And how what's come upon is manifest

---

[6] Iris Murdoch, *The Sovereignty of Good* (London: Routledge and Kegan Paul, 1970), p. 43.
[7] Ibid. p. 34.
[8] Iris Murdoch, *Metaphysics as a Guide to Morals* (London: Chatto and Windus, 1992), pp. 16–17.

Only in the light of what has been gone through.
Seventh heaven may be
The whole truth of a sixth sense come to pass. (*Squarings*)

But it is to Plato and the slave boy of the *Meno* that Iris Murdoch refers in this context, as he 'sees' an object that is, or was, invisible as something 'there'; 'as if he always knew and was remembering'. The idea of a gradual or relative unveiling is here, of a presence sensed in anticipation; the concept of revelation comes to the forefront of the analysis. And so, as happens in theological discourse also, the idea of faith accompanies the idea of revelation, for it is involved in the idea of anticipation. Iris Murdoch acknowledges at this point her indebtedness to Simone Weil, who described faith as 'an orientation of the soul towards something which one does not know, but whose reality one does know'.[9]

To wait upon, then, to attend to; attention is the characteristic quality of the true artist. Far from setting faith and reason, conviction and reflection against each other, it illustrates the fact that faith and increasing knowledge are contemporary sides of the same coin, or alternating stages of the same continuous process. A veiled presence attracts attention and thereby incites anticipation. This is itself a kind of trusting faith that is correspondingly and increasingly rewarded with an unveiling, and thereby strengthened rather than displaced. Faith is a kind of knowing that sees darkly as it waits upon light. The true artist, Iris Murdoch insists, offers the paradigmatic case of such attention, and of the achievement which in that case is always promised. This is the achievement of an ever broadening and deepening vision of a dynamic fabric of reality that simply transcends our permanent penchant towards an exclusive self-centredness, and thus provides us with a perspective upon reality which is essential to any true realisation of moral value within one and the same reality process. The one, only and whole reality process with which artist and moral agent have to deal.

It is in this way that art is enlisted by Iris Murdoch in aid of the

[9] The element of anticipation in a neonate's interaction with a significant adult was present in the Intersubjective First movement in developmental psychology described above. The role of anticipation in infant learning is part of the very structure of knowing which is exhibited most fully in the artist. For the infant already seems to know something that is to be known, seems to know its reality, as Weil puts it, in anticipation of disclosure of unknown extent through the cooperation of significant adults. In further conversation with Colwyn Trevarthen, concerning this striking combination of knowing already and (so) waiting confidently upon disclosure, which is anticipation, he talked about the natural development of that complex in life whereby as we grow older we revisit a correspondingly growing number of anticipations and their sequence of relative fulfilments, and so have our faith strengthened in a world of indefinite promise – or, of course, threat – to a point where some religious concepts begin to seem worth considering.

transcendence of moral value, a transcendence that carries equally beyond the individual human being's whims and humanity's whims, as and when humanity appears to act universally in the interests of that species, and to the exclusion of the interests of other species and entities. For the practice of art is characterised by attending to things, in that the artist concentrates and waits, anticipating the gradual unveiling. And the published works of art enable less visionary mortals to do this also. So that the dynamic development, the struggle and promise of the great universe of which we are (but) a part – or indeed its decline and promise betrayed – come gradually into the light; and we are enabled to see a grander project than ours, with which ours is nevertheless co-involved, to our fulfilment or diminution. Iris Murdoch often insists that it is only great art which can thus function as intimation of the transcendent; and that has left her open to objections against elitism. But the case must be conclusive for all true art; and that leaves open the very real possibility that there is something of the artist, and certainly some innate appreciation of art, in all of us.

That that great project, of quite incalculable height and depth and breadth, of which we humans are (but) a part, and which we anticipate little by little all our lives, from the womb, quite literally, to our last breath, is in fact a moral project; that reality in its entirety is a moral project, this Iris Murdoch seeks to confirm through the second of the twin themes mentioned above: the theme of the transcendence of the good. The kind of transcendence of the good which she has in mind, it is worth repeating, has nothing in common with those questionable ideas of transcendence which have been noted many times in the course of the critique of various kinds of dichotomous dualism, and which include in their connotation the characteristic of being separate from, extrinsic to, whatever it is that is said to be transcended. The Good, as Iris Murdoch sees it, is immanent everywhere. It is immanent in all of that which humans call moral behaviour, moral judgement, and indeed in the whole moral scene: 'disparate and complex beyond the hopes of any system . . . the good stretches through the whole of it and gives it the only kind of shadowy achieved unity which it can possess'. And with the immanence, as with the transcendence, we are asked to look beyond the human scene, and to see The Good 'evidently and actively incarnate all around us', and continually rediscovered in the course of our daily struggle with the world – where 'with' is not to be taken in the sense of 'against'.[10] It is in terms of transcendence and immanence as correlates rather than contraries, and

[10] Murdoch, *Sovereignty*, p. 97; *Metaphysics*, pp. 478, 427.

in terms of the immanence of that transcendent good in the whole of reality, that Iris Murdoch argues for what can then be called the absolute transcendence of The Good.

THE ABSOLUTE TRANSCENDENCE OF THE SOVEREIGN GOOD
A PLATONIC METAPHYSICS OF MORALITY

Iris Murdoch does make much use of the (in)famous Ontological Argument of Anselm in order to secure the reality of this absolutely transcendent–immanent Good. In the course of her long and elaborate use of this argument she reiterates the point that this Sovereign Good is not a thing or person amongst other things or persons, not 'one empirical phenomenon amongst others', not 'the old literal, personal "elsewhere" God'.[11] And in connection with that particular point she does elaborate more fully her balanced view of a role for traditional religion in morality.

She is as critical as others of the way in which institutional religion has frequently betrayed morality through coercion, condemnation and, at times, downright cruelty. But since that same institutionalised worship of a personal divinity did, and to an extent still may, provide essential support and inspiration for moral discernment and moral struggle, she is really calling for it to be demythologised rather than dismissed out of hand. And even demythologising seems to mean that it can retain its mythic forms and expressions, provided that the people who now use these do so on the explicit understanding that they are mythic, that is to say, means accommodated to the human condition that are designed to represent in the most concrete and memorable manner the unrepresentable. In this way a personal God can be regarded as an image or 'shadow' of a sovereign reality which is not a person. Rituals can be regarded as outward signs of inward, moral realities which are thereby kept before the community mind, identified and fostered. Prayer can be a kind of sustained, fervent, indeed supplicant, contemplative *attendance* upon the transcendent good, so as to increase its permanent magnetism on human life. Such in brief is a hint of the kind of demythologised religious myth which could restore to the good and to morality its necessary religious dimension, without the danger of idolatry and the detriment to morality which the worship of lesser go(o)ds inevitably entails.

But all of this could have been said without recourse to Anselm's distinctive argument; and it leaves us no further on than Hick's or

---

[11] Murdoch, *Metaphysics*, pp. 412, 415, 420.

Rothko's utterly indeterminate absolute. Furthermore, Iris Murdoch insists – and she insists that Anselm recognised this – there is an appeal to experience embedded in Anselm's argument. There is an appeal to a universal, recognisable moral experience. This consists in the orientation towards good (and evil) which is fundamental and ubiquitous in human existence. And it is just as fundamentally and ubiquitously accompanied by sequences of comparisons. For we gradually learn how unimportant was what we once thought important; how much more valuable are things and experiences and activities we at first could not see, beyond what we heretofore recognised as values, and now realise were lesser values, and our pursuit of them relative failures on our part. But this is an experience of goodness, or the good, operative everywhere in our world. An experience moreover in which we seem to be drawn constantly to higher and better values, so that our consciousness of failure is itself a source of knowledge, 'as we recognise and identify good and degrees of good, and are thus able to have the idea of the greatest good conceivable'.[12]

All of which makes one wonder if the elaborate appeal to Anselm's highly controversial argument leaves Iris Murdoch any closer to establishing the reality of Absolutely Transcendent, Sovereign Good than would the kind of Platonic metaphysics (with its similar problem of the existential status of the Forms) which shapes the more common hinterland of Iris Murdoch's philosophy. For the Platonic context in which Iris Murdoch sets her argument for the sovereignty of the good, as well as the parallelism between love and art as the named sources of that 'attending to' in which the intimations of the transcendence of the good are to be found, both suggest a certain view of the nature of art and of the artist's vocation which is still worth considering.

The account of the common service of love (Eros, passion) and art to the approach to the good, and the requisite transcendence of that comprehensive moral value, finds its most memorable expression in the history of Western philosophy in Plato's *Symposium*, in the instruction which Socrates receives from a 'wise woman', Diotima, one of those female embodiments of divine wisdom familiar in the wisdom literature of the ancient world from the Book of Proverbs to Boethius' *De Consolatione Philosophiae*. For in this context Beauty is added, as the third of the great transcendentals, to Truth and Good. The coincidence of truth and good has been analysed already in the course of a preferment of

[12] Ibid. p. 395.

practicalist theories of knowledge: it is in the course of practical interaction with the world, an interaction in which good or evil is realised, that we come to know the world. Each and every instance of a more speculative excursus in knowing is secondary to and derivative from this experience of practical interaction with reality. Hence, the process of at once recognising and realising good (and evil) is itself the process of uncovering truth (and falsehood). *Ens et verum convertuntur; ens et bonum convertuntur*; reality itself is at once a moral and cognitive enterprise. Plato, if anything, in a famous passage in the *Republic*, gives the priority to the good and its realisation in the coincident cognitive process of knowing reality. 'The reality that gives their truth to the objects of knowledge and the power of knowing to the knower, you must say is the idea of the good and you must conceive of it as being the cause of knowledge and truth.' And in that same passage he immediately adds to the notes of the true and the good, the note of beauty: 'Yet beautiful as knowledge and truth are, you must think of the good being more beautiful than these' (508d–509b). Now, it is by tying the note of beauty to that of the good that Diotima, in her instruction to Socrates, brings art into relationship with love in the process of realising the transcendence of the good.

The first thing she says about love, when she moves from myth (where she describes love as a *daimon*, a cosmic power rather than a god) to analysis and argument (*logos*), is that 'love is of the beautiful'. But when asked in effect, What then is beauty? – 'when a man loves the beautiful what does he love?' – she puts the word good in the place of 'the beautiful', and proceeds to explain how it is to the good that love drives and is drawn; that is to say, to the possession of the good and, moreover, to the everlasting possession of the good. Yet beauty straightaway comes back into the account as soon as ever the question is asked about the more concrete details of the actual process through which in love we are drawn or driven towards this everlasting possession of the good. For the answer to this more concrete question is this: in love we are driven and drawn to 'give birth in beauty'. This answer is quickly glossed in terms of our being repulsed by deformity, with the implication that beauty, the love of which drives us to give birth, to (pro)create, is in some important sense a matter of form.

There follows a typically Platonic progression in which this concrete and detailed process is illustrated by a sequence of such (pro)creations, ranging from the lowest bodily instance of the procreation of our children to the higher and higher forms of creation which involve soul or spirit more than, and ultimately instead of, body. Although, it is worth remarking incidentally, the desire for everlasting possession of the good of which Diotima spoke earlier is now glossed as the desire for immortality, and it is said to be in part at least achieved by every act of creation, including the procreation of our human progeny, 'the mystery of man and woman, which is a divine thing'. Nevertheless the love which drives one to the procreation of human progeny is always drawn towards the appreciation and creation of other 'children', the forms of virtuous living, the forms of the best laws and institutions of the state, the forms of science and wisdom; until one is finally drawn through all these lesser mysteries to a vision of the absolutely transcendent beauty that is immanent in all these manifold forms and in their human realisations; until one finds,

> under the boughs of love and hate,
> In all poor foolish things that live a day,
> Eternal beauty wandering on her way.
> (Yeats, *To the Rose upon the Rood of Time*)

Or, in Diotima's own words, 'beauty only, absolute, separate, single, and everlasting, which without diminution or increase, or any change, is imparted to the evergrowing and perishing beauties of all other things'.[13]

There are aspects of Diotima's account that are surely accessible to, and perhaps helpful for, those contemporary modes of analysis and argument concerning the transcendence of the good and the consequent appreciation of reality as a moral project which are just now in contention. These elements of Diotima's account are the conceptual linkage of beauty to the good, on the one hand, and to form, on the other, through the ubiquitous influence of Eros; the role of revelation in the vision that coincides with creating and being possessed by the beautiful-and-the-good; and the consequent role of art in the appreciation and creation of that which is simultaneously the beautiful and the good.

The first of these elements, even without the need which is felt by some authors at this point for an Aristotelian gloss on Plato, is immediately accessible from the discussion in the preceding chapter of this essay, on the manner in which emotivist theories of morality could be rid of their subjectivist, non-realist, non-cognitivist straitjacket, provided

---

[13] Benjamin Jowett's translation of the *Symposium* is used here, as found in *Plato's Symposium and Phaedrus* (New York: Dover, 1993).

only that far more extensive analysis be devoted to emotion or passion, and its essentially formed and informative functioning.

Aristotle pointed to form in the material universe as the source or locus of motion; hence as the e-motive entity. One does not have to add the insistence that Aristotle, as is sometimes said, brought Plato's forms back to earth. One needs only to forget for a moment the problem about the existential status of Plato's forms in view of certain things said about them in their transcendent mode. Or, alternatively, one needs only to recall that Plato's forms, even when described in the most transcendent terms, are simultaneously said to be 'imparted' to 'evergrowing and perishing . . . things'; so that there is a very real sense in which Plato's forms, like Hegel's Spirit, never leave the world. And then one can see that modern modes of thought, albeit far more scientifically sophisticated, and these ancient modes of thought in Plato as well as Aristotle, are mutually accessible to each other. One can then bring ancient and modern together to throw light on art and beauty and their relationship to a moral enterprise that is in and of this world.

All matter is always already formed. Even the most fundamental particle, the most common-denominator building block, of the whole universe, if such a thing there be, will when and if it is found have properties. That is to say, it will already be a formed entity. Otherwise it could neither be detected nor described. Form epistemologically and metaphysically precedes matter in both microcosm and macrocosm. A universe in which material particles which have as yet no form combine, at first perhaps randomly, in order to give rise to formed things is, quite literally, inconceivable; and inconceivable in a way that has nothing whatever to do with the enormous size of the probability, or improbability, quotient involved. Therefore in this constantly creative, that is to say evolving, universe, selection or, better, adaptation epistemologically and metaphysically precedes the operation of the so-called random factor, however obvious and large at least at some levels of physics and of evolution theory the weight of that random factor may prove to be.

The unified fabric of reality is composed of a continuously creative process constituted throughout all its parts and at all its so-called levels by the interaction of forms. Each individual form and each species form apparently driven and drawn to (or repulsed from) interaction with other forms of matter, in quest of fulfilment of one kind or another. In this constant and ubiquitous interaction of forms there is mutual in-formation. There is also mutual re-formation (eu-formation), or malformation. And there is mutual transformation or deformation. The mutual in-formation secures a place in reality itself for knowledge and truth, or falsehood; one thinks again of Deutsch's insistence on the place of knowledge amongst the entities that make up the dynamic fabric of reality. The mutual reformation or malformation secures the place of moral enterprise within that same dynamic fabric of reality. Equally and simultaneously, the mutual transformation or deformation secures a place for beauty and ugliness, its appreciation and creation, as a part of the fabric of reality of equal right and status with the other two.

It is the transformed that is sought by each formed entity which interacts with others in its vital efforts to pro-create itself or its kind. For beauty is first and foremost also a matter of form; and when Diotima says that the agent seeks beauty – 'for in deformity he will beget nothing' – although she is talking about the human aspirant to perfection, she is in fact broaching a general law of reality by which each form of reality seeks the transformed and attempts to avoid the deformed. In any case, beauty now joins goodness and truth as the characteristic of all creative and created things. It is in one and the same creative or destructive interaction of adjacent formed entities that beauty, truth and goodness – or ugliness, falsehood and evil – are at one and the same time encountered and engendered. In fact, Diotima hints at this broader view of the overall unity of this creative interplay of forms in the material universe. (For it could be that local interplays alone took place with the results of localised and unrelated creations and destructions; and then we should not have a universe at all, and not even a multiverse in Deutsch's version of it.) So Diotima speaks of pro-creation in beauty rather than in deformity, in terms of harmony with the divine. This can be interpreted in terms of a transcendent harmony that is sought through all interactive forms together, transcending all local interactions, that is to say, and forming a universe, which to Diotima is an affordance that derives from a creative and providential divinity, like the *demiourgos* of the *Timaeus*.

Eros, passion, emotion name the dynamic feature which characterises all form in that universal interaction by which forms appear both driven and drawn to other forms. And form names, well, the forms or shapes by which Eros is configured in this material universe. Is there an entity operative in this universe which is not itself a particular form like the others that we know, not additional to and separate from them, but is instead some all-encompassing, unbounded (infinite, in that sense) entity? And is it yet erotic in the original sense of that word, driven by its own passion (and drawn?) to creation? And how then could its relationship to the formed and interactive entities we know be construed? Diotima (Plato) had suggestions to make in answer to these questions. But answers to these questions at this point of the present investigation are still in the offing; and if past anticipations are anything to go by, they may not be forthcoming, if at all, until the universe as a whole is interrogated.

For the moment it is necessary only to note that the creative evolution which takes place continuously in this universe through this interplay of e-motive forms, is named in aesthetic terms as beautiful or ugly in so far as it is transformative or deformative according to degrees of perfection or imperfection achieved. It is named in moral terms as good or evil in so far as re-formation or mal-formation secures the existential fulfilment or diminishment of the needs or potentialities of those involved. And it is named in epistemological terms in so far as all transformation, deforma-tion, reformation and malformation succeeds in mutually in-forming those engaged in this universal process. Beauty and goodness are two sides of the triangle of which truth is the third. Exactly the same universal process, made up of substantial and accidental forms in continuous interplay, exhibits the perfection of form that enables us to admire and to further create. It exhibits the values that we encounter and then use to further evaluate. And it exhibits the truth of things which, because it is found in and through *interaction* of entities, enables each knower involved to be roused from individual dreaming – whether night- or day-dreaming – and to know both self and other in the manner and to the degree for which each knower is equipped to do so. Further-more, each of these processes that are reactive to the universal interplay of erotic forms is also reciprocally engaged with each of the others. Truth and beauty are valued morally as fulfilment of some of the most pressing needs and potentialities of life. The goodness and beauty of things form the truth that the knower craves. Truth and goodness in expression give rise to the admiration and appreciation that beauty calls forth. (One remembers that Descartes listed admiration first amongst the passions.) So much, then, for the first of the elements which Diotima's instruction to Socrates contributes to our current analysis.

The second, the role of revelation in the vision that coincides with possessing and being possessed by the beautiful and the good, and in being repulsed by the deformed and the evil, is more implicit in Diotima's speech, but it is important to note it nevertheless. It is implicit in the whole manner in which she describes how the degrees of beauty are gradually disclosed to the quester who is driven by his own Eros to 'procreate in beauty', until Eternal Beauty, in which all other beauty participates to the degree that beauty is imparted to them, is finally unveiled and possesses her. In fact, disclosure, unveiling, revelation, is the experienced prerequisite of all knowing, all valuing and all admiration or appreciation (there seems to be no clear word for the aesthetic side of the triangle, as there is for the moral and epistemological sides). In all cases something is dis-covered. Forms mutually in-form all formed entities, and in the process something of the invasive forms as well as something of the forms invaded is disclosed, revealed. I know even myself in the course of my interaction with other entities.

Indeed in the case of that kind of interaction which takes place between persons in (symbolic) communication, something that transcends all particular forms is co-revealed in the course of that particular in-formation – or so it seems. For, as was said in connection with reflective consciousness, and in discussing semiology also, personal beings forever transcend even the forms which fill their empirical consciousness. Yet they communicate that very transcendence of all form which is somehow theirs; and they do so in the very process of signing to each other, more than they do by means of any particular set of signs. Is there a clue here to the question awhile back concerning the operative presence in this universe of an entity which is not a determinate, formed and finite thing amongst others, and concerning its possible relationship to forms? That question must still await interrogation of the universe as such, in so far as it is humanly possible to interrogate it. For the moment it is necessary only to stress the principle that revelation is a constitutive part of all knowing. And the point of referring especially to the reflective consciousness that is characteristic of persons as we know them, is that it seems to cause a problem for the principle just announced. Indeed the most acute problem is caused for this principle precisely at the point at which one considers art as the intimation of that transcendence which secures the objectivity of moral value. To the extent that the artist (too) is going beyond the most empirical current content of reality disclosed, has she not also gone beyond the precept to attend to what is being revealed, and thus forfeited at least some of her claim to secure the objectivity of moral value in the world? Does not moral value once again turn out to be, in part at least, invented *rather than* discovered, to use the key terms in the cognitivist/non-cognitivist debate?

For, as has been said often already, that very ability to transcend all content of empirical consciousness which characterises such persons also entails their ability to construct ideas, formulae and, in the case of artists reflecting upon emotion in tranquillity, images and visions of things which go beyond any and all of their encountered forms. To that ability the creativity (freedom) of the moral agent and the creativity of the working artist has been attributed. But then, by the same token, must it not be admitted that the part of these ideas, formulae, images or visions which go beyond, which exceed, current empirical content is not constituted by any revelation, any contemporary disclosure; that it is instead an autonomous product of these reflective minds? Confining the question to art and artists here, is it not the case that their very creativity functions precisely so as to carry them beyond all that is revealed to their requisite attentiveness; that it carries them to the point at which the truly visionary dimension of their work resembles more a *creatio ex nihilo* than a vision in which the real is revealed? As Valéry once said about the work of art: *c'est le commencement d'un monde.*

ART AND THE ARTIST
THE EXTENT OF THE ARTISTIC REVELATION OF THE REAL
THE EXTENT TO WHICH THE REAL IS REVEALED AS A MORAL
ENTERPRISE

The key to the problem just now encountered is to be found in the same place as was the key to the problem of the objectivity of knowledge, once knowledge was seen to be a constituent element in the fabric of reality: it is to be found, namely, in the process of *interaction of forms* or, more generally stated, in that evolutionary, continuously creative process which consists in the mutual adaptation of forms of matter in this world. Looked at as a process of mutual in-formation, that process accounts for knowledge at all levels at which knowledge is deemed to occur. And it simultaneously accounts for the objectivity of such knowledge, since each form of being learns of itself and of other co-involved forms precisely from their experienced interaction with and upon each other (the practicalist theory of knowledge in its most adequate form). For the nature (*physis*) of any entity is known from the characteristic behaviour of its be*ing* in such continuous interaction; just as the individuals that compose any natural species are known from the distinctive forms and sequences of such behaviour in which they each indulge.

Consider that same cosmic creative–evolutionary process now from the point of view of ubiquitous trans-formation (or de-formation), rather than from the point of view of in-formation (or dis-information), and the key to the problem of the artist at her most creative, the answer to the question as to the persistence of objectivity in the very creativity of the work of art, is well within one's grasp. And with that, the key to the understanding of the continued role of attention and, as a further consequence, the key to the understanding of the role of revelation in the most creative work of art. So that, if the perpetual in-formational and trans-formational processes in which reality as a whole seems to consist can also be deemed eu-(or mal-)formational, that is to say moral processes, in that needs and potentialities are constantly fulfilled or frustrated, then art and artists can indeed fulfil the role which modern moral philosophers expect of them. They can act to establish such intimations of those trans(re)formational and de(mal)formational reality processes that carry us well beyond human individual and communal whim, while including, of course, the interests of humanity and its increasingly influential creativity. They can thus establish those intimations of the transcendent on which, as contemporary philosophers insist, the objectivity of moral value rests secure. And all of this while maintaining the necessary distinctions between art and morality, and without turning every artist into an *ipso facto* moralist.

Take again the common view that the object of art is beauty. This view is sometimes rejected as both unrealistic and too precious by half; but such rejection can be reversed by accepting that beauty here stands for its opposite also. Then take another traditional view that beauty is a matter of form (perfection or imperfection of form); not a matter of form only however, but a matter of light shining, of splendour (or incursive shadow) also; and there is already a remarkable coincidence of key terms between art and creation in general. In the first creation story in Genesis, for instance, form and light are the twin foundational images. Creation itself is a matter, first, of forming entities in (or out of) 'prime' matter, the no-thing, the empty, the void; and it is simultaneously a matter of forms coming to light. Light, the first reality to come into being, without which the emergent forms could not be perceived, much less their cosmic inter-relationship, and the dynamic future which that inter-relationship promises. It is not an explicit part of the Genesis account of that creativity which operates at the cosmic level of the entire cosmos, but it is surely a tolerable extension of it, to say that the forms then reflect the light. Their reflection of the light into which they have been brought reveals both the created things themselves in their current forms, and the creative power that continues to operate in them. But it also and inevitably reveals something of the prospects and promises of their future forms as a result of that continuous creativity.

This is clear enough in the case of the newly created human form, which is distinctly described as being in the image of the creator of the cosmos. And it is clarified further in the co-creative role given to human beings under the image of steward of the creation or, in the second creation story in Genesis, the image of the gardener who was to tend the garden – until, of course, as the subsequent story of the Wisdom Tree (the tree of the knowledge of good and evil) has it, they threatened the whole project by trying to appropriate divine wisdom to their own, instead of attending to the wisdom of the creator which was already shining for them also from the rest of the evolving creation. From such accounts of cosmic creativity, then, one can see that revelation, disclosure, coming to light, reflecting the light, can be coincident with creativity. And when one then notices the role of light in the very creativity of the artist, one can also begin to see that, even at the most creative point of that creativity, revelation is most operative, not least. And from that point of view, art as intimation of the transcendent in a manner that secures the objectivity of moral value is safe from suspicion.

'I am always shy of calling myself a poet', wrote the Irish poet Patrick Kavanagh (in a preface to his *Collected Poems*). He seems to mean that he shied away from thinking of himself as one who had a special craft, a particular technique which therefore enabled him to produce, to create, things which others could not produce, or produce so well. And he certainly included, amongst such things that such craft might mistakenly be deemed to produce, moral precepts or moral values. 'A true poet', he continues, 'is selfish and implacable. A poet merely states the position and does not care whether his words change anything or not.' 'There is something wrong with a work of art, some kinetic vulgarity in it when it becomes visible to policemen.' What, then, is the true source of his art? 'I wasn't really a writer. I had seen a strange beautiful light on the hills and that was all.'[14] He then 'innocently dabbles in words and rhymes and finds that it is his life'; and then, there is no doubt, he discovered techniques of production, or acquired them. But it was the light and his patient lifelong attention to it, his attending and waiting upon it, that is the true source of his works of art in poetry and prose. It was the strange beautiful light that made him an artist, and made of his art a channel of the revelation of reality, of the way things are together in their common

[14] Patrick Kavanagh's autobiography, *The Green Fool* (London: Penguin, 1975), p. 239. The other quotations in this paragraph are taken from the preface to his *Collected Poems* (London: Martin Breen and O'Keeffe, 1972). He also says in that preface: 'I have never been much considered by the English critics.' Yet the sheer spiritual depth of his best poetry may serve as evidence that the English are sometimes no more judicious in selecting Irish poets for honours than they were in selecting Hume from the ranks of Scottish philosophers.

world, transformed and deformed, mortal and immortal, just as they are and can be, as Heidegger would say, in their very be*ing*.

When describing reality as a moral enterprise, and noting the central-ity of Eros, it is often said that it is difficult to decide whether to talk in terms of being driven through need and potency, or in terms of being drawn by the attractive affordances of equally needy and potential entities in the environment. The decision is to talk simultaneously in both sets of terms; and this because of the ubiquitous interaction, the interplay, of all formed entities that is in turn an inevitable feature of the very mutual interdependence of all entities, by which they live, and live more abundantly, each by the others' grace and at the others' expense, and thus make up a true universe. This is the actual universe that we know, in which adaptation is the engine and random mutation the recurring opportunity. Eros is even more at the heart of the universe viewed now as an aesthetic enterprise.[15] It is equally difficult to say whether it drives from within oneself towards transformation-to-beauty, or is drawn towards the transformations (and repulsed from the defor-mations) of our co-activists in the creative evolution of our universe. But again it is best to say that it is both drawn and driven for the same reasons of all things living by each other's grace and expense; and it is possible, and useful at this stage, to make this point in terms of light.

Thinking of the interplay of forms in which this universe consists, then; thinking of this in terms now, not of re-formation in which needs are fulfilled, but of trans-formation in which increasing perfection of form is secured (or the deformity in which it is damaged); thinking of the light that shines from these forms forever engaged in mutually creative (or destructive) dynamism, it is necessary to see this light simultaneously shining forward from present to future from the point of view of the form first in perspective:

> What's come upon is manifest
> Only in the light of what has been gone through.

And simultaneously shining back from the future, from the perspective of the form that is to grace the first at its own expense:

---

[15] As we have seen in Plato's linking Eros and beauty and giving birth in beauty. Dante with his Beatrician experience is possibly the greatest subsequent exponent of this connection: 'the Love that moves the Sun and the other stars' has a particular affinity with the poets whom he calls *fideli d'Amore*. See Thomas Finan, 'Dante and the Religious Imagination', in J. P. Mackey (ed.), *Religious Imagination* (Edinburgh University Press, 1986). Kavanagh too is no mean exponent of the connection between suffering love and the art of poetry: see, for example, his poem 'Prelude' in *Collected Poems*.

Things in the offing, once they're sensed
Convert to things foreknown.

There is inevitably a gradual lessening of the light, according to the distance into which it reaches and from which it comes. This increasing shadow, this relative darkness, can represent many things. It can represent a further level of as yet unformed potential; a kind of inviting darkness that welcomes further reflection of light; on the analogy of a kind of transcendent consciousness positively open to indefinite degrees of empirical content. But the penumbra can also re-present, make powerfully present to us, either the cost to the forms involved in gracing each other, or the graceless incursion of positively destructive forces which the very same creative processes in which the universe consists can in our all-too-common experience unleash. In all events, it is the artist's métier to capture these mutually creative or destructive forms as they come to light, or move into darkness, and to allow these to be seen through the ensuing work of art by those of more prosaic vision. In so far as one can distinguish the aura light that shines into or from distance of time or space, from the clearer light of accomplished detail that reaches the more superficial eye from each activated stage of the be*ing* of the embodied forms, then one could say that the distinctive contribution of the artist by avocation consists in enabling the rest of us to see more clearly that aura of the continuing transformation or deformation of things. In bringing to form and visibility the aura light that shines from the ever-transforming fabric of reality, the artist is a visionary, also now in the sense of that word which connotes the shape of things to come, the form of what might well be, an increasingly ideal state of being or, of course, its very opposite.

Now, naturally, something of the artist's own creativity is superimposed upon the creative transformations that are continuously revealed. Yet even this feature of the artist's work, where it most reflects the artist's own distinctive creativity and particular vision, is still guided and ruled from the revelation vouchsafed by the trans-formative interplay of forms in the whole of reality as we know it. If only because the artist is by vocation most highly aware of the creative form of the human being as itself a pivotal player in the cosmic interplay of forms. For then the true, the good, artist, even at the most creative dimension of her own work, can be said to be revealing to others what is revealed to her from the penumbra of darkly seen possibilities of further human creativity (or destruction). A 'seeing', then, that is no less objective because it is human prospective creation that is represented, on the analogy of moral values which are coincidentally created by human action and discovered to be such by human perception. And all the more objective since the implacable artist always sees better than most the interactive participation of the human with the broader reality of which it is so much a part.

Hence the compelling nature of the artist's clearer discernment of forms as yet inchoate in the light that shines from things into or from the future of all, by dint of continuous transformation, is due entirely to the degree of attendance upon reality which the artist achieves. It is due to the artist's fidelity to the shining, to the revelation, then vouchsafed – for the response to revelation is faith – from whatever height or depth or breadth of an ever transforming world it has been vouchsafed, and in whatever ratio of clear or established detail of form at the centre of the revelation, to increasingly inchoate detail of form in the penumbra; it is to this that the claim on behalf of the artist to enable all of us to see reality as it is, to merely state the position implacably, as Kavanagh would say, is due. And upon this in turn rests the claim of art to offer intimations of the transcendent of the kind analysed above, which are said to secure the objectivity of moral value.

Now, that final claim depends entirely on the view of the works of art as channels of the revelations of the real to folk of weaker vision or poor attention or, more usually, both. Monet's *Water Lilies* allows such folk to see the lilies and the pond and the surrounding landscape as they would never otherwise have seen all of this. The painting itself is not the end product of a special kind of producer called a painter, the end or goal of which lies in the contemplation and enjoyment of the painting itself. This is the point made about poets and poetry by Patrick Kavanagh. And it is a point that can be appreciated more keenly by looking again at Diotima's qualified acknowledgement of the artists in their service to the pursuit of the really good. For Diotima does acknowledge the specific role of the artist in the activity and experience to which Eros drives and draws, that is to say, the activity and experience of (pro)creating in beauty. In her order of excellence of those who create in beauty, higher than those who procreate human children she places those who are 'more creative in their souls than in their bodies', those whose creations, generically named, are wisdom and virtue. And first amongst the latter she names 'poets and other artists who may be said to have invention'. But these are then quickly superseded in her hierarchy by those who creatively order 'states and families', just as Homer and Hesiod are said to be superseded by Solon; and finally by those who pursue together the love of wisdom to the point of beholding 'true beauty divine and simple'. Of these last she comments: 'Do you not see that in that communion only, beholding beauty with the eye of the mind, he will be enabled to bring forth, not images of beauty, but realities; for he has hold, not of an image but of reality.'

That, as it stands, seems to amount to a rather stark contrast between the artist, on the one hand, who is pictured confined to the production and contemplation of images of a reality which is good and beautiful, and, on the other hand, the philosopher, or principally the philosopher, who simultaneously creates reality as he contemplates the beauty and goodness of the real. Yet the careful reader of Diotima's speech will see that contrast modified in two ways. First, and earlier in her instruction to Socrates, Diotima had made the following significant admission: 'All creation or passage of non-being into being is poetry or making, and the processes of all art are creative; and the masters of art (*techne*) are all poets.' According to that passing piece of definition, all those who create, who bring something into being in a form in which it did not exist before, are artists and indeed poets, if only by extension of that term in accordance with its etymological root, which refers to making (*poiesis*). These general artists create realities, then, and not just images of realities. And they create in beauty, presumably; which must mean that they contemplate beauty also in reality and not in image only, as part of their activity and experience of creating. So, second, the implication is that the 'true beauty divine and simple' which both philosophers and all common practitioners of the arts and crafts get hold of in the very act and experience of creating in beauty, is entirely immanent in the universe, an eternal beauty wandering through all of its history, and yet entirely transcendent, as the process of imparting–participation which the Platonic Diotima uses would in any case imply.

On a finer critical analysis, then, what can be gathered even from the distant Platonic sources is this: in so far as the artist is obsessed with the work of art as the end product and itself the object of future contemplation, she is of second-rate importance in the creative knowing of reality itself. From the time of the pre-Socratics the complaint against the poets, the myth-makers, was that they tended to place imaginary entities before *ta onta*, the things that are. And the suggestion that the poets should be banned from Plato's ideal Republic is based on that same suspicion of their placing the image between us and reality. Yet artists are not in the end banned from Plato's

Republic.[16] They clearly have their part to play in it, even if that part, because of Plato's (like Hegel's) preference for philosophy, might to the cynical resemble too closely the official role of the dramatist in the old Soviet Union. And Plato's repeated case for the part that mathematics plays in the education of the moral agent might anticipate a preference for science over art in securing (*pace* O'Hear) the transcendent ground for moral values and their consequent objectivity. Even so, the point remains that it is in so far, and only in so far, as the artist succeeds in her work in opening our eyes to the revelations of (the goodness and beauty of) the real, that she enables us to create in beauty or, more precisely put, to play our part in that cosmic process in which reality itself creatively evolves, and simultaneously and increasingly realises the goodness and beauty that do and can characterise it.

And yet, all of that being said, there is still an impression abroad, from original Platonic times to our own time, that art is still secondary to science (metaphysics-philosophy) in providing intimations of transcendence such as would secure objective status for whatever we think to have or need such status. Say all of that. Say again that the work of art opens the eyes of the soul to deeper and more distant realms of the dynamic real. Because the true artist attends upon a light that comes, however dimly, from reaches of be*ing* that are deeper in the future and more distant than those occupied by human being. (In the ancient Irish tradition to which Kavanagh is beholden, the poet is a seer, and the practice is attested in which the poet spent days in darkness waiting upon a more rarefied light from such more distant reaches, in order to see the shapes of things to which the common light of day all but blinds the common man.) Say all of that, and some would still say more for science. Particularly when science is pursued to and through those more theoretical reaches at which the so-called theories of everything come into view, when physics can reasonably come to be called metaphysics. And more particularly still when this exponentially developing science is accompanied, *pari passu*, as it invariably is, by an equally exponential increase in the sophistication and power of human technology. Surely at this stage of the world's history the old Platonic preference is quite beyond dispute: the preference for (the scientist–philosopher–

[16] Because Plato wrote philosophy as dialogue in which he himself is not a participant, it is dangerous to take any view expressed by the participants as Plato's view; and this is particularly true of expelling the poets from the Republic. There are wider issues here, of Plato thinking of philosophy as a conversation between spiritual questers to be carried on down the centuries, and not as something to be congealed in a system; but these belong in another place.

technician) being enabled to get 'hold not of an image but of reality' and consequently to 'bring forth, not images . . . but realities'.

There is unquestionably a case for science–metaphysics–technology providing the kind of intimations of the transcendent which would in turn secure the objectivity of moral value in the universe. Science prides itself on objectivity, and there is no reason to doubt the fact that that objectivity also characterises those metaphysical reaches to which modern science increasingly extends. Science–metaphysics, then, by attending to that cosmic mutual in-formation in which universal be*ing* in fact consists, can plot the relative and evolving constructions and destructions of the forms of reality that are permanently co-involved. And these, read now from the point of view of the Eros-driven moral agent, coincide with the mutual fulfilment or depletion of needs and potentialities, and so with the moral good or evil that represents moral value in objective reality. Why then should one not continue to accept that those who deal directly with and through realities contribute more to securing the objectivity, the reality, of moral values in the universe than do those who deal with reality in and through images of it?[17]

Before attempting to answer that question in such a way as to support those who favour art in securing the necessary objectivity of morals, it is worth observing that both scientists and artists, in different ways and in varying degrees, resent being treated as moralists. The scientist does so by insisting that it is her business to discover how things work; and it is only when technology decides to put such knowledge to particular practical purposes that moral issues arise. The artist does so by insisting even more implacably on simply revealing, simply stating the position concerning the real. Both, it would appear, must have their pleas allowed. It can be pointed out to them, of course, that in the actual conduct of their professions they are subject to the same kinds of moral obligation to do good work rather than bad as they are in the rest of their lives, and as the rest of the human race is. And if they resent even that suggestion that they must be moralists to that most common extent – and they may resent even that, because of the fear that even this might bring the philistine censor to their laboratories and studios or, worse still, the religious believer armed with ready-made precepts purportedly from above – they may be mollified by the further suggestion that the authors of, and so the primary authorities on, the morality of any way of life are the practitioners thereof.

[17] The whole modern debate about imagination is caught up in these questions. See especially the articles by Mary Warnock and A. D. Nuttall in my *Religious Imagination*.

Yet, that proviso accepted and aside, the scientist's refusal to be seen
to be making and implementing value judgements in the course of
specifically scientific work is not quite as fully justified as is the artist's.
And for that very reason, paradoxical as this might seem, the artist may
argue a case to be preferred to the scientist in the role of securing the
necessary intimations of the transcendence of moral value within the
fabric of reality. For the practising scientist, precisely because she 'gets
hold' of realities, and long before the technologist 'brings forth' new
forms of realities; because of the experimental nature of scientific investigation and research, and the sheer and ever-growing range of actual
interference with the forms of reality which experimentation involves,
must always already invoke and implement moral guidelines.[18] Whereas
the artist, recollecting emotion in tranquillity, reflecting in her passion
for the beauty of form – and reflecting particularly perhaps upon these
very scientifico-technological processes amongst all the others that go on
in the world – does nothing more than image these forth in the creative
work of art which then enables all of us to view more deeply the cosmic
transformation and deformation in which reality consists.

The case is even clearer when it comes to crossing the line between
'pure' science and technology, at least in those instances where that line
can be crossed. For the line twists and turns and sometimes fades to the
point of disappearance; and it seems to do this more frequently as the
techniques of investigation increase in modern science. Try drawing a
line between research and technology in the case of contemporary
genetic engineering, for instance. Indeed the line is likely to disappear
completely as the human race comes more and more into control of the
continuous creation of the universe until, in Deutsch's envisaged eschaton for example, it can never be drawn again. Now here one begins to
see the advantage of the artist; and an advantage moreover that looms
larger as time goes on. For the artist gets hold of an image by attending
imaginatively–intelligently to reality itself in its very be*ing*, and produces
an image, a useless thing in straight utilitarian terms, which enables
others to see that reality as it truly and deeply and most objectively and
extensively becomes and is. Thus the artist lets us learn, through the
ciphers of the transformations and deformations of reality, through its

---

[18] Polanyi is most frequently mentioned as one who insisted on the inevitably human, and hence
even the moral, dimension in the procedures of science. He was reticent concerning any further,
religious, dimension, although Drusilla Scott in her *Michael Polanyi* (London: SPCK, 1996) tries to
extrapolate to that dimension also. See also Wilson Poon's review of Keith Ward, *God, Chance and
Necessity* (Oxford: One World, 1996), in *Studies in World Christianity* 4 (1998), 255–8.

characteristic categories of beauty and ugliness, and exclusively through these, what is and will be good and bad for any and all of the forms involved in the whole unified interplay of forms which constitute the continuously creative universe. The artist lets us learn of good and evil, without needing to use these moral categories at all, and thus without preaching or moralising.

That same advantage of the artist can be more pointedly put. By observing that the scientist–technologist, though she can be asked to be, and is capable of being, as objective as necessary in her necessarily entwined moral judgements in both her 'pure' and 'applied' science, is still quite naturally inclined to see herself, and to be seen, as the one who is in control of her interactions with the relevant forms of reality. And she and her fellow human beings are those whose good and wellbeing are, quite naturally again, uppermost in mind, in the whole course of scientific procedures, from initial research to resultant technology. It is therefore a matter of prudence, to put the matter no stronger, that such a one should be able to benefit from the less threatened objectivity of the implacable artist who, by attending to reality as such, without interfering with it or making anything of practical use from it, sees the promise and the suffering of every living thing, and of the living universe as such, and lets others then see it also. This is presumably the case that can be made for those who chose art as the intimation of transcendence, and of the consequent reality of the moral enterprise in the universe at large. And it is presumably also the kind of case that Iris Murdoch had in mind, for a vision of goodness that transcends humanity, and reveals a larger vista than any which could be caught in terms of *humanising* the real.

The gifted seer attends, gifted by a greater power of insight and further graced in consequence by greater revelation; waits upon reality, and then creates the work of art. Not a prescription for anyone's conduct, not a moral text in any such sense but, rather, an image communicated of what is seen, enabling those who will not or cannot look and see so well, to see the deepest and highest and widest cosmic interplay of forms; and in particular the apparently ubiquitous mixture of transformation and deformation that characterises the cosmos. In this way the artist succeeds, and in the work of art enables others to succeed, in widening the focus of attention to reality, the apertures accessed by the self-revelation of reality. The focus is then implacably upon reality itself, upon as much of it as humankind can see and bear; on the continuing revelation of be*ing*, as Heidegger, in recognising the poet's part, so well described it. More particularly still the focus is broadened beyond that narrowness which individual or communal whim imposes, or even the increasingly common, yet self-serving, whims of the whole human race. The artist, with this wider focus resolutely directed upon reality, all of reality and nothing but reality, enables others to see into the relative darkness of the inchoate forms of states of affairs in the offing, as well as the incursive darkness of impending and inevitably mutual deformation or destruction. Art, as a consequence and without prescription, subjects our inborn Eros to the lure of that cosmic process of transformation in which we play an increasingly significant part. It submits us simultaneously to the revulsion from deformation perceived or intimated in the cosmic drama in which our part is as objective as any other. Subjecting us willingly to these lures, doing this by letting reality as such appear to us in both practice and promise, and not in the least by moralising about it, art establishes the coincidence of transformation with eu-formation, as of deformation with mal-formation. Coincidentally it secures the transcendence of moral value to the point where that transcends humanity as a whole, its interests, achievements and influences. And at that level of transcendence it borders at the very least upon reality as such as a moral enterprise, in so far as a certain noticeable coincidence of transformation and eu-formation, of deformation and malformation, continues to accompany us as we are drawn beyond the blinkered views of our own human interests and agency.

INTIMATIONS OF THE TRANSCENDENCE OF MORAL VALUE
FROM ART RATHER THAN RELIGION?
THE RELATIONS OF ART TO RELIGION

Now, if this analysis and explanation of art and the role of revelation, or something like it, can secure those 'intimations of the transcendent' which O'Hear required for the subsistence of moral value, can we be sure of the other point that O'Hear and others seem anxious to make, namely, that religion is thereby replaced in such a role by art? Do we have O'Hear's 'non-religious intimations of the transcendent'? And what is then to be said concerning Iris Murdoch's quasi-religious status of the good? For, although she fully shares O'Hear's criticism of traditional theistic, principally Christian, religion, as well his appeal to art to secure the necessary transcendence for moral value, she still finds a role for religion, albeit a thoroughly demythologised religion. Could it not be that the transcendent intimated and indeed revealed, as it has been claimed, in the artist's work is itself of such a status as to justify the epithet religious? There is a large and growing literature on the relationship between art and religion which could be considered in the effort to answer that question. But in order to attempt the least unsatisfactory answer to this question which restrictions placed by the large range of this essay allow, it is necessary to conduct this further investigation by recourse to one sample, consisting of one prominent contemporary exponent of art as our access to a transcendent God, and one contemporary philosopher who is critical of that case.

Undoubtedly the most erudite and passionate argument in recent times for art as our access to God is George Steiner's *Real Presences*.[19] Not that his argument ever attempts to amount to anything approaching an apodictic proof, or a hypothesis that can then be scientifically or even satisfactorily well evidenced. His claim is more humble: that art allows us to 'wager on transcendence' (p. 214). Access or referral from art to this 'transcendent dimension is offered by all Western art from Homer to Kafka'; but music receives special mention as the source and provision of 'intuitions of transcendence'.

> Was music once a proof of God's existence:
> As long as it admits things beyond measure,
> That supposition stands. (Seamus Heaney, *Squarings*)

Transcendence, the transcendent dimension, the transcendent, seems to connote in Steiner's argument that which forever exceeds our intellectual ability to comprehend, as well as our empirical strategies of evidence and proof. As such the transcendent is intimated in our artistic tradition as a whole – though not of course in every work of art which goes to constitute that tradition – as something of an irreducible 'otherness' (p. 210). Thereafter Steiner simply seems to assume that the transcendent (dimension) so defined can be called God. The question as to whether God exists, he believes, is the 'one question ineradicable in man' (p. 220); and art offers the intimation of God's existence, enabling if not persuasively urging us to wager upon the truth and reality of God. There is, however, one additional element to be noted in what otherwise seems a tentative if tenacious argument of quite humble posture and outcome in Steiner's work. At one point, in reference to religious belief and commitment as a wager well supported by artistic vision, he issues something that might almost be construed as a threat: to this effect, that *si Deus non daretur*, or if we will not wager on God's existence in line with

---

[19] London: Faber and Faber, 1989. Page numbers in the text refer to this work.

universal artistic intimations, human thought and creativity itself will be indefinitely diminished.

It is on this last point that Ronald Hepburn first fastened in developing his criticism of Steiner's case. Human thought and creativity, he quite rightly responded, can continue to find meaning and value for life in this world, *etsi Deus non daretur*, and even if we cannot be persuaded that a wager on God's existence is really justified. One needs to be no more than a thoroughgoing agnostic to know this; though atheists of course may know it also. As a matter of fact art itself, in its substantial historical presence and provenance, provides the most persuasive evidence of humanity's ability to continue to find meaning and value in a shared universe, a rich and complex system of shared meaning and value arrived at by human thought and creativity, embodied and transmitted in language and other artistic media. And transcendence is glossed as that which takes us beyond all 'empirical confirmation and scientific demonstration'.

Then, in insisting that all of this is possible in a world where people are not persuaded to wager on God's existence, Hepburn made his own suggestion, crucial to his criticism of Steiner, concerning the manner in which the transcendence of God, or the transcendent that can be called God, is to be understood, at least in the philosophical tradition of the West. The Christian God at least, he suggested, does not emerge from the world to transcend its empirical structures in the manner in which meaning and moral and aesthetic value emerge as a result of human thought and creativity. The Christian 'God is not the world-soul'. Total meaning and the conservation of value in the universe might well depend upon there being a God quite other than and beyond the universe who makes it fully intelligible and who conserves all value through and beyond death. But our ability to find value and meaning increasingly in life and history, although it may well give precious hints towards such total prospect – hints which some people do take to be intimations of a transcendent divinity – could never yield the conclusion that the non-existence of such a one, or even the refusal to wager on its existence, could seriously diminish these achievements of our human thought and creativity. The transcendence towards meaning and value which art exhibits cannot, in the absence of some hard metaphysical evidence for God, act simply, and have itself described without further ado, as intimation of divinity on which we can be urged to wager.

Ronald Hepburn pursues this nicely balanced critique through a number of more concrete examples. To take but one of these examples, he evokes again the power of music to impart an experience of transcending time, generalised as the power of art in general to impart an experience of a transcendent stillness and repose at the heart of all the busy motion of coming to be and passing away. (One thinks here of Hugh MacDiarmid's poem *On a Raised Beach*, in which the stones exhibit in their stillness the greatest and most permanent power of being.) And that of course can arouse in us what Steiner called a refusal of the finality of death. But, once again, in the absence of metaphysical evidence for something or someone who could overcome the most apparent finality of our deaths, such refusal cannot rationalise a wager on our immortality.

Finally, Ronald Hepburn worked the same critique through two general themes which correspond most closely to the themes and treatment of the current investigation. He quoted Mikel Dufrenne to the effect that beauty, the object of art, can be defined as 'the plenitude of the perceived'. Art aims, perhaps asymptotically, at such plenitude of being. It operates always under the lure of that plenitude, through all perceived insufficiency and indeed exigency of being; offering of its nature both promise and intimation. And God is the name for the unsurpassable plenitude and density of being; the totality of the value-ideal envisaged. Further, and with particular reference to the properly creative element of our human part in the drama of being, Ronald Hepburn referred to the oft-used analogy between that and divine creativity. This analogy is often a spring board for the conviction that humanity is co-creator with such a divinity in a cosmic process that can therefore one day arrive at this plenitude of being which art of its nature intimates. But the 'plenitude of perception', that is to say both the plenitude of being and of its perception, at which art of its nature may be said to aim, cannot be said to exist or to be about to exist simply because it is an ideal of art; and much art is powerful precisely in its depiction of both 'ontological deficiency' and the consequent deficiency in our perception. And as far as the creative element in our art and our moral lives is concerned, in the absence of convincing metaphysical evidence to the contrary we can hardly be persuaded even to wager on a divine creator as our co-creator. 'We partly constitute the world, in perceiving it and contemplating it as we do: we are co-creators of it – *along with non-human, unconscious nature* – a collaboration, as it were, of the blind forces of nature and the human power of bringing to consciousness and synthesising in our own unique way.'[20]

---

[20] I have been using and quoting from Ronald Hepburn's lecture to a staff/graduate seminar in the Philosophy Department, University of Edinburgh, January 1996, entitled 'Aesthetic and Religious: Boundaries, Overlaps and Intrusions'.

The best way of mediating between these positions on art and religion is to take up again the troublesome term transcendence, concerning which Ronald Hepburn has also complained of much and frequent confusion in its use. It is significant, perhaps, that in discussing the transcendence which, according to Steiner, art both intimates and achieves, Ronald Hepburn concentrated on the materials of art and their *prima facie* powers: ink marks structured on a page, sounds arranged in a sequence, with their timbre and rhythm, and so on; and on the mystery of the manner in which they transcend towards meaning and value, towards a greater plenitude of the perceived and a deepening appreciation and respect. It is significant also that the only other possible collaborator available to us in this activity of transcending is named 'blind nature'. For when Ronald Hepburn then suggested that, after all, we may not 'infer from that anything momentous about the cosmos as such, as distinct from the little world of man' we are certainly left with the impression that meaning (at least any explanations and understandings beyond the most empirical scientific descriptions of 'blind nature') and values are distinctive human additions to reality, which themselves have no reality beyond that which they have in and amongst the conscious minds of human beings. That may seem a harsh conclusion to draw. But if Ronald Hepburn is right in thinking that the transcendence towards meaning of marks, sounds and so on is the only kind or level of transcendence that Steiner has in mind, then the conclusion would appear to be justified. Incidentally, it is not a conclusion that could be drawn from Ronald Hepburn's own philosophy, for he does provide ample evidence of allegiance to a realist or cognitivist position in the matter of morals. But the point would still be that the manner of transcendence as described above does not measure up to such realist convictions, and full clarity concerning transcendence is crucial to this debate. Transcendence confined to that transcendence by which an arrangement of marks on a page, pigments on a canvas, sounds and so on becomes signs can only remind one of that semiology which describes signs in isolation, and will not ask of what they are sign. Then reality is lost to view – or termed blind, perhaps by a kind of transference? – and moral value has not yet achieved its necessary objectivity. The little world of man looks once more at once too great and too small. Too great as to the human collaboration in the provenance of meaning and value; and correspondingly too small in the consequent assessment of the world's own affordances and of the promise and hope that these carry. And all the time the danger hovers of an unbalanced self-serving because of the apparent absence of moral value in 'blind nature'.

The kind of transcendence that needs to support the present investigation is not only that by which marks on a page are transcended towards meaning, but rather that also by which the sign (the marks with the meaning we give them) is transcended towards the reality it represents. On such a fuller view of transcendence the 'Platonic' criticism of art for concentrating our attention on an image of an image is overcome; and the sign, the artistic image, opens our eyes instead to the dynamic structures of reality itself. And then, as Iris Murdoch's argument enables us to realise, especially when we are enabled to see the essentially mutual needs and potentialities, and the interactive nature, of the transformations involved, the whole world and not just the little world of man appears to be engaged in the creation and maintenance of epistemic, moral and aesthetic values. (The rest of) nature is revealed, not blind but everywhere knowledgeable, prescient even; and all of it engaged inseparably with human beings in goodness and beauty, and of course in the opposites of all of these. For everywhere in this cosmic enterprise in which we have but a part, however prominent and perhaps increasing a part, and as the artist above all allows us to see it objectively, there is the human equivalent of falsehood, evil, ugliness. There is evidence of ontological deficiency, declension from that plenitude of perception which art envisages, and which art struggles to realise, even on those occasions when it must express a realistic pessimism, revulsion or even resignation. And there is not even an unchallengeable case to be made that evolving reality is going forward, ever onward, towards greater universal truth, goodness and beauty. Even the increase of self-conscious knowledge, valuation and appreciation of reality which we seem to experience from our human perspective does not appear to be by any means an unqualified boon. Yet, for all that, reality as a whole reveals itself to the artist to be a moral and aesthetic enterprise, and ours but a part in it.

Is the claim fully justified, then, that art offers no persuasive inference for a transcendent God, nor enough even for a wager on such a one? Certainly if the argument concerning transcendence is confined to the terms outlined above, that is the case. For then the choice offered is confined to a kind of world soul which emerges from or within the universe, on the analogy (or more than analogy) of the kind of transcendence by which 'meanings and landscapes and fugues emerge from signs', especially if these ever arrive at 'the total intelligibility of the actual universe'. A kind of world soul consisting of a human species-being and the totality of the meanings it had made for itself – but only for itself – by deployment of its squiggles and sounds and other artistic means.

But what if the transcendent revealed by art is not a world soul of any such kind which emerges from or within the universe? For the image of a world-soul is an image derived from a metaphysics in which a truly transcendent God creates a world and in doing so ensouls it. And in that traditional kind of Christian–Platonic metaphysics the world-soul or spirit emanates from the One God, rather than emerging from or in the world, and is one-in-being with that God, as the Christian gloss on this takeover of that Neoplatonic theological scheme insisted. So, what if art reveals a transcendence from which the empirical universe con-tinuously 'originates', rather than vice versa; a transcendence which transcends the human also, but a transcendence which operates always within the universe? Then Iris Murdoch would have her case sup-ported. Not by her peremptory appeal to the Ontological Argument – in which in any case her Absolute had to be defined in such negative terms that O'Hear's puzzlement at how such a One could interact with moral striving was strongly underlined – but by the Platonic-type epistemology–metaphysics with which she glossed the Ontological Ar-gument. 'What we cannot but think' is then translated into 'what we cannot but see' if the artist (or the scientist in the largest sense of that term) is our guide; namely, intimations of a transcendent which orig-inally, continuously and creatively transcends the whole universe from within it. A continuously creative source, from beginning to end, of its forms-in-movement; a creator that creates precisely by forming, and continually creates through the interplay of the dynamic forms which then make up the universe. A wager on such a transcendent agency, and soul of the world in that traditional sense, has not been ruled out by the terms of the critique of Steiner's case. Indeed its very possibility, at the very least in sufficient measure for the placing of a wager, is surely supported by the following features of Murdoch's Platonic restoration.

Art offers intimations of a transcendent, a transcendent moreover that lies (further) beyond those worlds of meaning, of aesthetic and even moral values, that already transcend squiggles on a page, pigments on a canvas, vibrations of violin strings. For the works of art transmit to all who would look or listen revelations of reality itself upon which the artist has waited, and has been rewarded with a dark light. One feels entitled to speak of reality itself, or as such, revealing itself, if only because of the sheer power of the 'seer' to locate humanity itself, or as such, within the unified fabric of reality, both in its present and in its possible states. Seeing reality as such as the continuous creation of form, yet eschewing the act of either scientific experiment or moral judgement, the artist creates the images which allow others to see reality itself as both an aesthetic and a moral enterprise. This fulfils the first requirement of O'Hear and company for a transcendent ground of moral value; but it does so by seeming to subject to question their second requirement, namely, that the transcendent so intimated be non-religious. For it prevents them from restricting the moral enterprise once again to human agency and human interest. In fact it positively mandates an inquiry after some wider moral agency in reality itself; in O'Hear's terms, it raises a question as to whether the darkness in Chardin's work from which the common pragmata of our world are seen to emerge might not represent the original light to which the eye of the seer is first and very gradually attuned; this rather than the utter emptiness, the engulfing abyss (of nothingness?) which he suggests is all that Rothko can portray. Certainly Iris Murdoch sees and names this wider moral agency, and appeals to art for vindication of this view. And if in her escapade with the Ontological Argument she seems to concur in a predominantly, if not purely, negative description of it, in her more Platonic philosophical mode it is immanent and active throughout reality. So that, if it cannot be defined in itself as in total separation, it can certainly be known and described from its immanent agency. She names it, simply, the Sovereign Good. But that cannot be good enough, for at the very least it prompts the question: The sovereignly good *what?* And that is a question worth pursuing a little further at this point.[21]

RELIGIOUS REVELATIONS OF THE TRANSCENDENT THROUGH ART

Reality as it is revealed is a unity; a seamless fabric of all the entities, elements, properties and procedures which make it up. Reality reveals itself, in these terms, as a universe. Even the multiverse hypothesis includes the unity involved in the interaction of the participatory universes, and is in that degree a universe of universes. If a universe

[21] A great deal of mere linguistic sleight of hand is passed off as philosophical analysis and argument by the simple ruse of distracting people's attention by capitalising first letters of words, and thus making into substantives such primarily adjectival terms as the Same (the same as what?), the Other (the other what?), and of course the Different in its various French forms.

exists quite apart from our universe/multiverse, we cannot by sheer dint of lack of interaction ever know anything about it. The same would be true of divinity which did not act in our universe/multiverse, and whose activity was not therefore any part of its processes.

Reality also reveals itself to be a perpetually self-transcending entity in all of its features of truth, goodness and beauty. It is an on-going aesthetic, moral and existential enterprise. That is best explained by saying that it consists of a unified interplay of forms which in-form, re-form and trans-form mutually and multiply. It is best known by participating entities which have the form of consciousness, and best understood by participating entities which have the form of self-con-sciousness, and these last kinds of participating forms contribute most effectively to the universal enterprise in which reality itself consists. They can also contribute most effectively to the evil and ugliness, and to the ontological deficiencies which relative failures all over the universal enterprise produce. But these are and must be called relative, for an ontological deficiency is by definition relative to an ontological suffi-ciency either in effort or in train; ugliness is a distortion of form which exists or is being created; and evil is a reversal of the fulfilment of the potentialities and consequent needs of one of the interactive forms, which usually occurs or is enacted in the process of the fulfilment of a need and potentiality of another.

It is necessary to repeat that all of this is not meant to amount, nor does it in fact amount to a cosy and rosy contention to the effect that goodness, truth and beauty initially and increasingly triumph over their opposites until, at the eschaton, their triumph can already be known to be due for completion. Much less does it amount to an endorsement of the picture sometimes painted by those engaged in theodicy, whereby the darkness of evil in the unified fabric of reality sees any moral objection to it neutralised simply by pointing to its necessary contribu-tion to the beauty of the chiaroscuro of the total picture. And less still does it do anything whatever to solve the puzzle of how we are ever to be able to evolve any moral precepts if the life and life more abundant of each interactive formed agent is always at the expense of the others involved. All that being said, though, what is revealed is that the fabric of reality as a unified whole – however it may end, and indeed if any sense at all can be made of talk of its end – is a unified, dynamic, moral and aesthetic enterprise throughout, in which the negative values are relative to the positive.

What is it, then, that is being revealed, however darkly, that contin-

ually forms this one universe precisely through this multiple, this pullulating, transforming interplay of forms? The question is unavoidable
for seer and would-be seer alike, as it is for the scientist of the very
highest ambition. And the answer? It can scarcely consist in some kind
of encompassing entity that acts as no more than a kind of container that
keeps the myriad forms of the world in touch with each other. That, if
we did even dimly perceive it – and one ventures to say we do not –
would not secure the intrinsic unity of the perpetual-motion universe we
do perceive. 'The universe itself' is scarcely a sufficient answer either;
although in terms of a frequently stated preference for immanence and
transcendence as correlates rather than contraries, a preliminary
answer might indeed talk of an eternally self-transcending universe. But,
again, something over and above the sum of the more immediately
perceptible forms that make up the universe is clearly involved, since the
mere sum of these does not create the universe, any more than their
mere juxtaposition does (as in the randomness-before-adaptation scenario). Charles Hartshorne in his introduction to *St Anselm: Basic Writings*[22]
comments as follows on Anselm's entity than which a greater could not
be conceived: Anselm had in mind, most likely, an entity that could not
be surpassed by another; but his argument would succeed just as well if
his famous phrase were taken to refer to an entity that could only be
surpassed by itself. And that places at the service of the present point in
the investigation the view from process theology of an entity that can be
said to be eternally self-transcending, if only as the power within, and
hence the source of, all other instances of transcending transformation
of forms according to each one's essence and prospects. In that sense this
answer to our unavoidable question can be said to be Anselm's 'that
than which a greater cannot be conceived'.

Thereafter the forms of the question can multiply, and the answers
become correspondingly more difficult to ascertain. Is that which may
now seem to appear to the limits of vision from the very edge of darkness
as the ever mediated, unifying (trans)forming force within the whole
interplay of forms in the universe – is it of the nature of mind? Or is it
(also) of the nature of matter? An answer can be approached while
explicitly rejecting any either/or impression which the sequence of
questions here might suggest to the unwary; an impression, in other
terms, of what has so often been called 'Cartesian' dualism. First,
remember that matter in and of itself must be conceived to be (as yet)

---

[22] See S. Deane's translation *St Anselm's Basic Writings* (La Salle, IL: Open Court, 1962).

unformed. For the instant we speak of some formed entity, however elementary and universal such a primary building block of the universe may be, we are already envisaging something more than mere or 'prime' matter. Then, that which may now be coming in view has this in common with matter itself, that it does not appear to be (in) a particular form, additional to all the other empirical forms that make up the universe; for it could not then operate in and through all of these. In Neoplatonic metaphysics both God and matter were called no-thing, nothing, for both, albeit at opposite extremes of be*ing* in these systems, were beyond the formed, and so could not be counted in the number of things – or of individual persons, for that matter.

Is it conscious? That is the most difficult question of all on which to hazard even the most tentative of answers at this point, but it may be worth rehearsing some of the considerations involved. Deutsch, it will be remembered, would call it, or some entity very like it in his scheme of things, knowledge. And he envisaged an eschaton in which such all-creative knowledge took the form of the combined and very reflective consciousness of vastly evolved successors of the human race. All of which, as was said at that point, raises the issue of the status or agency of that cosmic–creative knowledge from the outset of the universe. And similar and simultaneous questions can of course be asked concerning cosmic evaluation and aesthetic creation. Or are we with the animals the only conscious beings in the universe, and we alone the only ones endowed with reflective consciousness and capable of reflective knowl-edge? Posing that question from the point of view of consciousnesses which are predominantly receptive and reactive to limited numbers of forms of things, and only in a correspondingly limited fashion capable thereafter of creatively envisioning them transformed, it is all but impos-sible for us to conceive of the kind of consciousness that could transcend itself infinitely more creatively to all transforming form that has ever existed or will ever exist. That would be the kind of consciousness that would surely characterise the power or presence that so darkly appears to perpetually (trans)form the universe in and through all the forms perpetually engaged in the cosmic interplay.

Yet such an answer would envisage a subject and (or of) reality at the cosmic level, by dint of a metaphysics/epistemology which gives us back both subject and reality at the cosmic level, on the analogy of, or by extension of, the same kind of metaphysics/epistemology which gives us back both subjects and reality at the local level of the universe at which we humans currently operate. And we may have some hint of how we might envisage such a supreme consciousness, one that is not limited and so individuated as ours are, in the experience we have in our directly mediated consciousness of other finite persons. For this is already an experience of the limitlessness, literally, of the other's transcendent consciousness corroborating the always incipient limitlessness of our own reflective consciousness. A sense there, as Feuerbach so well analysed and understood, of consciousness infinite and operative within, and accessible especially to the intersubjective dimension characteristic of human personhood from womb to tomb – or, as Feuerbach would say in lieu of the intersubjective dimension, that level of consciousness which characterises, unites and is in some sense a common consciousness of humanity itself, the species-being. Could this intersubjective consciousness, this consciousness which always already has as its 'content' the consciousness of indefinite others – could this be an image of, perhaps even a participation in, the consciousness that forms universe?

Is it The Good? As the immanent, unifying power and source of all dynamic, transformative forms, it could appear as the mediated creative origin of all re-formation, but also of course of all de-formation. In that case its complicity in empirical evil is as open to question as its complicity in cosmic empirical goodness. At one's most sanguine Platonic best one could describe it as The (Supreme) Good, in the sense of the demiurge, the creator God of the *Timaeus*, in that it is the creative source of all that is good, while adding perhaps that the secondary causes through which it operates (and especially Plato's *anagke*) are responsible for all that is evil, once deduction is made of the losses sustained by the condition of all living and thriving at each other's expense. But in any case it does not support Iris Murdoch's cause, even if, as could well happen, it is described in terms which are personal, but not of the one-(very big)-person-among-others kind which she rightly wished to demythologise. For The Good which Iris Murdoch insisted we cannot but see is the objective value that characterises the whole of reality, particularly in its final perfected form, in so far as such can be envisaged. But what we should then be seeing emerge from the still darkest depths and heights of the universe is an original creative power and presence to which the epithet the good could be applied in a most apposite, though not in an exclusive, manner, rather than some entity which is defined as The Good as such, which Iris Murdoch's argument seems to require.

Is it God, then? So tentative and yet compressed a piece of concluding analysis and argument at this point cannot suffice for an answer to that question. All that can be safely concluded is that theological analysis and argument does legitimately, if not necessarily, develop from the kind of metaphysics which shows reality as a whole to be a unified, a moral and an aesthetic enterprise. And that kind of metaphysics, so this chapter has argued, is the adequate response to the revelation with respect to which both the artist and the scientist–philosopher is both receptive and transmissive. But there is a more persuasive reason for not attempting a peremptory answer to the god question at this point. The complaint is sometimes heard that philosophy of religion seldom, or only incidentally, deals with real religions; religions, that is to say, that are actually believed in and practised by the vast majority of the human race. Devoting too much time to the so-called proofs and disproofs of God's existence, and operating with a highly abstract definition of divinity which bears little enough resemblance to the God worshipped by any of the world's religions – such philosophy is thereby deemed to be incomplete at best. But for present purposes the more positive point is more important: it is surely essential to consider what at least one major religion has to say about the God allegedly revealed to its founder and/or practitioners, before answering the current question concerning divine status for the kind of entity which it is now being claimed may be revealed from the depth and height and breadth of the fabric of reality as we know it. Or, in terms of the general title of this work, it is essential to consider some theology from some major religion in order to see how these prospects for theological reason which have begun to emerge from within the discipline of philosophy – and in particular the philosophy of morality, aesthetics and science – fare when they are faced with some actual theology from a living religion.

CHAPTER 6

Revelation, religion and theology

It is not necessary to offer a critical survey of Christian theology in the modern era of Western history, not even as potted a survey as has been offered in Part One for Western philosophy. This is partly because the centrepiece of any theology, the concept of God, has continued to figure in such a variety of ways throughout the course of modern philosophy; and partly because there is a shorter route to our imminent goal. This is through a brief survey of the modern Christian theology of revelation, at the centre of which inevitably appears the alleged existence and nature of the divinity operative and revealed. For this final approach, apart from keeping the continuity with a concept which has become dominant in the analysis and argument at this point, enables the critique to come to more immediate grips with the prospects of the reaches of reason (*logos*) in conversation with a living faith; more immediate, that is to say, than if one had to work through a survey of the history of whole theologies in order to see how reason in its various modes – artistic, ethical, scientific–philosophical – appeared and operated within them. For even as brief an account of modern theologies of revelation as might be adequate for present purposes, if only because these theologies commonly consider revelation in relationship to that 'natural' reasoning of which philosophy is the epitome, will certainly test any claims to divine status for that 'entity in reality' with which the last chapter ended; and test these claims now under the heat of a close, actual and currently active religious perspective. Then we shall know as much as we are likely to know at this time and place about the very phrase theological reason; and we shall have come, as far probably as we now can come, in the critique of theological reason.

It seems fair to say that at the beginnings of the history of Christianity there is no hint of a dichotomous dualism of theology and philosophy, in

265

which theology was purely a response to divine revelation and philosophy was confined to the increasingly uncertain speculations of pure reason trying to pull itself by its own boot-straps to the heights of reality. Although with the inestimable benefits of hindsight it can now be said that some seeds were then sown which could with time and circumstance grow and finally blossom into such a dualism. This, in both parts, is because Christian apologists in that early world, at a period in the history of Western philosophy named as the period of Middle Platonism, took over a pre-existent and mainly Greek theology; and took over not merely its method, but a very great deal of its content. One need read only Justin Martyr's *First Apology* in order to get the clearest and fullest impression of this move and of his justification for it; for in the works of these apologists Christian theology took the shape of its contents for all future centuries. Centring his whole case on the image and concept of the *logos* – the very term on which Greek philosophy, from *its* very beginnings, centred its claim to rival myth in analysing and understanding the dynamism of all 'the things that are', from deepest source to furthest goal – Justin pointed to the Christian claim that the *Logos*, the Divine Word itself, had taken flesh in the founder of his religion. This enabled Justin to do two things simultaneously: first, to concede that the same *Logos* was already revealed in the Greek world history – the prologue to the Gospel of John said that the Divine Word enlightened everyone in the world – and that the *Logos* was truly seen by the best intellectual vision of their philosophers and the most insightful imagination of their poets; and, second, it enabled him to claim that the Greeks, of all people, should be able to see the truth of the Christian beliefs, if they would but bring themselves to look at these without the prevalent back-biting and bias, since the same *Logos* it was who shone for the Christians, now from the exemplary humanity of one Jesus of Nazareth. In this manner, then, Justin Martyr took over Greek theology, method and content, 'gold from the Egyptians', in a move designed to persuade the Greeks to continue their ancient service to the divine *Logos* by becoming Christians, or at the very least to allow the Christians to get on with it without further opposition. There clearly was at this point and for this kind of Christian theologian, no appreciable dualism between theology and philosophy, or between revelation and 'mere' reasoning, groping in a darkness in which no guiding light shone for it.

Justin, however, did have something else to say about the Greeks, and it is here that the hint of a split between Greek philosophical theology and a Christian theology focussed upon Jesus of Nazareth begins to appear. Like many who do not seem to be able to make a case for their own superiority without highlighting the occasional failures on the part of real rivals, Justin alleges that the Greeks allowed the revelation of the true divine *Logos* to be adulterated by demonic influences, and that their theology therefore needs to be corrected, and not simply to be opened for corroboration and further improvement by the revelation the Christians had received. In this way the issue of the relationship between theology and philosophy, revelation and reason, became entwined from the beginning with the issue of grace and nature or, to state the matter more precisely for the present context, sin and nature. The allegation is repeated in many forms in early Christian apologetics and other theologies. For instance, at the opening of the argument of the single most systematic work of Christian theology that came from his pen, the *De Trinitate*, Augustine accuses of the sin of pride the non-Christian philosophers whose theology he otherwise so fulsomely admires, and to that sin he attributes both their shortcomings and their downright errors with respect to the self-revealing God. Only those redeemed from sin, it would follow from this kind of allegation, can apprehend as clearly and fully as humans may, the revelation that comes from the one, true God; and these Christians are very clear indeed concerning the one source of redemption. The unredeemed are condemned in the very best of their philosophising to seeing and serving demons or idols perhaps even as much as, if not more than, the true divinity. And in that way also a split begins to appear between theology and philosophy, revelation and reason.

It would be quite superfluous to present purposes to try to trace here the full history in which this split, in some later Western philosophies and Christian theologies, opened to the extent of the dichotomous dualism which even the exponents of what is now called the science of religion do rightly attribute to Christians,[1] and which, like similar crude dualisms elsewhere, may well result in losing sight of one side or the other, if not sometimes of both. It will be sufficient for present purposes to draw on

---

[1] Exponents of the science of religion would say that this dichotomy between, on the one hand, theology as the study of the content of a special revelation given by God to particular people and, on the other hand, a science working with a particular philosophical method (the phenomenological method) which is at best utterly agnostic concerning the reality of God, constitutionally incapable of saying anything either true or false about that reality, is one that they have simply taken over from theologians, and these, in this culture of course, are mainly theologians of the Christian religion. Such exponents of the science of religion cannot then evade the critique which constitutes the main burden of this chapter. See, for instance, Michael Pye (ed.), *Marburg Revisited: Institutions and Strategies in the Study of Religion* (Marburg: Diagona, 1989), p. 15.

seven-league boots and land on some paradigmatic cases which still shaped this theme at the dawn of the modern era. Aquinas in his *Summa Theologiae* fully upheld the view which enabled Justin to support the theology of the Greeks, the view that God is revealed in the creation and that the lover of wisdom, the philosopher in all of us, can with patience and attention find God active there. Yet he also claimed that what Christian theology would call a special revelation, as distinct from a general revelation in the nature and history of the world, was needed and was in fact given directly by God to some people for transmission to all others. This was needed both because so many people simply could not attend sufficiently to the general revelation to gain its full benefits, and because there were additional features of God's nature which were not revealed in the nature and history of the world; and there were also aspects of God's activity in the world, crucial for making our way to the eternal happiness which God had in store for us, which we would otherwise not know. One of these aspects had to do with redemption from human sin.[2] This has remained roughly the Catholic theological position on the subject to the present day. It was confirmed authoritatively by the First Vatican Council in 1870, in response to positions perceived to be promoted by the Enlightenment, one of which we shall shortly see after the influence of Kant. And it could be characterised generally as a distinction between general and special revelation, to which would correspond a distinction between philosophy and theology, but a distinction which should attract the image not so much of a split as of a continuity across a thin dividing line.[3]

Calvin, odd as it might seem to say, remains quite close to that position, and it is only in his additional assessment of the ravages wrought by sin in human history that he then distances himself from it in practice. For Calvin is quite clear in his conviction that the original revelation of God in and at the creation of the world, and thereafter in its continuous creation, did and would have continued to suffice for human beings both to know the true God and to follow the path – wisdom as a way, again – to eternal happiness in the graciously bestowed fellowship of God. *Si Adam integer stetisset*, that is to say: if only

---

[2] Thomas Aquinas, *Summa Theologiae*, pt 1, q. 1, art. 1; pt 1, 2, 3; and for the Trinity, pt 1, 28, 1.

[3] The First Vatican Council of the Roman Catholic Church in 1870 solemnly defined that God could be known with certainty by the operation of the natural light of reason on and in the creation; the so-called Anti-Modernist Oath issued by Pope Pius X seemed to go even further when it added *adeoque demonstrari etiam posse*, since *demonstrare* can well be taken to refer to a rather apodictic form of proof. See H. Denzinger, *Enchiridion Symbolorum* (Rome: Herder, 1965), nn. 3004, 3538.

Adam had not fallen. But Adam did fall, and brought the whole human race not yet born into a state of sinfulness, destined thereby to eternal damnation. And yet it was not the case that, from an objective point of view, the revelation of God in God's continuous creation had ceased. Calvin waxes eloquent – at times far too eloquent for the liking of some contemporary Calvinists, who find themselves wishing that he had been a little more consistently *Calvinist* – both on what he calls the *sensus divinitatis* enjoyed by every human being born into this world, and on the evidences for God's active presence everywhere in nature and history. The former, the *sensus divinitatis*, he declares to be naturally inherent in the consciousness and conscience of every human being, evidenced for example in the universal sense of obligation and guilt; the latter follow some general lines of evidence of the so-called proofs, but without any pretence to prove, and the lines of Calvin's grand panorama of history in which, he thinks, whole civilisations can be seen to be requited for the good and the evil they have done. What is it that prevents the human race, like the still-innocent Adam, from seeing this powerful and permanent revelation of God in the nature and history of the world, and from then walking in the way? It is the blindness caused by sin, and which can only be relieved by the special revelation and (of) the redemption brought by Jesus the Christ.

There is a slight problem for Calvin, implicit in this general account: how can those who come after Adam and who have not been already favoured with the special revelation courtesy of Jesus the Christ be guilty of not seeing and following it? This is in one sense a special version of the general problem of explaining how those who came after Adam and are fallen because of his activity can be in any way guilty of being in a fallen state. But in this special case of this implicit problem, some interpreters of Calvin see an implicit solution, and in this they see the point of all the elaboration of the permanent revelation of God both in the human conscience and in the world at large. What Calvin's case amounts to, they say, is this: the blindness caused by sin is not quite total; as a consequence, humans can continue to see something of the permanent and still potentially blessed revelation of God in God's continuous creation; they can see enough of this to declare them guilty of not seeing more, yet not enough of it to put them, without receiving the revelation and redemption that came especially in Jesus the Christ, in the state of grace before God and on their way to eternal happiness. That, in any case, is the interpretation of Calvin's case in the *Institutes of the Christian Religion*, which justifies the view that he sees an ideal continuity between

the general revelation and the special Christian revelation, much as
Aquinas sees this, but then insists on opening something of a chasm
between them caused by the practical consequences of sin. How wide
that chasm is depends upon one's view of how great, even if not
complete, the sin-induced blindness is, according to Calvin. But this is in
any case an example of the manner in which it is the intertwining of the
theme of theology and philosophy with the theme of grace (sin) and
nature that causes the overall impression that theology based on the
special Christian revelation alone now deals in the true revelation of
God, whereas reasoning on the evidences in the continuous creation
leads only to further immersion in sinful idolatry.[4]

Kant can serve as our example of an Enlightenment view which saw a
rather complete dichotomy between theology and philosophy, revelation and reason, but which then concluded, in Kant's case certainly,
that the former could, and at this stage of 'humanity come of age'
should, be replaced by the latter; a dualism of revelation and reason,
then, in which loss from sight of the former was no great loss, and could
in a sense be positively recommended. Already in the preface of the first
edition of the first great work of his critical period, after he had been
awakened from his dogmatic slumbers by the gaucherie of Hume's
sceptical philosophy, Kant summoned the Christian faith before the
court of human reason – for it is the Christian faith he has mainly in
mind in writing of religion. In the preface of the *Critique of Pure Reason* he
wrote: 'Religion, on the strength of its sanctity, and law, on the strength
of its majesty, try to withdraw themselves from it [i.e. the court of
reason]; but by doing so they arouse just suspicions, and cannot claim
that respect which reason pays to those only who have been able to
stand its free and open examination.'[5] Twelve years later there came a

[4] *Si integer stetisset Adam:* John Calvin, *Institutes of the Christian Religion,* II, vi, 1. If Adam had retained his
original integrity, then 'the natural order certainly was that the fabric of the world should be a
school in which we might learn piety and by that means pass to eternal life and perfect felicity'.
The coincidence of this originally blessed knowledge of God from the creation with the
knowledge of God the creator reiterated in scripture is clear from the very structure of book I of
the *Institutes*, where chapter x actually argues the similarity of content of chapters i–v with that of
chapter vi. On the rather fine point that this revelation of God in nature is now sufficient only to
incur our guilt, but no longer after Adam's fall sufficient to see us safe to salvation, see Calvin's
commentary on Acts 14:17: 'this kind of testimony of which mention is made, is such that men are
deprived of excuse and yet it was not sufficient to salvation . . . men cannot be led to a saving
knowledge of God except by the direction of the Word. And yet this does not prevent but that
they may be made inexcusable without the Word, who although they be naturally deprived of
light, are yet blind through their own malice, as Paul teaches in the first chapter of Romans.' For
further analysis of these issues see E. A. Dowey, *The Knowledge of God in Calvin's Theology* (New York:
Columbia University Press, 1965).
[5] I. Kant, *The Critique of Pure Reason* (New York: Doubleday, 1966), p. xxiv.

work from his pen entitled *Religion within the Limits of Reason Alone*. He had
to defend this work in a letter to the king, Friedrich Wilhelm II,[6] for the
ecclesiastical censors were still very much abroad in both the Protestant
and the Catholic regions of that era, in accordance with the principle
laid down in the Treaty of Westphalia: *cuius regio eius et religio*, the religion
of one's king(dom) is one's religion. In the preface to the first edition of
that work Kant had diplomatically declared his willingness to submit to
the office of the theological censor; but with one important proviso: that
the office of censor conduct the examination according to the criteria of
academia, for no one, he suggests, would want a recurrence of the
Galileo case. And lest this might seem, as indeed it must seem, to tie the
censor's hands and pre-empt a judgement against Kant, he goes on to
explain that philosophical theology, that is to say, the critical study of
rational religion, a discipline of its nature independent, covers a good
deal of ground that is held in common with Biblical religion and
theology. So all he is asking, really, he seems to imply, is that the Biblical
theologian should not impose his criteria on the philosopher any more
than the philosopher has any right to impose his methods and results
upon the Biblical theologian.

We have no detailed information as to how the censor saw this rather
tendentious pre-emptive case for the defence, but it cannot have fared
badly, for the book was well and widely received; so much so that some
years later, in a preface to the second edition, Kant has grown much
bolder in behalf of the claims of philosophy and rational religion, over
against what as a good Protestant he would continue to call Biblical
religion and its theology. He begins with an image of common ground
or content: a circular plane of Biblical religion containing within itself
the smaller concentric circle representing rational religion. He then goes
on to consider the project of taking any part of that Biblical religion and
submitting it to rational investigation, in order to see if he cannot find an
actual coincidence of content with some part or theme of rational
religion. It then becomes clear that he envisages the final result of such a
project to be a rather complete coincidence of content of all that could
be called true religion, as between Biblical religion and rational religion;
that is to say, whatever is true religion in the Biblical record will also in
fact be found by the philosopher to be true rational religion. So that, as
he puts it, 'reason can be found to be not only compatible with Scripture
but also at one with it'.[7] Otherwise, he issues the very thinly veiled threat

[6] Kant, *Philosophical Correspondence 1759–99* (University of Chicago Press, 1967), n. 642.
[7] Kant, *Religion within the Limits of Reason Alone* (New York: Harper and Row, 1961), p. 11.

that we shall find ourselves faced with one (true, rational) religion and one cult, as he calls it, and these if one tries to mix them will act like oil and water, with the former always coming out on top.

Not that Kant wishes to deny that there are in the Bible instances of what he calls supersensible revelation – the image of the concentric circular areas on a circular plane is still in effect. But it now becomes clear, as suggested by the phrase supersensible revelation, that all that is additional to the coincidental content of Biblical and rational religion is mystery and miracle, that is to say, acts (miracles), including acts of communication, which are strictly speaking unintelligible as to process involved and perhaps content also (mysteries). Kant will not deny that such miracles and mysteries did in fact surround the Christ event, as the life, death and resurrection of Jesus is sometimes rather inelegantly called. But he has this to say, finally, about all of that:

> The person of the teacher of the one and only religion, valid for all worlds, may indeed be a mystery; his appearance on this earth, his translation thence, and his eventful life and his suffering may all be nothing but miracles; nay, the historical record which is to authenticate the account of all these miracles, may itself be a miracle (a supersensible revelation). We need not call in question any of these miracles and indeed may honour the trappings which have served to bring into public currency a doctine whose authenticity rests upon a record indelibly registered in every soul and which stands in need of no miracle. But it is essential that, in the use of these historical accounts, we do not make it a tenet of religion that the knowing, believing, and professing of them are themselves means whereby we can render ourselves pleasing to God.[8]

There could scarcely be a clearer case of a more dichotomous dualism of revelation and reason; or of special, supernatural revelation and that which is within reason's remit. (The latter could hardly be called natural revelation. For Kant there is no revelation of God in nature; indeed there can hardly be said to be a revelation of nature in nature.) There could scarcely be a clearer decision to the effect that the former, whatever evidence there may be of its occurrence, and whatever its value as a prop to the weakness of newborn conviction and commitment, is of its nature destined to be superseded and made obsolete by the growing strength of the latter. (The content of the rational religion of Kant, the good Protestant, was, it will be remembered, a pure faith in an otherwise incomprehensible God, the seedbed of which consisted in a combination of a natural desire for the *Summum Bonum* – the coincidence of moral righteousness and happiness – and a pure will, that is to say a

[8] Ibid. pp. 79ff.

will committed to moral virtue for its own sake, without the influence of any thought of reward or punishment. The content of cult, on the contrary, consisted in alleged but unintelligible acts of God, including acts of divine communication, as instanced for example in some views of the divine 'inspiration' of scripture.)

Finally, with seven-league boots, leap forward a century or more to Barth. For Barth offers a fascinating mirror-image of the dichotomous dualism of revelation and reason, theology and philosophy, which Kant has just presented. And he offers this mirror-image, in one foundational context at least, without as yet any entanglement with questionable theories of original sinfulness and fallenness. It is a mirror-image in that the roles are reversed. This time it is the special, supernatural revelation that so distinguishes itself from, and so supplants, all that human reason operating in and upon the nature and history of the creation could comprehend, that the latter must be entirely lost to sight, and certainly so if it pretends to the slightest independence of access to the true God.

When Barth's distinctive voice is first heard, it speaks in distinctly Kierkegaardian tones, determined to rescue true access to the true God from the culture of the Age of Reason, a culture which had crept too much into the Christian church and which sought to contain God within its own intellectual categories, and to measure divinity according to these. In this of course the age was doing no more in Barth's view than had always been done by the philosophers who prided themselves on their quest for the Absolute and on their increasing successes in the quest – Hegel remains a prime target for such Kierkegaardian protest. This, in one of his (mercifully) shorter works, is how Barth expresses the utter contrast between false and true access to the true God:

[First, when the human being generally speaks of God] he means the object of the universally present and active longing, the object of man's homesickness and hope for unity, a basis, a meaning to his existence, and the meaning of the world; he means thereby the existence and the nature of a Being who, whether in this or that connection with realities other than himself, is to be regarded as the Supreme Being that determines and dominates all that exists.

Second, in utter contrast, notwithstanding the fact that many of the philosophers and theologians of the Age of Reason (Schleiermacher as well as Hegel) had presented the God of Christianity as the true end of the long quest, when the true Christian speaks of the true God,

it is not that on the long road of human seeking and longing for the divine a definite stopping place has in the end been reached in the form of the Christian confession. The God of the Christian confession is, in distinction from all gods, not a found or invented God or one at last and at the end discovered by man; He is not a fulfilment, perhaps the last, supreme and best fulfilment, of what man was in the course of seeking and finding. But we Christians speak of him who completely takes the place of everything that elsewhere is usually called God, and therefore suppresses and excludes it all, and claims to be alone the truth ... What is involved is man's meeting with the Reality which he has never of himself sought out or first of all discovered ... God in the sense of the Christian confession is and exists in a completely different way from that which is elsewhere called divine.[9]

That is very much the mirror-image of Kant's position, with this possible qualification that, whereas Kant displaces one 'supersensible' revelation with a rational faith, while still leaving a very provisional role for the former, with Barth the displacement of human reason's role is total and without remainder. Furthermore, as with Kant, this position can be achieved by Barth without recourse to an explanation of the effects of original sin. Or, to put the matter rather differently and without the need to examine in any detail Barth's theology of original sin, the whole search and service in which human beings engage by dint of their own investigative reason in the universe, is itself sinful rather than being the result of some original sin, and it is also the source of yet further sinfulness in the form of evil perpetrated in and by humanity – one remembers, for example, Barth blaming natural theology for its alleged contribution to the ideology of the Nazis and thence to the evils they brought upon the world. Happily, however, from the point of view of the present context, that particular determination by Barth to displace every possibility of a theological dimension to the metaphysics achieved by attentive human reason (as examined in the last two chapters) is more positively approached by noticing the place and function of the idea of revelation in Barth's whole system, especially as the system finds its expression in his monumental work, the *Church Dogmatics*.

Barth opens his *magnum opus*, the *Church Dogmatics*, after the usual prologomena to any systematic theology, with the Christian doctrine of the Trinity. Mindful, perhaps, of Calvin's (and Hegel's?) strictures on entertaining some general concept of God, only later to move to the properties of the actual God – in fact the Triune God, which Calvin (and Hegel) recognised from the outset as the only true God operative in the world and its history – Barth begins his theology with the Trinity.

[9] K. Barth, *Dogmatics in Outline* (London: SCM Press, 1949), pp. 35, 36.

And yet, although the statement that Barth begins his systematic theology with the Trinity is literally true, it needs to be qualified in two significant ways. First, it is not the Trinitarian nature of God as such that provides the source and the abiding spirit of Barth's distinctive theologising. It is rather his awesome appreciation of the utter sovereignty of God that does this, the opposite side of the coin to his suspicion of the containing and measuring of God by the intellectual categories of the Enlightenment. The Lutheran principle 'let God be God' is the governing criterion for Barth's theology from beginning to end. Second, and as a consequence, the opening and foundational concept, or, perhaps better stated, the opening and foundational doctrine in Barth's system, is the doctrine of revelation. Chapter II of the *Church Dogmatics*, after the opening section on prologomena, is entitled 'The Revelation of God', and its three parts are entitled 'The Triune God', 'The Incarnation of the Word' and 'The Outpouring of the Spirit'; as he himself writes in a section entitled 'The Root of the Doctrine of the Trinity' (ch. II, p I, sec. 8, ii), 'the Christian concept of revelation already includes within it the problem of the doctrine of the Trinity'.

The quickest way to a simple understanding of this complex of opening concepts in Barth is through Calvin's edict to the effect that 'God alone is a suitable witness for his own word' (*Institutes*, I, vii, 4). In other words, only God can reveal God in any true instance of a claim to have acquired such a revelation; so that the utter sovereignty of God, God's safety, so to say, from all attempts to contain, and much more from all attempts to measure God against human concepts and images, is secured when divine revelation is so understood that God is in complete control of it at every point, from origin to reception. And then the 'problem' of the Trinity is already involved, in this way: in every instance and element of divine revelation God is the sovereignly free source of it, and not anything or anyone else; not anything left lying around in God's creation, for example. God as source, then, or Father. God is then also sovereignly free in choosing the medium, for want of a better word, of self-revelation; and God has chosen Jesus of Nazareth for this purpose, and become 'incarnate', as our imperfect words would have it, in Jesus for this purpose.

Nor can we add at this point: but surely God also sovereignly chose the world which God created, for purposes of self-revelation; for God in fact chose to create the world through this Jesus, and so Barth can write in one of his more accessible works, 'the world came into being, it was created and sustained by the little child that was born in Bethlehem, by the Man who died on the cross at Golgotha, and the third day rose again. That is the Word of creation by which all things came into being.'[10] This is in line with Barth's insistence elsewhere that scripture, by which in all his theology he is bound, gives us no licence to speak about a discarnate Word. And finally, even the reception or acquisition of this revelation does not escape the complete control of God's sovereignly free lordship, for the receiver needs the power of God as Spirit in order to perceive and receive the revelation of God through the medium God has chosen. All in all, God is source, medium and power of reception within the human spirit of God's own sovereignly free revelation: God is Father or Source, God is Son or Word, and God is Spirit. It is not, of course, one must hasten to add, that according to Barth one can analytically derive the idea of the Trinity from the idea of divine revelation; but rather that the actual experience of God's gracious revelation to us carries within itself the revelation of God's true triune being.

Now, it would be very difficult not to see this theology of Barth's as a case of the most dichotomous distinction between divine revelation and human reason, between true theology and a totally presumptuous and false philosophy. This is particularly so in the aftermath of Kant, Calvin's philosophical 'other', who displaced supersensible revelation with reason, albeit with a level of rational exercise which must be called faith or postulate, and this without any apparent role for what might be called general revelation in nature and history. Certainly none of the other options offered in the history of the topic of revelation seem to fit Barth's case: not the distinction between general and special revelation, either in the version in which the latter fulfilled the former, and was to a given degree coincident in content with it; or in the version in which special revelation also corrected the faults in the reception of general revelation due to human sinfulness, and simultaneously added a special revelation concerning the redemption of the sinners.

Of course there is a version of the linking of revelation and reason with sin and nature which Barth could and did in fact take over. This is the version in which the sinfulness in question is defined in terms of the common human practice of discovering, as they themselves would say,

[10] Ibid. p. 58, where Barth declares that the doctrine of divine creation is not a kind of 'forecourt of the Gentiles' to which all are equally admitted, whereas only the faithful can penetrate further into other aspects of the being and acts of God. He also insists in this context that divine creation is no different from Jesus' conception by the Spirit, as far as the need of revelation and faith is concerned. Although, as we may see later, there are diametrically opposite ways in which that last contention might be interpreted.

but in reality speculatively inventing what Barth knows to be false gods, or demons, and then engaging in the further evildoing which service of such idols inevitably entails; rather than the blindness to the revelation in the world of the one, true God being the result of deceit by the satan, the adversary of God, resulting in the service of the same satanic one throughout subsequent history. But that first version of the intertwined sin theme merely corroborates the interpretation of Barth's theology at this point as a raw opposition between reason and special revelation. For the sin consists precisely in the pride of human reason speculatively inventing a god which can provide for humanity and its familiar world a unity, a basis and a meaning, that seems to satisfy human need and longing for such things. But all of that is to be utterly displaced by the special revelation which came in and with Jesus of Nazareth. It has never been even partially displaced, and it never can be even partially displaced by some alleged general revelation in the world which came before, or is in any way subsidiary to, the revelation through God's sovereignly chosen medium, Jesus. Barth is as dismissive of semi-Pelagians as he is of Pelagians, and when one forgives him his implicit calumny against a decent Irish theologian, one can see the same point reiterated concerning the displacement of mere human reason by special divine revelation.

But what, then, is one to make of the following material from a much later part of the *Church Dogmatics*, the part in which Barth is broaching Christology proper, the theology of Jesus of Nazareth as the Christ, who is also the eternal Son of God?

This is the context in which Barth asks, 'how can we know God if we do not find the truth and power of His being in his life, and of His life in His act?' For Barth equates the very being of God with the divine activity: 'The whole being and life of God is an activity, both in eternity and in worldly time, both in Himself as Father, Son and Holy Spirit, and in His relation to all creation.' From our point of view, then, it can clearly be claimed that 'He creates us . . . to share with us and therefore with our being and life and act His own incomparable being and life and act.' In the sovereign freedom of the divine act, in which is the reality of the divine being and life, and which is shared with us, we may know God, and only in that may we know God. But how close, if one may ask, is this sharing? How close is eternity to time? How close is the divine being, life and act to human being, life and activity?

There are sentences in Barth which suggest a closeness between these two which amounts almost to equating them, if indeed these sentences do not literally equate them. Writing now in this very same context in terms of history, Barth says of God: 'He does not allow His history to be His, and ours ours, but causes them to take place as a common history. That is the special truth which the Christian message has to proclaim at its very heart.'[11] And later in the same Christological context, when the topic is atonement, a key concept in the Christian elucidation of all that Jesus is and did, both for God and for our human world, there occurs in Barth's writing a similarly uncompromising equating, as it seems, of the history of this divine act and history as we commonly speak of it in our continuously created world. 'The atonement is history. To know it, we must know it as such. To think of it, we must think of it as such. To speak of it, we must tell it as history. To try to grasp it as supra-historical or non-historical truth is not to grasp it at all. It is indeed truth, but truth actualised in a history and revealed in this history as such – revealed, therefore, as history.'[12] The repetitive insistence on this point must surely be taken as a sign of Barth's sense of its central importance and of the consequent need to impress it clearly and without the slightest chance of confusion on the reader; one cannot regard this passage as just another instance of Barth's well-attested proclivity for taking a thousand words to say what, if he had taken the time to do so, he could have said much more clearly in a hundred words. The divine act of atonement, God 'reconciling the world to himself', in some sense the pinnacle of divine activity in the evangelical Christian's view of things, is here insistently described as history in and of this world.

Does all of this amount to the assertion that the act in which we know God, and in which we find the 'truth and power of His being', coincides with what we commonly call history in this world? Such a conclusion could possibly be called premature, by pointing to the fact that Barth repeats in this context, indeed especially in this context, his conviction that only in Jesus of Nazareth can we truly see the true God truly acting in the world: 'what God does in Himself and as Creator and Governor of man is all aimed at the particular act in which it has its centre and meaning'.[13] This is the act which Christian theology has called the incarnation of the Word of God in Jesus of Nazareth. Therefore this statement is the theological equivalent of the contention that God creates the world in and through the divine Word which we then can

---

[11] Barth, *Church Dogmatics* (Edinburgh: Clark, 1975–), IV, 1, p. 6.
[12] Ibid. p. 157.
[13] Ibid. p. 7.

know in and as Jesus of Nazareth. But that is hardly sufficient to settle
the matter; if only because, where the concept of creation takes centre
stage in the discussion of this matter, it becomes extremely difficult to
assert that it is God-as-active-and-known-in-Jesus that is the only true
God the Creator and hence the one who creates the whole world, and
yet, without any further explanation as to how this could be done, to
deny all possibility of any knowledge of the one, true God from the daily
immersion of those who never heard of or do not wish to hear of Jesus, in
this same history of this same creation.

It is not surprising, then, that there are those who argue that Barth by
the time he arrived at the later, Christological reaches of his great life's
work, the *Church Dogmatics*, had indeed resiled from the purity of the
position originally attributed to him above; the position, namely, in
which a special revelation of God in Jesus the Christ entirely replaced
anything that could be attributed to human reason speculating in and
about our common world. And many of these quote in corroboration of
this contention an interesting lecture which Barth delivered in 1956, to
which he gave the intriguing title 'The Humanity of God', and in which
he actually used the term retraction. It is worth taking a look at that
lecture, and pursuing what might otherwise look like some obscure
problem of Barthian exegesis. Because Barth is undoubtedly the greatest
and most influential Christian theologian of this century; so that an
account, however brief, of his handling of the idea of divine revelation
over a long theological lifetime, during which he interacted constantly
with both what had gone before him and what was going on at the
growing points of twentieth-century theology, is likely to lead us most
directly to an assessment of the Christian idea of the true God, and of
the nature and mode of the revelation in which that God is truly known.
Thereby the task announced at the end of the last chapter might be
accomplished as quickly as possible, the task, that is to say, of submitting
to the test of encounter with a living religion the still problematic status
of the 'entity in reality' allegedly encountered, through the philosophical
investigation of morality and art, metaphysics and revelation.

Barth begins his lecture with his own description of the theological
position which, as one commentator put it, he dropped like a bomb on
the theologian's playground, particularly with the publication of the
revised edition of his commentary on the Epistle to the Romans in 1922.
The necessarily polemical–critical character of his necessary defence at
that time of the *divinity* of God, of God's sovereign lordship, gave such
prominence to characteristic phrases such as *totaliter aliter*, the utterly

other, and the 'infinite qualitative difference' between God and humanity, that some complementary and equally essential characteristics of the
living God, albeit never denied, were underrepresented to the point of
fading from view. So he now judges to be the case. Correspondingly, the
necessarily polemical–critical treatment of what he called the an-
thropocentrism of the prevailing theology – the pretence to meet and
measure God according to the powers and prospects of human religious, even 'Christian' religious, experience – resulted, despite some
positive reference to humanity, and even to Platonic humanism, in the
impression of a negative sign set over all that was human. Thus the stark
contrast between the sovereignly free revelation of God on the one hand
and, on the other, all that was human, and in particular human reasoning at what would otherwise appear to be its highest achievements, filled
a picture which was true to reality as far as it went, but which left in
obscurity further reaches of the same reality.

Barth then asks of himself and of those who followed him enthusiasti-
cally in rapidly increasing numbers: 'did we not largely fail to perceive
that the *divinity* of the *living* God – and it was with him that we wanted to
deal – has its meaning and power only in the context of his history and of
his dialogue with *humanity*, and therefore in his *togetherness* with humanity?' And his answer is very much in the affirmative, for 'God shows and
reveals who he is and what he is in his divinity, not in the vacuum of a
divine self-sufficiency, but genuinely just in this fact that he exists, speaks
and acts as partner (undoubtedly the absolutely superior partner) of
humanity. He who does that is the living God. And the freedom in
which he does *that* is his divinity.'[14] The full connotation of Barth's term
the humanity of God is to be found, then, in the analysis of that term
togetherness. And it is this that needs to be added to, or at least to be
made far more explicit in, his original and very polemical insistence on
the unqualified divinity of God, if the whole truth of the Christian faith
as he sees it is to be as fully expressed as is possible at this time. For when
this is done, and only then, there will no longer be any danger of the
divinity of God being seen as abstract, and in some sense even inhuman.
A too-exclusive insistence on the awesome and untrammelled sovereignty of God, although in one sense that divine characteristic cannot be
exaggerated, can create the same impression as those abstract definitions of God as omnipotent, omniscient and so on in which the more
rationalist philosophies dealt.

[14] Barth, 'The Humanity of God', in Clifford Green (ed.), Karl Barth: *Selected Writings* (London:
Collins, 1989), p. 52.

But correspondingly now when we speak of the actual, living God in terms of the humanity of God's very divinity so understood (God's partnership with humanity in history), we must also abjure all temptation to think of humanity too in abstract terms. For then we should be thinking of humanity in general and of human reason in general and, starting out from these, without already taking into account any of the actual interventions and conditionings, and especially those that originate in the freedom of God, in the course of history, we should find ourselves returning again to the 'little bit of religion and religious morality' which results from the practice of the principle of 'man as the measure of all things'. Whereas, of course, it is in the actual concrete, historical and historic humanity of Jesus of Nazareth that God's divinity and humanity (in Barth's connotation of the term) are simultaneously revealed. That is a fact of history and a crucially conditioning factor for humanity-in-the-concrete; it is apprehended by those who are inspired to do so by the Spirit of the same God; it is to be proclaimed prayerfully by these to all of humankind, principally by living in community according to it, however imperfectly, in what is called the church. In the real world, and in its actual history, God in the sovereign freedom of absolute divinity, decided to be together with humanity through a definitive togetherness with Jesus of Nazareth. Thus Barth is, and we should be, thinking in our theology of an actual, living God and of the actual, historical human world. Thus also, in God's humanity as just now defined, God's divinity as Barth first proclaimed it (again) to the tail-end of the Enlightenment, is fully intact. Thus, finally, as Barth continually suggests in the course of this lecture 'The Humanity of God', he has not resiled in the least from his earlier position; he has simply filled out an integral part of it which for polemical purposes had earlier been left underdeveloped. His retraction is from the underdevelopment, and from nothing else.

The matter cannot altogether end here, however, with Barth's continual protests of his own consistency. For there are in Barth's more fully developed theology implications for the assessment of humanity itself, of its historical cultural achievements, and even of the theologising of his predecessors and his opponents – implications which he himself actually draws – which could raise all over again the issue of resiling or not resiling. Because of this togetherness with humanity, sovereignly chosen both as to its substance, locus and mode by God alone; because of this sympathy, dialogue, partnership, intercourse, history with humanity (for all of these terms and more are used to gloss togetherness); because of this humanity of God (so defined) which, far from detracting from God's divinity, is the very characteristic which God in sovereign freedom gives to divinity in concrete reality; because of this humanity of God, certain consequences follow for our assessment of humanity itself in creation, and it is a number of these consequences for assessment, which Barth himself merely sketches in the concluding part of his lecture, which finally focus the question as to whether he has resiled or not from his earlier stark dichotomy between divine revelation and human reason.

First, because God in the unqualifiedly sovereign freedom of his divinity has chosen to partner humanity through the particular partnership with Jesus of Nazareth, human nature, both in all that it has in common with the rest of the creation and in all that is distinctive to it, is good. Barth's conviction is here as unqualified as God's freedom, and it is delivered in reference to the fall: 'This gift, their humanness, is not extinguished by the Fall of humanity, nor suffers any diminution even of its goodness.'[15] But this judgement, Barth hastens to add immediately, is not to be confused with an optimistic anthropology, with an assessment of humanity that is ignorant of, or blithely indifferent to, the monstrous evils that humanity has caused and continues to cause in the history of the world. In the theological terms already used of original sin above, in Barth's view original sin coincides with the blindness to the one, true God, and all the other evils that follow on revering some other entity – a personification of power, or some such idol – in place of the one, true God; rather than this blindness to the one, true God, and its moral entailments, being caused by some original, in the sense of previous, fall. And the sin is then original in the sense that it takes its origin from the very highest and best of which humanity is capable, its power of reasoning and its pride in the results of this; and in the sense that the unqualified reverence for and imposition of these results on the world is the origin of so much of the evil that is done. But the goodness of the humanity that is at once God's gift and partner is still the premise of all the evil that is done by it, and it therefore maintains the promise that things may not be as bad, and might even be better, as the vision of true God and true humanity is restored and the partnership functions with less interference.

Second, the humanity of God, understood as God's partnership with humanity, enables us to assess positively the distinction thus conferred

---

[15] Barth, 'The Humanity of God', p. 58.

upon, and really characteristic of human culture, in the production and consumption of which all human beings participate. As Barth puts it: 'God as *humanity's* Creator and Lord is still at liberty on occasion to make of human activity and its results, in spite of their problematic character, *parables* of his own eternally good willing and doing.'[16] And finally, and of most relevance to present purposes, there is an even more generous assessment of the theology of the very theologians whom in his more polemical mood Barth had so critically condemned. He takes Bultmann's existentialist theology as his example in the lecture for this more generous assessment. For although he may still have some reason to fear that we have in Bultmann only 'a repristination of the theology of the devout individual, engaged in self-reflection (this time about one's authenticity or inauthenticity), self-expression and self-explanation', which might 'lead us back into the old error that one could speak of humanity without having first, and that very concretely, spoken of the living God', nevertheless Bultmann's theology can already be credited with reminding us 'of the elements of truth of the older school in impressing on us again and yet again that one cannot speak of God without speaking of humanity'.[17]

All in all, then, and even if we are not very clear about what Barth means by parables; if we take together these more positive assessments of human nature in its distinctive powers and faculties, of human culture in general, and of those theologies which look so much like theological dimensions of some of the higher cultures, we would seem at first blush to have here a fairly rounded revision of his original, rather absolute dichotomy between the results of divine revelation and the results of human reasoning. It now looks as if what he is really complaining about is that these culture theologies condemned to an underdeveloped state (if they did not entirely lose from view) the sovereignly free divine initiative. For they looked too exclusively to the human side of the partnership; in contrast to Barth, who himself had once left underdeveloped the human side of the partnership with God and had thus left out of clear focus the humanity of God. The former mistake might of course be considered to be very greatly more grave than the latter, and one for which no comparable extenuating circumstances obtained. Nevertheless, the measure of the mistakes is still a relative matter, as is the need and extent of the necessary retraction, and it leaves intact the prospect of some true knowledge of the one, true God from rational reflection on

[16] Ibid. p. 59.
[17] Ibid. p. 60.

humanity in its history. If humanity is truly God's gift (creation?) and
God has in fact always worked with it in what must then be a shared
history; and if human reason reflecting on earthly humanity and its
history (including especially the history of Jesus and Christianity) claimed to see something of God's act, and thence of God's being, in all of
that, the resulting image or concept of God might indeed be limited by
human powers of perception, imagery and idea, and flawed by the
human propensity for misperception and misrepresentation; it might
well be said to see more of what Barth calls the humanity of God than of
God's awesome and incomprehensible (literally incomprehensible) divinity; but that could hardly justify the statement that the God so 'found'
and 'discovered', in Barth's earlier words, is utterly 'suppressed and
excluded' by the true Christian proclamation. Conceptually completed
in a truer Christian theology, very possibly; corrected, perhaps; but all
and entirely suppressed and excluded? Hardly that.

The interest at this point of this essay, however, lies not in trying to
prove that Barth, despite his protests, had resiled from his original
position concerning divine revelation and the human quest. For Barth
might even now insist that whatever human reason could see of God in
the world's history is solely due to God's act in Jesus; and as a consequence, his dichotomy between sovereignly free divine revelation and
questing human reason could still stand. Yet all that Jesus was and did,
said and suffered is, after all, part and parcel of our common history;
and whatever of it is still available in the succeeding centuries of that
history, should it not be equally available to all? So that it is still
necessary to pursue the questioning of the Christian religion on the
matter of divine revelation; and it is more important to know exactly
what is being said by Barth and his opponents than to attempt to
adjudicate between them. Ask, then, what precisely is the relationship
between Jesus of Nazareth and the rest of the history of humanity, if not
also the whole 'natural' history of the world inclusive of human history?

The moment one presses that question, one realises that, in Barth at
least, there would appear to be two connected ambiguities that need
some clearing up. There is first of all an ambiguity in Barth's talk of a
common history of God and humanity. To put the matter perhaps too
bluntly (for the sake of brevity), it is the ambiguity of the 'with' and the
'is'. In the lecture that just now has been analysed, the 'with' is altogether dominant. Just as God's sympathy, sharing, intercourse, togetherness and so on are said to be 'with' Jesus in particular, and
through him with humanity in general, so God's history is said to be

'with' ours. Whereas in the contexts visited above from the *Church Dogmatics*, it is the 'is' that is dominant: the atonement, as surely an act of God as any act might be, 'is' history, and that means the history that we partake in and know in this world; for Barth is anxious to add that the atonement is not supra-historical or non-historical. In the first of these formulations there is the possibility that what is being claimed is that there is a kind of divine history running alongside, or even within, human history, and interacting with it, but not otherwise coincident with it. And in that case, one might begin to suspect that the means of coming to know that divine history could well be claimed to be additional to, different from, those by which we know our own history in the world. One might even suspect, further, that the history of Jesus, or at least the story of the acts of Jesus as the Christ, the incarnate One, could be claimed to be additional to, or different from, those ordinary acts of human living in which he also engaged and which constitute the common history of us all; and then a similar claim could be made about knowing *that* history of Jesus. In the second formulation on the contrary, where the 'is' is dominant, there seems to be a clear suggestion of a quite uncompromising identification of the history of God and of humanity. What God does in Jesus, and through Jesus in us, simply is history, one and the same history, part of the common and ordinary history of the world.

Or perhaps the whole of it? For now the second and connected ambiguity comes into play. The world was created, according to Barth, by the man who died on the cross at Golgotha. That indeed is good Christian and Biblical teaching. Paul, for instance, identifies the *Logos* by which we live and are saved, which is the very creative and re-creative power of God, as the crucified one, and he does so in one pithy phrase, *ho logos ho tou staurou*, the Word of the Cross (1 Corinthians 1:18). And those who have even the minimum of theological acumen necessary to realise that the incarnation does not refer simply to some hidden act of mysterious insemination in the womb of a Jewish maiden (for it takes a little more than that to become fully human); those who realise that incarnation refers rather to the whole being-and-act of God taking form and activation in the whole being-and-act, the whole life and death of an individual human being – those are the people who can see that this is indeed good Christian and Biblical teaching. But if that is the case, how can there be a gap between creation, the so-called natural world, and history, any more than there can be between a special history of God and our common history, alongside of which it is thought to be running?

If God is known to us in God's life and act, and it is in and through Jesus that God continually creates the world, how is it not possible, at least in principle, and if humans could even occasionally overcome their error-prone ways, to know something not just of some abstractly defined creator god, but of the living, actual, incarnate God from this same continuous creation? Yet, and here is the ambiguity, Barth is constantly reminding us that the Creator God reached by philosophical inquiry, the God who appears to be known by our ranging far and wide over the world, has '*nothing whatever to do* with Jesus' message about God the Father whether or not the term "father" be attached to it'.[18]

If the rather cumbersome terminology used up to now were to be dropped, then instead of talking about the nature and history of the world or of the universe, one would talk simply of the history of the world. On the ground that, although there is a valid distinction between nature and history hinging on the prerogatives and prospects of free, creative, self-conscious agents, there is also a natural history of the universe, as it is called, which is partly our prehistory and in many ways continuous with our history. Then too the combined upshot of the two connected ambiguities could be stated as follows: it seems at times, on reading both Barth and his opponents on the topic of divine revelation, that creation has to be separated from history, and that a special history of God's has to be separated from common human history, although in both cases these two are very much with each other, sharing some common space and time, and interacting in a variety of ways. Yet on other readings one gains the contrary impression: that these separations do not obtain at all, and that there is instead a coincidence amounting to an identification of continuous creation with history in its most general and cosmic sense. On the first view divine revelation takes place in a special history of God somehow introduced into this world; on the second, it takes place as the history of the world. The complaint here is not about contradiction, much less self-contradiction, but about ambiguity, and about a consequently large residual lack of clarity concerning divine revelation.

The cause of this persisting confusion may well lie in the fact that, from the beginning, Christian theologians have been making bold and quite specific claims about divine revelation: that it is to be found here but not there, that it is there but ineffective due to human self-induced blindness, and therefore that it is effective only here where that blindness can be overcome, and so on, and so on. But they have seldom, if

---

[18] Barth, *Church Dogmatics*, I, I, pp. 390–1.

ever, provided a thoroughgoing analysis and explanation of the actual process of divine revelation. They are always telling of what has been unveiled, and when and where; but apart from impressions we may glean from these tellings as to how precisely they think the relevant communications took place, there has not been a full and frank examination of the precise means, of the actual procedure adopted by the divine revealer. René Latourelle, in a book that was to herald the reverse of that neglect with a vengeance, remarked on that odd fact of theological history, pointing out that none of the histories of Christian theology which had become popular since the rise of the science of history, not one of them, contained a section on the theology of revelation. A brief visit to the recent Christian theologies of revelation, which came hard and fast, like a gushing rebuff to Latourelle's complaint, might help resolve the ambiguities which still impede our progress in this part of Christian theology. That prospect is all the more enticing in that the recent and intense decade of Christian theology of revelation concluded – though some would prefer to say it petered out – with a theory of revelation as history.

THE RECENT CHRISTIAN THEOLOGY OF REVELATION
REVELATION AS HISTORY

At the beginning of the debate opened by Latourelle's book the most common impression of the nature of the actual process of divine revelation, conveyed by almost all of the talk and writing about it in Christian circles, was that it consisted in some kind of divine speech to chosen human hearers. Since the content of this divine speech, in the modern context in which the revelation claims were issued, was most usually thought to be doctrines of the Christian faith, this became known as the propositional theory of divine revelation. Even though, it must be repeated, we are faced for the most part, not with a theory properly analysed and argued, but rather with an impression conveyed. And the writers on divine revelation during the intense decade of debate which followed Latourelle's book, if they are united on nothing else, are united in rejecting the propositional theory of revelation. The contexts in which the impression of the propositional view of revelation came about and strengthened are many and complex – beginning with *Logos*, translated 'word', as the name for the Creator–Revealer incarnate in Jesus – but it is impossible to pause even to list them here.[19]

---

[19] For an account of some of these contexts, see my *The Problems of Religious Faith* (Chicago: Herald, 1972), pp. 118ff.

Yet the connection between the Christian faith and common history had been raised already by that particular feature of the Age of Reason which saw history emerge as a fully fledged science. That connection proved to be the core problem of the so-called quest of the historical Jesus;[20] it was as unlikely to go away as it was to be sent away by the thundering of the authorities in any of the Christian churches, or indeed in all of them put together; and least of all by thunderings to the effect that divine revelation, in both process and results, was something immune from human history. In actual fact, as far back as the eighteenth century the phrase salvation history began to appear particularly in Biblical theology, although it was not adopted in the Roman Catholic Church until well into the twenthieth century. And that proved to be one of the precedents followed by Latourelle and those who engaged with him in the intensive discussion of the actual process or processes of divine revelation in recent years. So that the recent and sustained theology of revelation was characterised from the outset by a move away from the assumed impression of divine revelation as a propositional activity – textbook theology defined divine revelation simply as a *locatio Dei*, a divine speech – and a move towards seeing the process of divine revelation as consisting in historical events.

When Latourelle himself, towards the end of a long historical and theological analysis of the theme of divine revelation, comes to his own view of it, he summarises that view as follows:

The process of revelation, in its totality, is thus made up of the following elements: (a) Historical event. (b) Interior revelation which provides the prophet with an understanding of the event, or at very least the reflection of the prophet directed and illuminated by God. (c) The prophet's word, presenting the event and its meaning as objects of divine testimony. It is the complementary character of historical event and event of the word (God's word to the prophet and the prophet's word to the people of Israel) that makes revelation grow. Thus the moments of revelation in the history of Israel are always marked by the appearance of one or several prophets. The presence of prophets always means that God is at work in history. The structure of revelation in the New Testament is not essentially different from that of the Old. Christ is He who has come, accomplished the work of the Father, and who, for this reason, has been exalted to the Father's right hand. The first credos of Christianity are the statement of these historical facts and their bearing on salvation.[21]

---

[20] For a brief account of the modern quest for the historical Jesus, see my *Jesus the Man and the Myth* (London: SCM, 1979), ch. 1.
[21] R. Latourelle, *Theology of Revelation* (New York: Alba House, 1966), pp. 349–50.

Now, there are several features of that summary which would suggest that, despite the length of the book, we have not come very far at all from where we started. The term to be defined in detail itself occurs as a central part of the definition: if 'interior revelation' is part of the process of divine revelation, we are still in as much need as ever of knowing what precise process is involved in this interior divine revelation; for otherwise we are not much closer to understanding any better the process of divine revelation. Further, the formula which was at the centre of the old impression of the revelation process, God's word, occurs here also as a gloss on the interior revelation which the prophet enjoys. The gains then would seem to be restricted to these: historical events are part of the process of divine revelation, but – at least implicit in this account – this refers to a very select sequence of historical events, those that concern Jews and Christians (how odd of God to choose the Jews, and even odder to add the Christians?); and yet, however and in whatever sense these events may be special, the presence of prophets is required for them to be revelatory of divinity.

Within a year Pannenberg was editing a volume entitled *Revelation as History*, which took matters forward by some significant steps. First, an important general point is pressed home, to the effect that, if we are to remain faithful to the Christian Biblical point of view, we shall not talk about God's self-revelation. For that is not given in history, or not yet in any case. As suggested in the New Testament, where the Greek word translated 'revelation' is transliterated as 'apocalypse', the full unveiling of God as God is in God's own being, the resulting face-to-face knowledge of God, the knowledge of God as subject, as Hegel would say; that belongs to the eschaton, to a time or, better, a state in which time and history are overcome. What is revealed in history is God's mighty acts and the promises entailed in them or, in other words, God's will and intentions for the creation – which can, of course, be resisted and frustrated, as we well know. The point is important, although the distinction once again must not be too dichotomous, for, as Barth said, God's very being is involved in God's act; yet the point does preserve the experience of the gradualness of the unveiling, of the essential image of the journey, and of the necessity of time. Second, those epiphanies of God which are recorded in the Bible are to be seen as etiologies of cult and cultic places, or once again as pointers to God's mighty acts in history. That is true even of the story of the making known of God by name to Moses in Exodus 6:3. For words, and even words placed on the lips of God, are really acknowledgement formulae which of the very nature of the case can and do become words of promise; for what is acknowledged is God's mighty acts in history, and these contain in themselves the highest promise possible for all creation.

Finally, although prophets undoubtedly play a crucial part in the process by which people of good will come to see the revelation of God's mighty and promising acts in and as historical events, the Bible itself clearly does not regard the presence of a prophet to be absolutely necessary for the divine revelation to occur and to have its proper illuminating effect. That might answer a question left over by Latourelle when he transfers his description of divine revelation from the Old Testament, as Christians call it, to the New, where prophets play a very minor role (unless he sees Jesus as also fulfilling the vocation of prophet). There is a sense conveyed by the contributors to this volume,[22] then, that a sequence of historical events, culminating according to Ulrich Wilkins, in the resurrection of Jesus of Nazareth as an earnest of the general resurrection of all, do themselves constitute the divine revelation such as it has so far been granted and received. This relative demotion of the necessity of the prophet, however, is more crucial than it might at first sight seem for the coherence and intelligibility of the theory of divine revelation occurring through the process of historical event. For it focusses the critical eye more closely on the selection of a particular sequence of such events as those in which divine revelation, or at the very least some very special divine revelation, took place. Schillebeeckx, for example, had already argued against any such demotion of the role of the prophet in the process of divine revelation in this common Christian selection of historical events. He did so on the grounds that these selected events in all outward appearances resemble any number of other events which might be selected from world history, but which are commonly regarded as being simply 'of this world', bearing no particular charge of divine revelation.[23] It is not necessary, in order to feel the force of this point, to think that this theology so far had thrown such light on the role of the prophet as to advance our understanding of the process of divine revelation.

Because no such advance is visible, because we still do not know what God allegedly does in and through the prophet, the problematic point remains all the stronger; the point, namely, that the selected historical events of the chosen Judeo-Christian sequence do to all effects and purposes resemble in all outward appearances any number of events

---

[22] W. Pannenberg (ed.), *Revelation as History* (New York: Macmillan, 1968).
[23] E. Schillebeeckx, *Revelation and Theology* (New York: Herder and Herder, 1967), pp. 8–9.

that any other person or people might choose. A nomadic people, more or less enslaved for a time by one imperial power, escaping, wandering, capturing a little land for themselves, forming a kingdom situated unfortunately perhaps along a route joining more natural arenas of imperial power, becoming pawns of these until they finally lost their independence entirely; and a wandering preacher born into this people, with a striking and distinctive religious message, even something of a wonder-worker, ending up, even if innocent, on a Roman cross between two other Jews. Events like these are a ha'p'orth a dozen at any point of human history. Even the alleged resurrection of Jesus, were it to be the very best-attested of historical events, would be one of many, precisely as an historical event, that is to say, as the bringing back to life of a dead man.[24] For if that is not adequately paralleled by the reviving of other dead people in the course of history – and there are a number of other examples in the Bible – it is paralleled more than adequately by the bringing forth of life from 'dead' matter in the history of the universe in general. The point here is not to deny or denigrate in the least the revelatory power of all of these events in the common history of the world, and least of all of the last; nor is it to deny that this may be seen by those who have the gift of the seer as the revelation of the power of something very deep, as deep as some unifying source, some holding centre of all our universe. The point is that, on the account of the matter that is now before us, there is no apparent reason why other selections of events from the pullulating variety offered by the history of the world should not be equally brought forward as instances of divine revelation. To think of the process of divine revelation without remainder as historical events is to leave one logically open to that broad prospect, whether one likes it or not. That is what Schillebeeckx argued.

To make a long story short, there were others operating on the theology of revelation during that intense decade who also felt that their Christian tradition did not require a prophet at all points of their foundational divine revelation; yet felt something else was necessary, over and above the simple exposure to historical events, even select

---

[24] This is wildly controversial country; for a fuller treatment and support of what is said here the reader might consult my *Jesus the Man and the Myth*, chapter on resurrection; my *Modern Theology* (Oxford University Press, 1987), pp. 78ff, 'Resurrection, Eucharist, Divinity'. But to clarify a little here: if the resurrection of Jesus is taken to mean more than (merely) reviving a corpse, if it is taken to mean his raising to Lordship, a lordship which has its experiential counterpart now in empowering us for life, life more abundant, eternal life even, then the parallel is in the power that produces and promises ever evolving being and life, and that is palpable in every 'event' in the world's history, both natural and human.

historical events, or well-attested stories concerning these. Monden, for example, berated the Pannenberg circle for suggesting, as he read them, that historical events recorded in the Bible were in and of themselves so revelatory of the divine that they could yield the faith by which we live and hope. On the contrary, he insisted, it is only by faith that anyone can see the revelation of the divine action and of its awesome promise in these events.[25] Once again, however, and as in the previous case of the role of the prophet vis-à-vis historical events which might otherwise come across as quite common, there is no corresponding analysis-in-depth of this faith which apparently allows some people but not others to see selected events as God's mighty acts in history and revelations of the divine will and intent. Of those who saw the three on Golgotha on that Friday afternoon, what was it that allowed the Roman soldier to confess that the one in the middle was the Son of God, while to others he was a failed pretender to a Jewish throne, rightly executed between two freedom-fighters (or terrorists, of course, depending on your political point of view), or just an unfortunate man innocently condemned to death in one of those tediously frequent miscarriages of justice? Must the answer to that question bring us back again to some interior revelation, or inspiration, or illumination, back to something like the prophet again, and back to the beginning once again of the question about the precise process in which divine revelation is thought to consist?

Moltmann, finally, was the most uncompromising in his challenge to Pannenberg and his circle, in that the addition of faith was in his view insufficient to make even select historical events revelatory, in and of themselves, of the divine. In a book, *The Theology of Hope*, which owes a good deal more than was ever formally acknowledged to the work of the great Marxist philosopher Ernst Bloch, and to the latter's deep analysis of the epistemological and metaphysical structure of hope in cosmic history (*Das Prinzip Hoffnung*), Moltmann carries forward to theological completion Pannenberg's thesis concerning the essentially eschatological nature of the revelation of God. Not surprisingly, as a practitioner of a good Protestant ethos, Moltmann decries any attempt to see a self-revelation of God in the cosmos. 'A "natural theology" of this kind', he writes, 'in which God is manifest and demonstrable to every man, is not

---

[25] L. Monden, *Faith: Can Man Still Believe?* (New York: Sheed and Ward, 1970), p. 153. H. R. Schlette, *Epiphany as History* (New York: Herder and Herder, 1960), also followed the Pannenberg line while adding the necessity of faith; although in the case of the resurrection of Jesus, Schlette really did not need to stress the *aporia* caused by intractable uncertainty concerning the events which are said to have taken place after the death of Jesus, in order to make room for faith, as Kant might have said: pp. 64–5.

the presupposition of the Christian faith, but the future goal of Christian hope.' But he is not happy with the idea of history as revelation either, whether this is taken to mean that the whole succession of events in history, or some selection of them, can reveal God or God's activity to the inquiring mind or, alternatively, that some 'reading into' these events from some special viewpoint of religious faith or illumination would reveal the presence and the plans of God. As he himself puts it, he does not wish to have to face an 'alternative between a complex of saving history which is a product of history, and unprovable retrospective projections of faith which are the product of subjective faith'.[26]

Moltmann is particularly critical of the treatment of the resurrection of Jesus by Pannenberg and his co-contributors to *Revelation as History*. A proleptic event, they seem to think. That is to say, the definitive and final mighty act of God in the whole history of the cosmos had already in fact taken place in the case of Jesus, and it stands there as the earnest of the great general resurrection of the eschaton in which both history and the divine self-revelation will at the last be completed and accomplished. But that, it seems to Moltmann, is to make the believer or the inquirer like a dog chasing its tail: the tail is already behind, but the dog is chasing after it, and when the dog catches up with it the circle will be complete. To think of history in this way is, first, to give an indefensible status to the resurrection as an historical event (rather than an event which of its nature transcends history); and, second, to regard a select part of recorded history as a completed series in which the features of God could in principle be discerned as clearly as the Greeks of old thought they could discern the features of the *Logos* in the created cosmos. As far as Moltmann is concerned, the appearances of Jesus after his death – for these form the substance of the resurrection kerygma – simply caused his disciples to hope that, as God had thus *appeared* to vindicate Jesus even beyond death – for these were *appearances* to chosen people, like Paul on the road to Damascus, who *then saw* (the language is of special revelation and corresponding vision) – a future eschatological event awaited them all which would be a true future for Jesus also.

What, then, is Moltmann's own last word on divine revelation? The revelation of God in the cosmos is postponed to the eschaton, whatever and whenever that may be; and the same seems to hold of the 'complex of saving history', unaided as he insists by 'subjective faith'. Is there no revelation in the past or present world? Moltmann comes close to such a

---

[26] J. Moltmann, *The Theology of Hope* (London: SCM, 1967), pp. 282, 154.

position when he addresses the atheism of our times, and especially when in this very context he comments once more on the resurrection of Jesus of Nazareth.

If this very atheism – as it has been most profoundly understood by Hegel and Nietzsche – derives from the nihilistic discovery made on the 'speculative Good Friday,' that 'God is dead,' then the only real way of vindicating theology in face of this reality, in face of this reason, and in face of a society thus constituted, will be in terms of a theology of resurrection – in fact, in terms of an eschatology of the resurrection in the sense of the future of the crucified Lord. Such a theology must accept the 'cross of the present' (Hegel), its godlessness and god-forsakenness, and there give practical and theoretical proof of the 'spirit of the resurrection'. Then, however, revelation would not manifest and verify itself *as* history of our present society, but would disclose to this society and this age for the very first time the eschatological process of history.[27]

Ignore the questionable reading of Hegel. For it *is* questionable if, as it seems, it suggests that Hegel thought the Absolute was not progressively known and thus unveiled in the history of the world; Hegel's references to crucifixion and resurrection find their place and meaning in the practical process of continuous transcendence towards the ultimately transcendent; a process from which the Absolute is never absent. Then Moltmann does seem to say that divine revelation is absent from the world and its history, and even from its so-called salvation history, as such. And still he claims that revelation discloses, even to this atheistic age, 'the eschatological process of history'. So that there is revelation after all, and revelation of the divine, since the eschaton in fact will consist in the self-revelation of God? Moltmann operates throughout the book with the category of promise, something which is held for us in history, and crucially in the resurrection of Jesus of Nazareth. This category seems to coincide with some form of revelation of the divine, however inchoate. But once again, as has happened with categories such as interior revelation, illumination and faith – faith which enables one to see God in the history of the world, or 'subjective faith' Molt-mann calls it, rather than faith which names the kind of knowledge that results from divine revelation in or as history – once again, as has happened with these other categories, this category of promise is left without analysis of precise process involved. With Ernst Bloch promise is the category that secures the objective character of hope; for it is the category that coincides with our experience of life in our universe flowing in and through and by us, flowing through death itself, ever renewing itself, ever capable of advancing towards limitless horizons,

---

[27] Ibid. p. 84.

towards the ultimate *Humanum* that becomes progressively visible –
especially to the prophet! – though never predetermined.[28] Hope, then,
for Bloch is a kind of practical knowledge that could well be called faith
– keeping faith, or not keeping faith, with a future ever in genesis – and
in fact it is the distinctive and crucial form of knowing for human kind,
however neglected it continues to be in the epistemology of the various
philosophical schools. What for Moltmann corresponds to life for
Bloch? If it is God, how can there not be some current disclosure? And
how can he then avoid the dilemma of either having to admit that the
disclosure is in or as historical events as such, or having to provide us
with some analysis of a process by which the disclosure is added, as it
were, to these events?

In the end it was Gabriel Moran in his second book on divine
revelation in six years, during that intense if belated period of analysis of
the topic, who seems to have adopted the most uncompromising view of
history as divine revelation, but to extend it, as Pannenberg and his
circle would not be prepared to do, to the natural history of the world, as
it is called. For his second book can be read towards that conclusion,
although it is a difficult book to understand, devoting as it does so much
space to probing the depths of human experience in the world, already
under investigation by scientists of various kinds, and by ecologists and
liberators.[29] Divine revelation is now an ever present category for our
experience of the world in all its relational complexity. It can therefore
be said both that there is universal revelation of the divine, and that
there are an ever increasing number of particular instances of it in the
history of the universe. The uniqueness of Jesus and of the revelation
seen in his life and person, is attributed to Jesus' unique receptivity for
the divine communion. Special revelations of the divine are particular
points or peaks in the omnipresent, universal revelation. And it is
significant too that for Moran divine revelation, in a sense, has no
object: certainly not in the form of propositions of a doctrinal kind, and
not in the form of concrete historical data either.[30] Rather at a certain

---

[28] See for example E. Bloch, *Man on His Own* (New York: Herder and Herder, 1971), p. 48.
[29] Gabriel Moran, *The Present Revelation* (New York: Herder and Herder, 1972). His first book on the
subject was *Theology of Revelation* (New York: Herder and Herder, 1966). Piet Fransen's 'Divine
Revelation: Source of Man's Faith', in P. Surlis (ed.), *Faith: Its Nature and Meaning* (Dublin: Gill
and Macmillan, 1972), provides what might be an interesting parallel to this position on
revelation. His fundamental category is grace (corresponding to Barth's description of human
nature, and presumably all other nature, as God's gift; Latin *gratia*) and our experience of the
natural world and its history as grace.
[30] It is perhaps worth remarking at this point that a crude propositional view of divine revelation is
not part of traditional Christian theology. Aquinas, the greatest medieval systematician of
traditional Christian theology, borrows Isidore's formula for Christian doctrines or articles of the

depth our basic relational experience in the history of this world is open to the transcendent and the holy, the numinous, and we are then in touch with God, as well as being on a journey towards God.

It is difficult to offer a single assessment of this intense decade of theology of divine revelation, even one that would suffice to meet a humbler need, the need to clarify on this point the most powerful Christian theology of this century, the theology of Karl Barth. For every assessor willing to say that there was a single outcome, and willing to say what it was, there is at least one other who would rather think that the movement, rather than reach any agreed conclusion on the nature of the process known as divine revelation, simply petered out and left the world no wiser on the matter than it had been before. And there is much to be said for the latter assessment, although it might be added as an extenuating circumstance that the movements in Christian theology which both overtook and succeeded this brief concentration on the theology of revelation, can be seen to have carried forward some of the central themes of the latter, and in particular the most central theme of all, the theme of the relationship of history to what Christians considered to be the definitive divine revelation. For the movements which overtook and succeeded this recent movement devoted to the theology of revelation were centred on what came to be called the new quest of the historical Jesus, a new quest undertaken despite the best that Bultmann could do, by the best of his erstwhile students. And this quest, and the controversies which surrounded it, opened on to a more general topic on which a great deal then came to be written, namely, the general relationship between history and Christian faith.

There is good reason to take it, then, that the clearest and best-attested theme of all this recent theology is the theme of history as divine revelation. This may be so mainly by default; by default, that is to say, of any success in analysing and explaining in detail any of the processes which were sometimes said to be necessary additions to raw historical events if the latter were to prove revelational of the divine: prophecy, illumination, inspiration, 'subjective' faith. Yet the fact of these defaults can itself be taken as indicative of the strength of the one clear conception of divine revelation which emerges both from the specific theology of revelation and from those cognate areas of theology which overtook

Christian faith, as constituting a *'perceptio divinae veritatis tendens in ipsam'*, a humanly formulated perception of divine truth which is still on the way to (perceiving) it: *Summa Theologiae*, pt II–II, I, 6. Moran's point about revelation of concrete historical data refers to taking literally as divine actions some very specific selection of events allegedly fully historical.

and succeeded it. At the very least there is enough here to give us licence to inquire as to what light might be thrown on the theology of Barth, and what case might be made for his consistency from beginning to end of his life's work – for he himself was convinced of that consistency – if the clear and simple theme of history as divine revelation were taken at face value as the best outcome of the recent theology of revelation. We should at least then be in tune with Barth's own repeated insistence that God's being and life consists in an activity, and that God's activity and ours form a common history. In fact we should be taking the reference to common history in quite a literal and unqualified sense.

THE HISTORY OF CREATION AS DIVINE REVELATION
THE ROLE OF RELIGIONS

Recall that Barth's first and last theological principle, and the one which never declines in the least from its dominant position in all of his theology, is the principle of the utterly sovereign freedom of God, the divinity of God, as he calls it. One entailment of that principle, the one which concerns the concept of divine revelation, is this: even in the acts of divine revelation God is not given over into our possession. In other words, with divine revelation we shall not have defined God – philosophers of religion and other provers and disprovers of God's existence beware! In yet other words, God is not a thing amongst, or even infinitely above, other things, not a form or a formed thing, for all formed things are finite, limited to or by their forms, and so defined, or at least definable. When Barth adds, under the complementary principle which he states as that of the humanity of God, that God's definitive revelation took place only in Jesus the man, in an historical individual who lived and died as we all do, then, if we are to be fair to Barth's finest theological insights, we must neither take this to be a qualification of God's divinity as God's divinity has just now been explained, nor take God's freedom now to be a mere euphemism for divine caprice. Barth really does mean to say that God's act, and hence God's being, is actually disclosed, and disclosed definitively, only in a mortal man like ourselves, a man called Joshua or Jehoshua of Nazareth (or Bethlehem), of uncertain date of birth, in a remote district of the Roman Empire called Galilee, some two thousand years ago. Genuinely revealed, actually disclosed; and yet we are still not enabled to define God; but that is because of the nature of the being of God, and not because of any flaw in the revelation.

So we cannot then conclude, as some of us in the past have been tempted to do, that Barth is saying God reveals God while revealing only that God is revealing and therefore really revealing nothing. We cannot conclude that God's free choice of Jesus is the final confirmation of the fact that God reveals while revealing nothing; because Jesus the man as the medium of the divine revelation was indeed a man like all others. And so God's much-vaunted sovereign freedom is thereby proved to be a classic instance of caprice, which of its nature reveals nothing of God. That is clearly not what Barth means to say; and if his case is to be assessed fairly, it becomes necessary to find a content for this concept of sovereign divine freedom more positive than the idea of caprice; and yet one that can encompass the exclusive focus on Jesus of Nazareth as the definitive revelation of God's divinity. Now, the clue to a successful solution to this problem of Barthian exegesis and of Christian theology in general, and to a solution which can keep intact the dominant perception of history as divine revelation, may well lie in a point that was made about freedom when morality was at issue, and the status of the fabric of reality as a moral enterprise. The point then made was that freedom, often conceived to be the hallmark of morality, is best understood when it is placed within the more encompassing concept of creativity. For then a free will can shed its thin spectral character as something hovering and at first unmoved (unmotivated) between alternatives that have somehow cropped up, and acting, it must then seem, rather arbitrarily on one alternative rather than the other(s). Creativity, on the other hand, understood as the interplay of dynamic forms, positively incorporates motivation – for motivation is a matter of mutually informing, influencing and attracting forms in motion – in a mutual adaptation which is evolutionary, and which thus brings about something which is partly, but really, new; something which a determinate system could never promise. In that creativity lies the realistic element of freedom in which, in turn, the essence of morality consists.

But would this same point apply to the sovereign freedom of God if God is not a form amongst other forms, not definable, no (one) thing? It is difficult to see why it should not, even if it puts us to the pin of our collars to conceive of such an entity. We do have some analogy for this – and perhaps it may later prove to be more than an analogy – in a feature that lies at the depth of our own consciousness. Although in our case what has been called the transcendent consciousness is never available to us except in and through the empirical consciousness – *pace* Sartre's distinction of the prereflective Cogito from the Ego – we can experience something of the manner in which the transcendent consciousness, 'bending back' and thus 'going over' and thus potentially beyond consciousness's successive contents, is the special source of that greatly extended and accelerated creativity of which the human species is capable, particularly when compared with the other species of things that together make up the fabric of reality. There is at least a hint here of how a greater and greater creativity could come to characterise a more and more transcendent consciousness. That is all that is necessary at the moment in order to secure the conviction that in divine being also creativity is the positive substance of sovereign freedom. And once creativity is in place as the comprehensive concept of which freedom is a functional expression, there can no longer be any difficulty about the prospect of a real revelation of the divine act and being occurring, for all Christians accept that God is revealed in creation. Then the phrase 'but nothing is revealed', can only mean that God is no thing amongst other things, so that no (additional) thing is revealed.

What then of the distinctive Christian theme of the definitive divine revelation solely in Jesus of Nazareth? The subsuming of the idea of divine freedom into that of divine creativity can help here also; and it can conserve the consistency which Barth himself assumed throughout his writings; for Barth remains from beginning to end the most uncompromising of proponents of that distinctive Christian theme. Now the story runs as follows.

True divinity is revealed in the man Jesus of Nazareth. That is to say, in the human being; for it would not make sense to say that true divinity is revealed in what the tradition called the divinity of Jesus. The divinity, the one true divinity, is what needs revealing; it is revealed according to the Christian claim in the man Jesus. Now, if instead of saying: God chose to reveal his true divinity only in Jesus (for this sounds quite capricious, Jesus the man being and doing and suffering much as many other humans have been and done and suffered), say: Jesus in all that he was and did and suffered is God's creation, and, precisely because of the fact that – and certainly not despite the fact that – all that Jesus was and did and suffered is recognisably on the human scale of things, God is thereby revealed definitively in him. When the story is told in this way, and it is in this way that the Christian story is and should be told; when the story is told in terms of creation, rather than being told simply in terms of divine sovereign freedom, then the suspicion of caprice may well disappear. But there emerges instead an issue to be clarified;

otherwise the disappearance of the impression of caprice may be no
more than the result of sleight of theological hand. The issue concerns
the relationship of special creation (revelation) to general creation (revelation). The God whose creation Jesus is, is the God who created
everything, according to the Christian creed. Why then is not the same
creator God equally revealed in everything that is created?

The first part of the resolution of this issue undoubtedly consists in the
recognition of the fact that the human species is itself the most creative
species in the universe – or that at least appears to be the case, as far as
our current knowledge of the universe and its various inhabitants goes.
The whole evolution of the universe represents in effect a process of
continuous creativity. Yet considered in abstraction from the human
species, it is a slow and ponderous process, too much at the bidding of
random event and of the tedious process of trial that lacks the anticipation and the reflective oversight of the whole process of which humanity
has become increasingly capable. Now, it would appear to be a fair
assumption to make that the creativity of God would be more clearly
and fully disclosed in the more creative of created entities. Since the
substance of divine sovereign freedom, and therefore the substance of
divinity, subsists in creative action (if such talk of substance does not
mislead one into thinking of God as another thing or kind of thing); since
God's being, as Barth would say, is in God's act and God's act *par
excellence* is creation, then God is most clearly and fully disclosed in
creativity. Further, it would seem to follow logically, the greater the
creativity in which God is claimed to be disclosed, the fuller must the
resulting disclosure be. In the first creation story in the Bible, it is said of
human beings, and of them alone amongst all the species there said to be
created, that they are in the image of God. And in a story the main
theme of which is divine creation, it is a fair implication that the
correspondence of image to imaged centres upon creativity; that humans are in God's image and so image forth God because they are so
distinctively creative (and for this reason also they are placed by God in
charge of a continually created and creative world).

But this would allow only the conclusion that the fullest revelation of
the divine in the universe takes place in the human race, in all that it is
and does and suffers in the same universe; and that the more general
revelation of God in the rest of the creation is inchoate with respect to
this and subject to refinement through it. One is still some distance from
understanding, let alone accepting, the conviction that the definitive
divine revelation occurred in one human being rather than in the

human race as such; at the very least in the sense that divine revelation in the rest of the race was inchoate and in need of final refinement with respect to the revelation in this one human being; and furthermore that that human being was in fact Jesus of Nazareth. What now if one were to test this final form of the Christian conviction in terms of creation and creativity? For what Christians call the New Testament does make more explicit in the case of Jesus the connection implicit in the first creation story between being an image of God and exercising creativity.

The New Testament regards Jesus as the image of God *par excellence*; and when it speaks of what Jesus achieved, or rather of what God achieved in and through Jesus, it speaks of a new creation, a new heavens and a new earth. It is mainly in the use of Wisdom literature, as it is called, and of its central imagery, that the ideas of Jesus as image *par excellence* of God – of Jesus, that is to say, as God's creator agent in quite a unique sense – come together in the New Testament. Wisdom, *Sophia*, in what Christians call the Old Testament, is God's own creator of the universe, God's first-born through whom all things were made; and the application to Jesus in the New Testament of the central imagery of that tradition implicitly applies a claim for creator-of-the-world status in the case of Jesus.[31] The same claim concerning Jesus, with the same cosmic, creation-wide dimensions to it, is also made in the magnificent passage of Paul's Letter to the Romans, 8:12–23. It is made there in terms of Jesus' title Son of God (which, together with the titles Lord and Christ, is one of the key titles of the king in the tradition into which Jesus was born); and the fact that the imagery of spirit is used in this context should not mislead the reader into thinking that a different kind of claim is being made here than that which is made in the Wisdom tradition and imagery; for in the latter tradition spirit, word and wisdom are, despite the predominance of that last, and hence the naming of that literary tradition, virtually interchangeable. In Romans 8, then, it is claimed that, because the spirit of sonship is abroad, the very same spirit of sonship which made Jesus what he was and empowered him to do what he did, we can all hope to be sons (and daughters, of course) of God in the likeness of Jesus. Indeed, the claim continues, the whole creation is

---

[31] See Proverbs 8:22ff, where God creates the world through God's first-born, Wisdom; the Wisdom of Solomon 7:25, where Wisdom is the mirror, reflection, image of God; John 1:1–14, where God creates the world through the Word incarnate in Jesus; Revelation 3:14, where Jesus the Word is the 'beginning' of God's creation; Hebrews 1:3 and Colossians 1:15–16, where Jesus is the reflection, stamp, image of God, and again first-born of creation; Galatians 6:15, 2 Corinthians 5:17, 1 Corinthians 15:28, where what is called the new creation in and through Jesus ends with God being all in all.

groaning with that hope of liberation from its present bonds, thus sharing fully in the hope that will be realised in and through Jesus and those who will be sons and daughters also, co-heirs as Paul puts it with Jesus, of what God continues to create anew. If, in accordance with all of this, one turns the claim concerning God's definitive revelation in Jesus into the terms of the corresponding claim concerning God's creation and creativity exercised through Jesus, is it any easier to understand the claim to definitiveness and uniqueness made in favour of Jesus? The question of understanding the claim, needless to say, is prior to any question of accepting it.

An understanding of this Christian claim in terms of creation which images forth divine creativity might be approached initially through the hypothesis that as there is a history of creation there is also a history of revelation. This is only to be expected, since creation and revelation are now two sides of the same coin. Creation names the sourcing of the unified interplay of forms that constitute the universe both as a work of art and as a moral enterprise. Revelation, as well as referring to the act of disclosure, refers also to the apprehension of what is disclosed; for without the latter there is no disclosure, no revelation. Revelation includes in its connotation, then, the knowledge of the source that is at work in the world. In fact, the coincidence of creation and revelation is even closer than that. At its most foundational and essential level knowing, it has been pointed out, consists in praxis. Form(-in-motion) in its perpetually adaptive interaction with other form comes to know that other (and itself) through that same interaction by which the other in-forms, reveals itself to, it. Correspondingly, in the case of the human form, it is by engaging with the world that the world and all that is operative in it, including itself, is known; to the extent that it is or can be known. This engagement with the world is at once moral, artistic and heuristic; or, in one of those exercises made possible by reflective consciousness, it can be quite predominantly artistic, or quite predominantly heuristic (scientific–philosophical); and these processes can accelerate almost exponentially the corresponding processes of participative creativity in which the whole universe and all that are operative within it are continually engaged. The history of creation and the history of revelation coincide as closely as can be, and this principle of epistemology applies to any continuous creativity of a comprehensive or sourcing kind which we might be able to identify and thence designate divine, as much as it applies to local creators and their creativity. An ultimate source creativity which appears (necessary) to make into a *uni*verse the pullulating interaction of a myriad of finite forms, might itself be deemed to be formless, known only in its presence and power through all other forms. And perhaps known also on the analogy (or more than analogy) of the most transcendent dimension of human consciousness. But the principle of the intrinsic coordination of form-seeking (to know), and form- or formless-impacting (revelation) remains secure.

It follows that the greater the creative engagement of which any intra-mundane agent is capable, the greater will be the revelation and knowledge of the universe and of all that is operative within it. Already with the dawning of reflective or self-consciousness signing, language in the very broadest sense of the term became possible: as consciousness could bend back over its current content and so envisage this imitated, or altered, or absent, it could have a representation of this content with which to communicate. But there are apparently further stages in what is called the immanent transcendence of consciousness, stages which facilitate abstraction and analysis, and at which even greater creativity becomes possible. Some relate the development of such stages in human history to leisure, and simultaneously to an ever developing creativity of reflective consciousness which gained more and more control over the necessities of human life, for these two causes are clearly connected. Some who are involved with the history of religions talk, like Karl Jaspers, about an axial age, usually located round or about the fifth century BC. This was an age, it is claimed, at which simultaneously across many countries people appeared capable of taking a universal view. Reflecting on all kinds of things of which they were already reflectively conscious, they could see more than was common to classes of things and thus come upon universal categories; and amongst these would be the dawning inklings of a universally operative 'source' creativity. The accounts of this axial age, so called, are sometimes cast – and it may be said unnecessarily – in that combination of universalist and individualist categories which characterised the rationalist individualism of the Enlightenment.[32] But before taking up that point, it is worth noticing a comparable account of the history of religion, albeit this time confined to the Judeo-Christian tradition.

In the course of the argument of his *Essence of Christianity*, Feuerbach traces the stages by which the Israelites reached the conviction that God was more than the patron of the tribe (the miracle stage), and more than

---

[32] See Anthony O'Hear's reference to the axial age as used by Hick, and with this Enlightenment-type gloss upon it, in Michael McGhee (ed.), *Philosophy, Religion and the Spiritual Life* (Cambridge University Press, 1992), p. 54.

manipulator also of neighbouring peoples (the providential stage), and
was in effect the source of all that happened in the universe (the
creatio-ex-nihilo stage). For Feuerbach, and this is his relevance to this
context, these stages of knowledge, revelation correspond to the stages
in the conscious creativity of a people who can at first manage and
envisage managing only their own tribal affairs, but successively envisage the management of other centres of power, and then that of the
whole world (when their 'way' will be a light to the Gentiles, to light the
same way forward for all – the Jewish claim, still heard today, to have
discovered ethical monotheism). If one prescinds once again from a
particular philosophical gloss, or in this case from a theological gloss
upon the theme, one can see illustrations of a history of revelation, and
in particular a history of the revelation of what people felt they discovered as the divine, but in any case a history of knowledge of the
universe revealed to them, that quite coincided with the history of the
developing creativity of the engagement of these same people with the
world of which they formed such an integral part. And it is crucial for
present purposes to note the pivotal role played by individuals in both of
these histories of religion. The individuals that see the emergence of the
axial age are usually named as Confucius, Lao-tzu, Gautama Siddatha,
Mahavira, Socrates–Plato; and although it is the nation of Israel that is
the Son of God at the precise point of history known as the axial age, the
individual voices of the great prophets are thought pivotal for the axial
revolution in that case also. Then, of course, the individual in which
Feuerbach's history of religion culminates, at least proleptically, is Jesus
of Nazareth accepted and worshipped as the incarnation of God.

   The interpretation which the rationalism of the Enlightenment – still
very much with us in so many forms – would and did put upon such an
allegedly axial age, and in particular on the individual roles within the
corresponding revolution, is as follows. These individuals discovered a
few universal truths, universal in the sense now of being quite ahistorical
or supra-historical, and discovered even these in either a very emaciated
or, as Feuerbach would say, an alienated form. Thus the Jesus of the
Enlightenment – of Renan as well as Kant – is a precocious teacher of
the rule of universal rational moral precept, centred upon the commandment of love of (God and) all humankind. Thus the universalist–
individualist formula of the Enlightenment is fulfilled. Rational principles are universal by nature of being ahistorical, and are thus available
in principle to every individual of every time and place; and it is these in
their moral form that provide a social ordering of these same individ-

uals; and it is these and these alone, stripped of all local and temporal colour and content, that can order the whole of humanity into one harmonious society.

But there is a better and truer interpretation of an allegedly axial age and of the role of the individual within it; an interpretation in which no ahistorical element appears; in fact, quite to the contrary. In this interpretation, attention is paid to the apparently universal phenomenon in the history of the world, in which the truly creative occasion occurs through some change in some individual or individuals, however haphazard the change may appear to be. A change which, although in many other instances nothing other than destruction or failure followed, in this case triggered a creative response in the individual or individuals concerned. A creative response which then became general precisely because of the intrinsic interconnection of the individuals concerned within the unified fabric of reality. A creative response through which the power of the newly (pro-)creative thereby expanded exponentially from the individual to the local and, depending upon the nature of the newly evolved–creative element, potentially to the whole universe.

Here is the relevance of the Intersubjective First position with regard to humankind; and of Deutsch's case for the universal relevance of the origin of life in general, and intelligent life in particular, despite its present and seeming confinement to an incredibly tiny and obscure part of the universe. And in general, in addition to those particularly impressive scientific–philosophical systems, here once again is the relevance of that modern sense of the whole of reality as history. Such that even if we do insist on distinguishing 'natural' history from the 'real' history which begins only with the origin of the species *Homo sapiens sapiens*, we shall but see the role of individuals more pivotal in the latter than it is in the former, as the account of the continuing creativity in which the history of reality consists unfolds. If only because the vastly increased creativity of which human beings are capable coincides completely with the manner in which the pre-existent social structures of intersubjectivity generate more, rather than less, individuality in the members of that species. And this in turn is simply the inversion of the principle which states that, far from human community being created, far from new individuals being socialised by application of formulated and allegedly universal truths and in particular moral truths, human community is continually formed to as general an extent as may be, and perfected as much as it can ever be, by the free play of creative communicative co-operation, in essence emotional communicative co-operation between always already mutually interconnected individuals. In such terms, particular and general, one can at least understand the pivotal role of individuals in the history of creation; and within that general understanding, the claim for a definitive role for an individual in the history of divine creation and revelation, where the coincidence of creation and revelation is closest of all.

But why *Jesus* as the definitive creation–revelation of God? If it was odd of God to choose the Jews how much more odd must it seem that God made a final, definitive choice of the Jew, Jesus? For all that has been said so far might make more understandable the claim that special revelations of the divine are initiated and sourced through particular historical individuals, through those named above as belonging to the axial age, through Jesus, and through many others perhaps whom the same vagaries of history which threw up such people afterwards left nameless. It might then be more acceptable to claim that each of these individual founders of religious traditions contributed, as other like individuals may continue to contribute definitive insights, all of which must eventually add up to the definitive revelation of the divine, whatever that may be and whenever it may be deemed to take place. It would certainly be more acceptable if that latter kind of claim were to be made without attempting to impose any hierarchical order on the revelatory individuals identified in this ecumenical manner. Divine revelation would be deemed to increase with the history of creation, but as a cumulative rather than as a serially corrective process.

The characteristic Christian claim that in Jesus of Nazareth, and in him alone the definitive revelation of the creator God in human history has already occurred seems to run counter to that last eirenic claim. And if that last eirenic claim is understandable in terms of the history of creation, surely the characteristic Christian claim concerning Jesus is rendered unacceptable, if not also unintelligible, by these very same terms. Despite such surface appearances, however, the characteristic Christian claim concerning Jesus of Nazareth in the terms here offered for such a purpose can actually prove quite understandable, provided only that the claim is kept in line with its own original, Biblical perspectives. Whether, in addition to being understandable, the claim is also acceptable is a matter which depends upon factors which are not germane to the purpose of this essay. Hence the following attempt to prove the Christian claim intelligible within its own original perspective and in terms of the history of creation is not offered as a result of any apologetic intent, but rather because it can contribute further insights into the nature of creation and revelation as history. The task of rendering the Christian claim understandable from its own original perspective and within the terms of the history of creation can be accomplished most expeditely by three kinds of consideration, and the final conclusion concerning history as creation–revelation can then be drawn – together with an assessment of the insightful and consistent nature of Barth's theology.

First, it is necessary to say something about Jesus himself, since the claim is to the effect that his human life, death and destiny are a creation and revelation of the divine in some definitive fashion. Now, of course, given the two-centuries-old quest of the historical Jesus, and the amount of literature which continues to appear on the subject, it would be foolish to attempt here anything other than a brief and purely illustrative cameo of the allegedly distinctive features of Jesus' human existence. Let the following suffice then, purely for the precise purposes of the present context, while further inquiry must be referred to the extensive and still-growing literature on the subject.[33]

Jesus was informed, as all can be, by the coordinated dynamic forms of the continually created world in both its natural and its social dimensions. His understanding of reality and his active attitude towards it were formed by the sight of the sun that warmed the good and the bad, and the fall of the rain that refreshed alike the virtuous and the wicked. He was also formed and informed by the living memory of the kings, those sons of God, those cosmic figures who were thought to channel divine power and wisdom down through society to the natural world of promise and plenty, those original Adams who freely enjoyed and disposed of, to the benefit of their subjects also, all the supports of life and life more abundant which all that rich world afforded. In these ways he was formed and informed by continuous creation, and formed and informed so thoroughly by the creative power that held it together and permeated it all, that he apprehended creation as being in the nature of a gift or grace poured out to all without distinction of moral worth or social status; and as he then gave extension in his own life to that kind of creativity by which he was formed and informed, he experienced it to be in its definitive depths an emptying of self[34] in which – paradoxically as it

---

[33] My own attempt to deal with this subject, for what it is worth, together with references to other literature and discussion of the problems of relating history and faith, and so on, may be found in *Jesus the Man and the Myth*, especially ch. 7, and in sections of *Modern Theology*, especially pp. 53ff and chs. 3 and 4; and also in *Power and Christian Ethics* (Cambridge University Press, 1994), ch. 4.

[34] David Turner's 'Aboriginal Religion as World Religion', in *Studies in World Christianity* 2 (1966), pp. 77–96, contains a fascinating account of an Aboriginal view of creation as consisting

might seem, at least until one is ever more informed of the nature of
transcendent self, or at least privileged with an experience of pure
human love – the greatest truth and fulfilment of selfhood itself is found.
In this way he could envisage kingship, and indeed all social authority,
as having the form of service to others; and he lived out this creative
insight from creation by calling a community around him which would
exercise no authority within it except that of service, the self-emptying
again, the dying to self that would find true self. And when the powers
that were saw this vision and praxis of his as a threat to the embodiments
of the kinds of power they termed divine – as indeed it was – he was
inspired and enabled, by the same creative forming of his very being and
life, to make the final self-emptying of his mortal life and breath, in
fidelity to that cosmic creative power as well as to the community which
at that point he could not otherwise serve. That definitive act of his
well-defined life was then, quite understandably, experienced by those
who attended to it, as a dying into that creative power or spirit by which
he had been formed and lived (in terms of their religious symbolism,
God who continuously created his life without hindrance from him, now
raised him to God's right hand); and they simultaneously experienced it
as the definitive breathing into their own present and future of the
power or spirit by which he had lived (in Paul's language of resurrection,
Jesus became life-giving spirit, or son of God in power).[35]

In all of this creative living and dying Jesus experienced and gave
expression in his community to the source creativity of the whole
universe; and on reflection he verbalised and otherwise symbolised this
(in the breaking of bread, the staff of life; and in pouring out the wine, for
example), thus adding to the social influence of his life and death a
powerful definition to the formative memory of the race. In this way,
then, so the claim goes, Jesus of Nazareth came to experience, by
embodying it in the life and death of a thoroughly human being, the source

essentially in the expulsion of forms. Taken in conjunction with Turner's more substantial
account of this Aboriginal theology in books referrred to in this article, it can be seen to have
achieved quite the level of sophistication which we find, for example, in certain Jewish mystics'
description of divine creation in terms of God's retraction or withdrawal in order to make space
for the creatures thus fashioned or formed. Creation, in short, as a self-emptying which,
paradoxically perhaps, makes the self in question all the more realised as self. See J. Moltmann,
The Trinity and the Kingdom of God (London: SCM, 1981), p. 110.
[35] See Acts 2:14–26; Romans 1:2–6; 1 Corinthians 15:45. The author of the Fourth Gospel sees the
death of Jesus – when he is 'raised up' on the cross – as the moment of his reaching the definitive
status of life-giving spirit (John 28:30 can be translated 'handed over the spirit' more accurately
than 'gave up the spirit'); and each of these two symbols, raising up and breathing spirit into, can
be the equivalent of the idea of resurrection.

creativity of the whole universe, the divine being-in-act which, not being a form amongst other forms (as his tradition insisted, it can neither be imaged nor named), if it can be said to be a self, is a self that continuously empties itself of dynamic forms into others, who can only return to it by emptying themselves in turn in order to reach the stature of (the one?) true self. Creation, incarnation, revelation.

The second and third considerations relevant to this issue have to do with the connotation of the term definitive; perhaps more with what it cannot be taken to connote than with what it can. For it would seem from the Bible that the term definitive must be understood neither in the sense of exclusive nor in the sense of something already finalised, over and done with.

Secondly, then, the claim that God is definitively revealed in the life, death and destiny of Jesus of Nazareth, a claim outlined in some such terms as those offered above, has nothing in common with a claim that God is exclusively revealed in Jesus[36] – however tardy Barth may have been in issuing the necessary qualification, under the heading 'The Humanity of God', to the impressions left by some of his more extreme formulations. Quite to the contrary, the same divine creativity–revelation which finds embodiment–expression in the life, death and destiny of Jesus is at work in the whole of the universe and in the whole of history; in particular in the whole of the history of humankind in and with the universe. The Word of God incarnate in Jesus, according to the prologue to the Fourth Gospel, enlightens everyone. The divine revelation in Jesus is definitive in that it is the same divine revelation that is everywhere in the history of the universe, for those who can and will experience it. In one very real sense, then, what is distinctive about the revelation which is at the origin of Christianity – however well or ill it may have fared in the course of the history of Christianity – is that it takes itself to be something which is not in principle or at source distinctive of any time, place, person or people.

If 'definitive' does not mean 'exclusive', what positive connotation can it be given in the case of Jesus? Creation–revelation may be said to be definitive in the case of Jesus in that it takes the form of a thoroughly

---

[36] See J. D. G. Dunne and J. P. Mackey, *New Testament Theology in Dialogue* (London: SPCK, 1987). Dunne in ch. 3, with reference to the Wisdom theme in New Testament Christology, shows that John 14:6 ('Jesus said to him, "I am the way, and the truth, and the life; no one comes to the Father, but by me"') expresses 'not an exclusiveness which denies God's presence anywhere else, but an inclusiveness which gives a means of recognising it everywhere' (p. 78). Corresponding to this and in support of it, in ch. 4 I challenge Hick's exclusivist reading of the Christian doctrine of incarnation, and try to show that it requires quite the opposite kind of reading.

human life, death and destiny. Primarily so, in any case; for the other forms of its expression, the verbalisations of it in scripture and tradition and the other symbolic, mainly ritual forms of it, must be deemed to be secondary to this. Now, creation–revelation which takes the form of human being must be definitive for human beings; and if humanity is destined to be the highest form of being in the universe, other than divinity itself, then that form of divine revelation must be definitive for the whole universe. Provided of course (and this is the second positive note in the connotation of the term definitive in the context of the Christian claim) that there was nothing in the life, death and destiny of Jesus which could have distorted or even partially darkened the divine creativity–revelation which was operative in and through him. It is a crucial part of the claim concerning Jesus, therefore, that he did nothing to distort or darken the divine creation–revelation that operated in and through him – in the religious symbolism of the tradition, he was without sin. 'Definitive', then, means that the divine creativity–revelation which is everywhere in the history of the universe is embodied and expressed without distortion in the full and true humanity of Jesus of Nazareth, in all that Jesus was and did and suffered.

Third, as 'definitive' does not connote 'exclusive', neither does it entail the idea of something already finalised, over and done with. For then the history of divine creation, which, it is now suggested, is the history of divine revelation, would have to be thought already ended some two thousand years ago. A comparable confusion to the confusion often encountered in theological treatises on creation, from which one gets the impression that creation refers to a specific divine act which took place only at the remotest origins-in-time of the universe; an essentially deist idea, or at least one in which the universe thereafter needed only some kind of occasional, providential management. But in fact in neither case is divine creativity properly thought to have ended at some point of the past. In the case of Jesus, it is one thing to say that universal divine creativity operative in and through the whole interplay of forms that make up the fabric of reality, so forms and informs one human life that it is embodied without distortion in that human being, and embodied in it precisely as a thoroughly human life and being. It is quite another thing to say that that same divine creativity, embodied in that historic human life and, given the intrinsically intersubjective or social dimensions of human existence, inevitably motivating and inspiring, forming and informing others, nevertheless brought the history of divine creation–revelation to a close. Many of Jesus' earliest followers took it that with

Jesus' life, death and resurrection the end of the history of creation was imminent; just as many of his much later followers have been known to talk of divine revelation ending with the death of the last of Jesus' apostles. The former we now know to have been mistaken, although it is a little more difficult to dissuade the latter. Indeed it is not even possible to say that Jesus brought the history of divine creation–revelation to a close proleptically, in Pannenberg's understanding of that formula; and Moltmann was undoubtedly correct on this point. For then, as Moltmann pointed out, Jesus' followers would be struggling along in the wake of what is already behind them in the history of creation.

Certainly those who take themselves to be the followers of Jesus must show themselves, if they are at all serious in this matter, to be empowered by his spirit, still working through the community that took his name and title. They must show themselves to be formed and informed by the selfsame self-emptying divine creativity that is everywhere operative in the universe, and that for them took definitive human form in Jesus of Nazareth. Further, they who are thus empowered are themselves creative agents in history, contributing since the age in which the creative interplay of forms in the fabric of reality evolved their self-conscious species, to the greater and greater historical conditioning of the creation as a whole. Hence, empowered by the same Creator Spirit, as they would capitalise it, which reaches them now through Jesus of Nazareth and the community which they regard as his body in the world, they are in one sense aiming at achieving no more than Jesus achieved, that is to say, to let that Creative Spirit form their lives and all their being in the universe as thoroughly as it formed the human life, death and destiny of Jesus. But in another sense they must aim at achieving more; for creativity still has a history, and the human race continues to gain in creative (or, of course, destructive) control over nature and society, and within the total fabric of reality. Those who claim to be the body of Christ still breathing his spirit in(to) the world, must continue to co-create the world to degrees that increasingly transcend those that can be recorded at the dawn of the Christian era. That is what is meant by saying that they must achieve more than the historical Jesus and his first followers could or did achieve. For that is what is envisaged, surely, by the passage in the Epistle to the Romans already referred to: Jesus' historic embodiment of divine creativity, symbolised as his sonship of God, working in and towards the sonship of God of all humanity, until the whole of creation is liberated from its bonds and for its fullest promise.

One is tempted to think here again of the role which humanity plays and may yet play, according to Deutsch's theory of everything, and particularly at the approach of the eschaton. Not that we can take Deutsch's theory to be finally true; the history of science–philosophy would caution against any such foolishness. But it is in terms of the best-founded and most persuasive scientifico-philosophical systems of a particular time that one can best test those theological systems which – quite in accordance with views now expressed on history and revelation – are also developing at that time. Think, then, of Deutsch's account of what is called artificial intelligence. This is at once something which is clearly in the process of being created by human beings, and as often feared by human beings almost as a rival and future displacement, like some recently born but rapidly growing and threatening god. Looked at more positively and without fear, however, this process of the development of artificial intelligence can be seen just as easily as the increasing endowment of the formed matter of the universe with faculties of informed and indeed creative knowledge–formulae, which can at one and the same time represent an increasing spiritualisation of universal matter itself, and hold out the prospect of the creation of that universal (virtual) reality-generator which would result in the creation of eternity in an instant of time, and not as an infinite length of time.

Yet Deutsch's theory of everything can be the kind of theory that could render more understandable, if not also corroborate, the kind of theology of creation–revelation that is now under discussion, if two supplements are added; especially since it can then be argued that the theory needs these two supplements in any case. First, it needs to be supplemented by the scientific vision of Trevarthen and company, who see this same process of human creativity in the universe as a moral process as much as a scientific–technological one, an intersubjective (e)motional process of persons communally engaged in creating their common and universal history. Second, it needs to take more into account the evidence to the effect that the universal (virtual) reality-generator is already in operation in the universe(s) before human beings are taken into account. So that humanity is then seen as that through which this original universal (virtual) reality-generator, or creator simply, operates *par excellence* and increasingly. And that does imply that the creator is increasingly dependent therefore on the free creativity of humanity for the bringing about of eternal life – Christians would say dependent on the obedience of Jesus and the ones who follow and fulfil his mission in the world. But that in turn, provided one does not contrast immanence and transcendence in the old misleading manner, can be taken just as much to mean that humanity too is the creation of the original (virtual) reality-generator, and that in depending on humanity's freedom the creator is depending on its own highest continuous creation, on the highest embodiment and expression of its own creativity. A god not to be feared as a tyrant, but to be appreciated as a source of empowerment and grace.

However we attempt to envisage continuous creativity in the universe, and the eschaton in which it may finally end, the point of importance at this stage of analysis and argument is this: to insist that divine creation–revelation did not end in the time of Jesus is to reinforce in effect the prior conviction that the claim concerning definitive divine revelation in Jesus of Nazareth entails no exclusivity. For this final insistence simply gathers together a number of well-established convictions which might otherwise remain isolated and without their full impact. These are the conviction that creation consists in the activity known as the dynamic, adaptive interplay of forms, and in the activity of whatever it is that keeps these forms in one evolving and, above all, *uni*versal interplay;[37] the conviction that there is a history of creation; the conviction that creation is revelation both with respect to that which initiates and that which receives (for it is by creatively interacting with others that one knows these as well as oneself); the conviction that humanity is the most creative species that we directly know in the universe, and that there is a history of its creativity also, within which can be detected an axial age in which the individual came into fuller focus coincident with, rather than contrary to, the increase in intersubjective cooperative creativity, and at the epitome of which can be expected the highest participation possible in the comprehensive being and act which has always accounted for the universal interplay of forms; the conviction that the comprehensive source being/act, conventionally called god, therefore, conducts the creative interplay of forms primarily and increasingly through human creativity; the (Christian) conviction that God's creative interplay of forms and the privileging of humanity in

---

[37] In much Christian theology creation as fashioning out of the formless (the void and empty deep of Genesis) is thought to be inferior to the abstract idea of creation out of nothing – an abstract idea which, incidentally, some Christians think they invented, failing to realise that, as in many other cases, the Greeks had it before them. This is a mistake, for the former construction is in fact the exact counterpart in imagery of a conceptual construct which, without it, would be virtually devoid of any intelligible content. The key to understanding this contention is to be found, again, in an analysis of the meaning of nothingness. Some of this analysis is already present in the first part of this essay; and before the end it may be supplemented by treating it again in the context of the most creative transcendent consciousness.

314 Critical–constructive

this continuous creation of the universe takes place axially, and is axially revealed in the humanity of the individual Jesus of Nazareth in his full humanity and in nothing but his humanity; and, finally, the conviction that as humanity increases asymptotically its creativity in and of the universe, and so participates to the fullest degree possible for it in the source of the coordinated creation of forms that make up the universe, that source will be thereby most fully and finally revealed in and to it. Humanity will then know the original creative power in the universe, as it itself is known by that creative power, that is to say by the fullest participation possible in the source creativity which creates it also.

What the faithful followers of Jesus proclaim, then, most particularly in their most characteristic doctrine of the incarnation of the original creative power in fully individualised and as fully socialised humanity, is the continuous creation–revelation of God in the whole universe, and pivotally and in the end completely in humanity fully and finally formed and informed by that continuous divine creativity, to the point at which humanity participates, as fully as it is possible for humanity to do, in that same creativity by which both itself and the universe is created. (This is what the Greek Christian theologians in particular called the divinisation of humanity.) In saying this, the emphasis must remain upon the faithful followers of Jesus, and not upon the Christian religion as such. For what is being proclaimed, one must insist once more, is an historical creation–revelation process which is accessible to all at all times, and can be rendered inaccessible at any time only through weakness or destructiveness, culpable or inculpable. And what is being proclaimed by the faithful followers of Jesus in their lives, as it must be, as much as in their preaching about it, is that this universal creation–revelation process, in accordance with its own increasing historicality and concomitant foregrounding of the individual in the grand community of things, took definitive form as a human being in Jesus of Nazareth, an origin and earnest of the final stage in the whole process which would be completed when the human community achieved simultaneously the greatest degree of individualism and social cohesion (all co-heirs with Jesus) and the greatest degree possible for it of participation in the source creativity of the universe (God all in all). What is being proclaimed, then, it is important to repeat, is not the definitive status of the Christian religion, much less of any of the Christian churches which continue to foist their rival claims upon an already sufficiently confused human race, but the definitive act of creation–revelation, in the sense explained, in Jesus of Nazareth.

For the Christian religion, like any other religion, is a human construct, an elaborate construction erected, maintained and continually modified by history-bound human beings, in response to an allegedly divine revelation. Therefore, any religion is itself an expression and a faithful communication of that revelation only to the extent that the common fallibility, the persistent waywardness and the recurring obtuseness of the people involved may allow. A religion comprises a creed, a cult, a code and a constitution; where the creed can be taken to include sacred scriptures as well as formulaic doctrines, and the constitution is the legal and structural form of the community of co-religionists. Seen as such, the Christian religion can scarcely be said to be distinguishable from, or indeed to have existed independently of, a movement within Judaism, until the second half of the second century BC. And from that time onward, with the relative exception of its sacred scriptures – if one ignores the process of continually editing and translating these down the centuries – Christians have constantly remodelled and reinterpreted each of these elements: creed, code, cult and constitution. This has been, and continues to be, an on-going process of relative and at times impressive fidelity, and of relative and at times grievous infidelity to the always and still-on-going divine revelation in continuous creation which, this religion proclaims, found definitive form in the thoroughly human existence of Jesus of Nazareth. Now, if that is the case, and it appears very much to be the case, a final word might be added at this point, but only in passing, about the proper relationship of the Christian religion to other religions.

Given the apparently endemic waywardness and infidelity of Christians and given the fact that other religions also respond to a divine revelation which coincides with the whole history of creation and with, presumably, a similar mixture of fidelity and fallibility, the relationship of Christianity to these religions must be one of dialogue rather than any attempt at displacement.[38] For if the truth which Christians proclaim, namely, that in the humanity of Jesus God has revealed that the final and complete creation–revelation will occur as the consummation of an increasingly human-made and humanised universe; and if that truth is also in the process of being revealed to all by the selfsame creative–

---

[38] *Studies in World Christianity* (Edinburgh University Press, 1995–) has its distinctive focus on the cultural conditioning of Christianity in particular, and of its more general encounter with other religions of the world. It is this focus which holds out the best prospects for seeing the truth in other religions and the mutual benefit they can be to each other, and for encouraging dialogue rather than confrontation.

revelatory process which constitutes the history of creation, then the infidelities of Christians are as likely to be corrected in part by other religions as are these likely to be further enlightened by the surviving fidelities of Christian proclamation. Christians at their best, and only at their best, can then be seen to be opening more fully the eyes of others to what is always shining for them also through the lenses of their own religious traditions, from the selfsame historico-creative process, the creator word that fashions and thus enlightens everyone. And at their best, of course, Christians will also be at their humblest, willing to have the beams in their own eyes removed by what, over certain reaches of the truth-beauty-goodness–creating process that shines for all, may be obstructed only by motes in the eyes of others.

HISTORY AS REVELATION
THE ROLE OF THEOLOGY

The unshakable twin pillars of the theology of Karl Barth – the greatest Christian theologian of the twentieth century – are these: first, the living God is the sovereignly free creative source of existence and life for all that is, was or will be; and before this real divinity no speculative constructs of human definition of the divine may be allowed to stand (the first commandment). This he refers to as the divinity of God. Second, the living God is definitively revealed in the humanity of Jesus of Nazareth; Jesus is the living 'word' through whom the living God creates the world from beginning to end. (A characteristic way in which Barth puts that point is to say that the scriptures give us no licence to theologise about a discarnate Creative Word, that is to say, a divine creative 'word' that is not, or not yet, in human form.) This Barth refers to as the humanity of God. Barth admits, as has been noted above, that his earlier almost exclusive insistence on the divinity of God could have unwittingly closeted him with those who speak as of some abstract conceptual human construct instead of speaking of the living God. Now, to insist that the only real divinity is one which creates and is thereby revealed in the full and unqualified humanity of one individual is to imply, to put the matter at its very mildest, that that same one and only true God is revealed in the whole creative process that went into the creation of that individual before that individual was conceived, and in the continuing creative process which accompanied and followed on from that individual's appearance in the world. For every individual entity, and *a fortiori* every human individual, is brought into being as an integral part of the seamless fabric of this universe, a temporary crystal-lisation as it were of the creative interplay of its myriad dynamic forms. This was understood from the beginning by those followers of Jesus who wrote of the divine creative power, word or spirit which creates the whole world, creating for its own and final creative purposes, and out of the people and religious culture of Judaism, the man Jesus of Nazareth. It forms the substance of those concessions by Barth when, in the course of the argument of 'The Humanity of God', he revises his assessment of human nature and human culture.

Indeed it now seems possible to claim that this interpretation of Barth – to the effect, namely, that in his very insistence that the one real God is revealed definitively in the humanity of the individual Jesus, he implies that the same God is truly revealed in the whole history of creation – is even more intelligible and indeed corroborated the more we modern and postmodern people understand better the evolutionary and histori-cal nature of this continually creative and created universe. At the end of the last two chapters, which were concerned with the cogency of an analysis of the whole fabric of reality in terms of a unified moral and aesthetic enterprise, there seemed to hover almost within grasp the vision of some entity, not itself a particular form, which accounts for the (origin and) orchestration of the forms through which, in their continu-ous and mutual reformation and transformation, the continuous cre-ation of the universe came about. The resonance of that imagery with that of the dominant Judeo-Christian creation story in Genesis, and indeed with that of many if not most similar creation myths, is quite striking. The imagery of creation as a fashioning or *forming* of things by establishing their formal relationship with other things (light and dark-ness, dry land and sea, distinguished from formlessness and ordered in relationship to each other, and so on) is strikingly similar to the image of forming all that exists in the whole fabric of reality by orchestrating an interplay of forms. And it is precisely that foundational creative process that is so much better understood as the study of the evolutionary history of the universe progresses.

For example, we now understand on the analogy (or more than analogy: exemplar?) of the carbon atom how at some stage of this dynamic interplay of forms, the reduplicative processes necessary for life came about. We seem closer to discovering from the most recent studies of the brains of animals and humans, especially by those who simply refuse any dichotomous dualism of mind and matter, how at another emergent stage this kind of reduplicative process gave rise to that

phenomenon in which consciousness seems to consist; and perhaps also
how at a further emergent stage, that further bending back over its own
very content which we call reflective (self-)consciousness occurs.[39] At
that last stage the selfsame continuously coordinated interplay of forms
in the cosmos results in the creation of *Homo sapiens sapiens*, the most
creative entity in its own right of all the continuously created entities that
we know directly in the world; an entity whose essentially communal
creativity increases exponentially the creation of the future of the universe. In this way we understand ever better how the entity which
coordinates the interplay of forms is always operative in a single seamless history of creation, and even how creation through an individual
which proves to be both pivotal and proleptic can be an integral part of
that seamless history of (divine) creativity. So that the implication from
the definitive creation–revelation in and through an individual human
being to the conviction that this is the same creation–revelation that
occurs in the whole universe is indeed made more intelligible and
convincing.

   All of this, incidentally, is consistent with a common contention of
Christian theologians, to the effect that what God brings about in the
history of the creation is brought about through what this theological
tradition calls secondary causes, that is to say through mundane forms.
That, in any case, is all that can be said at this stage in order to make at
least understandable the contention that God created and continues to
create the world through Jesus of Nazareth, God's Word, a man like any
other who lived in full transparency, in all that he was, did and suffered,
this divine creative power that made him what he was; thus giving
definitive, pivotal and proleptic expression to this divine creative power,
in line with other individuals such as the Hebrew prophets, yet in this
kind of definitive individual instance which evolutionary emergences
exhibit. But his, so the claim goes, was *the definitive* achievement and
expression of the nature and presence of divine creation and the consequent revelation of the divine; for he lived and died a fully human life in
the fullest conscious and undistorted presence of this divine power and
purpose, and so it was fully though not finally revealed in his life, death

[39] See for example some recent scientific investigations along these lines, into the nature and
structure of selfhood: Jaap Panksepp, 'The Periconscious Substrates of Consciousness: Affective
States and the Evolutionary Origins of the Self', *Journal of Consciousness Studies* 5 (1998), 556–82;
Colwyn Trevarthen, 'Brain Science and the Human Spirit', in James B. Ashbrook (ed.), *Brain,
Culture and the Human Spirit: Essays from an Emergent Evolutionary Perspective* (New York: University
Press of America, 1993), pp. 129–81; Ulric Neisser (ed.), *The Perceived Self* (Cambridge University
Press, 1993).

and destiny for those who could see it. It would be finally revealed when all of humanity reached his stature as co-creator with the divine and brought the whole universe with it to an eternal perfection.

History, then, all of history and nothing but history is divine revelation. Barth can only be consistent if, when he says God's history is *with* Jesus' history and ours, he means that it takes place in and through Jesus' history and ours; and so God's history *is* ours. Or, more plainly put, God, Jesus and all of humanity have a truly common history. Then, to take the second of the ambiguities in Barth already noted, he can only be consistent if, when he says that the God discovered by human reason ranging over the world has nothing whatever to do with Jesus' revelation of the true God, he is taken to be talking only of the errors that abound in the history of human religious speculation, errors that are common also in the history of the Christian religion. This latter point Barth is only too happy to imply when calling Catholics Pelagians, for instance, whereas in the case of his own 'Biblical' theology it was merely a matter of an understandable unbalance at the beginning which he rectified later on. But this rectification, if it is to be serious, must elide to disappearance point any general attempt at dichotomous distinction between reason and philosophy on the one hand, and revelation, faith and theology on the other. It became clear, in the course of that modern theology of revelation as history, that if something else was necessary, some infusion of special divine light or religious faith for instance, in order that the divine be revealed in historical events, then it was not history that was truly revelationary after all, or at least it was not clear on what grounds revelation was described as history.

Unless of course such special divine light is taken to refer to nothing more, or less, than the dark shining of the originating and unifying source of the pullulating interadaptive forms in which continuous creation exists. Special, then, only in the sense that it is the darker light of that former source rather than the light more visible to the human form in which it shines, the light of all those other forms through which it is at work. Or special also perhaps in the sense that it is seen better by those seers (prophets, poets) who wait upon it and then enable others to see it as they could always potentially see it.

Indeed, in that same modern theology of revelation, the nature of this religious faith which might make historical events revelatory of the divine could also be quite unclear. Is it some especially infused conviction simply, or additionally some extra information concerning the origins or implications of the events in question? Those who, it is claimed, had received the infusion do not appear to be any clearer on this matter than those who, for some unknown reason, do not appear to have received it. It is quite possible, however, to give an intelligible account of both religious faith and divine revelation, on the basis of a thoroughgoing and unqualified theology of history as revelation, such as Barth's twin foundational principles of Christian theology, as well as his clearer statements concerning a common history of God, Jesus and humankind, would seem to support. Whether or not it is true that the whole of reality is a truly moral enterprise – and this would seem to be the case only if the entity which unifies and keeps coordinated all the interacting forms of which the universe is composed, is itself of the nature of a moral subject – it is in any case true that human beings come to know all they will ever know both of the universe and themselves by engaging with the universe for their own and its concomitant betterment. The fundamental form of knowing, of discovery by rational animals, and hence the fundamental form of reasoning, remains always a matter of praxis rather than theory; such that, for all the exponentially increased creativity which the very possibility of theory promises, the verification by increase of beauty, goodness and truth remains itself once again a matter of further practical experience. Hence every advance in knowledge begins and proceeds by an act of what can only be called faith – a fundamental trust at the heart of all engagement in the interplay of forms which constitute the universe, that despite all failures in previous forms of one's own engagement, and despite all betrayal by others interactive on the scene, goodness, truth and beauty will prevail and increase.

This is not a blind faith or an unfounded trust; on the contrary, although often deterred by failure and waywardness, and undermined by sheer destructiveness, it is sustained, inspired and increased by the constant revelation of the common beauty and goodness that is cosmic in achievement and extent, and particularly by the deeper, if at first dimmer and less penetrable, light of ever further potentiality and promise that shines in all of this. Faith and revelation, then, are the common coordinates of humanity's part in this cosmic drama. Divine revelation and religious faith are then no different in kind from common or garden-variety faith and revelation, operative in and as the history of creation. What justifies the addition of the adjectives divine and religious is the perception that what seems to be revealed from the depths of the universe as a whole, and what seems to beckon from heights of its furthest promise, is so comprehensive in its presence and influence, so ultimate and sourcing of all that goes on, that it qualifies, by convention, for the titles of divinity. Common human faith and cosmic revelation, in short, become respectively religious and divine when they are operative at that level of depth and height and comprehensiveness. And on this understanding of the matter it makes little difference whether one says, with some modern theologians, that divine revelation in history is dependent on the exercise of faith, or that human religious faith results from divine revelation.[40] Faith and revelation are causal coordinates, not to be contrasted, the one as cause and the other as effect. Committed engagement gradually reveals reality to its ultimate depths and heights and comprehensiveness; revelation correspondingly sustains, inspires and increases the engaged commitment until those same levels are reached at which the adjectives religious and divine are justified.

Theology, then, is the study of the whole history of creation, so named at that point at which the study attempts to ascertain the most comprehensive, the most original, agency – in the sense of 'origin' which has the connotation of 'source' – detectable, however dimly, within it. In that way it is a natural and inevitable part of the discipline of science, particularly at the point at which the scientific quest itself becomes philosophical; the point at which it seeks a so-called theory of every-thing, a theory which must accommodate the inherent role of humanity and of moral enterprise within its overall compass. Although it is often

[40] In both published work and private correspondence – see my 'The Theology of Faith: A Bibliographical Survey', *Horizons* 2 (1975), 207–38 – I took issue with Gabriel Moran's insistence that revelation was the more fundamental concept in Christian theology, faith the secondary and derivative concept. In *The Problems of Religious Faith* in particular, in the course of what one reviewer called a kind of Copernican revolution, I argued that, as 'faith' is a term for the most basic and general heuristic enterprise which corresponds with what Heidegger called the 'thrown project' that human being is in this world, 'revelation' had to be a term for what was progressively unveiled as that project proceeded. Faith was thus the more fundamental concept, revelation the secondary and derivative. I still think that argument was necessary at a time when revelation in Christian theology was thought of predominantly, if not exclusively, in terms of special acts of divine revelation before which human reason was purely passive and receptive. Now, some thirty years later, I think a fuller and truer account would picture human faith and divine revelation as thoroughgoing coordinates, following the paradigm of the interplay of forms in which the whole of continuous creation consists. For on such an account and paradigm, and on the understanding that knowledge is foundationally praxis, the process in which any active agent 'informs' is the selfsame process in which it is 'informed'. This would mean further that the distinction between general and special revelation is no longer such as would support any more of these tiresome arguments against 'Pelagianism', nor would it make Barth's fulminations against 'natural theology' look any less foolish than some quixotic tilting against imaginary windmills. A distinction between general and special revelation could only be fashioned from the common evolutionary perspective in which the whole evolutionary process, in all its physical and spiritual dimensions, proceeds through 'mutations' which are at first quite particular, and in that sense special, but then spread through a 'new' species of whatever genus (say, religion) one is analysing and tracing through the history of the world.

the artist, attending upon the light that shines from the still-darkest depths and furthest prospects of a living universe, that manages to take our common vision and inspiration beyond the interests of community and kind which too often act as restrictions on the working scientist also.

Theology is philosophy; it is by nature a philosophical discipline. And that means in turn that there are lessons here for the nature and practice of philosophy also, and in particular for what is usually called the philosophy of religion. It is a lesson that has been implicated earlier in this essay and in other ways. It reads: as philosophy in general must come to grips with the historical or, if one must insist, with the evolutionary and historical nature of reality, so the philosophy of religion must consist of a critical study of the history of the alleged revelation of the divine in that same history of creation. This must, then, include the study of the alleged intimations of the nature and existence of the divine that are represented in the history of the world by the actual religions of the world, for these represent in their turn the parts of the on-going quest for the uncovering (discovery–revelation) of the comprehensive–originary agency which the terms divine and God connote. It is never, once again stated, a matter of issuing some abstract conceptual definition of God and then attempting to prove or disprove the existence of that defined being. The so-called proofs of God's existence which textbooks in the philosophy of religion are wont to record and to classify in the two or three categories of metaphysical, moral and aesthetic, are in effect not proofs in that intended sense at all. They are, rather, expressions, distorted by rationalist minds, of the process by which a human engagement with the universe which is at once heuristic, moral and aesthetic seems to receive gradually at the depths and heights of the whole fabric of reality, intimations of a comprehensive agency operative within it. God is the commonest name people have for the most comprehensive or original entity uncovered in the universe, not a name for something first defined, the definition then to be followed by a search for suitable evidence for the existence of just that thing. In that sense philosophy is asking what, if anything (or any no-thing), is God, as it quests through the history of creation in an effort to see what, if anything, continues to hold it all in its drive–attraction towards goodness, truth and beauty; towards life and life more abundant. A question as inevitable for philosophy as theology is inevitably philosophical.

Epilogue

John Searle's latest book, *Mind, Language and Society*, is aptly subtitled *Doing Philosophy in the Real World*. It has been widely and well reviewed in philosophical reviews as a fine summation of his case against both reductivist materialism and the 'Cartesian' dualism which is at once its context and contradiction. Or, put more positively, it is received as a summary of possibly the best attempt currently available to solve the problem that has plagued modern science, ethics and philosophy, namely, the mind–brain or consciousness-and-the-physical problem. Philosophical reviews also laud him, and quite rightly, for persistently insisting on our massive experience to the effect that causality is not purely physical. It is economic, social, political and hence somehow mental, as the making of the world we inhabit increasingly illustrates. (An acknowledgement here of the role of the conscious communal creativity of humanity in the coming-to-be, or the gradual destruction, of the world; a role which loomed increasingly large in the argument of this essay.) And Searle is lauded further, and equally rightly, for his acid critique of those computer-program-type systems which are sometimes supposed to somehow accompany as epiphenomena the physical–chemical processes of the neural system – similarly and simultaneously in numerous discrete individuals? For apart altogether from the fact that these fail to correspond to our full experience of being conscious agents engaged in communal praxis with a world we thus both increasingly create and understand, they resemble too much those semiotic systems which in some branches of science (artificial intelligence, cognitive science, linguistics) and in postmodern philosophies seem to sit in some no-man's-land between mind/consciousness and (the rest of) reality. And they cannot thereafter account either for the interaction of these or for any knowledge of the latter on the part of the former. Searle is rightly commended, then, for saving from reductivist moves a view of communal conscious (creative) praxis in the simultaneous knowledge and making of our world. So, along lines similar to those adopted in this essay, effective intentionality (moral agency) is secured as part of the real world for which Searle wishes to philosophise; and ethics has its place within the realm of verifiable philosophical discourse.

So much celebrated positive result, it seems, when Searle approaches from the side of communal causality the great mental–physical conundrum which 'Cartesian' dualism both crystallised and bequeathed to us. Yet almost immediately Searle's philosophical reviewers sound a more critical note. And it may be significant to observe that this seems to be sounded when the puzzle of interactive relationships between the mental and the physical is now approached primarily from the point of view of the latter. For now when Searle tries to say more positively what we know consciousness to be – in addition to saying what communal consciousness causally and, in some sense, cosmically effects – the appeal to subjectivity resumes centre stage. As Honderich pointed out, in the review referred to at the beginning of this essay, a closed circularity of argument then ensues. Consciousness is that which has a first-person mode of existence, whereas objective entities have a third-person mode of existence. And a person is defined as an entity which supports states of being, amongst them consciousness, which non-persons do not support. So a person experiences consciousness as a state which depends upon its being a person; but any number of persons can experience objective (physical?) entities like mountains.

Now, this analysis, apart altogether from its circularity and its apparent reliance on an otherwise rejected dualism, leaves out of account what might be termed second-person modes of existence. As another reviewer, Kenan Malik, in the *Independent on Sunday* (25 April 1999) pointed out, Searle here seems to assume that subjective states are located inside our individual heads. Whereas in fact they are located in relationships with our fellow humans. Now, that inter-personal location highlights a feature of mind/consciousness to which the experimental results of the Intersubjective First position in developmental psychology are directly relevant, as are, more distantly, parts of the somewhat flawed analyses of Husserl and Sartre. It is a feature of mind/consciousness which can actually join a 'first-person ontology' of consciousness, to use Searle's own phrase, to a third-person ontology of the physical world, rather than see these two ontologies fall apart and lose sight of each other. It is a feature which Honderich seems to envisage, however dimly and reluctantly, when he suggests that the only way out of circularity for Searle is the 'mad but fruitful idea . . . that for me to be conscious . . . *is for a world in a way to exist'*. It is a feature, finally, which suggests a return to Searle's more fruitful approach to this contemporary conundrum, from the point of view of communal, personal, creative and even cosmic causality.

For what is it in any case that could make us assume that we know, and could progressively know better or more 'objectively', the physical rather than mind/consciousness? What indeed could make us separate these to such an extent that our answer would have to choose one over against the other? Talk of invisible or dark matter, and even of intangible universes, undermines even the Newtonian picture of reality made up of pieces of matter, the properties and interactions of which can all eventually be known. Particles now behave like waves, and a space–time continuum with various 'fields' finally emerges as a picture of that deeper and more comprehensive reality of which matter in its various 'packets' and their interactions are merely the concentrations of its energy. To be sure, mathematical values can be attributed to these different parts of the geography of the space–time continuum. But, apart altogether from the fact that one is increasingly haunted by Kant's insistence that space and time are forms of an essentially mental activity, such values, such intelligible formulae, do seem to belong more to the realm of mind than to the realm of matter, or of the physical – once again, to the extent that the latter can be separated from mind/consciousness.

The same question could be put in another form. Follow a hint from the ancient Greeks when they described as no-thing, no formed and hence finite entity, both matter and the One who was creative source of all. And then ask: If this at first formless matter, or formless reality of a different name (say, energy), is the primal potency that gives rise to all subsequent forms, and through these to all the interactive adaptations of these forms in which the whole of evolving reality consists, what is now the difference between, on the one hand, calling this the creator and, on the other hand, a seeming preference for calling some other no-thing source of all, the creator god? Particularly since the continuing creativity characteristic of the evolving universe is intelligible, and hence attracts to the source-reality the idea of intentionality. And more particularly still since, according to the concept of emergence, this is not a determinate form of cosmic causality or creativity, but one which continues to operate very much in and through the concrete and adaptive creativity of the forms of which it is the source.

The fact of the matter is that from the very beginning of our conscious lives and our human quest for knowledge, what we first experience and subsequently come to know at greater depth and comprehension, is a conscious organism engaged with other conscious organisms in a joint practical project in and with the wider world of reality. More precisely we know these conscious organisms to be endowed with a level of transcendence – of being able to see and go beyond any current content of their empirical consciousness – which makes them truly creative co-agents in a truly evolutionary universe. It is this which makes us persons, moral subjects, responsible to others in that cosmic creative project of which we are increasingly so crucial a part. Our knowledge is therefore subjective, since it is in and of the subject. But it is also objective, for it is embodied consciousness of the creative interactivity that each participates in and that makes a world to be. And particularly and crucially so in the special case of our foundational knowledge of other transcendent subjects with whom each of us communally constructs and construes a world. In and with this second-person ontology of our immediate experience of intersubjectivity, then, a third-person ontology and epistemology is always already secured.

Inevitably, at some stage of development, the members of this intersubjective community of human beings realise that the construal and construction of a world is not all their own doing. They realise that knowledge-bearing and creating agency, of such a kind as to keep the fabric of evolving reality together in the form of a universe, reaches far beyond their occupancy of their little segment of the space–time continuum. (Here is the true significance of strict Sabbath observance: by keeping their busy little grimy hands off it for one day of the week, human beings acknowledge in a very powerful ritual manner that a greater than they continues to create the world.) They receive dim intimations of this source agency operative within the whole cosmos, from and through a combined effort at looking outward to the continuous cosmic creativity which constructs a universe through the adaptive interplay of all intelligible forms of reality; and looking inward to the apparently limitless dimensions of a transcendent consciousness in which each intersubjective instance seems to participate. (This is as likely a candidate as any for Calvin's *sensus divinitatis*, which, following the prologue to the Fourth Gospel, he insists every human being enjoys.)

It sometimes seems as if Eastern philosophers, especially those of the Advaita Vedanta school, will pursue these intimations through the inward route, and Western philosophers through the outward route. But apart from the fact that this appearance may be due more to a difference in emphasis than to a genuine difference of substance, the reality of the case is the more holistic one; namely, a world-creating transcendent human consciousness, whose knowledge of the world coincides with its creative engagement with it, encounters in this very process intimations of a world-creating consciousness which transcends it also, and yet is ever creatively operative also within those locally circumscribed selves. However the matter is put, the least that can be said is this: just as Kenan Malik, in the interests of an Intersubjective First position and its communal dimension of consciousness, had to inform Searle that he had a more radical step beyond current categories to take in order to achieve his most laudable ends, so Honderich must be told that his mad but fruitful idea to the effect, namely, that to be conscious is for a world in a way to exist, may drive him to a madder but even more fruitful idea if he too pursues the philosophical inquiry beyond the unsatisfactory stage where Searle left him. It may drive him beyond the very human construction of a room, which he takes as his example in formulating his mad but fruitful idea. It may drive him in fact through the ever receding limits of the space–time continuum, until his formulation of the mad but fruitful idea reverses its formulation and reads: for a world in a way to exist is for a transcendent cosmic, construing and constructing consciousness to exist, ever operative within it.

So much in retrospect from the point of view of philosophy. But from the point of view of Christian theology, its dialogue partner in this essay?

A subject, a consciousness entirely self-referring and replete within itself, could not without further ado be known by any subject in this world. Nor could it without further ado know of this world. A subject, a mind, a source and container of unchangeable ideas of every thing and event which constitute this world, if God were so defined, would yield a deist divinity and a mechanistic universe utterly different from the one we know we inhabit. A mix of these two ideas of divinity would simply combine their problematic features. Quite rightly, then, much of the negative theology of modern Western philosophy rejected such divinities squatting beyond the world, separate and transcendent in that crude sense, and creating and occasionally providing for the creation across that infinite distance. And postmodernism – in particular when at its best, and before some of its own excesses brought it to the borders of (literal) non-sense (no truth at all) – replaced the logocentrism of such unsophisticated theology, and the accompanying authoritarianism, with images of meaning and truth (goodness and beauty) constantly in the making, as befits a universe which is characterised by the constant creativity of evolution. But this idea of truth is not at all incompatible with a subject that is source of all entities that make up the empirical universe. One that knows all that is or will be precisely by creating all that will be, in and through all that is created. One that is known by conscious creatures like ourselves; creatures who enjoy an analogous kind of transcendent consciousness evolutionarily imparted to us. One who is known to us, then, in the same manner as we are known; that is to say, by increasingly cooperative creativity, a participation in the divine transcendentally conscious creativity.

This account of creator and creation is rendered all the more intelligible when the act of creation is understood as forming, giving rise to forms and coincidentally to the whole space–time continuum; and endowing the forms, inevitably, with its own creative energy (Eros?), so that the evolving universe of forms that we know comes into being, a moral and aesthetic enterprise through and through. We cannot know this ur-creative consciousness before or outside of its immanent power and presence within the space–time continuum. And indeed the words 'before' and 'outside', make no sense in that sentence. We may not be able to comprehend the absolute ontological beginning of this process of the creation of form by this formless subject; and may only come as close to such comprehension as is possible for us in some Deutsch-like eschaton when we cooperate to create, out of some cosmic cataclysm perhaps, an infinite space–time. But that fact does not compromise in the least the absoluteness of the Source–Subject which the concept of *creatio ex nihilo* was designed to protect. Nor does it allow the uniqueness of the Source–Subject to disappear gradually into the undifferentiated mists of some vague pantheism. For creation out of nothing still means all that it ever meant, namely, that the creator does not create the formed universe out of any independently existing material; nor is the creator itself some kind of material out of which the space–time continuum is merely moulded.

And we can as little comprehend a final end of creation. There is Deutsch's picture of the eschaton; which must be suitably modified to take account of that reality-generating entity and process that always anticipates, and therefore always will anticipate, our mightiest efforts at (virtual) reality generation. Something like that picture must now replace those pictures of judgement day, hell and heaven which derived from earlier cosmologies; and that picture will no doubt be superseded as future cosmologies develop. Nor can we comprehend much better the final end of each one of us, individual subjects that we are; the final end that takes the form of each one's death. Suffice it to say that a far too familiar soul–body dualism posed the problem in this respect of believing that an essentially bodily creature would spend some 'time' after death as a purely spiritual, disembodied person, only to be somewhat artificially recreated as a bodily being at an eschatological general resurrection. Now, however, with the idea of consciousness (mind, soul, spirit) forever immanent in the physical, and with the concomitant idea of imparting–participation which binds reflective consciousnesses, particularly in their most transcendent functioning, with the absolutely transcendent Source–Subject, there is the possible image of the individual's return to the earth as a continuing participative union with the Source–Subject forever creatively operative within that same earth and throughout the whole space–time continuum. The final un-selfing of each individual human self which allows the fullest participation possible with the most selfless subject; and without having to await Deutsch's eschaton, or to depend on the wishes of his end-time creators. (Rahner somewhere suggested that human souls at death were united with the World Soul, which was for him a cipher for the persona of the creator God as continuous fashioner of the world.)

Finally, it might be worth indicating briefly the kind of Christian theology which would meet the lines, developed in both the historical and constructive parts of this essay, on the nature and prospects of theology today; and indeed to point to some theologies which have been appearing along these lines.

First, the foundational form of Christian theology must continue to be the investigation of God the creator. Further, the concept of creation must be the clearest common denominator in Christian theology, from the theology of revelation to what is called moral theology; a concept of creation, moreover, that is best illustrated from the continuous creativity characteristic of the evolving universe. The so-called naturalist theologies that seem to increase in strength and prominence at this time, whatever their remaining imperfections, obey this first commandment.

Second, that central and, some would say, constitutive area of Christian theology known as Christology/soteriology, the investigation of Jesus the Christ as God's incarnate Word, must keep to the fore at all times the same idea of creation: God's universal creativity working in some definitive sense in Jesus, and hence in history. Too often in (more usually Protestant) sin-driven rather than creation-driven theologies, the beginning and end of Christian theology has Jesus redeeming from sinfulness. To the point at which it sometimes seems as if a different God is put before God the creator. Those who obey this second commandment can of course accommodate in full seriousness the satanic, adversarial forces of destructive evil. But they see the prospect of overcoming this in the bespoke spirit of Jesus, and not in juridical or legal terms of satisfying divine justice, or even in unilateral declaratory terms of waiving the same. Rather do they see the overcoming of evil in terms of the same cooperative creativity that is made possible by God and (Christians would say) through Jesus, in a universe which is evolutionary–historical by dint of divine creativity throughout the whole of its fabric.

The recent theologies which obey the second commandment also are of a number of different kinds. There are, for example, the theological investigations of the relationship between faith and history, centred quite naturally upon the one who is both the Jesus of history and the Christ of faith. There are, to take a quite different example, the Christian theological investigations of other historical religions; at least those investigations that avoid equally an intolerant exclusivism and an unrelievedly relativist pluralism. For these theologies increasingly understand that what is creatively operative and so revealed in what they believe to be a definitive human form in Jesus, is what is also creatively present in the whole history of reality. The continuous creator is revealed to all who can see, and is cooperated with, expressed and celebrated in these communal combinations of code, creed, cult and constitution called religions. So that each religion, from all that is best in it, but only from what is best in it, could enlighten the others, and on occasion correct what is worst in them.

That in general is the kind of Christian theology which the modern era certainly allows; if it does not in fact positively call for it. And for all the fragmentation of all the stop–start efforts at Christian theology in recent times, the time must now be approaching when one could draw on all the best of these efforts, together with the best of what the modern movements in science and philosophy (and art) have to offer, and give a more comprehensive and systematic account of it.

Index

Advaita Vedanta 76, 326
Aitken, K. J. 156–7
Althusser, L. 49, 52, 53, 91, 93, 95, 104
Anselm 233–4
Aristotle 49, 121, 149, 209, 237
  Aristotle's God 68, 74, 76
art 166–7, 181
  and morality 221–33, 241–52
  and religion 252–64
Athanasius 78
Augustine 3, 32, 36, 198, 267
Ayer, A. J. 19, 185

Bacon, Roger 24
Barth, Karl 3, 4, 273–86, 297, 298, 300, 309,
  316–17, 319, 321
Barthes, R. 54, 79, 95, 97–102, 111, 112, 114
  Barthes' God 100–1
Beckett, Samuel 6
Blackburn, Simon 191, 195
Blake, William 229
Bloch, Ernst 294–5
Boyd, Richard 202
Bräten, S. 153
Burke, Seán 53, 104–5

Calvin, J. 268–70
Cockburn, David 117

Dancey, Jonathan 192
Dawkins, Richard 126, 137–8
  Dawkins's God 126, 179
Derrida, J. 54, 79, 95, 105–10, 113, 167, 177,
  183
  Derrida's God 108, 180
Descartes, R. 4, 5, 8–16, 20, 21, 30, 35, 49, 51,
  84, 162, 170, 193–4, 198
Deutsch, David 37, 47, 50, 127, 128–50, 181,
  218, 220, 262, 305, 312, 328
  Deutsch's God 144, 146, 147–8, 172–3, 179
Dilman, I. 9

Douglas, Mary 93–5
dualism ('Cartesian') 5–7, 8–15, 21, 23,
  46, 48, 53, 62, 65, 66, 74–5, 78–9, 85,
  91, 113–14, 119, 136, 151–4, 162, 261,
  323–4
Dunn, J. D. G. 309

Eco, Umberto 52, 53, 110, 118
emergence 127, 130, 138–9, 140, 145, 182,
  193, 212
emotions 11–16, 155–8, 163, 167–8, 193–204,
  209, 214, 218, 229, 325
Engels, F. 44, 45, 48–50, 91

faith 231, 246, 276, 292, 293, 294–5, 296,
  319–21
Fenwick, Peter 8, 14, 51
Feuerbach, L. 41–3, 167, 171, 219–20, 303–4
Fiamenghi, G. 159–60
Foucault, M. 54, 79, 95, 102–5, 112
  Foucault's God 104–5, 179
Fransen, Piet 295

Garner, Richard 202
Geertz, Clifford 96
Gilligan, Carol 151
Gregoire, F. 40

Hardwick, C. 128
Hartshorne, Charles 261
Hazard, Paul 24, 25
Heaney, Séamus 230–1, 252
Hegel, G. W. F. 31–41, 42, 43, 46, 51, 52,
  58, 109, 115, 172, 178, 199, 219, 229,
  294
Heidegger, M. 4, 53, 54, 58–62, 105–6,
  167, 251
  Heidegger's God/divinity 54, 61, 79, 86,
  108, 177
Helmreich, S. 147
Hepburn, R. 254–6

Herrenstein Smith, Barbara   127
Hick, John   224–5, 228
Honderich, Ted   9, 324, 327
humanism (secular)   226–8
Hume, David   16–21, 23, 26, 28, 30, 114
Husserl, E.   53, 56–8, 114, 166
    Husserl's God   78, 177
Huxley, Thomas   25

Jaeger, W.   122
Jaspers, K.   303
John Scotus Eriugena   125
Justin Martyr   266

Kane, R.   126–7
Kant, I.   16, 21–3, 26–30, 35, 52, 102, 149,
    270–2
Kavanagh, Patrick   243, 246
Kerr, Fergus   58, 61, 205
Kokkinaki, T.   159–60
Kolakowski, L.   92

Latourelle, R.   287–8
Levinas, E.   86–90, 168, 171
    Levinas's God   90, 180
Lévi-Strauss, C.   95, 96
logocentricism   105–6, 180, 327

MacDiarmid, Hugh   255
McDowell, John   192
McGhee, Michael   223
Mackie, J. L.   190–1, 195
Macmurray, John   81–6, 168
    and God   86
Malik, Kenan   324, 327
Marx, K.   26, 41, 43–9, 52, 92, 100, 115, 116,
    167, 220
    Marx's God   43, 179
Marxism   91–6, 98, 99, 103–4, 111, 114, 177
materialism   47–50, 53, 78, 91–5, 111, 113, 154
metaphysics   129, 133–50, 182, 184–5, 189,
    190, 207, 248–9
Middle Platonist divinity   78, 148–9
Moltmann, J.   292–5
Monden, L.   292
Moore, G. E.   184–8
morality   131–2, 167–8, 180–2, 184–214
    and art   221–33
    and religion   219–20, 221–2, 224–5, 233,
        252, 264
Moran, G.   295, 321
Muller, Max   94
Murdoch, Iris   228–34, 251, 258, 259, 263

Neoplatonist divinity   187, 258

Nussbaum, Martha   124, 198

O'Connell, R. J.   124
O'Hear, Anthony   222–6, 227, 228, 259
O'Leary, Joseph   122

Pannenberg, W.   289
personalist philosophy   80–91
phenomenology   53, 56–79, 114, 177
Phillips, D. Z.   8, 9, 14, 51
Pinker, S.   126
Plato   3, 8, 35, 79, 187, 196–7, 231, 234–6,
    246–8
Plotinus   32, 187
Polanyi, M.   250
postmodernism   4–7, 41, 47, 53–5, 75, 91, 96,
    97–110, 177, 327
practicalist theory of knowledge   204–7, 208,
    210–11, 234–5
pre-Socratics   121–4, 207
Pritchard, H. A.   185
Protagoras   123
Pye, M.   267

Rahner, K.   329
Reddy, V.   151
revelation   231, 236, 239–41, 246, 251–2,
    259–60
    in Christianity   265–314
    in other religions   315–16
Robertson Smith, W.   94–5
Rose, Gillian   41, 89
Rose, S.   126
Ross, W. D.   185
Rougement, Denis de   202
Russell, Bertrand   18

Sartre, J.-P.   20, 53, 56–76, 84, 86, 104, 114,
    115, 166, 167, 171, 177
    Sartre's God   70, 179
Saussure, F. de   96, 97, 98–101, 108–9, 110
Scheler, Max   154–5, 193
Schillebeeckx, E.   290–1
Schlette, H. R.   292
science   4, 6, 24–7, 31–2, 36–7, 60, 92, 93, 107,
    118, 120
    physics   133–50; and philosophy/
        theology   120–30, 134, 144, 147–9,
        170–4
    psychology   150–67; and (moral)
        philosophy/theology   160, 162–3,
        167–74, 207–19, 264, 321
Searle, John   8, 9, 323, 327
Socrates   123–4
Spinoza, B.   117

Steiner, George   253–4, 256, 258
Stoic divinity   147–8

Thales   122, 124
Thomas Aquinas   268, 295
Tipler, Frank   128, 144
transcendence/immanence   115–18, 122–3,
    124, 129, 179, 222–3, 226–8, 229, 232–3,
    242–3, 247, 253–4, 256–9, 261, 313,
    327–8
Trevarthen, Colwyn   150–3, 156, 159–62,
    169–70, 174, 183, 312
Turner, David   307

Turner, Frederick   107–8, 183

Vlastos, G.   124

Warnock, Mary   186
Watson, Gerard   68
Weil, Simone   117, 231
Whitehead, A. N.   68
Wilkins, Ulrich   290
Wittgenstein, L.   204–6
Wood, Ananda   76

Yeats, W. B.   236